AF538361

BRUNO LUCCHESI

BRUNO

SCULPTOR OF

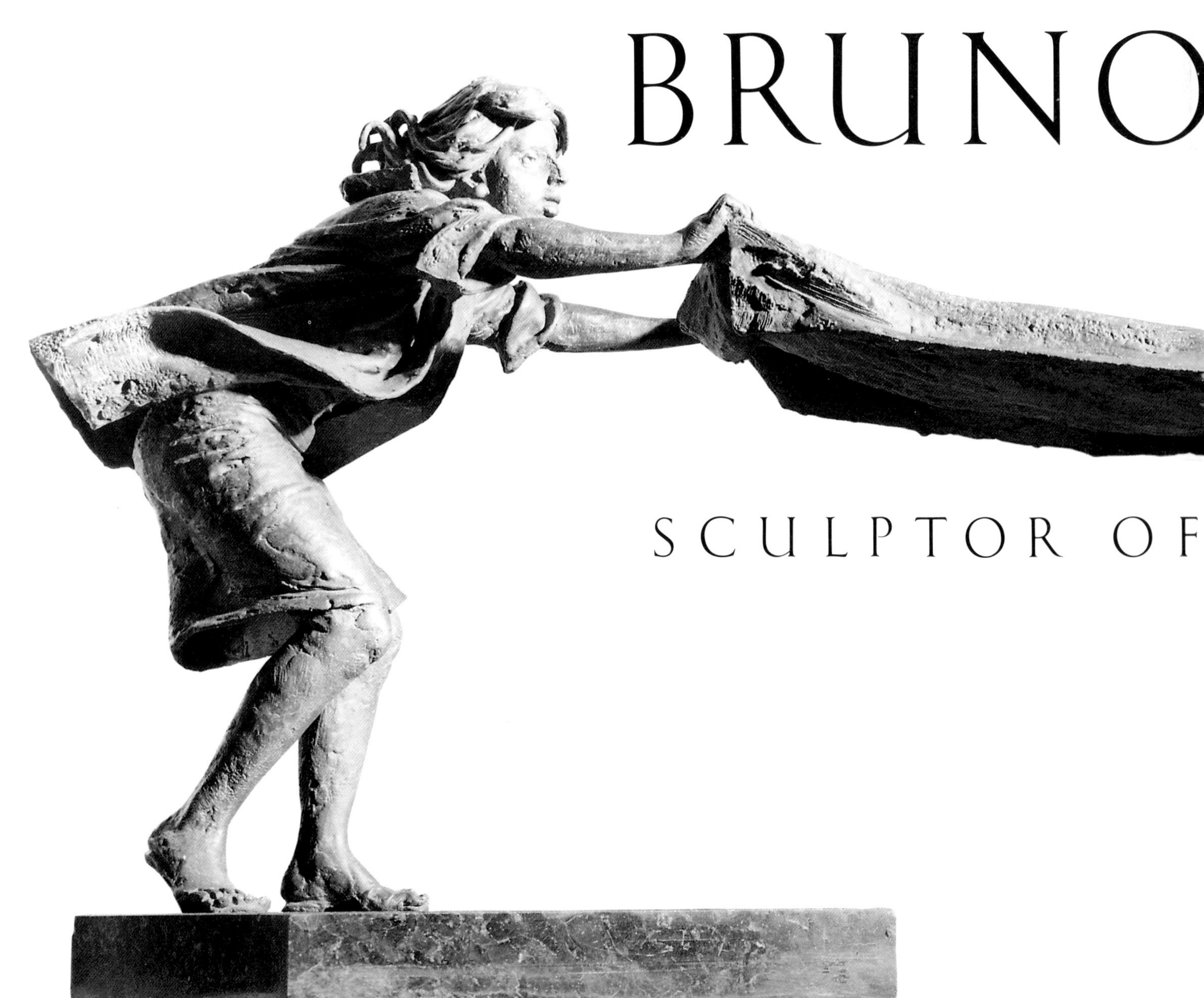

PHOTOGRAPHS BY David Finn

TEXT BY Dena Merriam

LUCCHESI

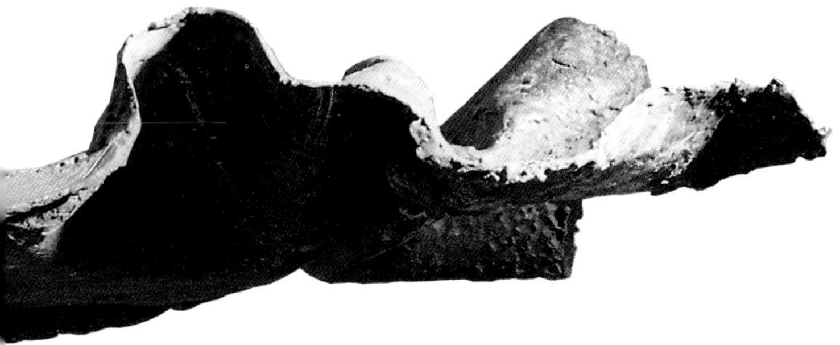

THE HUMAN SPIRIT

HUDSON HILLS PRESS · NEW YORK

FRONTISPIECE:
Spring Cleaning, 1985, bronze, 15 x 33 x 20 inches. Forum Gallery, New York.

RIGHT:
Janice Joplin, 1978, bronze, 19 x 9 x 9 inches. Forum Gallery, New York.

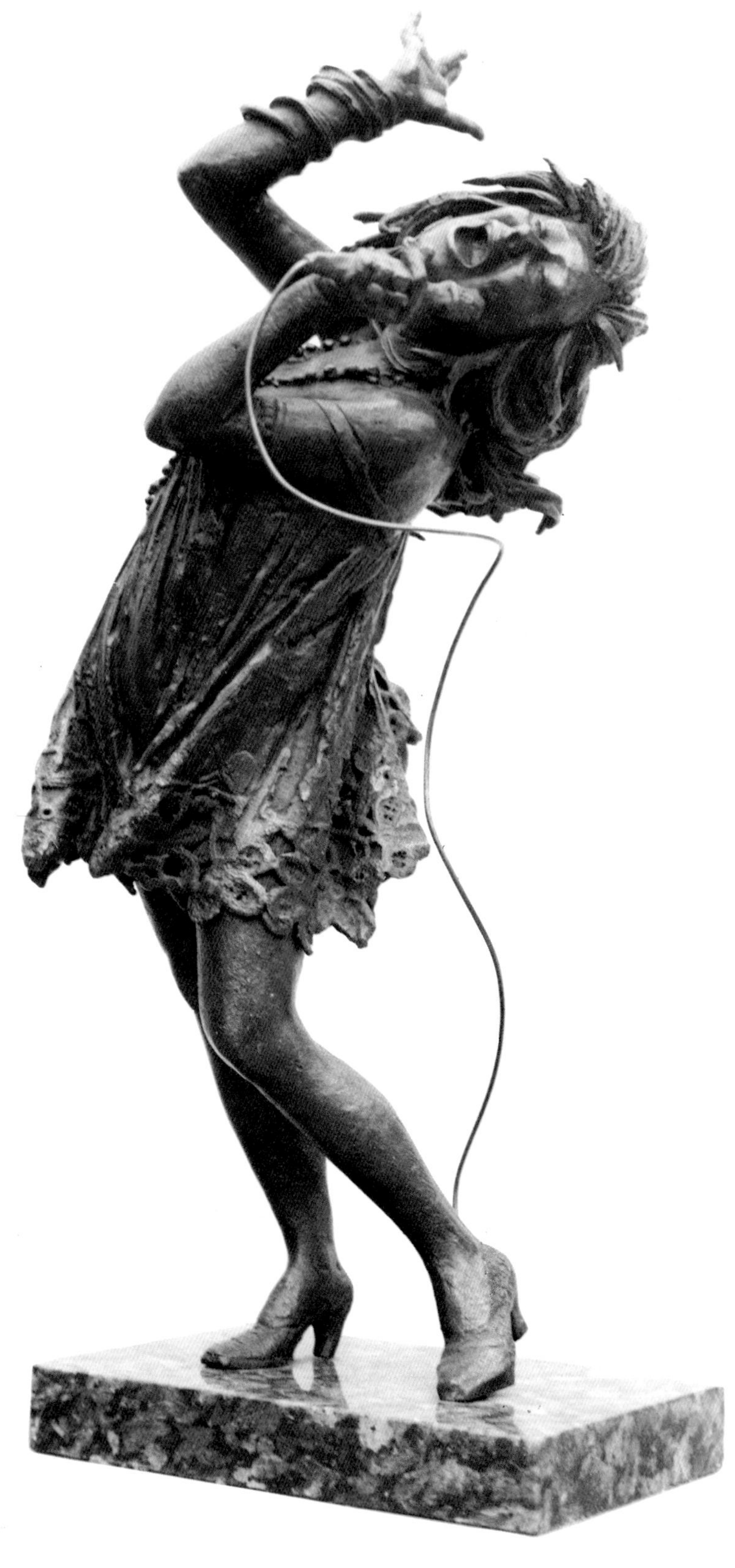

First Edition

Published in the United States by Hudson Hills Press, Inc., Suite 1308, 230 Fifth Avenue, New York, NY 10001–7704.

Distributed in the United States, its territories and possessions, Canada, Mexico, and Central and South America by Rizzoli International Publications, Inc.
Distributed in the United Kingdom, Eire, Europe, Israel, and the Middle East by Phaidon Press Limited.
Distributed in Japan by Yohan (Western Publications Distribution Agency).
Distributed in South Korea by Nippon Shuppan Hanbai.

Editor and Publisher: Paul Anbinder

Senior Editor: Virginia Wageman

Indexer: Gisela S. Knight

Designer: Nai Y. Chang

Composition: TGA Communications, Inc.

Manufactured in Japan by Toppan Printing Company

Library of Congress Cataloguing-in-Publication Data

Merriam, Dena.

Bruno Lucchesi / Dena Merriam: photographs by David Finn.—1st ed.

p. cm.
Bibliography: p.
Includes index.
1. Lucchesi, Bruno. 1926– —Criticism and interpretation.
I. Finn, David. 1921– . II. Title.
NB237.L8M47 1989
730'.92'4—dc19 88–32351
CIP

ISBN: 1–55595–021–3 (alk. paper)

CONTENTS

COLORPLATES

SCULPTOR OF THE HUMAN SPIRIT

In an era when sculptors have been exploring new forms, new media, new concepts, new ways to interact with nature, Bruno Lucchesi has focused his eyes and his sculptor's tools on the people he sees around him. Sometimes they are people he loves, sometimes people who arouse his sympathy, sometimes people he imagines in his mind's eye. Always he catches them in an unexpected moment, as if he had a hidden camera with which he peeks at friends, neighbors, passersby, or even mythological characters, freezing an unconscious gesture. He discovers his subjects when they are not looking and depicts them suspended in time.

It is difficult to find a niche into which Lucchesi's work fits. He has been called "the last of the Renaissance sculptors" because his remarkable facility with the human figure is reminiscent of the great fifteenth- and sixteenth-century sculptured pulpits, monuments, and doors of Italy. But there is something Gothic about the little touches of everyday life he incorporates into his sculptures, while his vigorous flowing forms are very much in the tradition of the seventeenth-century Baroque. His graceful nudes owe a good deal to eighteenth- and nineteenth-century romantic and neoclassical sculptures, and one wonders how he could have done his "street people" without the realism of Honoré Daumier.

Whatever his influences, Lucchesi seems to have an inexhaustible source of new images in his head, and those who have followed his work over the last several decades know that it has developed its own distinctive character that is always recognizable. He has revealed an aspect of the human condition rarely depicted.

Lucchesi is not a genre sculptor in the strict sense, for scenes of daily life are not his major interest. His emphasis is on the people in these scenes, not the settings themselves. In this respect he is more like Jan Brueghel than Jan Steen, for it is the character of the individual rather than their actions that is portrayed in his figurative sculpture. The environment seems almost incidental, although that too is often brilliantly shown. Even when he models a nude young woman lying on a couch talking on the telephone [pages 70, 71], he is demonstrating a new insight into an archetypal personality rather than merely representing an anecdotal moment.

The flair Lucchesi has demonstrated in his work derives from his background—his early years in Lucca and Florence, his life in America since the late 1950s, his innate modesty, his good nature, his sense of humor, his capacity for friendship. He laughs when asked where he thinks he fits in the great tradition of sculpture. "I never thought of myself," he says, "as doing work that could in any way be compared with that of Donatello, Ghiberti, or Michelangelo. I just do what I like to do. That's all." And what about the sculptors of our own time? He shrugs and gestures the question away. It is not for him to say.

His lack of pretension shows itself in the story of his life. Born in 1926 in a small mountain village named Fibbiano Montanino ("Little Mountain"), not far from Pisa in the province of Lucca, he spent his boyhood as a shepherd. In this community of about two hundred people, mostly farmers, life had changed little over the centuries. Like other villagers, the Lucchesi family grew their own food, made their own clothing, and used their extra crops to help buy items they could not produce such as sugar and salt or a pair of shoes.

Lucchesi says he did his first carving on sticks while tending the sheep—making animal heads and other designs that appealed to him. He had no special ambition to be an artist, but he did have an appetite for learning. At the age of ten he left his mountain village to study in the monastery in Lucca. There he saw, for the first time, sculptures in churches and cemeteries, and he became aware that creating figures and forms could be more than carving playfully while tending sheep or decorating wooden bowls and other household items. Fascinated by the act of making art, he learned what it was like to be part of the process when a local artist asked him to be a model for a mural he was doing for the monastery.

A few years later Lucchesi returned home to resume his duties on the farm, but the learning experience at the monastery had been a critical one. The exposure he received to the world of art enabled him to look at life around him with a new eye. Lucchesi's childhood memories of Lucca figure again and again in his mature work. His later sculptures of farm women and country peasants preserve the character of the people he loved, doing their daily chores of washing clothes in nearby streams, selling wares in local villages, caring for children. His depictions of city street scenes show an affection for the same kind of people—humble, ordinary folk whose earthiness and simplicity reveal an inner beauty that ennobles the human spirit.

Lucchesi spent the next several years in Fibbiano Montanino helping his family with the farm. The war came, and it was during the war years that he made the acquaintance of a refugee Yugoslavian artist, a former director of the Academy of Belgrade, now a barber in the small mountain village. When the war ended, the refugee artist set up a studio in Lucca, and Lucchesi would regularly bicycle down from the mountains to study drawing under his tutelage. Recognizing his student's talent, the artist approached an uncle of Lucchesi who lived in Lucca and urged him to arrange for more formal training. In 1947 the young sculptor was enrolled in the Art Institute of Lucca.

While attending school, Lucchesi lived in the back room of his uncle's vegetable store. In exchange for room and board, he would rise at five o'clock and go with his aunt to purchase vegetables at the general market. The activities of the marketplace were fertile ground for his creative mind, and later sculptures of women buying and selling their wares in the market are reminiscent of those early days.

The program of art education at the institute was a classical one. Italy had a rich heritage in the decorative arts, and the institute trained artists to be craftsmen in a tradition that went back hundreds of years. They learned to model classical figures and make plaster casts of clay models, to make figures for monuments in cemeteries and churches, and to fashion stucco ornaments for ceilings. The institute gave students the tools they would need to make their living through art.

Lucchesi completed the program at the age of twenty-four and from there went to live in Florence. He had no difficulty finding work. His first job was making ceramic models for the Paternino Reproduction Company. The figures he created covered a range of human types, from madonnas and saints to pirates and soldiers. They were sold throughout Florence, and one can still find some of these models in the shops of that city today.

The sculptures, made primarily for the tourist trade, were not particularly distinctive or original. However, Lucchesi's bent for more imaginative work became evident when he invented a new technique, called *sfoglia* (from the word *foglia*, which means leaf), for creating realistic folds and the texture of clothing. Using this process, he first made a layer of clay as thin as a pizza and then pressed it over the mannequin to give it a fresh appearance. By thus modeling the clay he was able to simulate clothing, and through the use of this technique Lucchesi developed a remarkably realistic treatment of the figure.

It was during his years in Florence that Lucchesi also began his career as a teacher of art. He joined the faculty of the Art Academy in Florence and soon was appointed assistant professor of architecture. He remembers taking his students to study the great architectural structures of Tuscany and working with them to make scale models of the various buildings. Later, in America, Lucchesi continued to work with students, receiving teaching positions at the New School for Social Research and the National Academy of Design, both in New York, and holding seminars on sculpture all over the country. His love of teaching eventually led to his collaboration with Margit Malmstrom on three books about the craft of sculpting: *Terracotta* (1977), *Modeling the Head in Clay* (1979), and *Modeling the Figure in Clay* (1980).

The opportunity to do his own work came when Lucchesi received his first commissions for outdoor sculpture in Florence. Two of them, *Madonna and Child*, 1953 [page 164], and *Saint Francis of Assisi*, 1956 [pages 18, 164], are typical of other sculptures that decorate the corners of buildings in Florence. The madonna figure is conventional in style, but the Saint Francis with his two acolytes kneeling before him shows a tenderness in the posture of the figures that foreshadows Lucchesi's mature style.

His most ambitious commission in Florence was for two ceramic murals on a kiosk for a gasoline station in the Piazza Donatello [pages 14–17]. One mural was on an exterior wall of the station, and the other was inside the small office used by the gasoline attendants to make change. Both had to do with the concept of transportation. These murals were the first works to demonstrate the facility and the wit that have become characteristic of Lucchesi's style. It also seems especially appropriate that Lucchesi's first

Bather, 1958, bronze, 24 inches high. Collection of Bernard Osher, San Francisco.

memorable work was done for such a pedestrian and commonplace location as a small roadside gasoline station.

In 1957 Lucchesi married a young American art student studying in Florence. He had always assumed he would live in Italy, but soon after the birth of their first child, he decided to bring his family to New York where his wife's parents lived. The vitality of the city appealed to him, and the couple decided to try to establish themselves in America. Lucchesi's first job in New York was making mannequins in a Bronx factory. A few months later he left to take a job in a ceramics factory in the Pocono Mountains of Pennsylvania.

During that first year in America, Lucchesi had little time for creative work. In Italy he had enjoyed working on the few commissions he received, but there seemed to be no similar opportunities in New York. So he started making small sculptures on weekends for his own pleasure and satisfaction.

It so happened that Lucchesi's father-in-law had a frame shop in Greenwich Village, and when he saw these small figures he decided to display some of them in the window of his store. The sculptures sold quickly, and before long Lucchesi was making more money from the sales in his father-in-law's frame shop than from his work at the factory. For the first time Lucchesi was in the position to devote himself seriously full time to his own sculpture.

Most of the buyers of Lucchesi's works were artists and collectors who lived in Greenwich Village. One was the owner of a well-known jazz club who used to purchase a sculpture by Lucchesi whenever he wanted to give someone a gift. A small following developed, and word of his work began to spread.

One day Lucchesi received a call from a member of the staff of the Whitney Museum of American Art in New York, who was looking for new artists to be included in the Whitney Annual. Lucchesi's name had come to his attention, and he was interested in coming to the sculptor's studio to see some of his work. Lucchesi was thrilled, but he was unprepared, working as he had been out of his home. Reluctant to lose the opportunity of showing his work to the Whitney, he immediately took a studio on Forty-sixth Street and Sixth Avenue, a neighborhood then popular among musicians. Lucchesi invited the museum curator to his new studio, now filled with sketches and sculpture. The visit was a success, and one of Lucchesi's sculptures, a bronze piece of 1958 entitled *Bather*, was included in the 1960 Whitney Annual.

During the course of the exhibition the piece was purchased by a banker named Bernard Osher. Osher was impressed with the quality of Lucchesi's work and requested to see more of his sculpture. After visiting his studio, Osher made Lucchesi a proposal. Convinced of the young sculptor's talent, he wanted to help him work toward a one-man exhibition. Lucchesi felt confident that if he returned to Florence to work, in a year's time he could produce enough sculptures for an exhibition. Osher agreed to sponsor him, and Lucchesi returned to Italy with his wife and son, Carlo.

Upon arriving in Florence, Lucchesi took a studio in San Gallo. He worked steadily, and when the year was finished he had completed fifteen new sculptures and cast them in bronze. His subjects were the people he saw in the cities and villages of Italy, people engaged in everyday activities—a mother feeding her child, a girl pausing on a bicycle, a woman hanging laundry, a girl jumping rope. These rituals of ordinary life were portrayed with affection and sensitivity. Capturing the beauty of the unnoticed moment, Lucchesi's sculptures were moving portrayals of contemporary life.

Several galleries were interested in displaying Lucchesi's work, and Bella Fishko, who was planning to open her new Forum Gallery, offered him a one-man show as the inaugural exhibition in 1961. The exhibition proved to be a remarkable success; twenty-one of the twenty-nine pieces sold.

Already in these early works Lucchesi showed his ability to render people in the middle or on the verge of action and to convey the feeling of time's continuum, the flow of one movement into another. In a 1976 Forum Gallery catalogue, Thomas S. Buechner, former director of the Brooklyn Museum, wrote of Lucchesi's uncommon capacity for combining the specific moment and the timeless gesture: "His moments are specific, accurately portrayed in the instant of their occurrence; but the gestures, crazy and twisty or settling and serene, are as timeless as an Egyptian

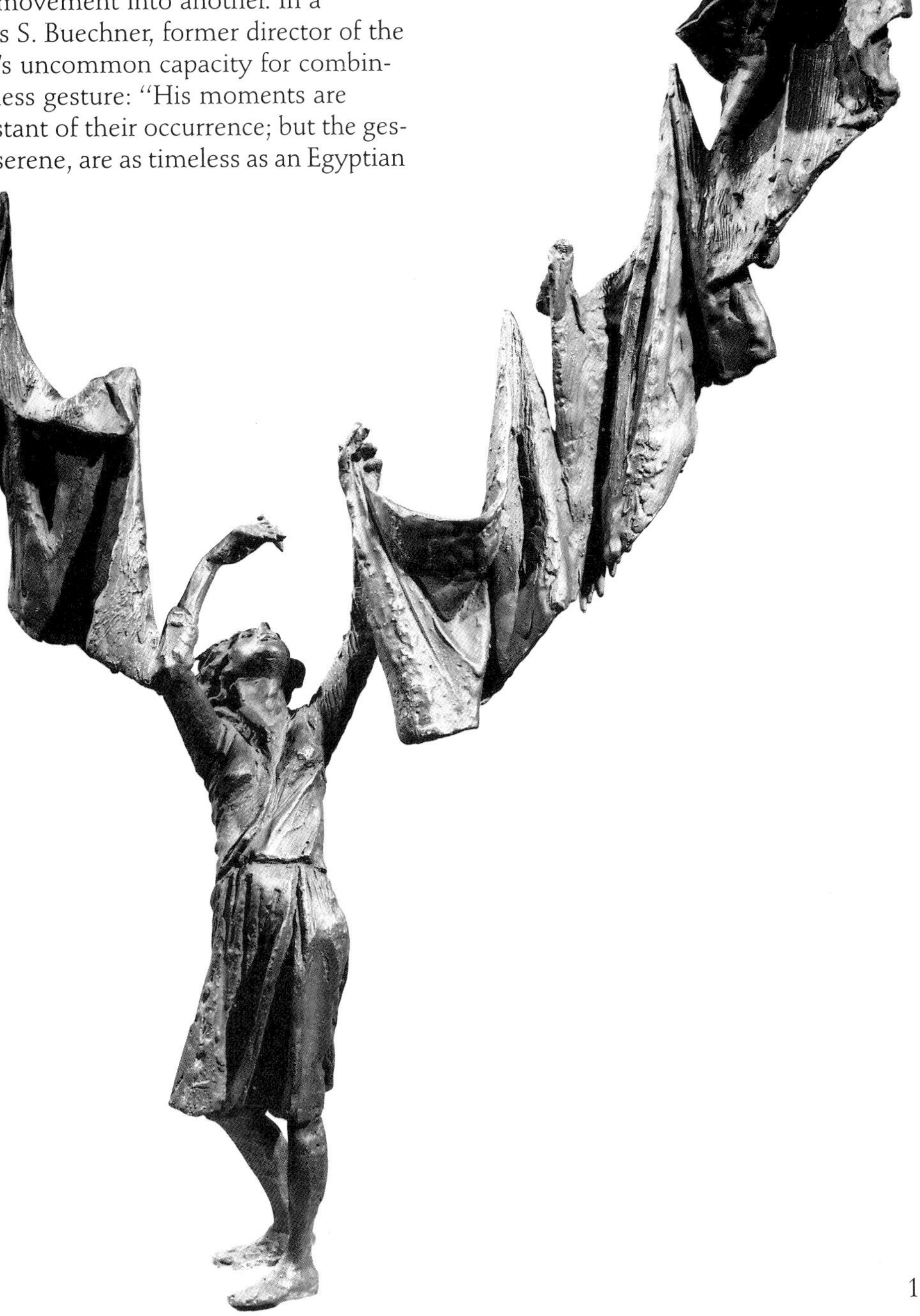

Study for Washline, 1972, bronze, 21 inches high. Forum Gallery, New York.

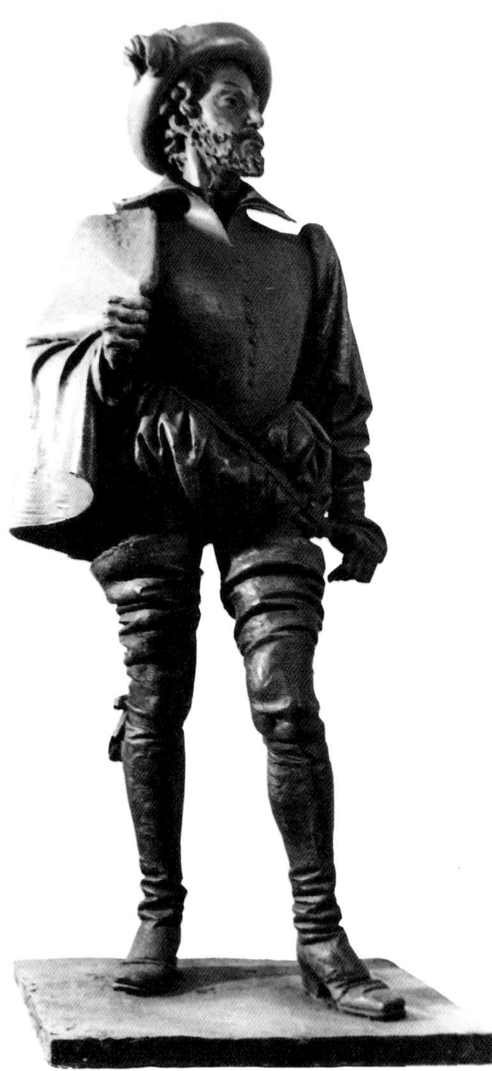

Model for Sir Walter Raleigh, 1976/84, bonded bronze, 16½ x 6 x 5½ inches. Private collection.

bas relief." Using the example of a sculpture depicting a woman vigorously brushing her hair, Buechner remarked, "This one gesture, so common to all hair brushers, seems as if it could be held forever."

John Canaday wrote a glowing review of Lucchesi's work in the *New York Times*, and he was hailed in the *Christian Science Monitor* as "one of the notably talented young sculptors of this generation." Suzanne Kiplinger praised him in the *Village Voice* for his "love of the human" and called him "certainly one of the most loving sculptors we have."

Following the Forum exhibition, Lucchesi received his first U.S. commissions. One was for a large frieze for the National Westminster Bank USA on Fifth Avenue at Forty-eighth Street. The thirteen-foot piece, which rests on the back wall of the bank, depicts a group of people waiting on a bank line [pages 124, 125]. Many of the figures are portrayed in motion—a woman bending to scratch her leg, a child leaning forward, a woman holding open a newspaper—and the gestures bear an unmistakable Lucchesi touch. The style of the sculpture is less realistic than his later work. Its rough surfaces, sharp lines and planes, and stylized forms indicate a tentative move toward cubism.

Another commission Lucchesi received during the 1960s was for the J. Walter Thompson advertising agency in the Graybar Building on Lexington Avenue and Forty-third Street. This life-size bronze piece depicts a scene with a writer and secretary. Again, the composition of the sculpture incorporates movement and the unexpected gesture. One of the female figures is bending backward, increasing the tension of the piece. The facial characteristics of the figures are stylized, and parts of the human figure are almost caricatures. However, Lucchesi's eye for the colloquial is evident. He depicts the writer with a pencil in his hand and a woman with a pendant hanging from her neck.

In the succeeding years Lucchesi received a number of commissions. One was from the city of Raleigh in North Carolina for a large sculpture of Sir Walter Raleigh, and another was for a large bronze bust of Walt Whitman for Arrow Park in Monroe, New York.

In 1963, two years after his successful one-man exhibition at the Forum, Lucchesi had a second show at the gallery, displaying twenty-six new pieces. The style of these works was more realistic, less revealing of "modern" or "cubist" influences. Lucchesi describes his goal as "seeking to capture an honest portrayal of people." Again, reviews praised his work as a sensitive depiction of contemporary life. They commended his eye for the unusual gesture and his skill at showing figures in motion. The reviewer for the *New York Herald Tribune* described Lucchesi as a sculptor "who has looked at Gothic art and has transformed medieval saints into secular men and women who read a paper, shake out a bed sheet or wash a window."

The moments of daily life became the hallmark of Lucchesi's work. "I was dealing with the human condition," says the sculptor, "with the way people interact with each other. More than anything else, I was trying to capture the gesture, the unexpected twist of the figure that says so much, yet is so common. But it was different, nobody else was doing it."

Over the decade of the 1970s Lucchesi began to turn his attention more and more to his immediate surroundings, life in New York City. The

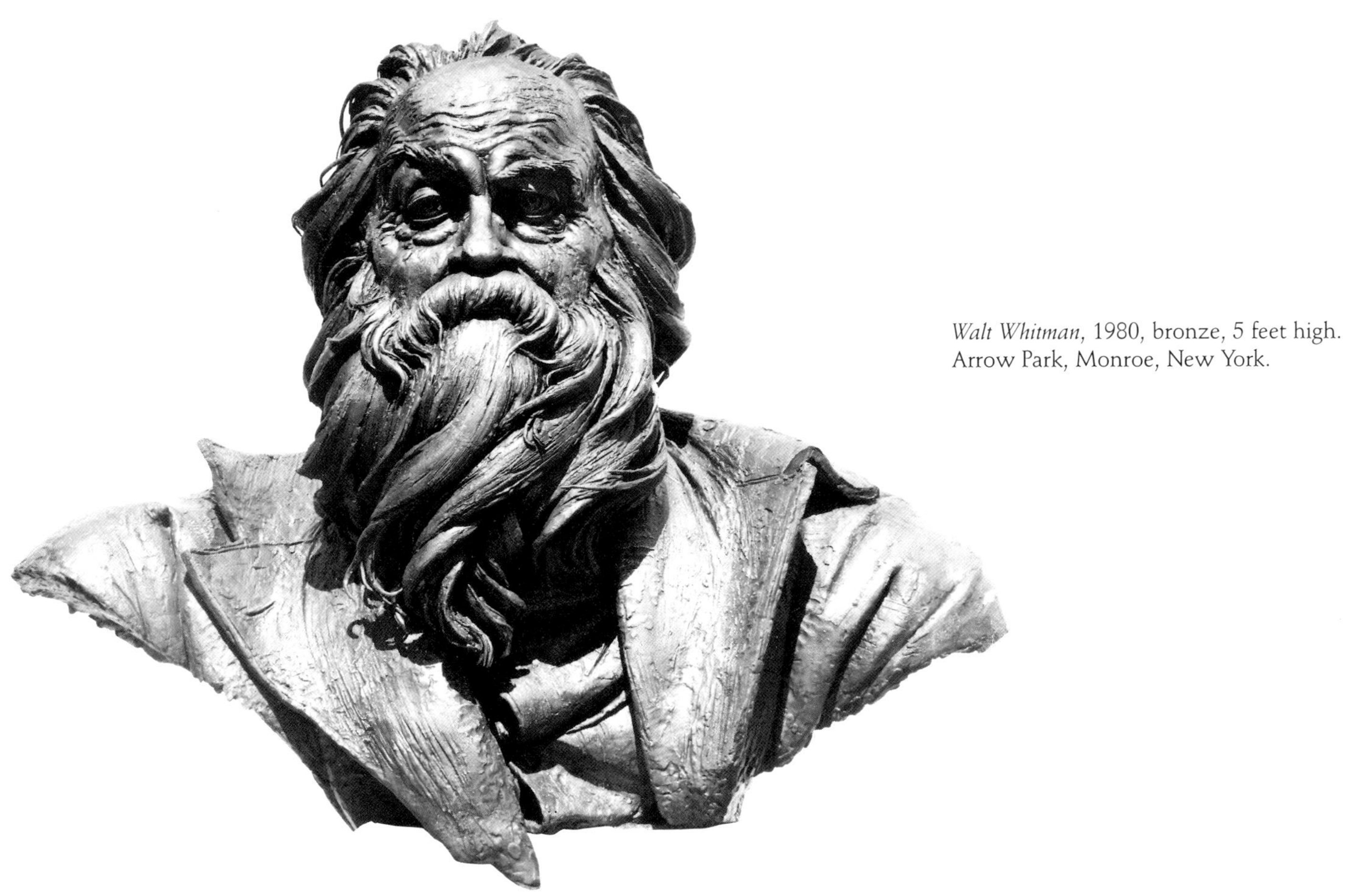

Walt Whitman, 1980, bronze, 5 feet high. Arrow Park, Monroe, New York.

themes of his sculptures encompassed the broad range of urban life—women in a bathhouse, a young woman at a pay phone, teenagers on line for a concert, bus stops, subway scenes, department stores, rock-and-roll stars, the homeless. In all of these scenes, Lucchesi was looking to capture the human spirit. "I like to see into the eyes of people," he says. "I wanted to get communication into a piece of sculpture. If it's not with a look in their eyes, then it's in the intertwining of the forms."

Despite the great variety of subject matter, Lucchesi describes his ultimate concern as being less with the particulars of a piece than the overall form. When working on a sculpture, he views the chunk of clay as an architectural frame and molds it until the silhouette looks as he wants it to. It is the aggregate, the larger form, more than the individual parts, that intrigues him. When describing the process of creating a work of sculpture, Lucchesi alludes to this fascination with form: "I rarely make drawings first, but if I do a sketch I do it on a tablet of clay and make a bas-relief. From that bas-relief, it keeps growing. I look at it from a distance. It has to look right from all angles. A lot of people see only the subject matter, but I pay more attention to the architectural frame. What interests me most is the overall look of the piece."

Whether Lucchesi is depicting a man trying on a coat, a woman shaking out the bedsheets [pages 2–3, 102], or a girl bent over to fix a shoe strap [pages 47, 84, 85], the silhouette of the sculpture is of paramount importance. Yet the viewer is always acutely aware of the people within the

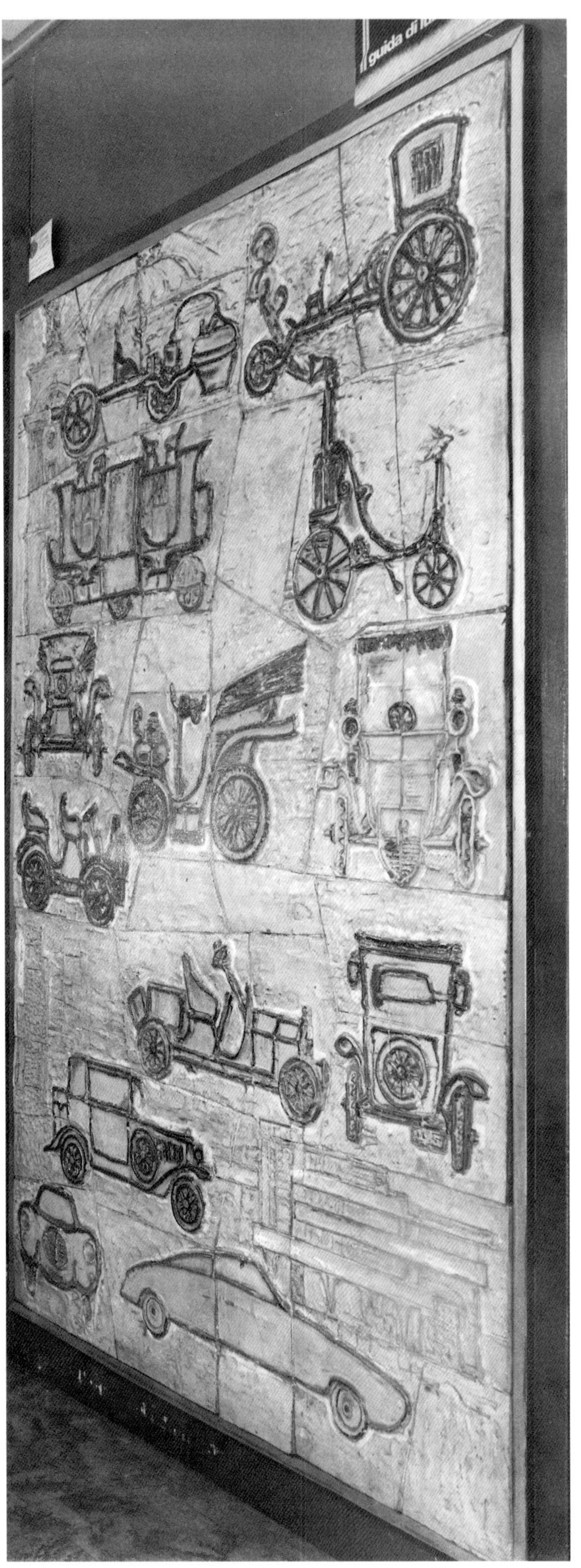

Gasoline Station, 1954, ceramic. Piazza Donatello, Florence.

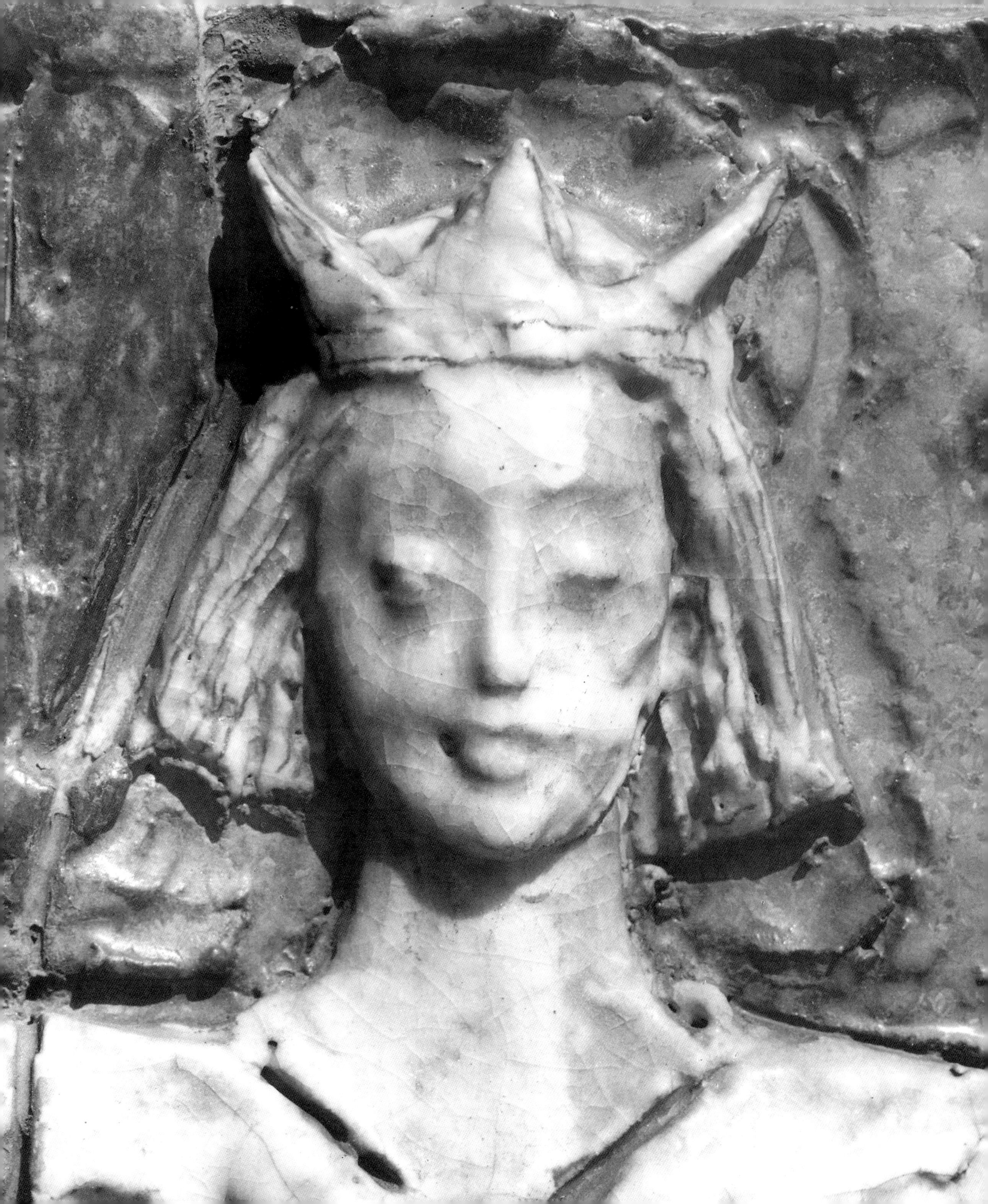

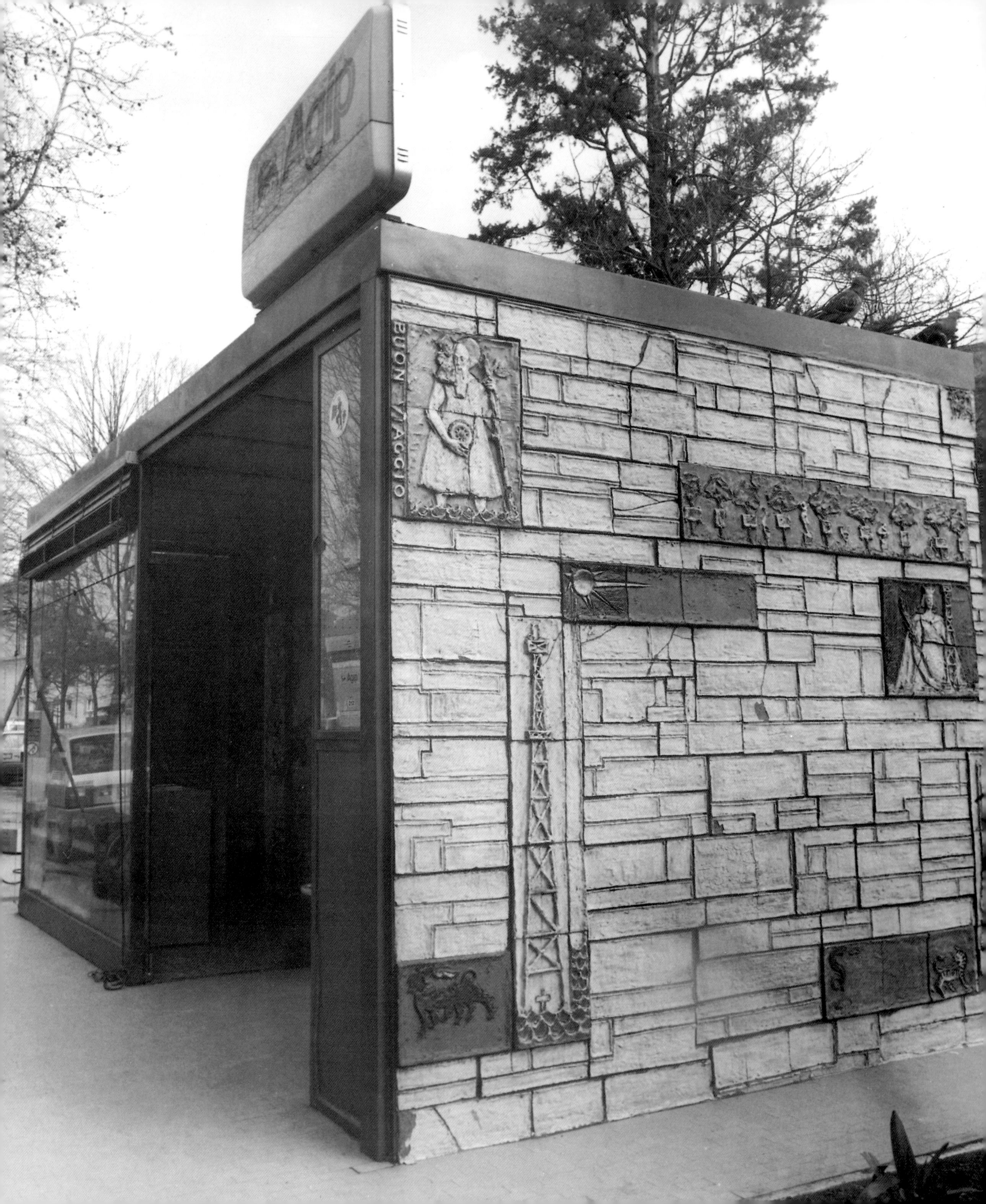
Agip
BUON VIAGGIO

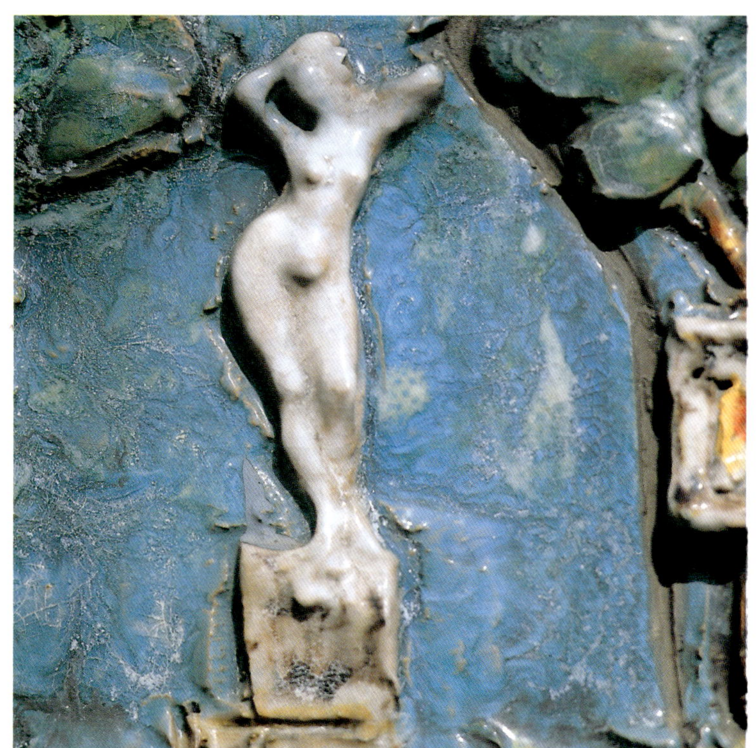

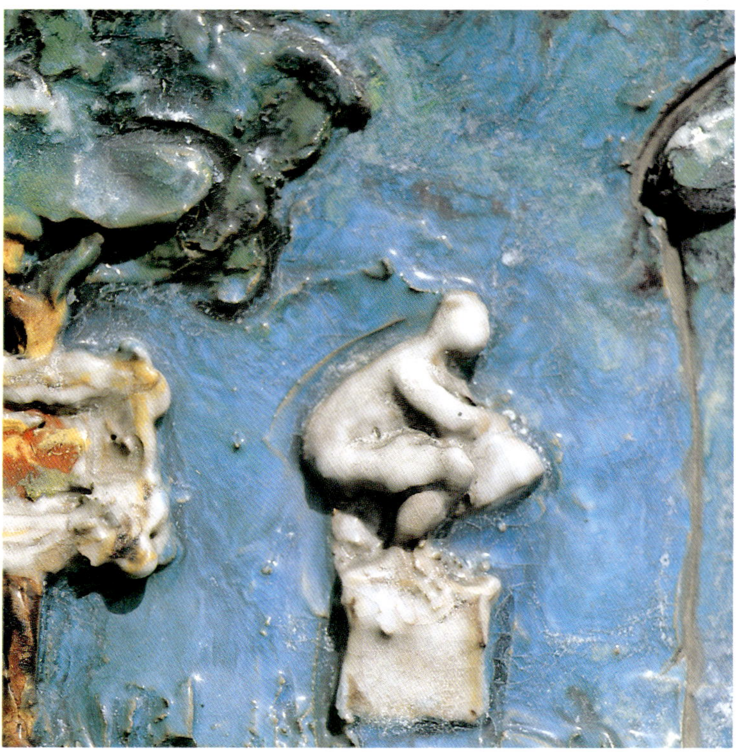

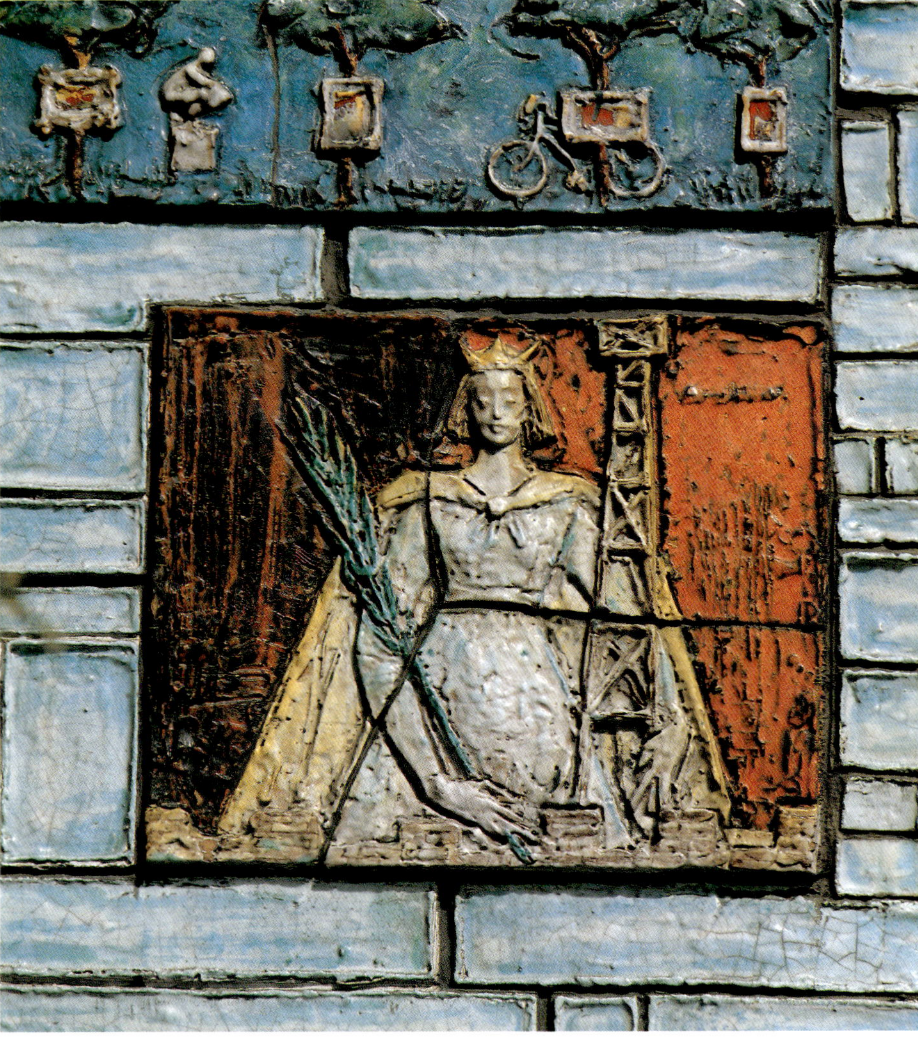

Gasoline Station (details), 1954, ceramic.
Piazza Donatello, Florence.

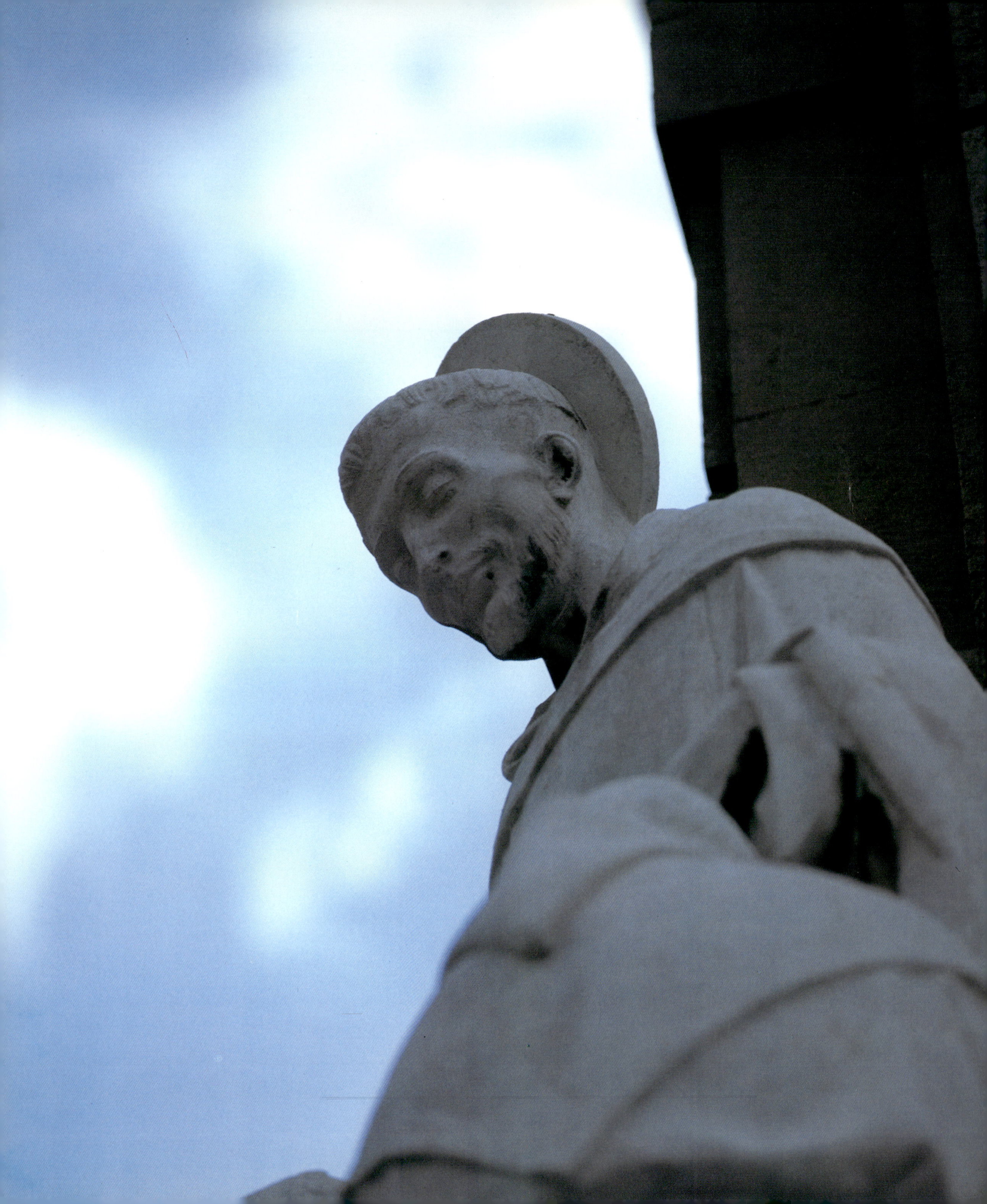

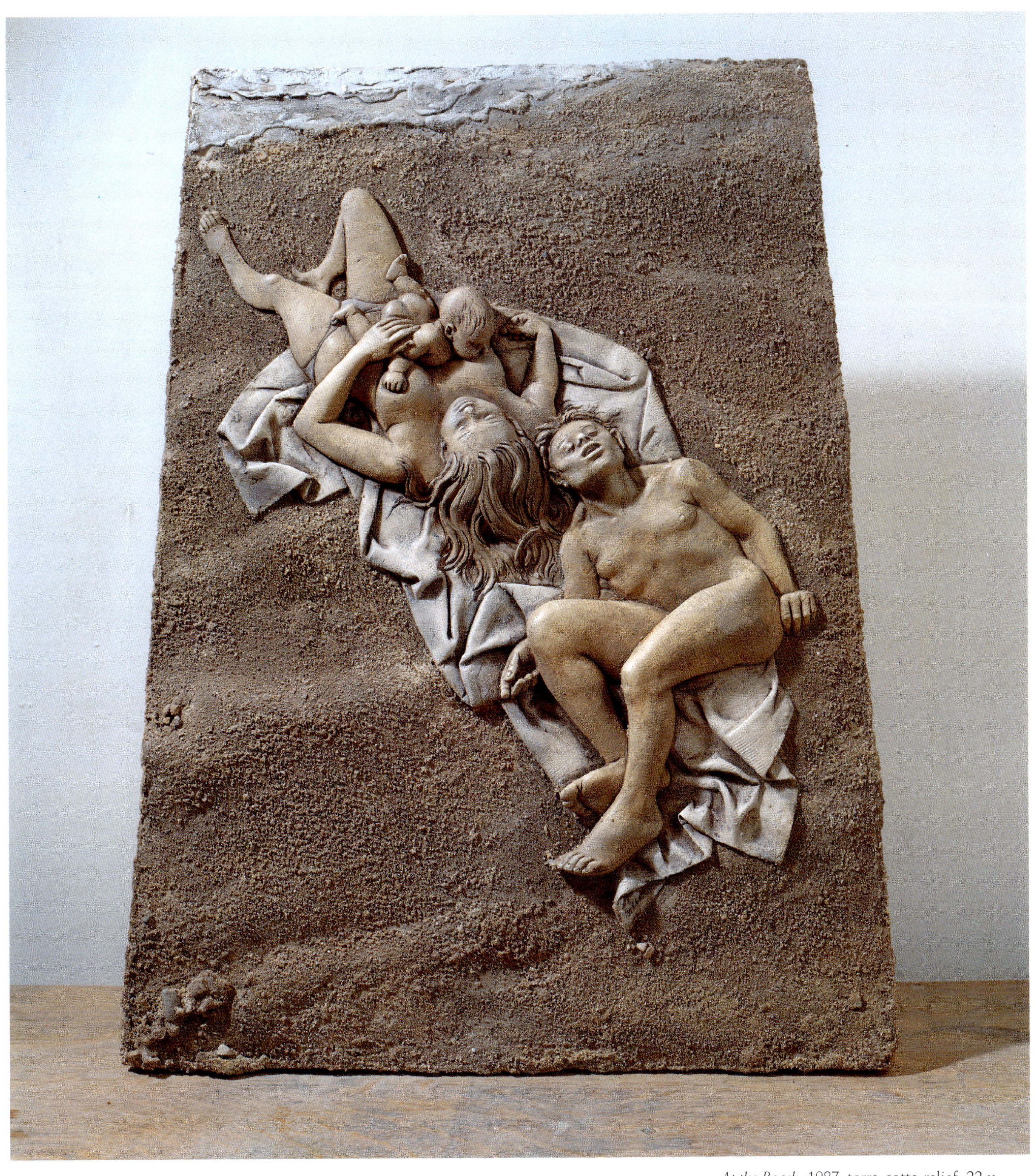

Saint Francis of Assisi (detail), 1956, marble, life-size. Florence. (See also black-and-white illustration, page 164.)

At the Beach, 1987, terra-cotta relief, 22 x 15 inches. Forum Gallery, New York. (See also black-and-white illustrations, pages 42, 43.)

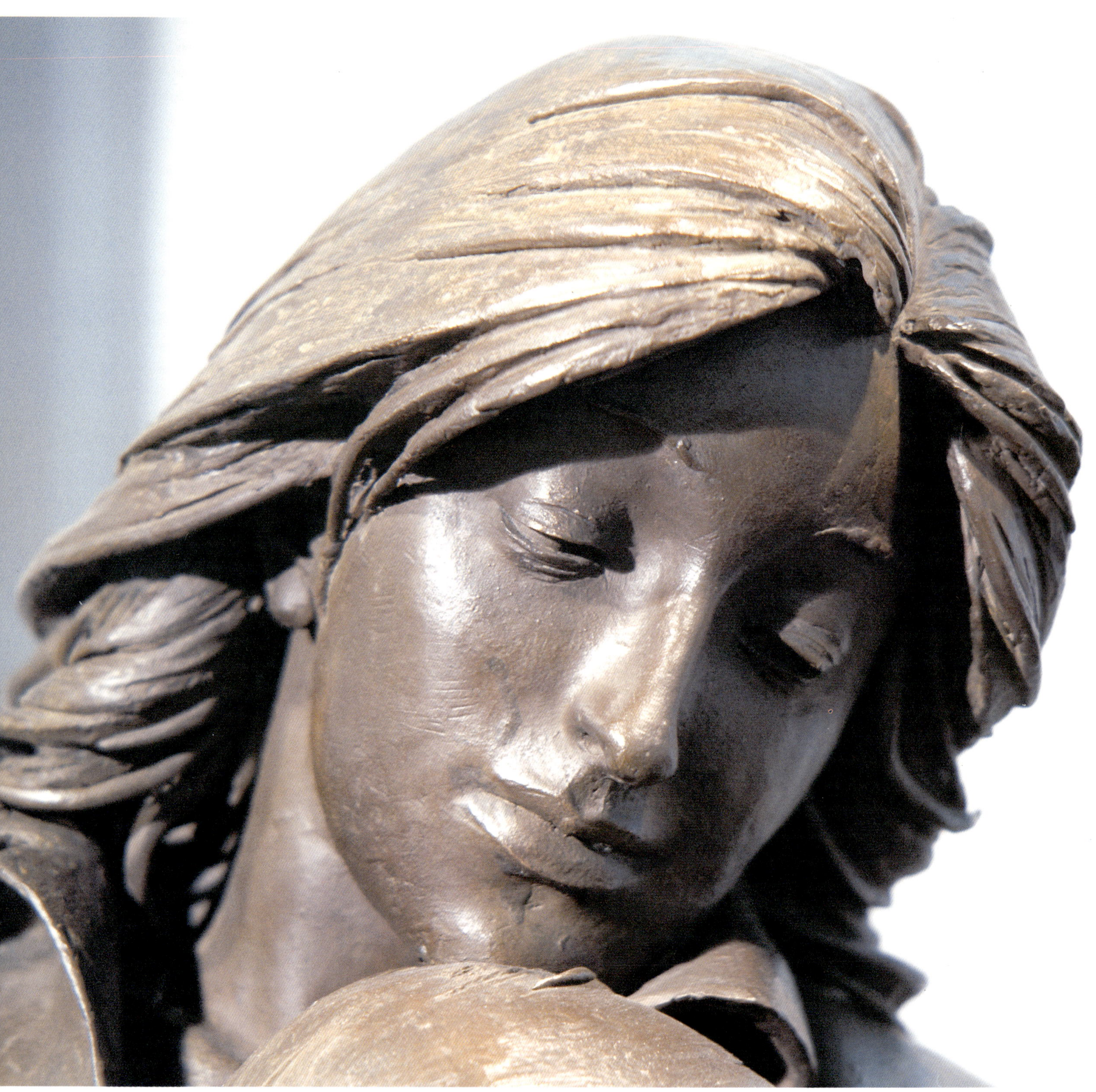

frame and the human qualities and conditions they convey—the warmth of motherhood, the sensuousness of nude women, the playfulness of rotund children, the resignation of the city's poor.

According to Lucchesi, it is the viewer, not the sculptor, who is essentially responsible for the interpretation of a piece. A sculptor may have a general theme in mind, but it is the viewer who enriches the work by bringing to it his own special perspective. "First comes the composition," maintains Lucchesi; "the philosophical statement comes after. The artist looks differently at a piece of sculpture when he's doing it. He doesn't think about the interpretations people will give it."

Over the years Lucchesi has also turned his attention to famous classical themes, but to these stories he gives his own special touch. One of his sculptures is a treatment of the celebrated *Judgment of Paris*, done in 1982 [page 156]. "In the sixteenth century," says Lucchesi, "everybody did the Judgment of Paris. It was a common theme. I wanted to try a different interpretation, so instead of making the women alive, I made them as statues. Paris is giving the apple to the best-sculptured woman." In *The Trojan Women* of 1974 [pages 154–55], Lucchesi shows Donatello-esque figures huddled together in their grief. "They are throwing down the body of Achilles," Lucchesi explains. "I had the body of a baby on the ground at first, but I took it out because it was too gruesome. So it became just women in sorrow. It could be at the base of a crucifix, a Deposition, but my original idea was the Trojan women."

Lucchesi also gives fresh interpretations to common biblical themes. In his *Annunciation* of 1980 [page 163], the madonna is depicted in bed. "Everyone who does an Annunciation makes it very dramatic," says Lucchesi. "I tried to do something different. During the Renaissance, Mary was always portrayed leaning on a pew with a book, reading. I don't think it happened that way. There weren't any pews or books then, so I put her in bed. I think that's where you should be if you are dreaming of a baby. She was probably scared and wondering how she could go through with it."

Susannah and the Elders is another famous theme to which Lucchesi gives a new twist. The elders are traditionally shown simply as old men, but Lucchesi presents them as old shepherds in his 1980 terra-cotta, adding a touch of the pastoral [page 162]. This sculpture includes an extraordinarily skillful and imaginative rendition of bushes and rocks, behind which the shepherds leer at the young woman bathing below, her towel draped over a nearby ledge. A typical Lucchesi touch is a small figure of a goat sitting in the bushes at the very top of the sculpture.

In *Jacob's Ladder* of 1978 [pages 160, 161], Lucchesi presents an original interpretation of Jacob's dream, and the ladder has the appearance of twisting upward into the sky. "Everybody did this scene," Lucchesi says, "with clouds and marble steps. But I figured he was sitting at the base of a tree, so I made the ladder out of wood like a tree, with some angels going up." To give the feeling of the ladder disappearing in the distance, he created a sense of perspective, making it smaller as it rises into the air.

Periodically Lucchesi works with models, but he always strives to find a universal look within the particular individual. "When I use models," explains the sculptor, "I try to make the piece more universal looking, with not too much character to the face. Maybe I'm wrong, but I like it to be

After Shopping (detail), 1979, bronze, life-size. Private collection. (See also black-and-white illustrations, pages 34–37.)

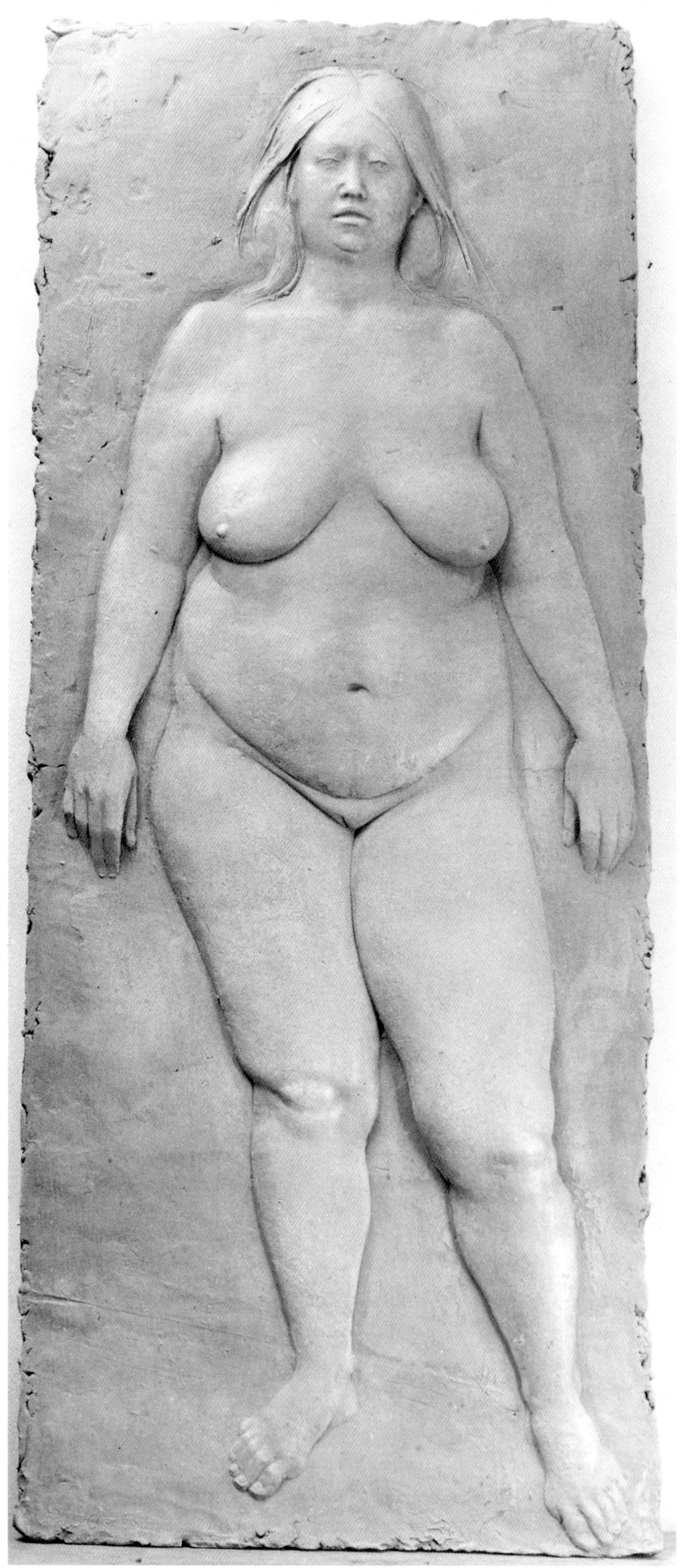

general, symbolic." In recent years Lucchesi's models have been people he comes in contact with in the East Village of New York, where he has his studio. In one case the model was a local pregnant woman. Another model was a heavy-set woman who also lived in the neighborhood. One of his most sensuous reclining nudes was made quickly of a model during a demonstration for students; the results were so striking that Lucchesi keeps a photograph of a detail in his home.

Patty, 1973, terra-cotta relief, 60 x 20 inches. Forum Gallery, New York.

In other sculptures Lucchesi has shown a remarkable facility for doing portraits from memory. One of the most touching such portraits is a relief of his aunt gesticulating through a window while his mother listens attentively [pages 94, 95]. They have an earthiness about them, both in appearance and manner. The aunt has a kerchief tied around her head and is wearing simple farm clothes; the mother is dressed similarly, and Lucchesi made no attempt to hide her wrinkles and jowls. The direct honesty of the figures touchingly shows the artist's affection for his subjects. Characteristically, he chose to depict them in their everyday attire, not in their Sunday best.

In another sculpture Lucchesi shows a beautiful young farm woman pensively looking into space, with one arm to her chin and the other holding a farm implement used for gathering hay [pages 80, 81]. This was his sister when she was a young woman, again done from memory. In still another Lucchesi portrays the aunt he lived with while he was an art student in Lucca; she is at a table selling vegetables in the marketplace [pages 100, 101]. "She's sitting there," Lucchesi explains, "waiting for her next customer. You can still see people like her in the marketplaces of Italy." A photograph of her remarkably sensitive face was once featured on the cover of the *National Sculpture Review*. Again Lucchesi chose her because she was typical of so many other women of his native country.

One of Lucchesi's most moving sculptures, *Pietà*, is of his mother on her deathbed [pages 110, 111]. There is a figure flung across the foot of the bed with her arm hanging down and her head buried in the bedcovers to hide her grief. When Lucchesi was asked who the young woman was, the artist replied, "She is the spirit of my soul mourning."

Most of Lucchesi's figures, however, are created out of his imagination. There is a distinctive look about his young women that represents Lucchesi's ideal of feminine beauty, and it appears over and over as one of the unmistakable characteristics of his work. It can be found in the faces of young women crouching, reclining on a chair or bed, reading a book, talking on the telephone, riding a bicycle, or holding a child on their laps. One of his favorite gestures is a hand resting on the chin, suggesting pensiveness. He describes this as "musing" and says this is "the position that people take when they are holding themselves in thought."

In the great tradition of figurative sculpture, Lucchesi has a fascination for drapery. He often makes the figures nude to begin with and then puts clothing on afterward. This generally gives the sense of tight-fitting garments, particularly on women, and the folds in the cloth add to the movement and drama of the sculpture.

Lucchesi's nudes, which are almost always female, have a lovely, soft sensuousness about them. This is particularly true of the young girlish figures, which he does beautifully. But his sympathy and sensitivity extend to the heavier-set women whose bulges and creases are treated with equal affection.

The men in Lucchesi's sculptures do not have the same distinctive characteristics as the women. They are rarely shown as the centerpieces of his sculptures, but almost always as accompaniments to the women he portrays. In one sculpture of nude men in a public bathhouse, he seems to be looking at his figures with a sense of amusement [pages 140–43]. For the most part they are fat, ugly figures who do not realize how funny they appear to observers.

As with Lucchesi's women, his babies always have something in common. He is one of those sculptors who has found the key to rendering the faces and figures of small children with great charm and lovableness. Whether they are sleeping, holding their mother's hand, or bouncing on their mother's lap, Lucchesi depicts them enjoying the happiness and security of childhood.

One of the more remarkable examples of Lucchesi's facility with clay and his sharp eye for the scenes around him is the landscapes that he introduces into his sculpture. This is particularly true of his reliefs, where he shows, in one instance, a beach scene with clouds in the sky and waves rolling in on the sand; in another, women on the banks of a river bending over to wash the family clothes [page 122]; and in still another, two lovers lying on the side of a hill with their bicycles lying on the ground nearby [page 118]. He is equally adept at indoor scenes—one sculpture depicts a diner counter with customers seated on stools, the waiter standing behind the counter, and the cook seen through an opening preparing some food [pages 138–39].

Perhaps what Lucchesi has become most noted for is his use of the technique of cantilever to show objects hanging in the air. When a woman is seen shaking out a sheet, one has the feeling that the sheet is actually suspended in space [pages 2–3, 102]. In another instance a woman leans comfortably on a rail, but the rail itself hangs in midair [page 86]. The same is true for a ballet dancer leaning over a barre that is not attached to anything [page 87]. A woman talks in a telephone booth, but the booth itself is mysteriously unattached [page 89]. In another sculpture a woman is standing on a chair washing a large window [pages 98, 99]; although she is connected to the ground by means of the chair, the window is suspended. A particularly impressive sculpture shows a life-size figure of a woman lying languorously on a hammock with one foot touching the ground and the two ends of the hammock reaching up into space [pages 72, 73].

The tension created in these tours de force is due to the contrast between the weight of the figures and the apparent antigravity suspension of the objects on which they are resting. Lucchesi has been very successful with this technique, but he uses it sparingly, only when it seems particularly appropriate.

Since the 1960s Lucchesi has had an exhibition regularly at the Forum Gallery every few years. For one of his more recent shows, in 1985, he was inspired to do a series of sculptures on street life in New York City. These sculptures were a departure for Lucchesi, who for the most part has concentrated on idealized figures, even when they are peasant women from Fibbiano Montanino. But in this particular series he showed the crowds in the graffiti-filled subways of New York [pages 133–37] and people waiting for a bus [page 123] or standing on line to get into a movie theater [page 132]. He showed a homeless man sprawled on the ground next to a garbage can, a shopping-bag lady, a hot-dog vendor, disheveled men relieving themselves at a public urinal [pages 146, 147]. These were not popular subjects, but they showed Lucchesi's sense of humanity in a new context. They were the work of an artist who never tires of looking at the world around him and finding subjects that enable him to express his sensitivity to the human condition.

Curiously, it was about the same time as the New York street figures that Lucchesi did some of his most profound religious sculptures. In the mid-1980s he did a group of sculptures for a church in Massarosa, a small mountain village near where he was born. These included a life-size wooden crucified Christ, a large bronze candlestick with figures at its base, a lectern for a bible also with figures, several angels, and two reliefs [pages 167–77]. In 1986 Lucchesi was commissioned to make an altar for the cathedral of S. Martino in Lucca. The altar, which consists of four friezes, is placed in the center of the cathedral [pages 166, 178–88]. The front of the altar depicts Saint Martin with Lucchesian saints. On the back is Saint Regolo accompanied by a religious procession of contemporary figures. The combination of an early saint and twentieth-century villagers produces an extraordinary effect, and the friezes, which were installed in the church in 1987, are an impressive complement to neighboring works by such famous Renaissance artists as Matteo Civitali, Fra Bartolommeo, and Jacopo della Quercia.

Lucchesi is justly proud of the results of his work in Lucca, for the reliefs are among the most powerful religious sculptures produced in our era. The individual figures are beautifully drawn with all the grace of Lucchesi's finest work. There are striking lifelike portraits of Bishop Giuliano Agresti [page 182] and other figures who played an important role in the history of Lucca. The scenery of the town is wrought with great skill and fidelity. The details of hands, clothing, religious objects, books, beads—all contribute to the total effect of what is clearly one of Lucchesi's finest achievements.

In contrast to the altar in Lucca, Lucchesi's most recent commission, completed in the spring of 1988, is of a contemporary subject, a football player. A group of residents of Elmira, New York, commissioned him to compose a portrait of Ernie Davis, a black football player, born in their town, who died at a young age of leukemia. The sculpture is a six-foot bronze piece standing atop a three-and-a-half-foot base. It shows the athlete in casual dress, with one hand grasping a football, the other holding some books, in honor of his years at Syracuse University. Davis was the first black man to win the Heisman Trophy, a much-sought-after award given in college football.

Unlike many of Lucchesi's other works, the athlete is depicted in a stationary pose, without the suggestion of motion or activity. The strength of the piece is in the straightforwardness, the honesty and sincerity, and the enthusiasm emitted from the face. Before beginning the sculpture, Lucchesi read Davis's biography and focused on the qualities he thought best characterized the football player—his goodness, strength, humanity, and love.

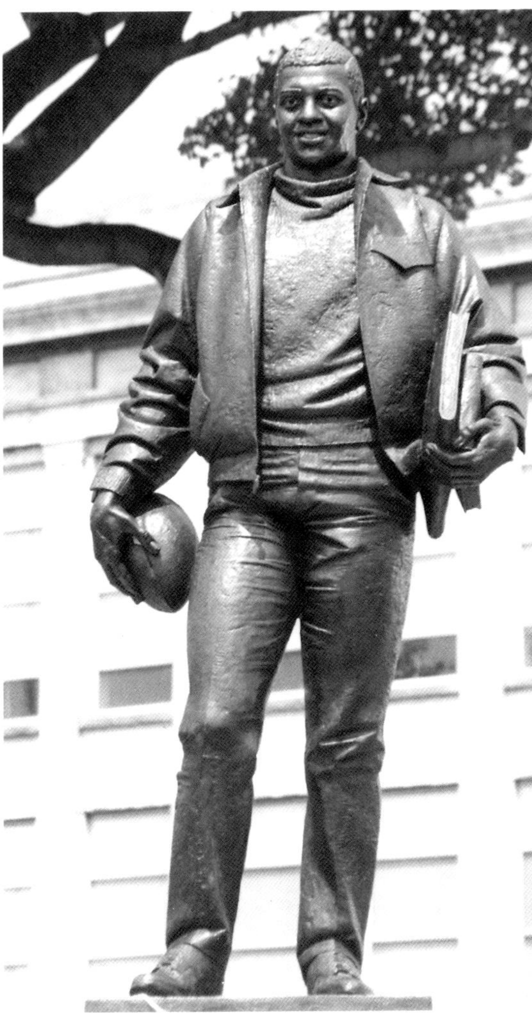

Ernie Davis, 1988, bronze, 6 feet high. Ernie Davis Junior High School, Elmira, New York.

These qualities are successfully captured in the smile, the eyes, and in the overall facial expression of *Ernie Davis*. The sculpture is a fitting addition to Lucchesi's collection of images depicting contemporary American life, and it is an apt expression of Lucchesi's concern and caring for his fellow man.

Over the course of his career Lucchesi lost whatever self-consciousness he might have had as a young artist when he was trying to make his mark in the competitive world of art, where there is a premium on "originality." In his early years as a sculptor, he was striving to develop his own distinctive and individual style. But as time went on, he followed his passions more directly and devoted himself to doing sculptures of subjects that moved him most deeply. He was less interested in building a "reputation" than in creating sculptures with integrity and truthfulness that conveyed an insight into some human quality, or gave a deeper appreciation for an aspect of daily life.

As a result, Lucchesi mastered the ability to express his innermost feelings and concerns through his own special world of people. The impact of his work demonstrates the power of his creative mind and the lengths to which his probing eye and skillful fingers can go in order to portray his remarkably compelling image of life in our time.

THROUGH THE CAMERA LENS

Bruno Lucchesi's sculpture is a photographer's delight—at least for this photographer. I have known his work for over twenty years and have been continuously surprised and fascinated by his marvelous inventions. Although there is always something recognizable about his sculpture, there is also a new discovery in everything he does, for his mind keeps darting around the world of people that surrounds him, continually looking for different ways to portray the life we lead. His subject is every man and every woman, but it is also each of us individually since we are all part of a universal humankind. And perhaps most of all it is Bruno Lucchesi himself, for by showing us what he sees in other people, he reveals something profound about the kind of person he is.

The forms Lucchesi creates of people bending, stretching, leaning, crouching, talking, thinking, sleeping translate beautifully into two-dimensional images. The figures have an easy grace that captivates the eye as one looks through the camera lens. Faces have a fine sensitivity that expresses the artist's love of the people he portrays, and the invariably thoughtful eyes seem to reflect the world within as well as the world outside. This is as true of his angels as of his subway passengers, of his mothers dreamily fondling their children as his women waiting on street corners.

When Lucchesi includes a group of people in one of his sculptures, each person seems to retain his or her self-awareness as an individual, and the camera can isolate them into separate figures. There is always some special quality about each one of them—their posture, their build, their clothes, their expression. By being selective, the photographer can create portraits, showing how distinctive and memorable each figure is. Although Lucchesi says that while working he is primarily interested in composing the figures and creating an interplay of forms as he manipulates the clay, what emerges is a sense of character and personality in each individual. They become archetypal portraits of the people we see every day as we walk the streets or look at our friends or think of ourselves and those we love.

There is a certain quality about Lucchesi's work that is unmistakable—the kind of face that he creates, the graceful movement of figures, the virtuoso handling of things in space. I never realized his uniqueness more clearly than when I visited the small church in Massarosa, Italy, where I went to photograph some of his works. When I arrived there was no one in the church who could point out which sculptures were Lucchesi's. The church was empty, and there was no one home in the priest's apartment. But when I looked around I realized that I did not need a guide. The flying figures holding up the lectern and others at the foot of the candlestick, the graceful angels in the four corners of the altar, and the relief of the Last Supper—these could not have been done by anyone else. The only work I missed was the life-size Christ, carved in wood, high up on the cross, which was less obviously Lucchesi's work, but fortunately the priest arrived just as I had finished and I was able to photograph it with the long lens of my Hasselblad camera.

Later that day when I arrived at the great cathedral of Lucca, with its superb tomb of Ilaria del Carretto by Jacopo della Quercia that has rightly been described as one of the greatest masterpieces of the Renaissance, my heart sank. In the center was an enormous altar, poorly lit, covered with relief figures that looked from the distance to be completely undistinguished. But as soon as I placed my lights on the side of the reliefs to bring out the sculptural qualities, I discovered that they were vintage Lucchesi, and I spent several exciting hours enjoying all the details through my camera lens.

I photographed many of the works for this book at the Forum Gallery in New York during various exhibitions, but I also had the pleasure of photographing some of the sculptures in Lucchesi's East Village studio. When I arrived at the comparatively small space where he does most of his work, I was surprised to find dozens of wonderful sculptures that seemed to be waiting for the camera. I asked Bruno if he would help me make a selection. "Think of me as dead," he said half seriously. "You pick out what you want to photograph without any influence from me." And he stood by watching, not saying a word as I made my choices—a task I found extraordinarily difficult, for there was hardly one I was willing to leave out.

Showing Lucchesi prints of my photographs was an experience in itself. He was always astonished to see how beautiful the sculptures looked. "I didn't know they were that good!" he said in disbelief. "They don't look like my sculptures! The photographs make them look better than they are." I insisted that the photographs could be no better than the subject, but I doubt that I ever quite convinced him.

The gentleness, kindness, simplicity, modesty of Bruno Lucchesi are ever present in his work. His people are wonderful to behold and a privilege to photograph. His genius is to express a joy of life even when he shows conditions that create misery and suffering, for Lucchesi's subjects seem to feel that being alive is its own reward. His gift to us is that as observers and lovers of his people, we feel their sense of gratitude in our own hearts.

DAVID FINN

MOTHER AND CHILD

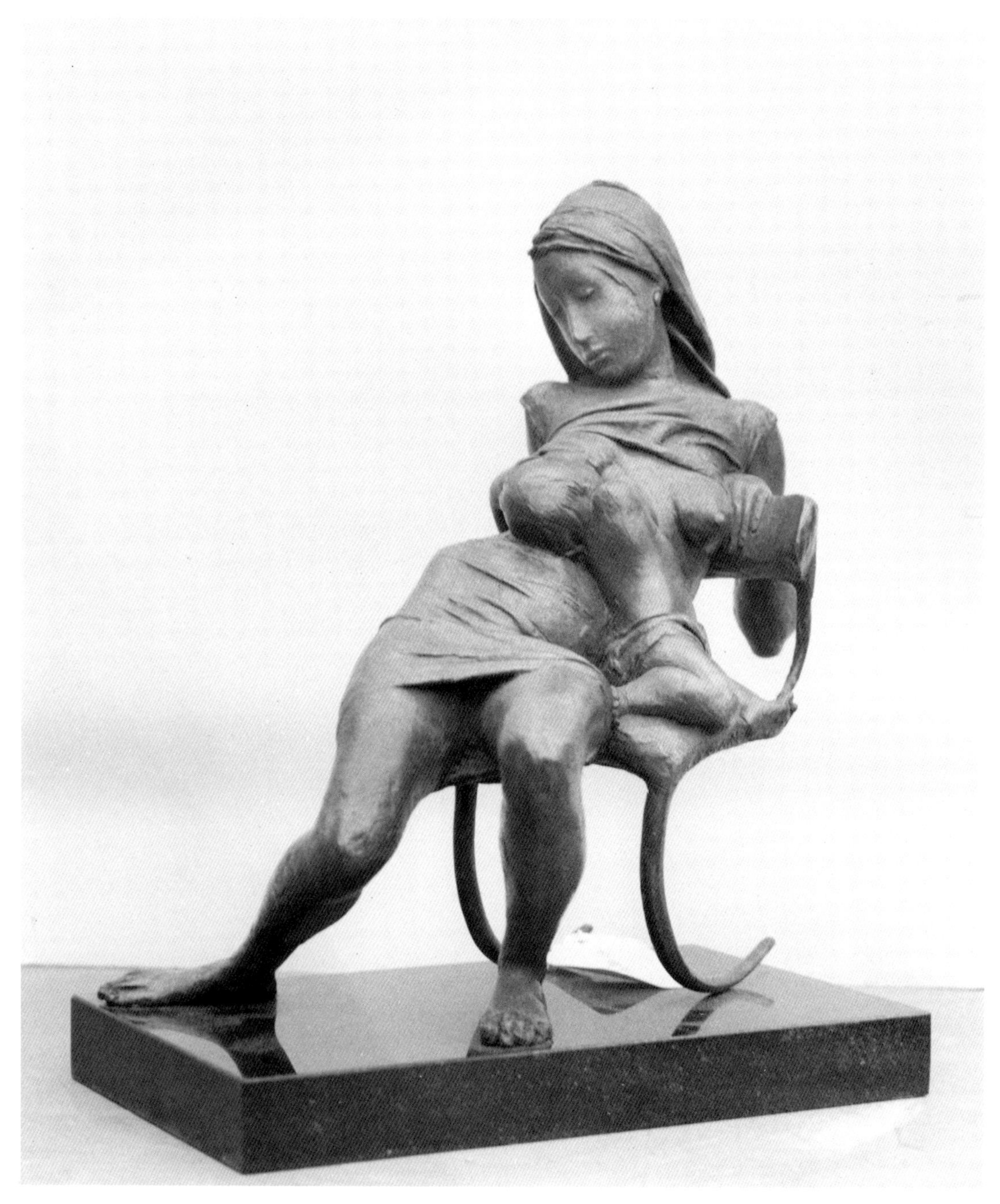

Nursing Mother, 1967, mixed media, 27 inches wide. Private collection.

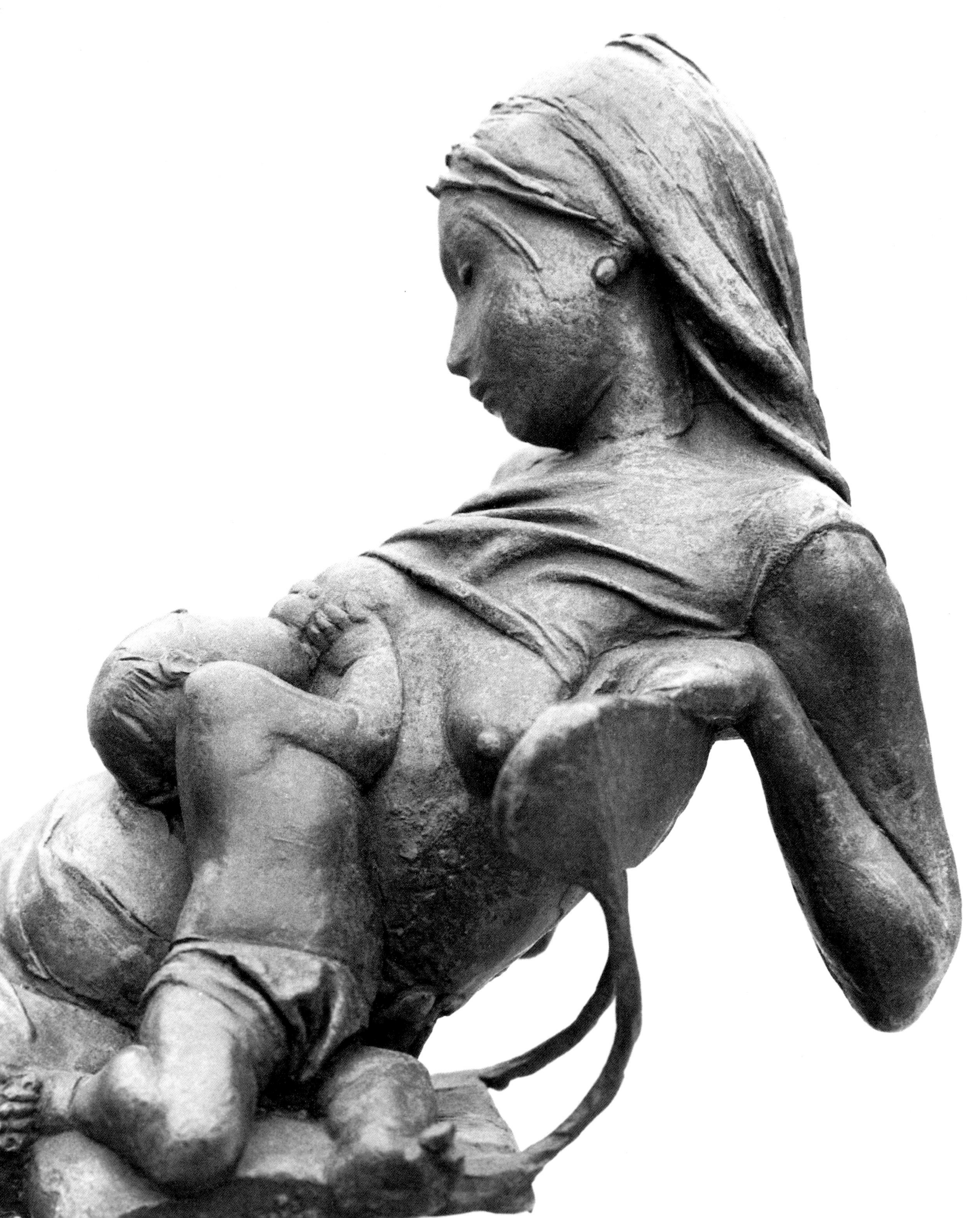

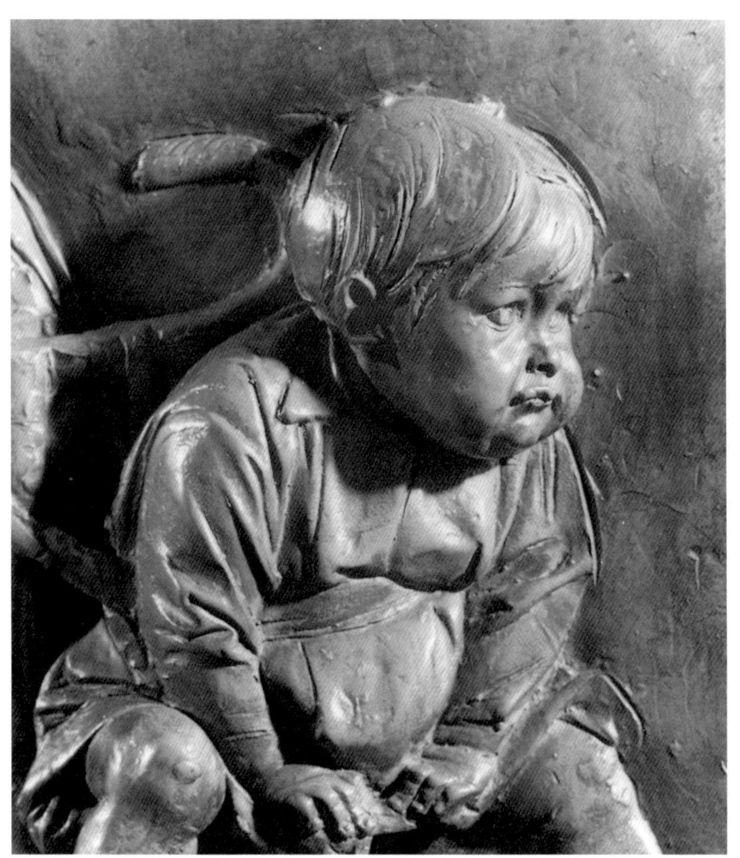

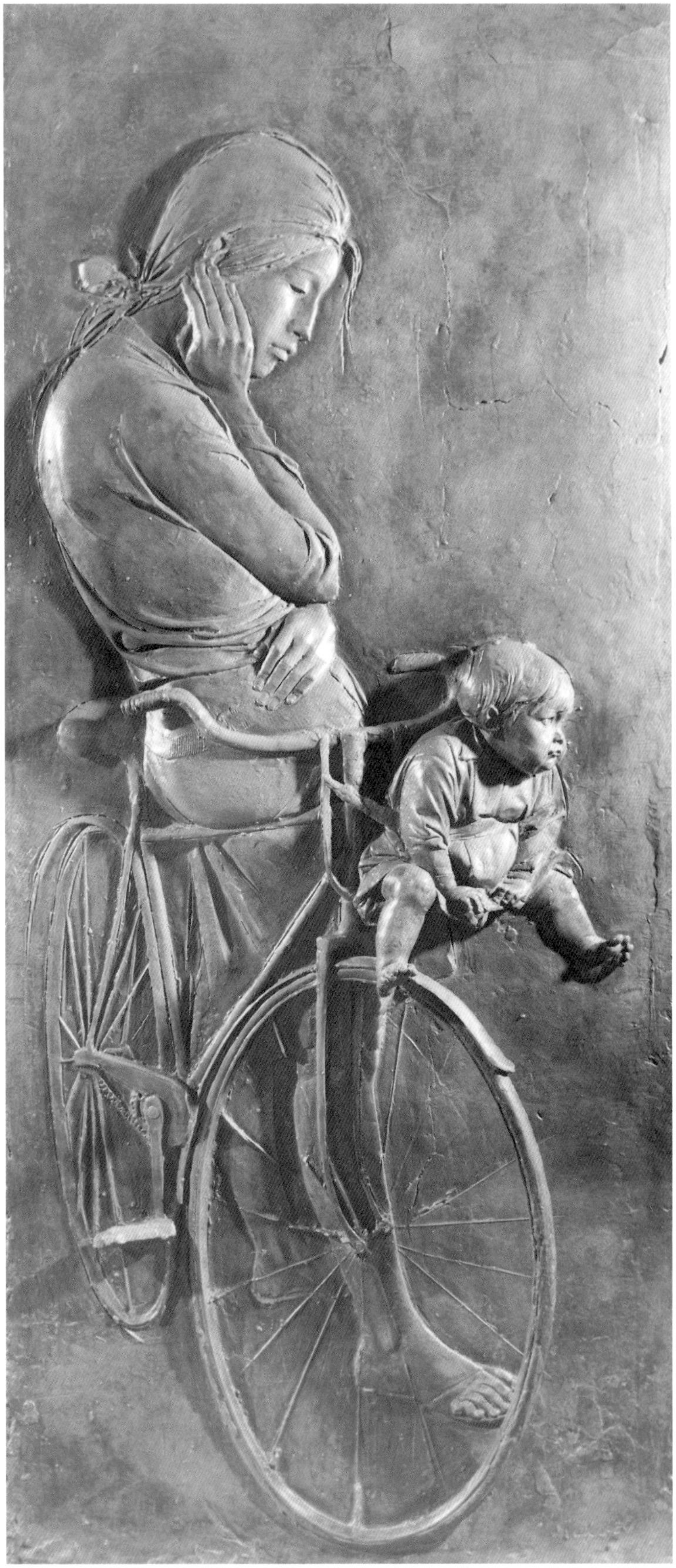

Mother and Child on Bicycle, 1967, bonded bronze relief, 61 inches high. Collection of Bella and Sol Fishko, New York. (See also colorplate, page 45.)

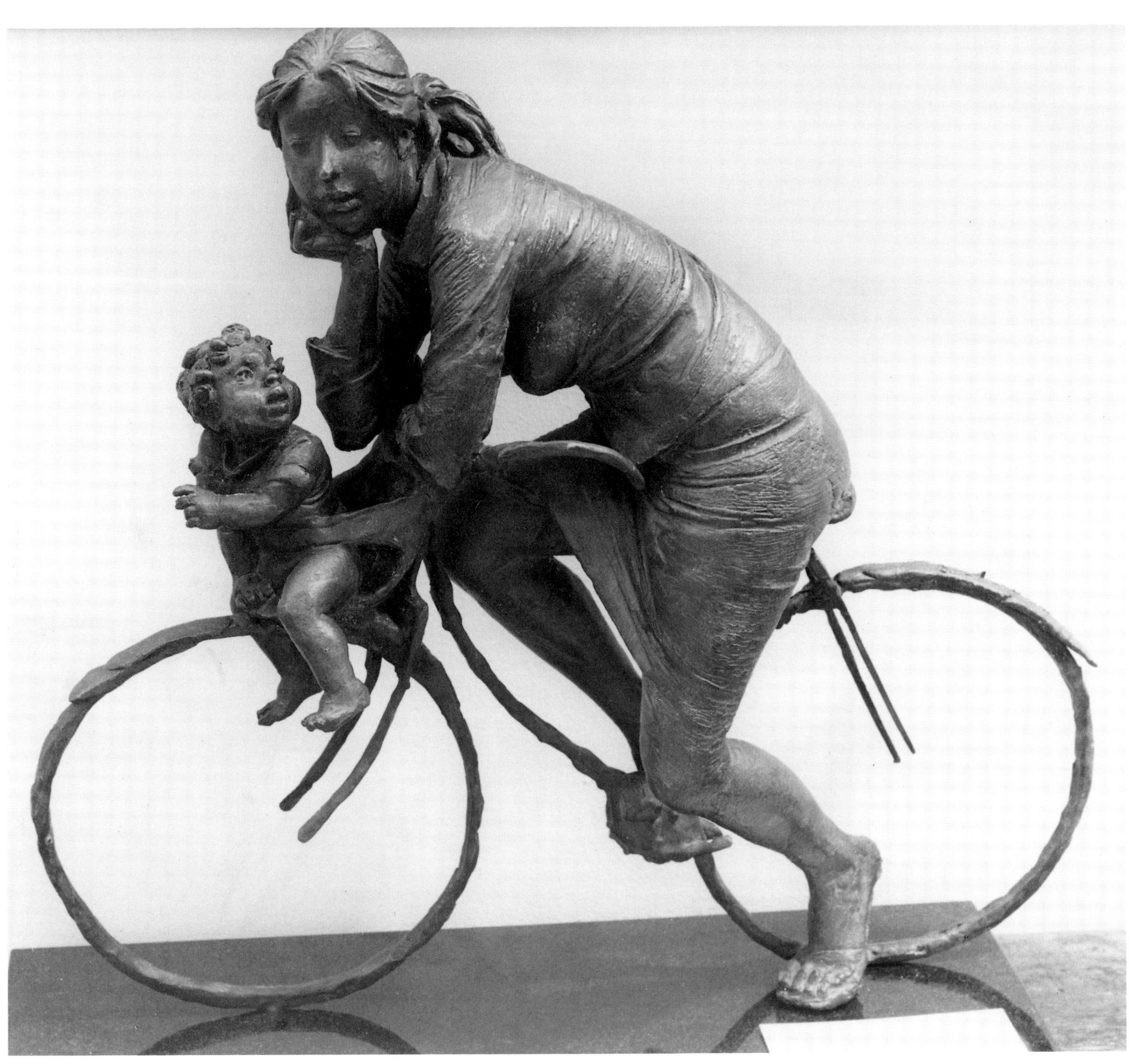

Woman and Child with Bike, 1980, bronze, 14 x 15 x 5 inches. Collection of Mayer Silvera, Hong Kong.

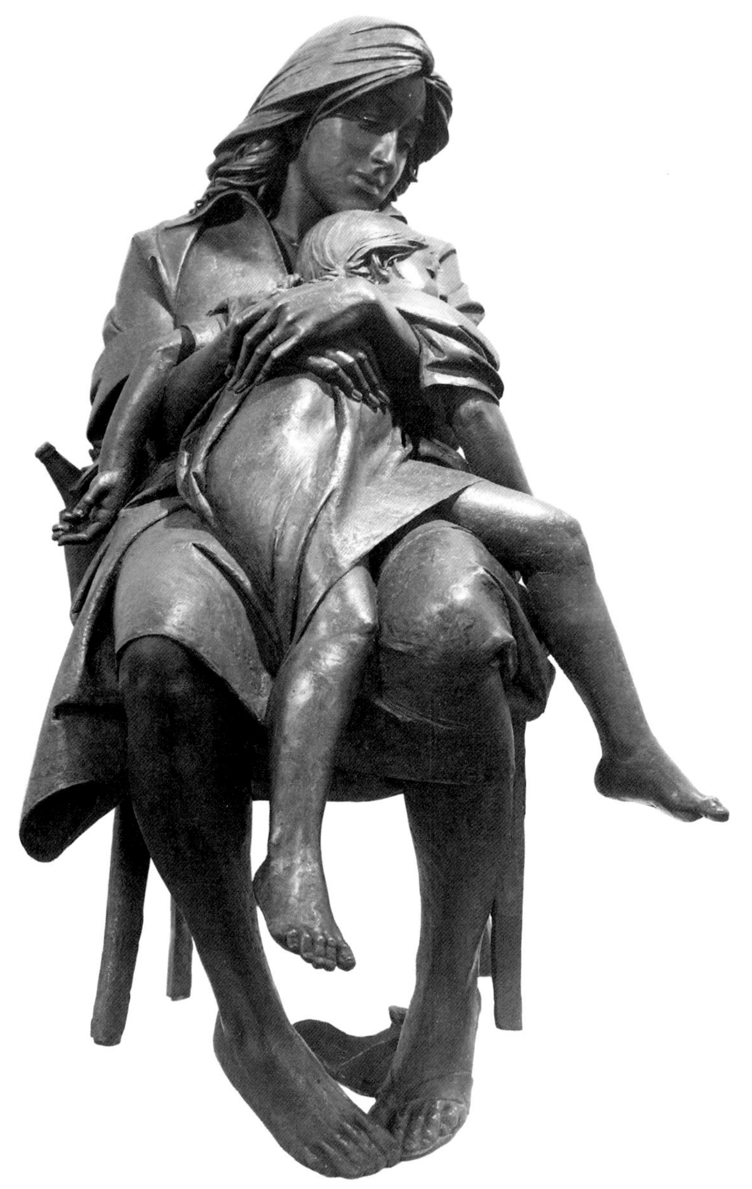

After Shopping, 1979, bronze, life-size. Private collection. (See also colorplate, page 20.)

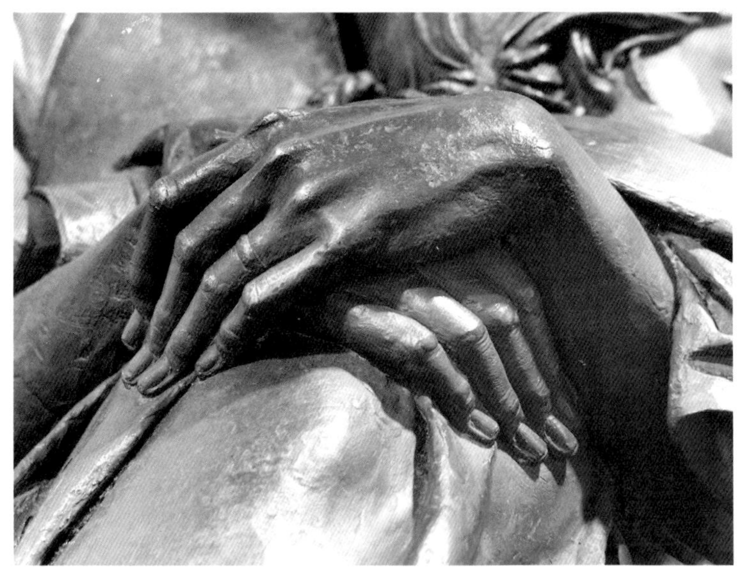

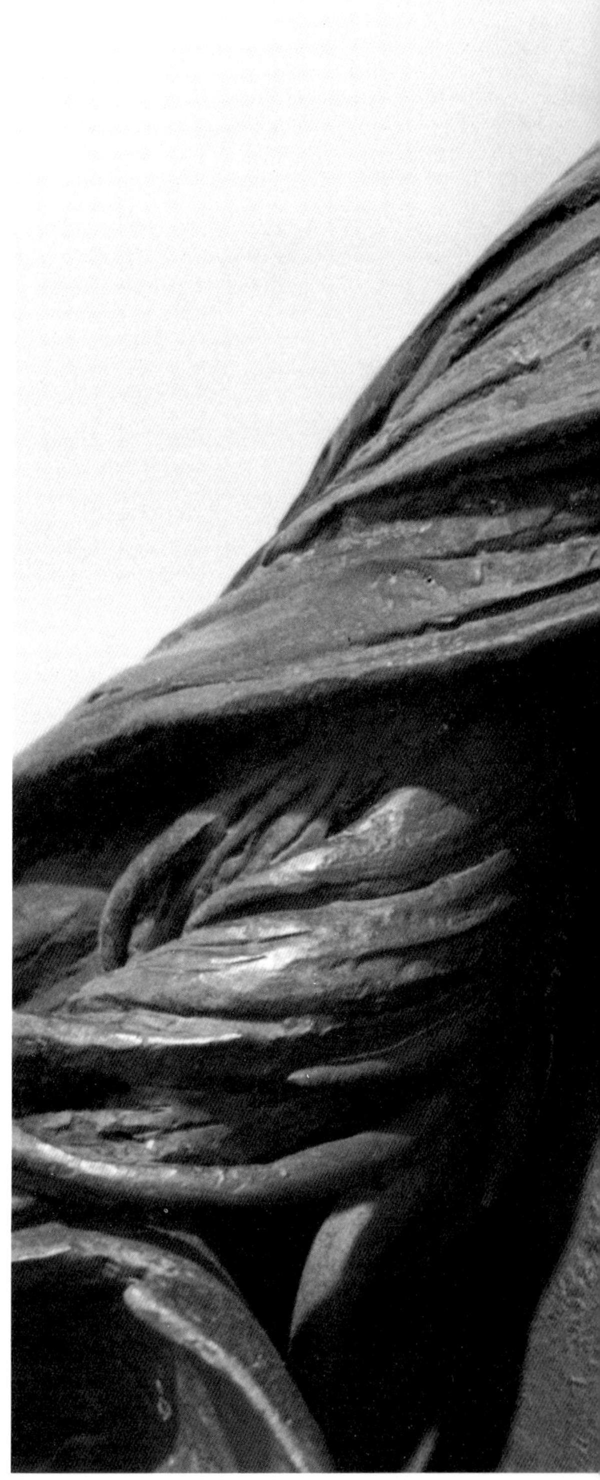

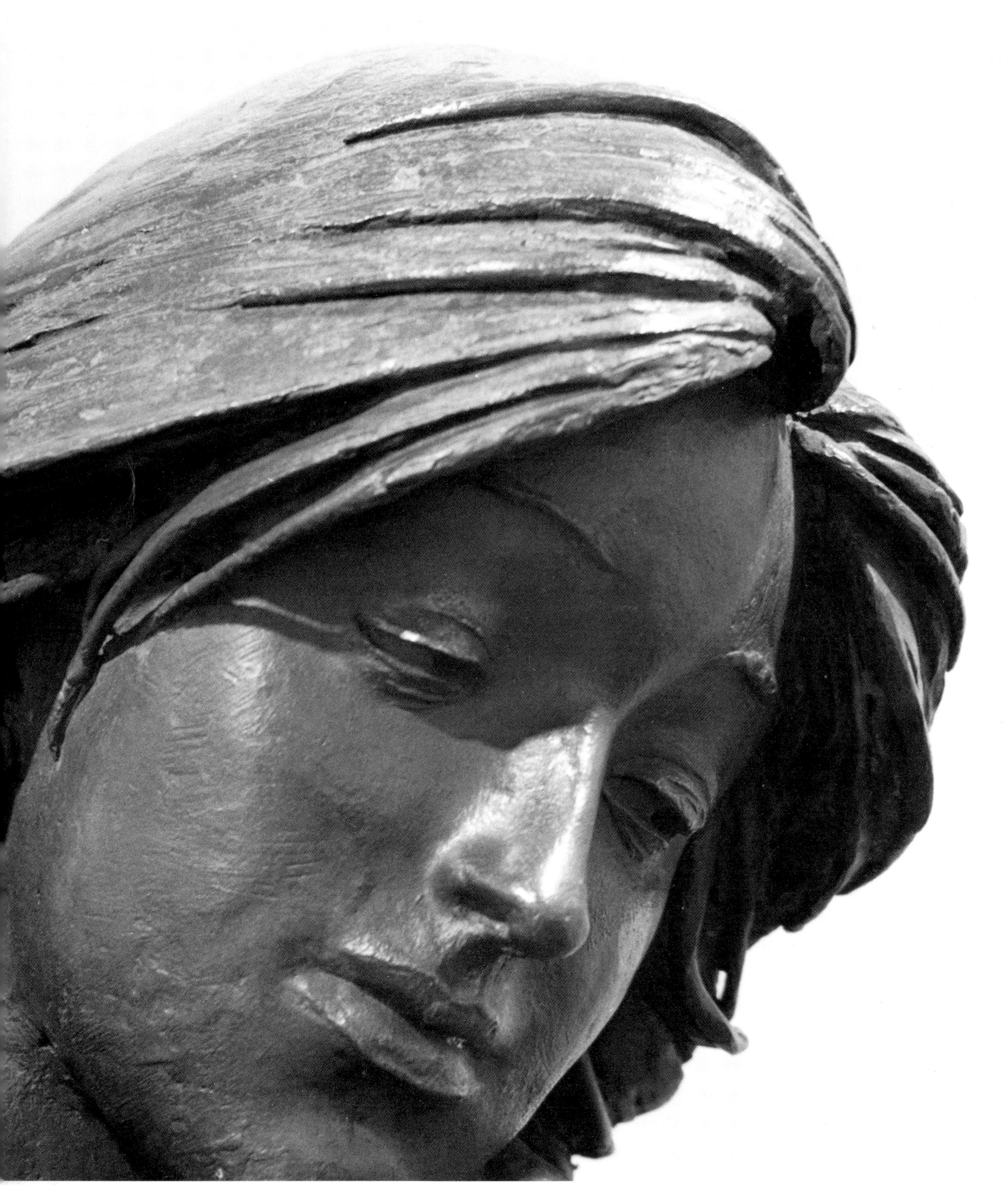

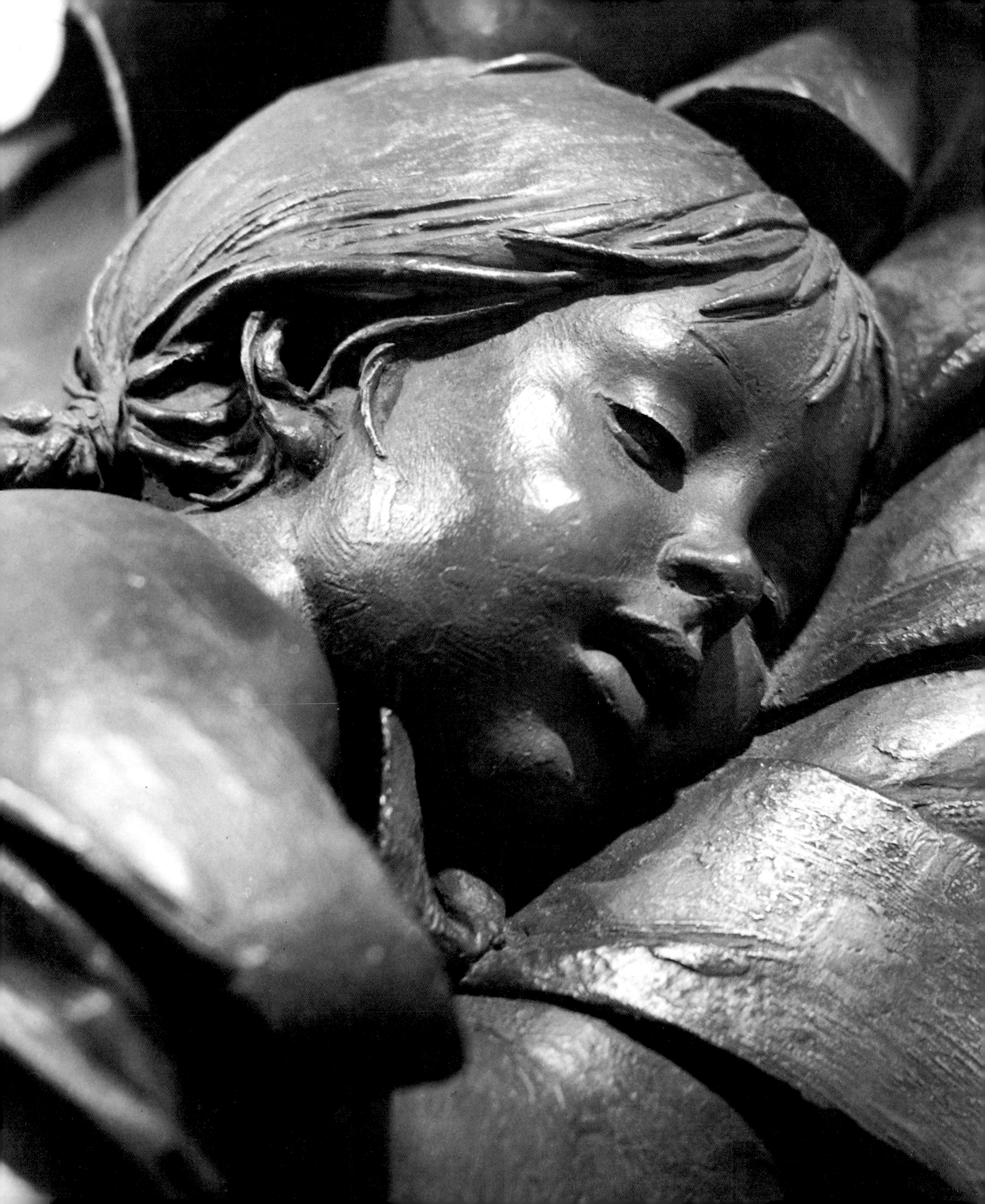

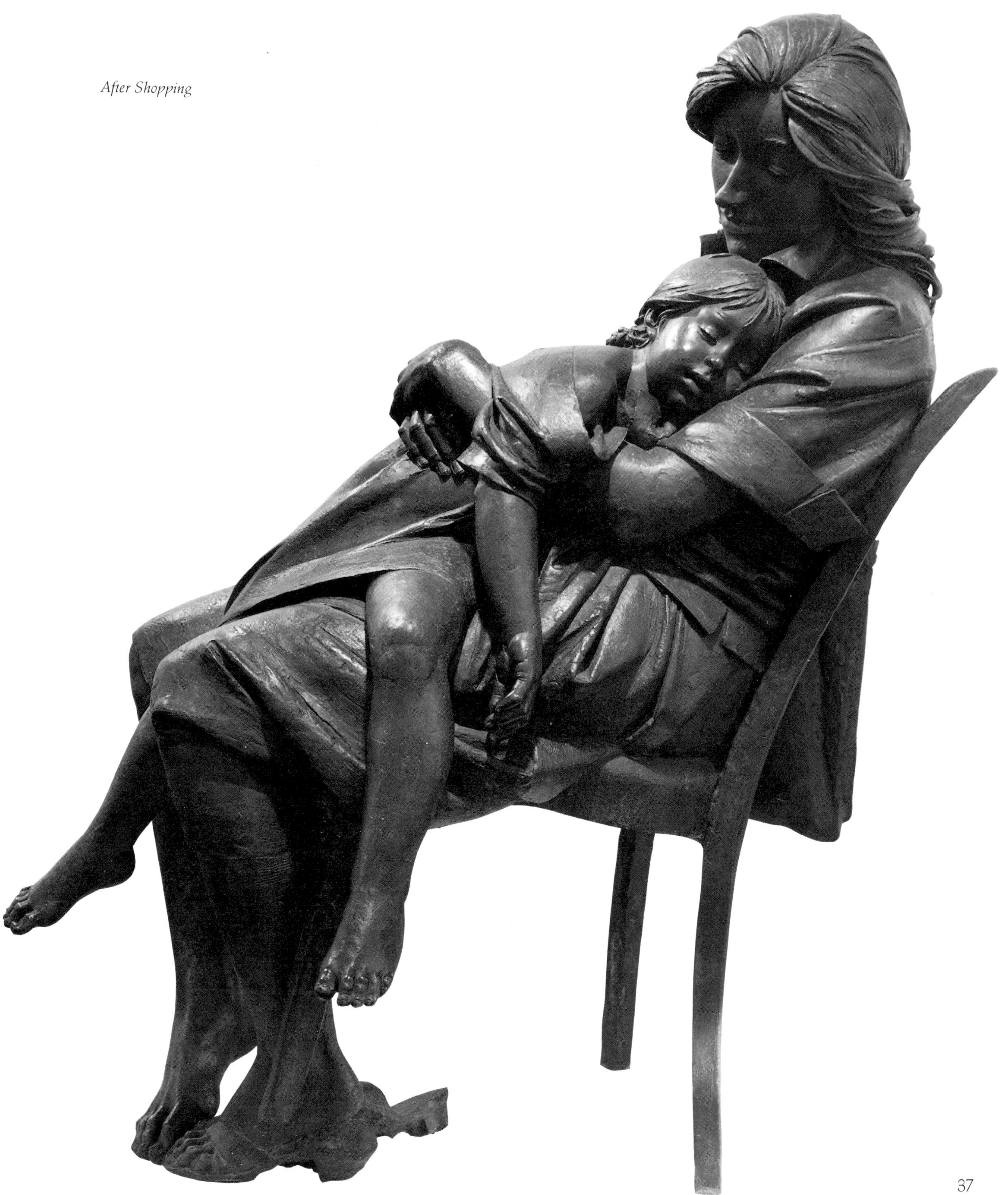

After Shopping

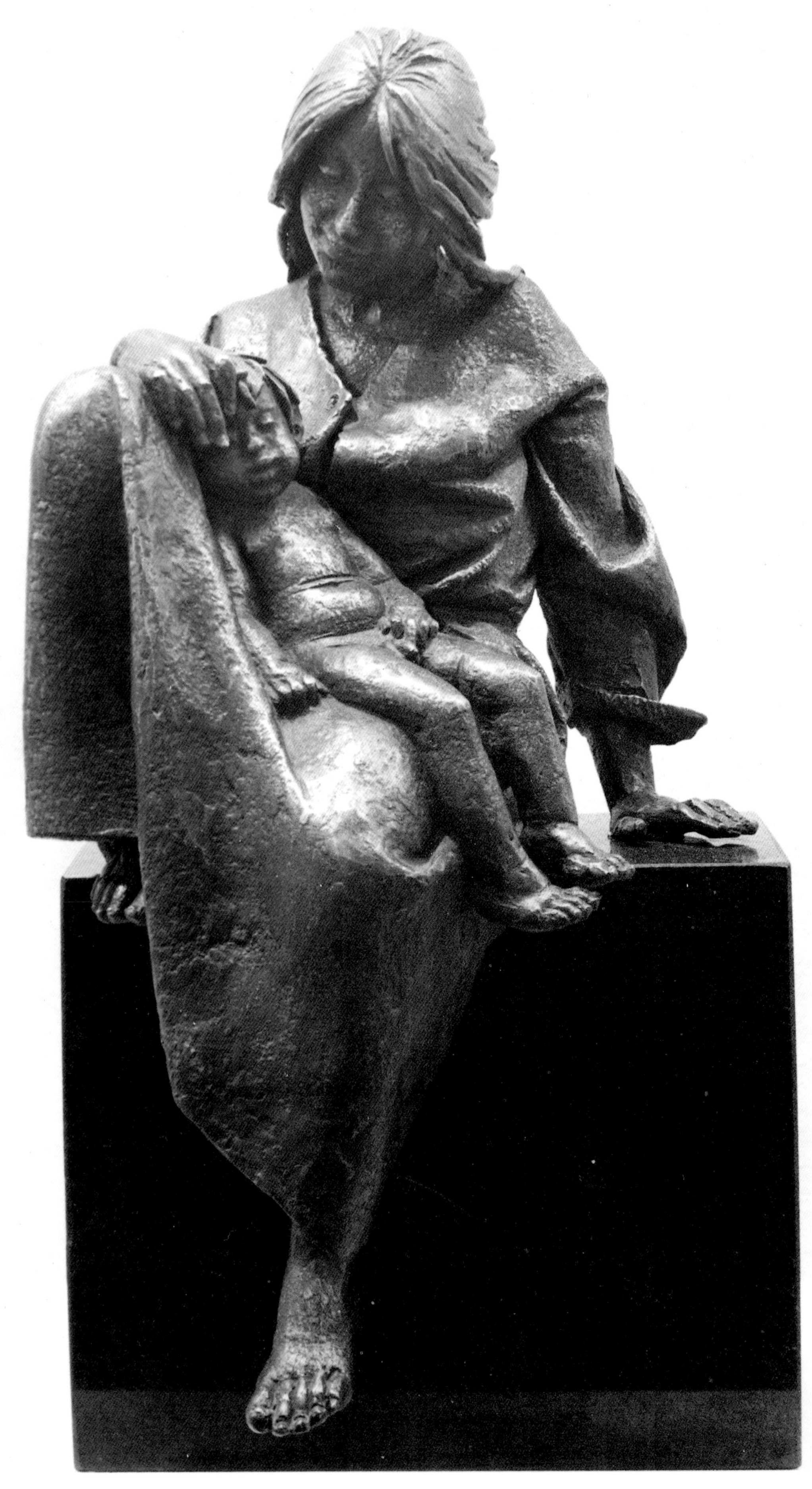

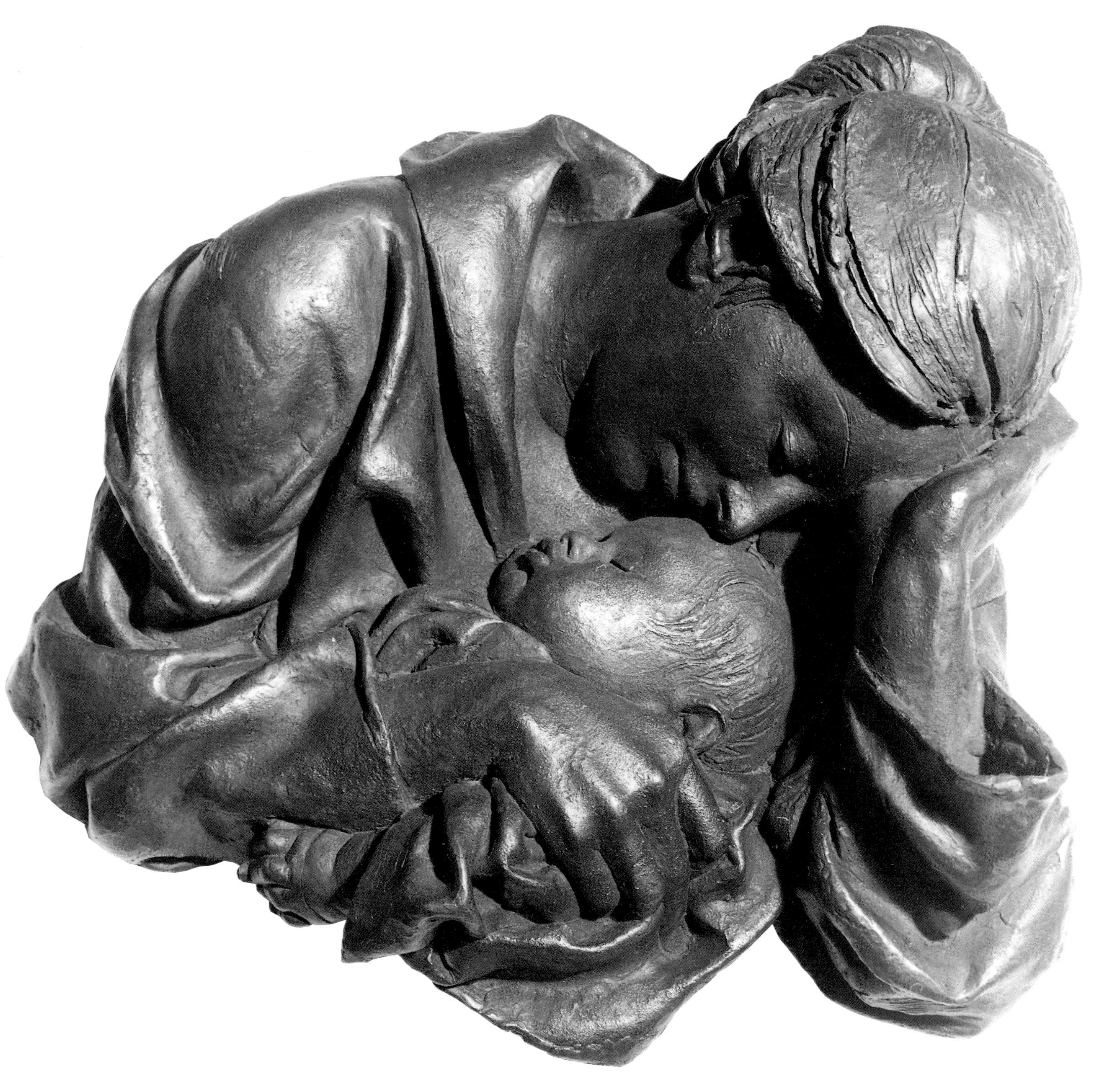

Madonna, 1973–74, high-relief bronze, 14 x 14 inches. Collection of Dr. and Mrs. Ralph Binder, New York.

Mother and Child, 1983, bronze, 14½ inches high. Private collection.

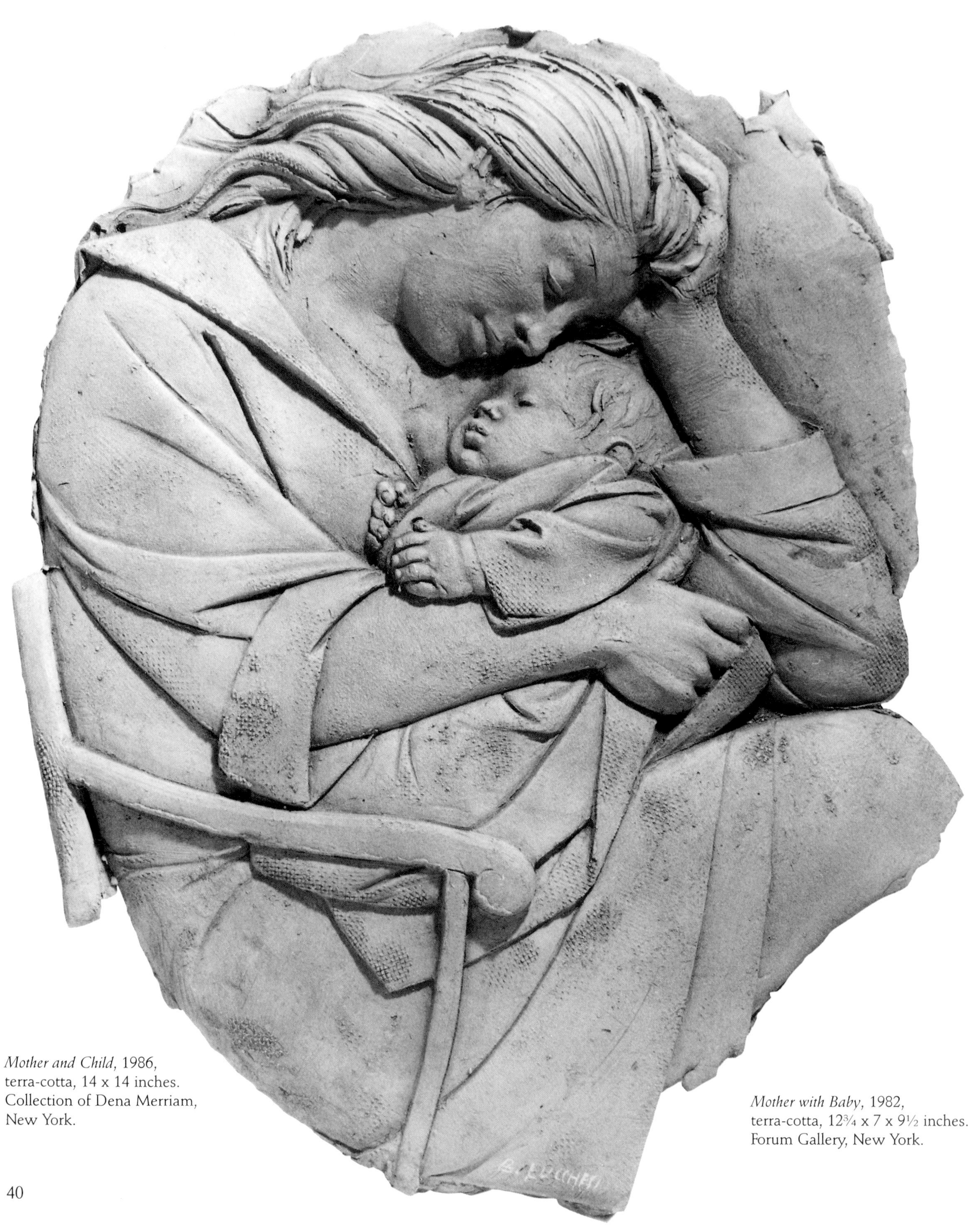

Mother and Child, 1986,
terra-cotta, 14 x 14 inches.
Collection of Dena Merriam,
New York.

Mother with Baby, 1982,
terra-cotta, 12$\frac{3}{4}$ x 7 x 9$\frac{1}{2}$ inches.
Forum Gallery, New York.

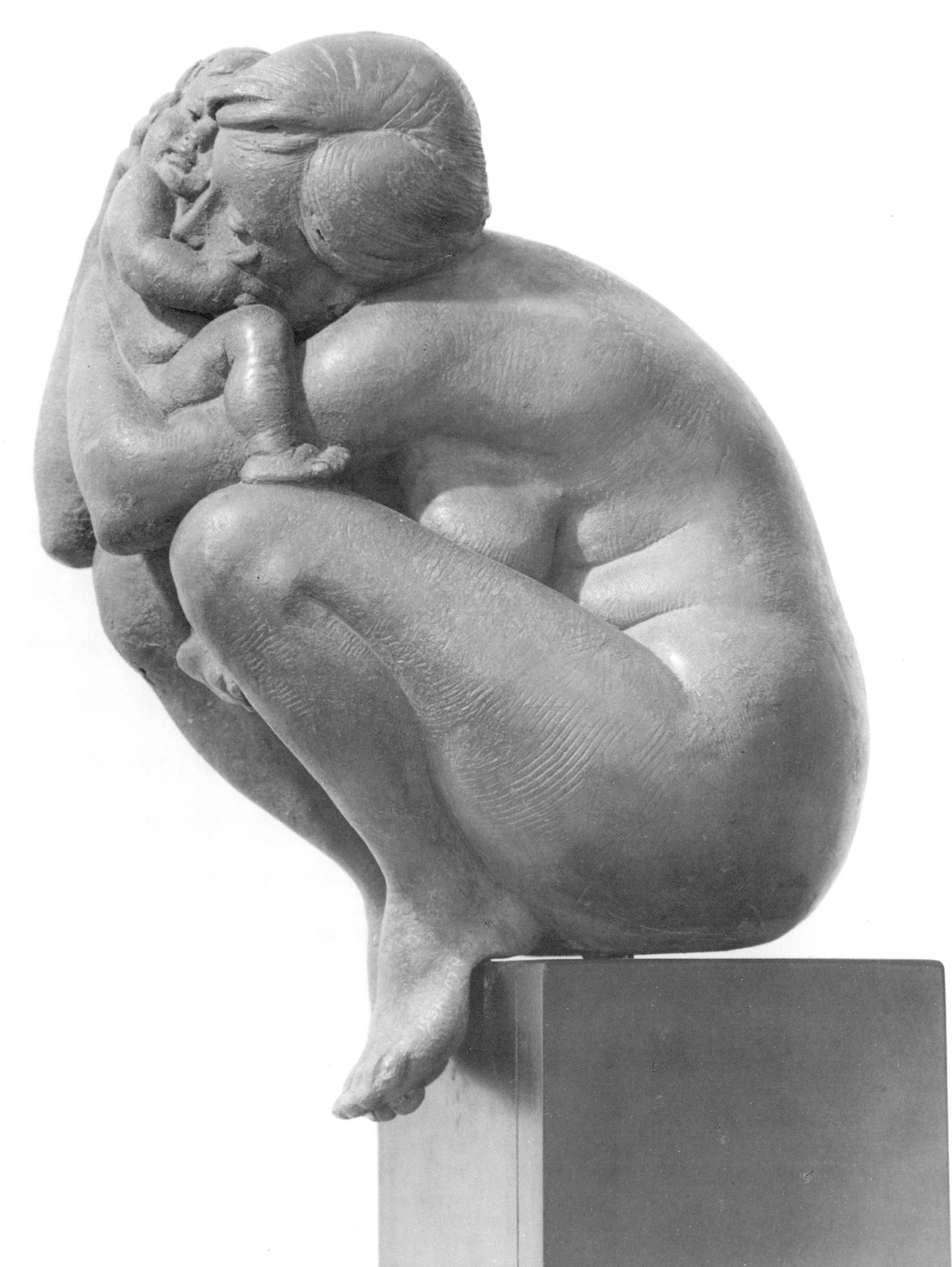

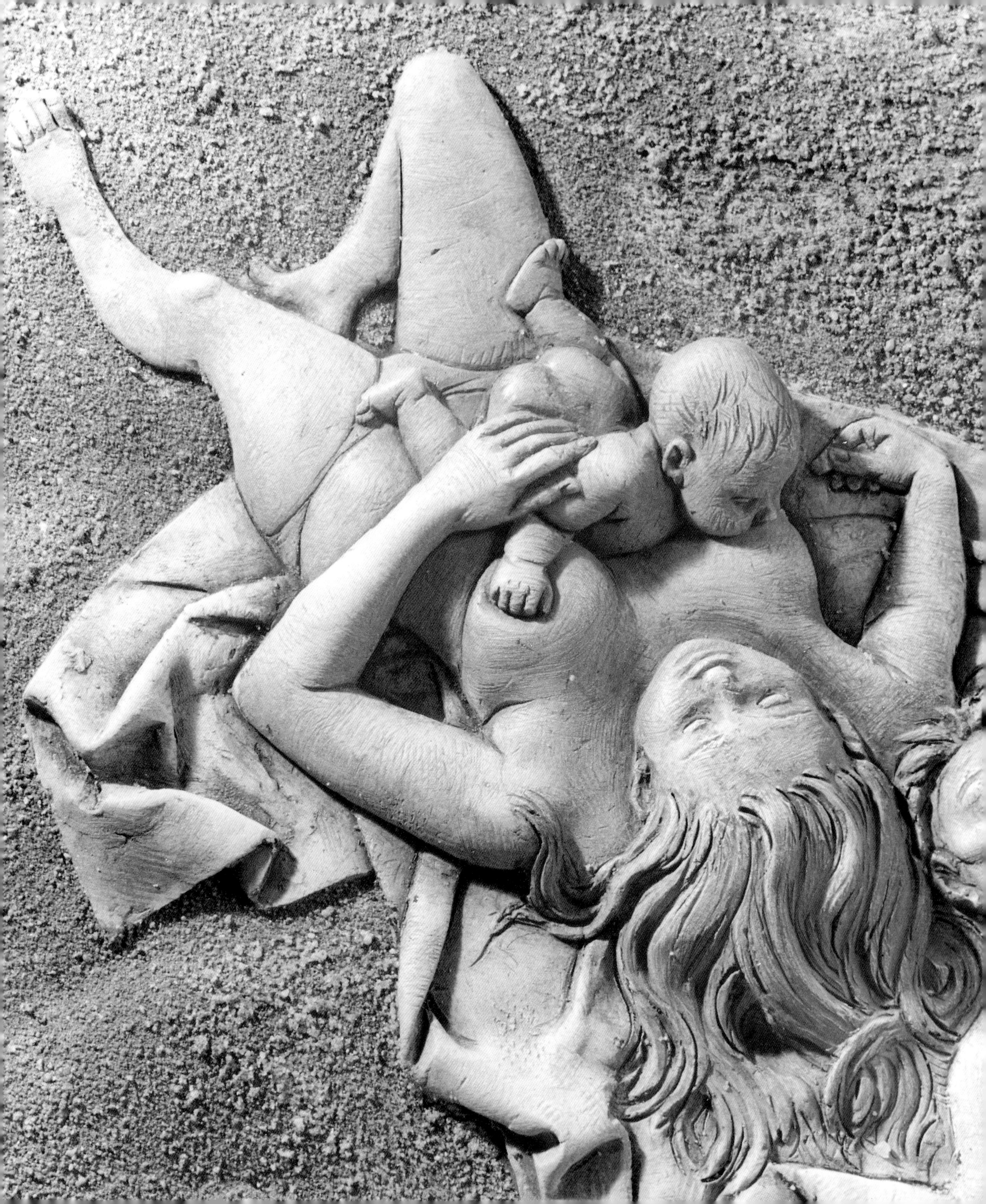

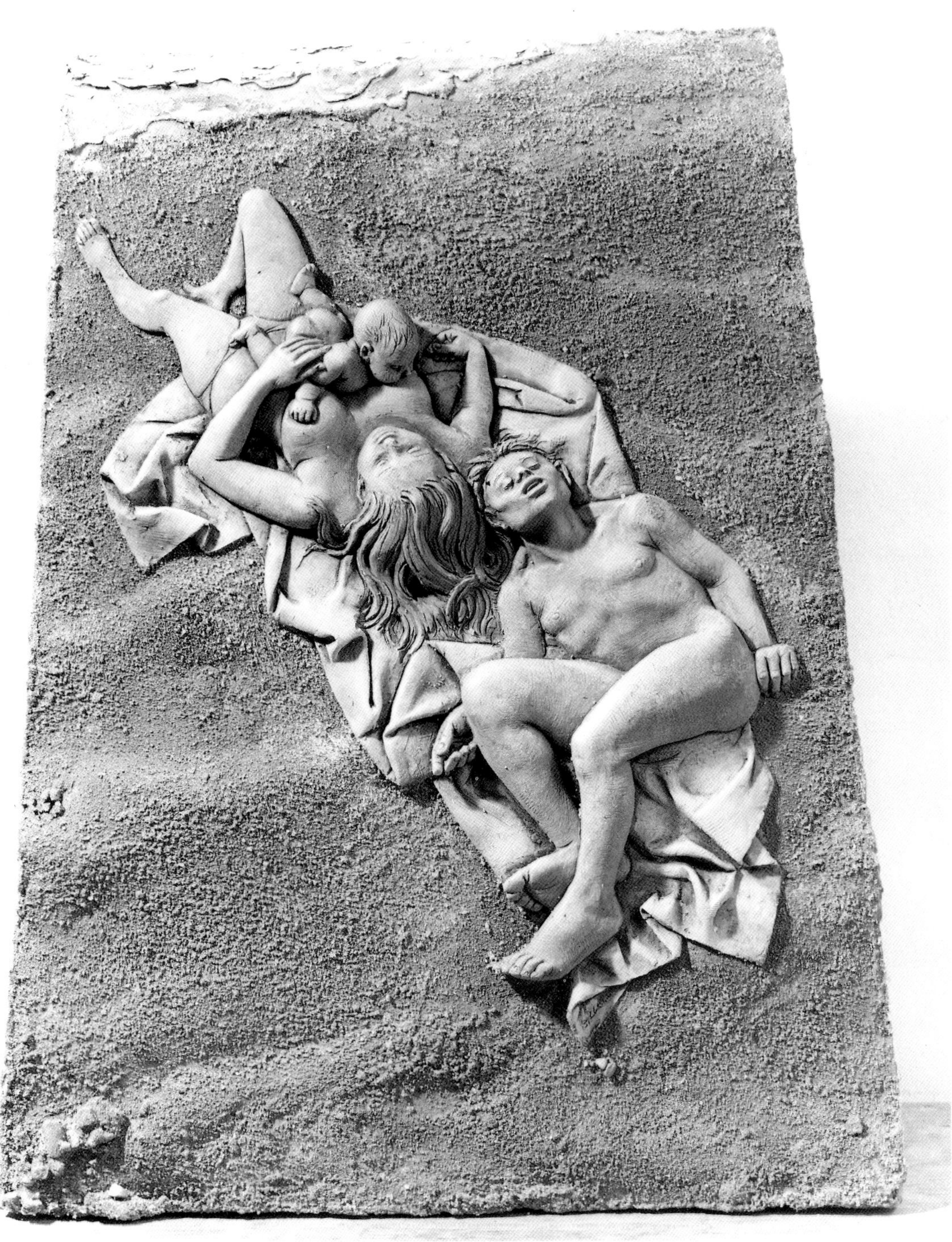

At the Beach, 1987, terra-cotta relief, 22 x 15 inches. Forum Gallery, New York. (See also colorplate, page 19.)

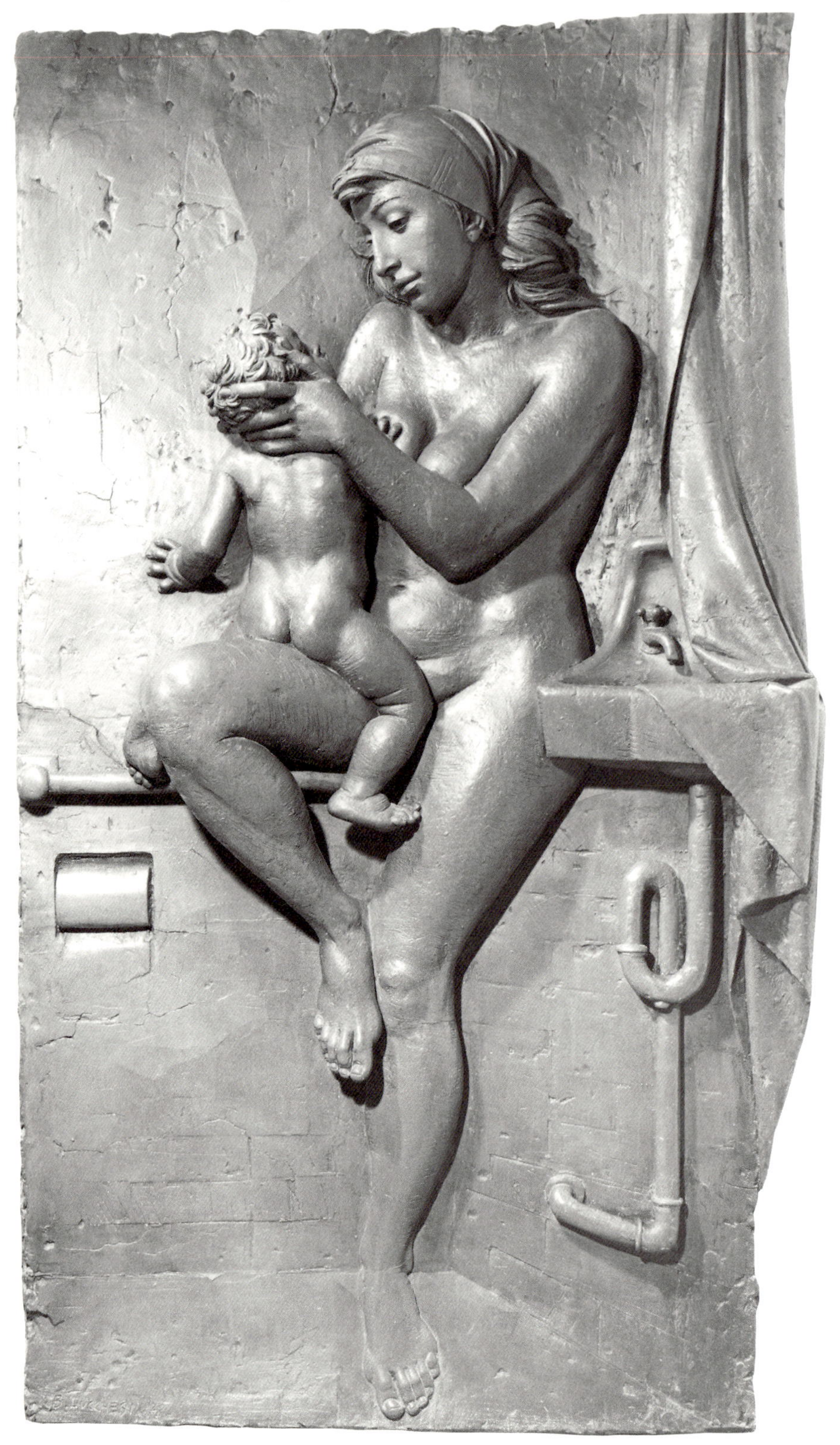

Bathroom, 1980, bonded bronze, life-size.
Forum Gallery, New York.

Mother and Child on Bicycle (detail), 1967,
bonded bronze relief, 61 inches high.
Collection of Bella and Sol Fishko, New York.
(See also black-and-white illustrations, page 32.)

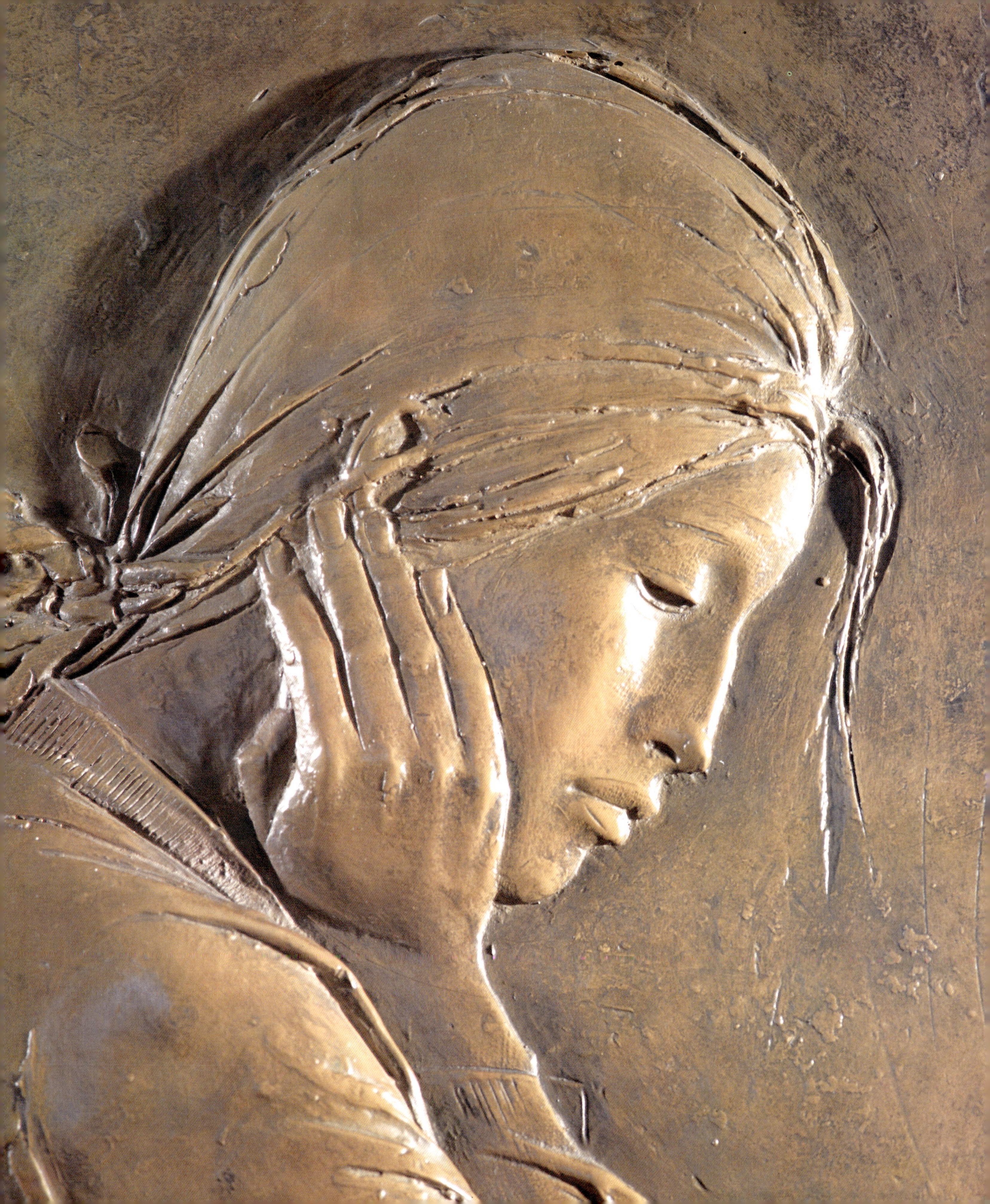

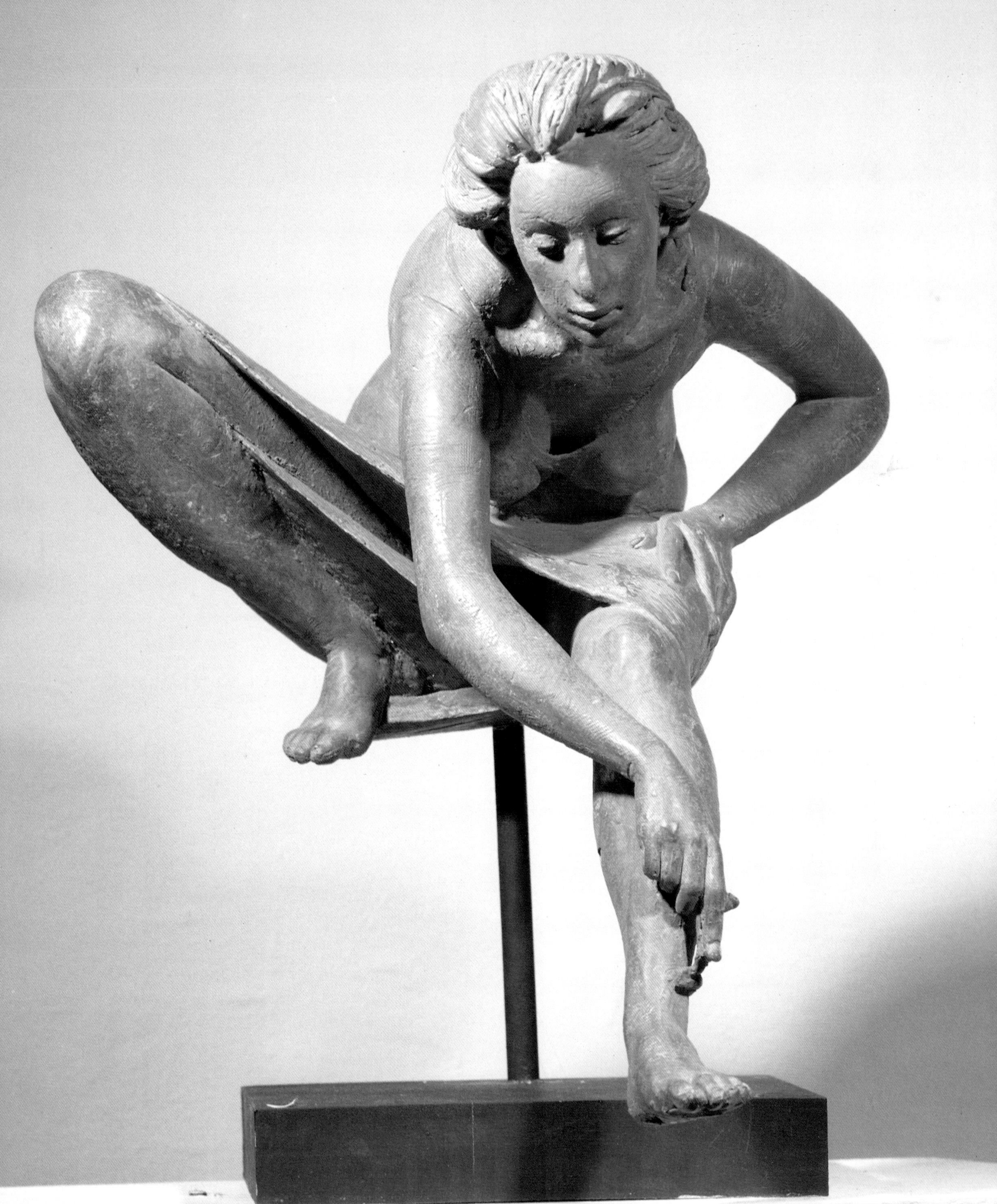

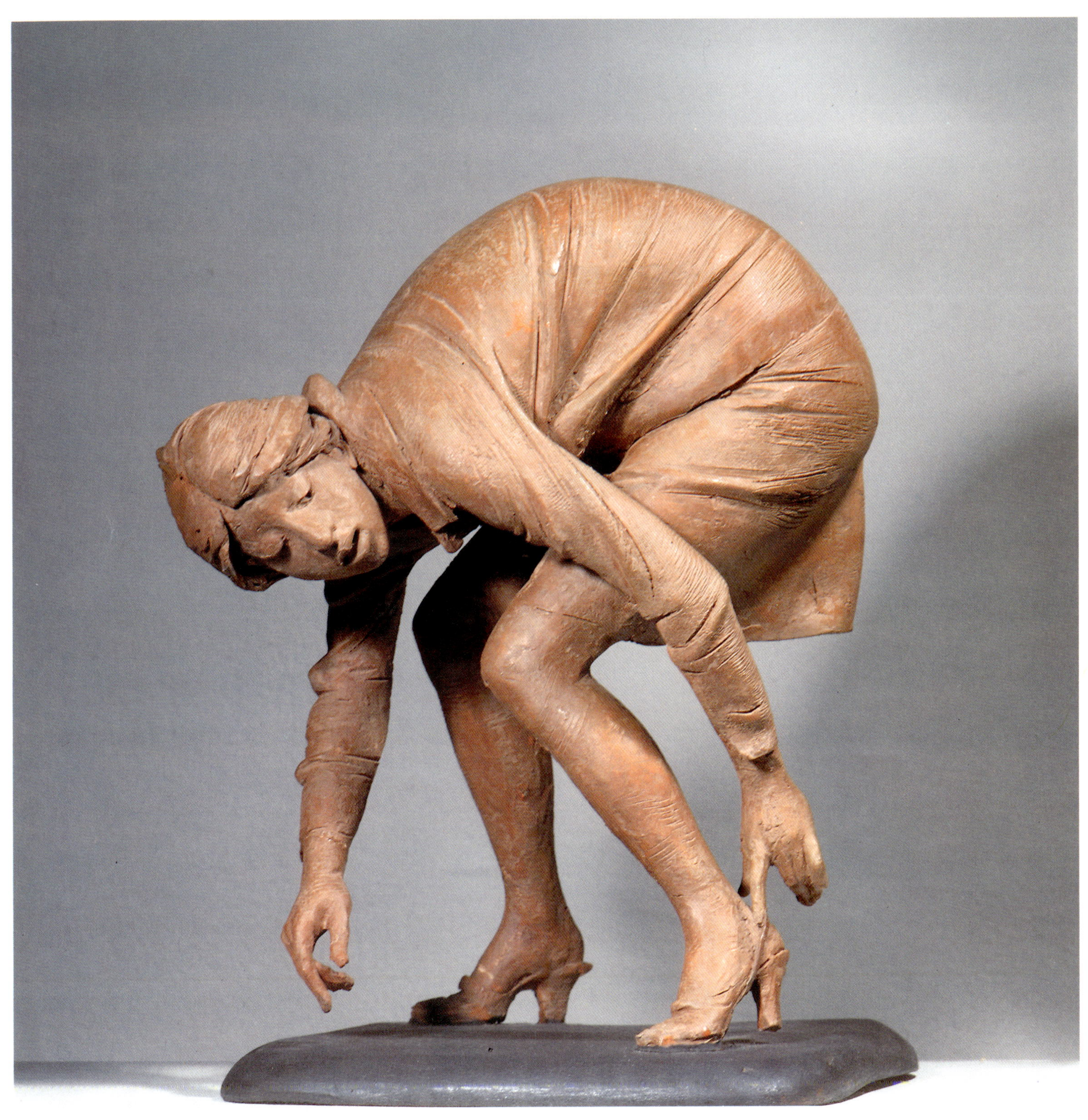

Woman Adjusting Her Shoe, 1979, terra-cotta, 13 inches high. Forum Gallery, New York. (See also black-and-white illustrations, pages 84, 85.)

Toilette, 1979, terra-cotta, 16½ x 14½ x 15¼ inches. Forum Gallery, New York. (See also black-and-white illustrations, pages 60, 61.)

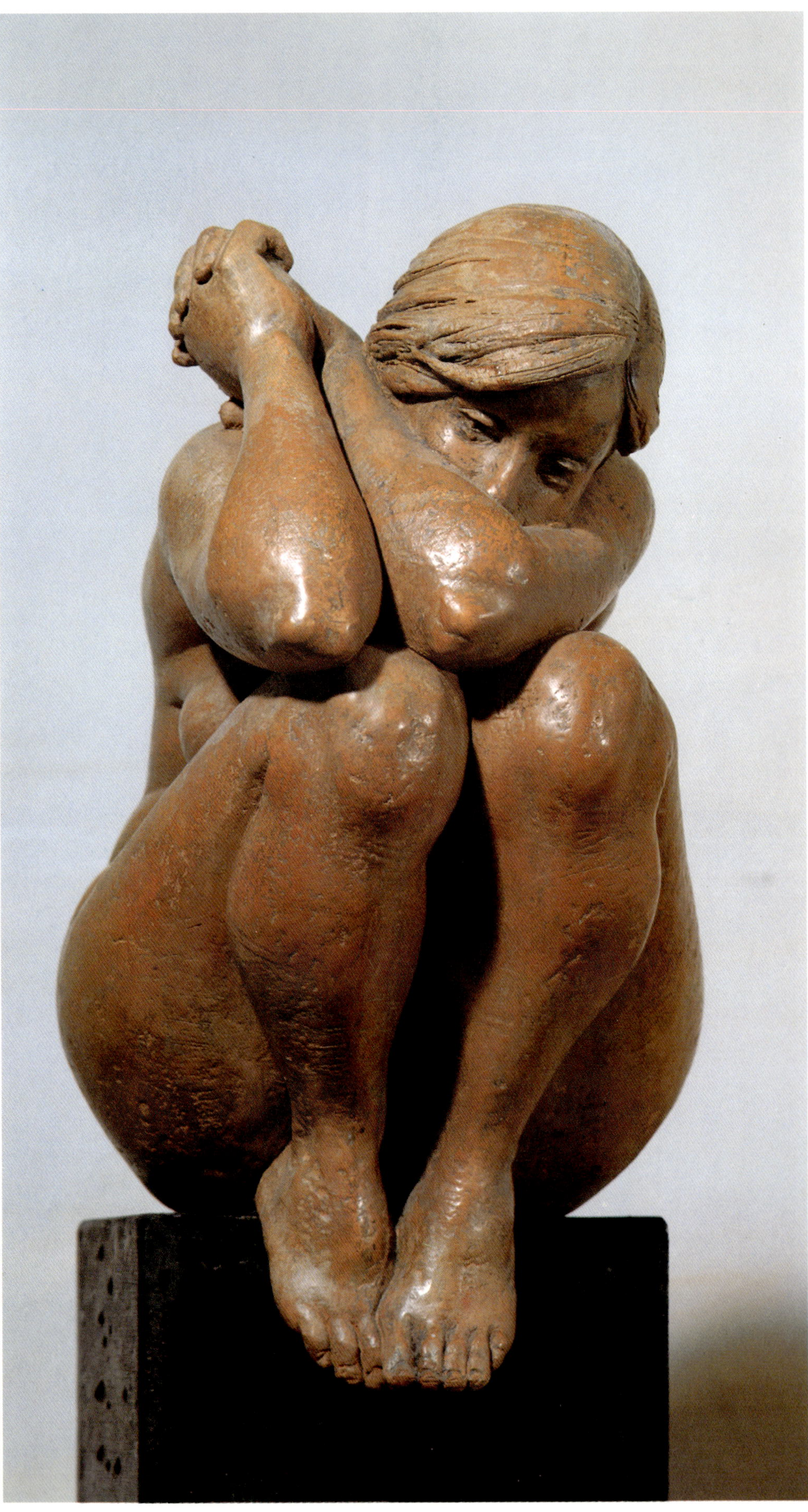

Musing #2, 1977, terra-cotta, 18 inches high. Forum Gallery, New York. (See also black-and-white illustrations, pages 56, 57.)

THE
FEMALE FIGURE

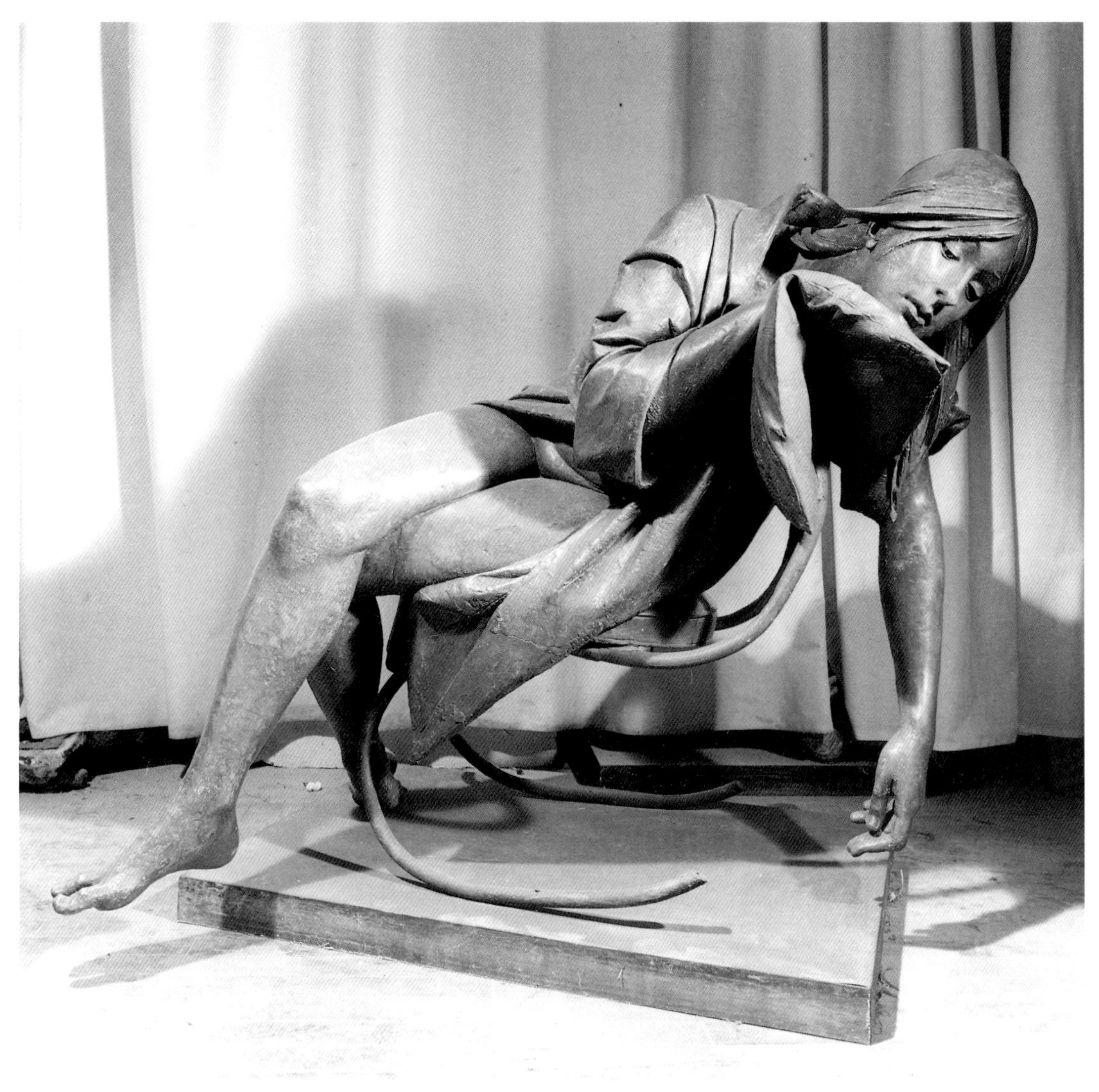

Resting, 1969, fiberglass, life-size. Forum Gallery, New York.

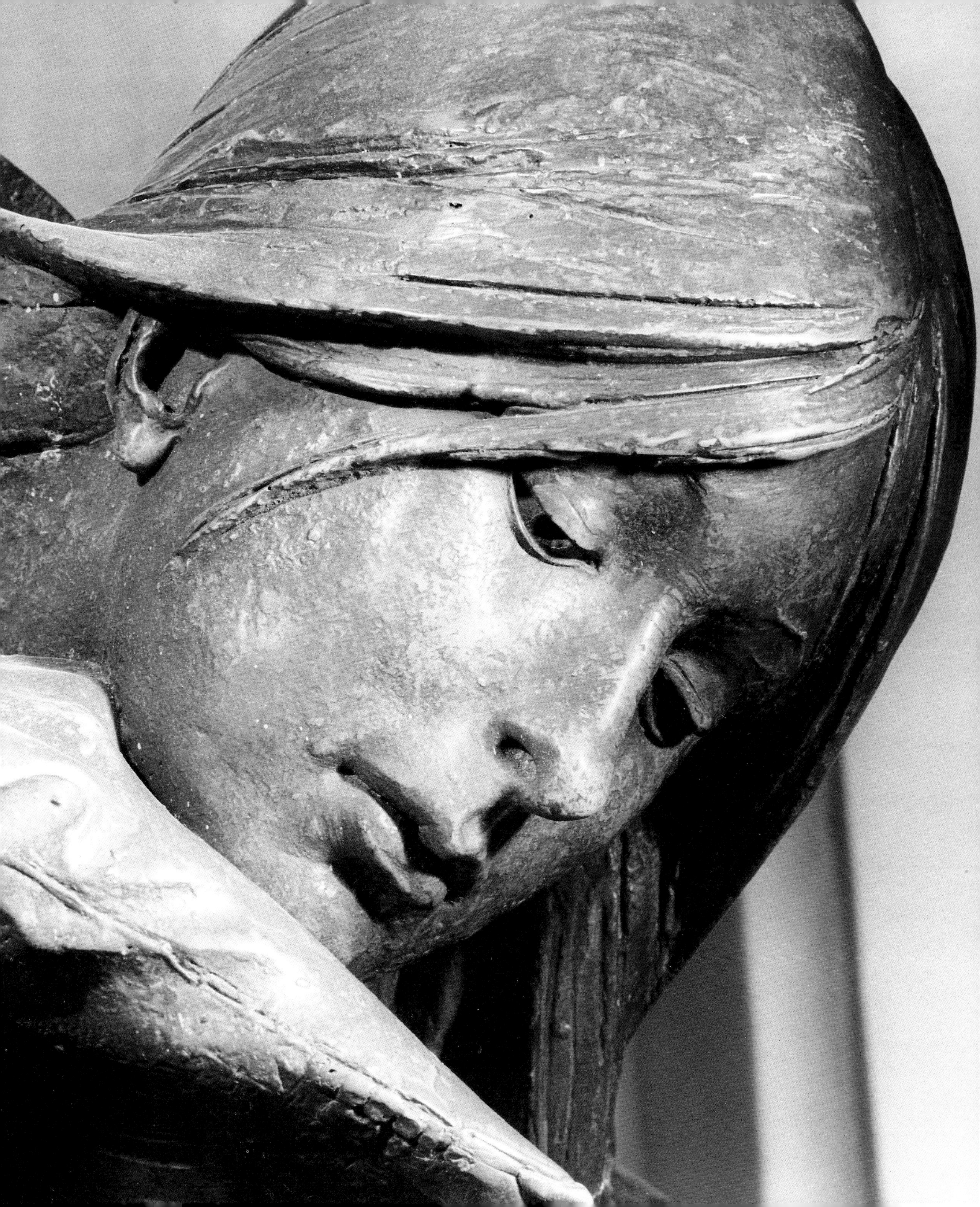

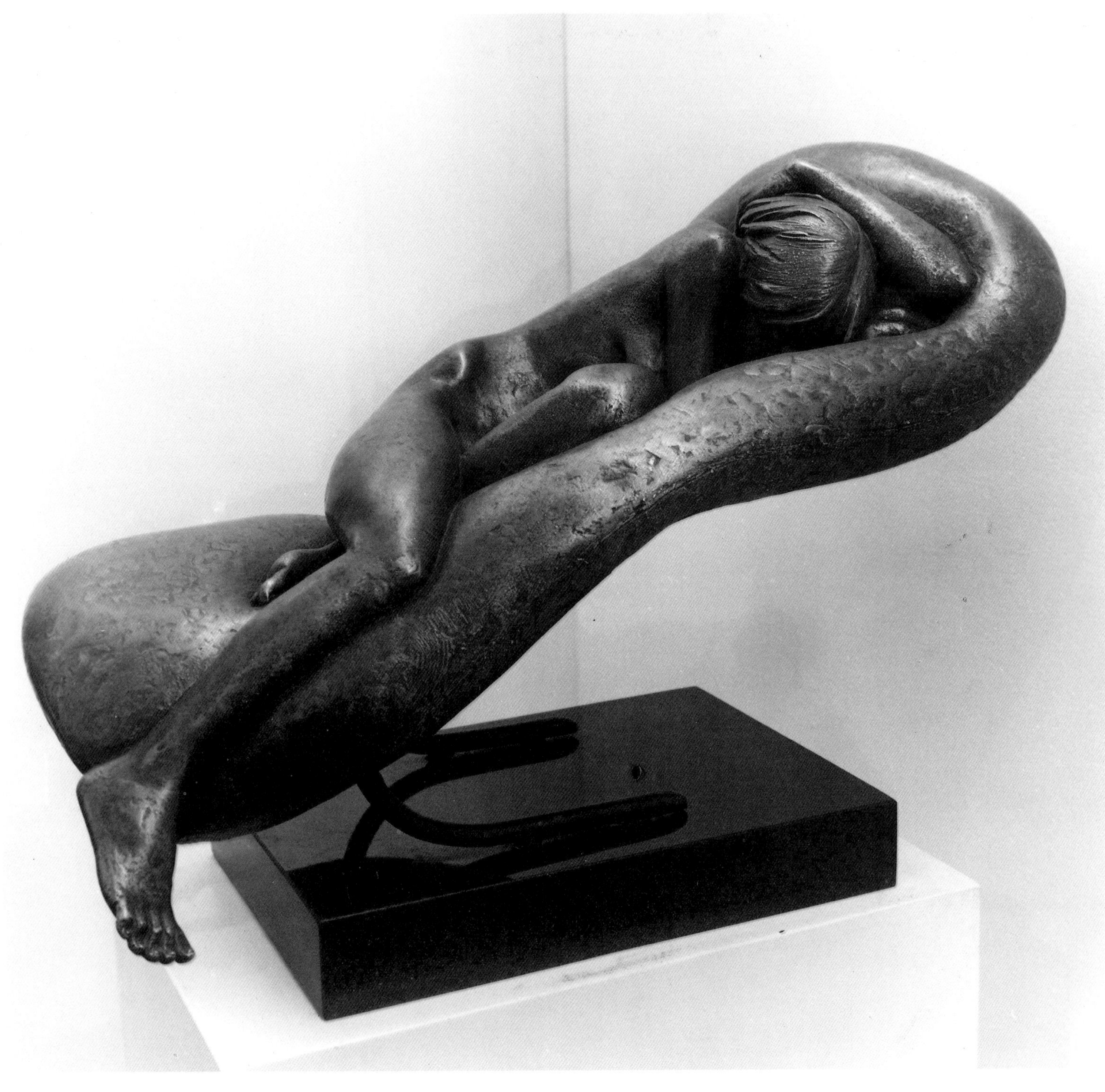

Sleeping Nude, 1970, bronze, 25 inches wide. Forum Gallery, New York.

Cat Nap, c. 1972, silver relief, 10 x 8 inches. Collection of Mr. and Mrs. Robert Ostrow, Largo, Florida.

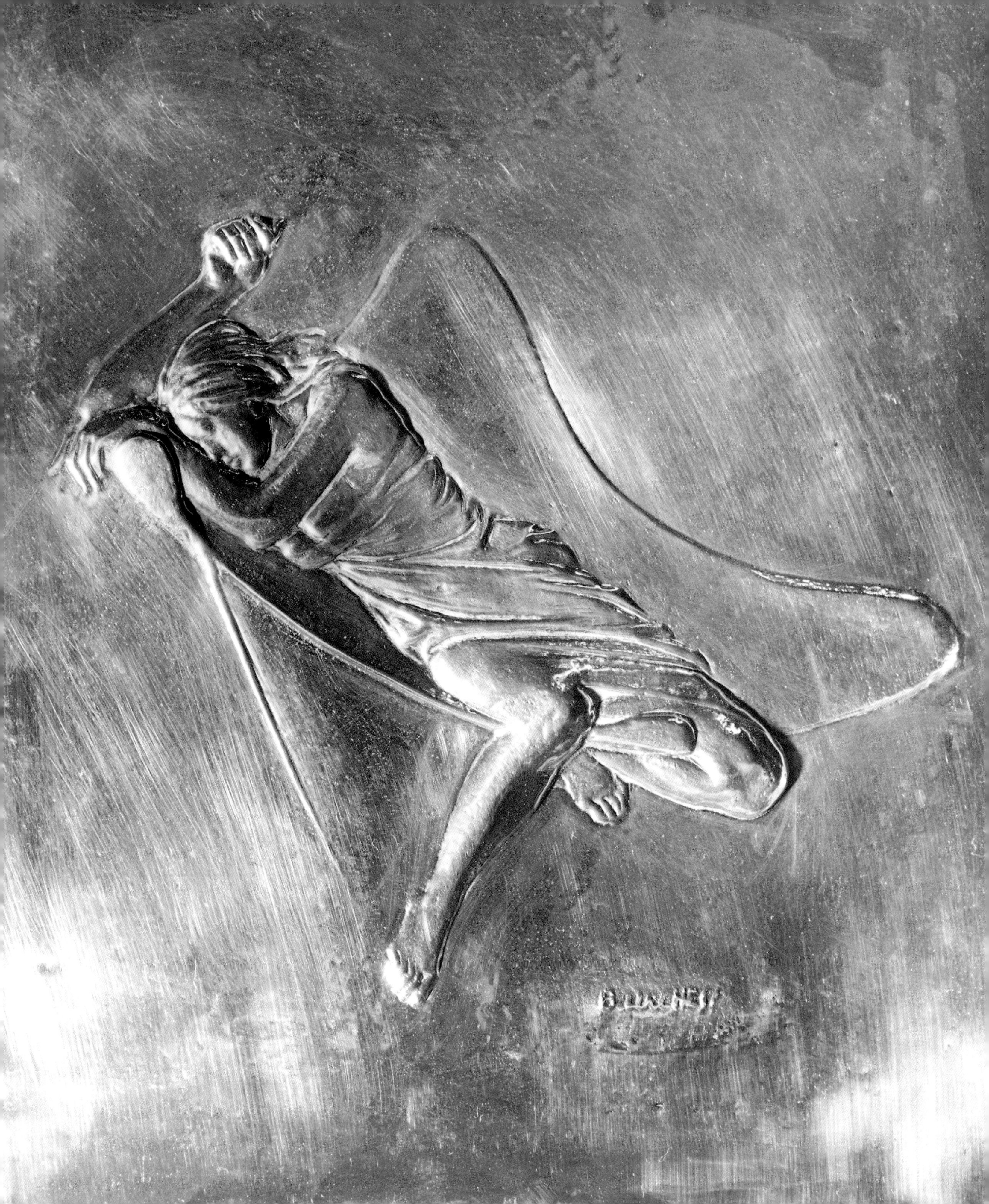

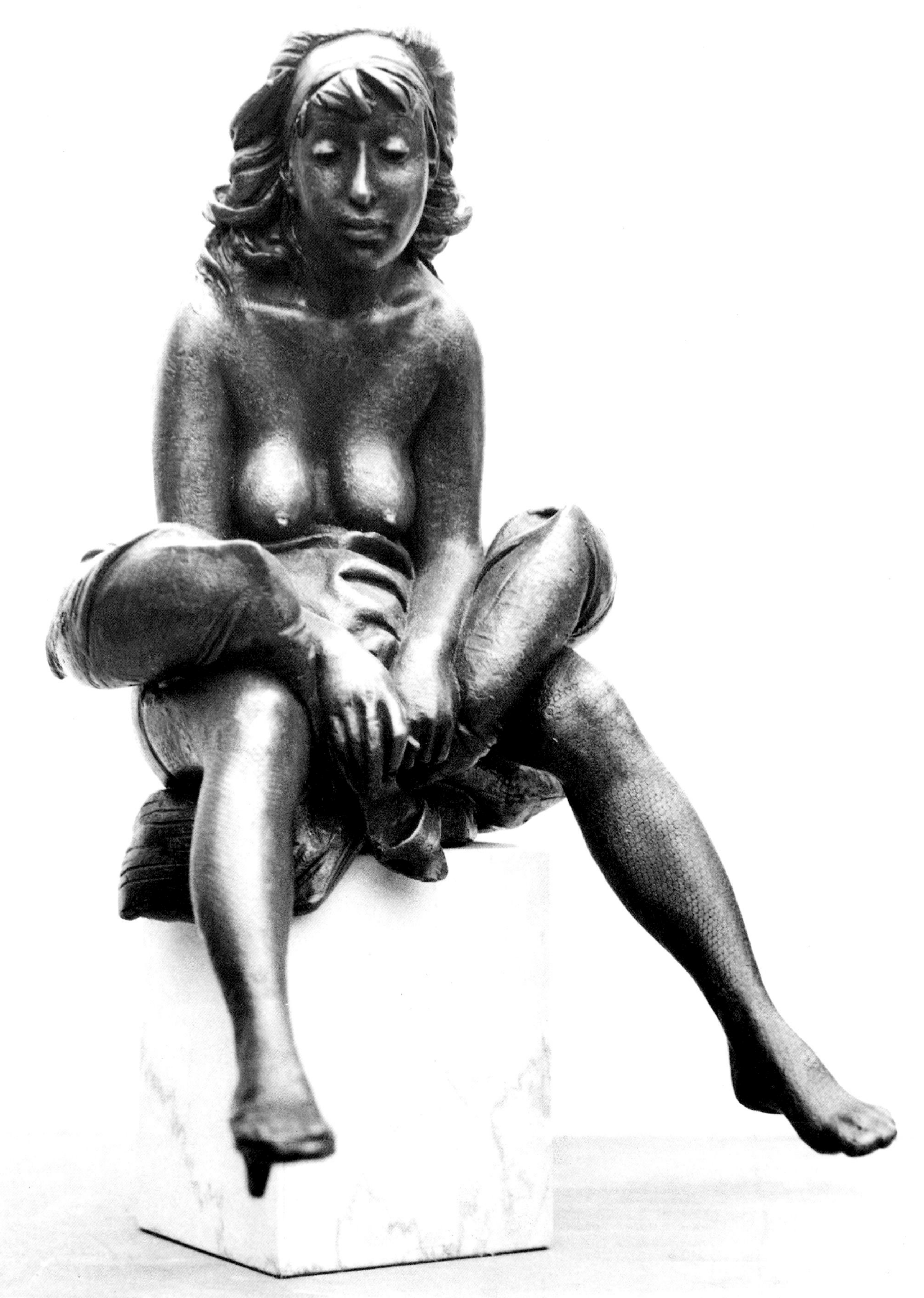

Model, 1979, bronze, 14 inches high.
Forum Gallery, New York.

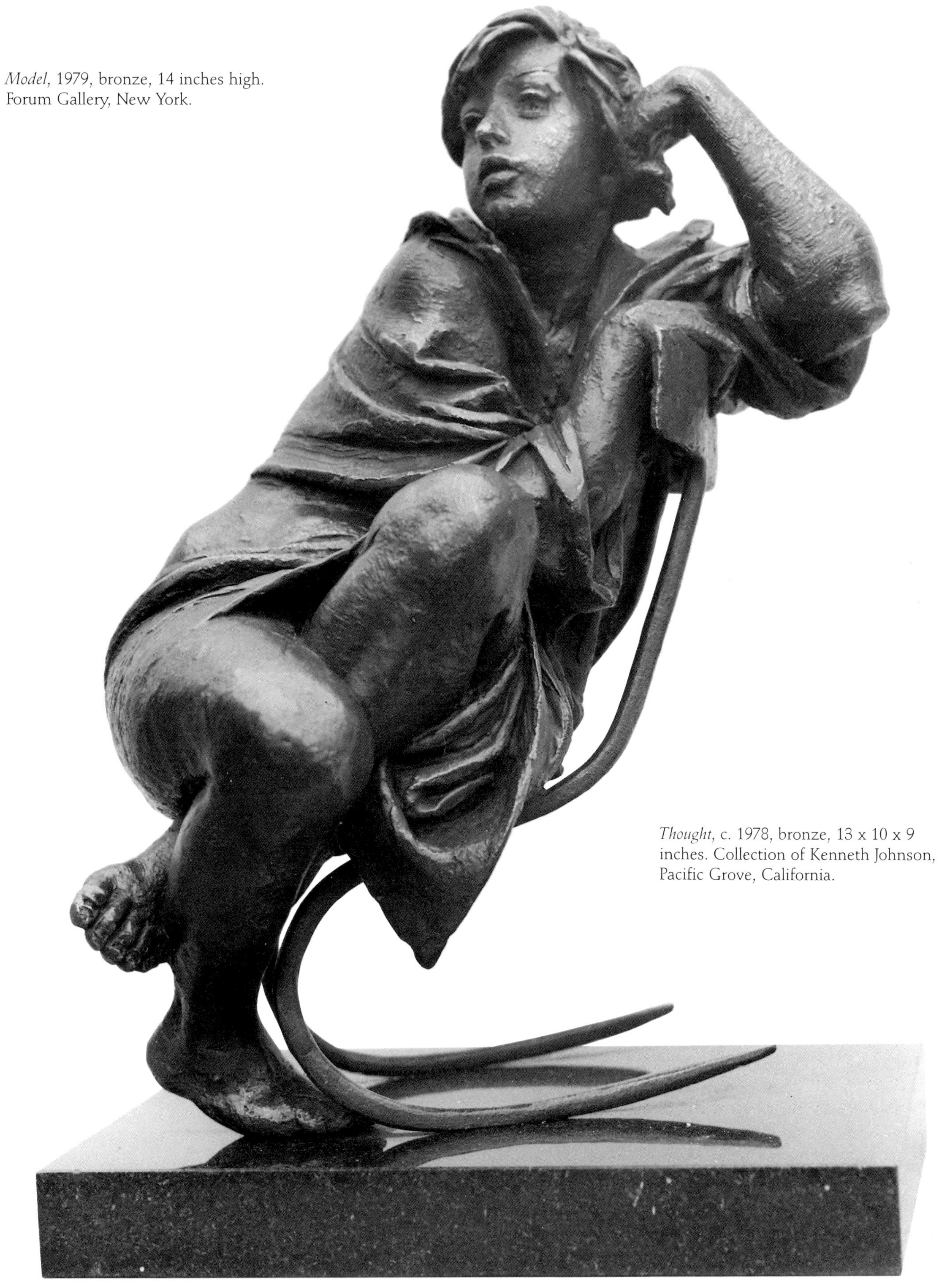

Thought, c. 1978, bronze, 13 x 10 x 9 inches. Collection of Kenneth Johnson, Pacific Grove, California.

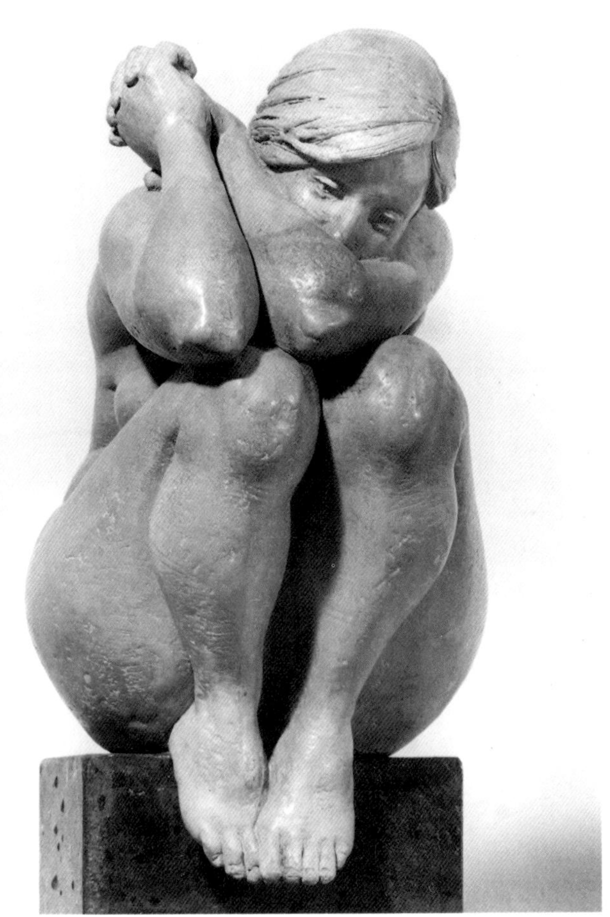

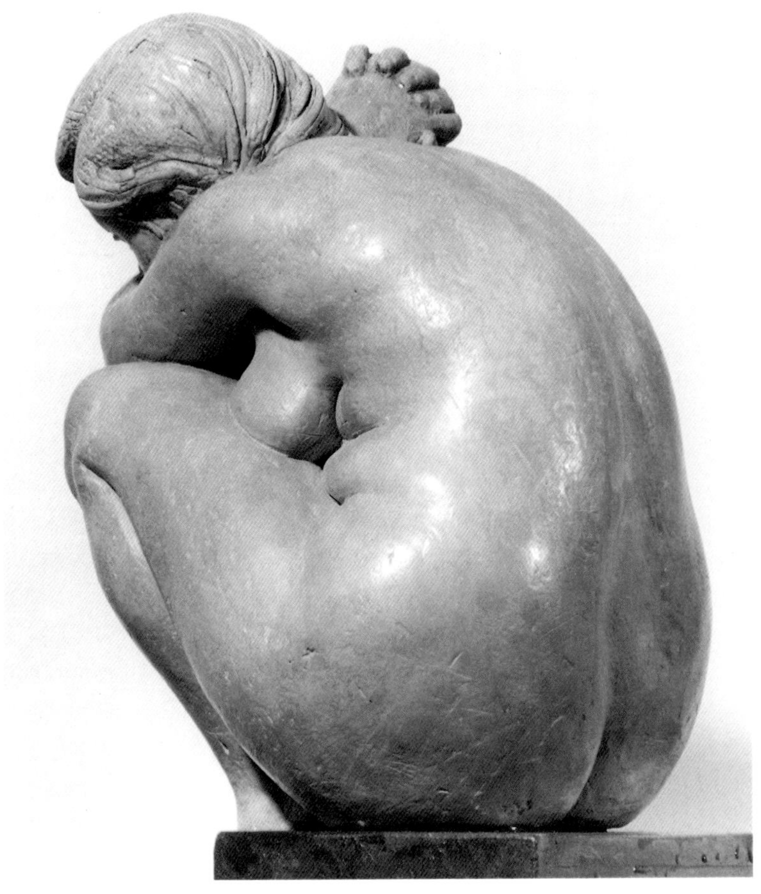

Musing #2, 1977, terra-cotta, 18 inches high. Forum Gallery, New York. (See also colorplate, page 48.)

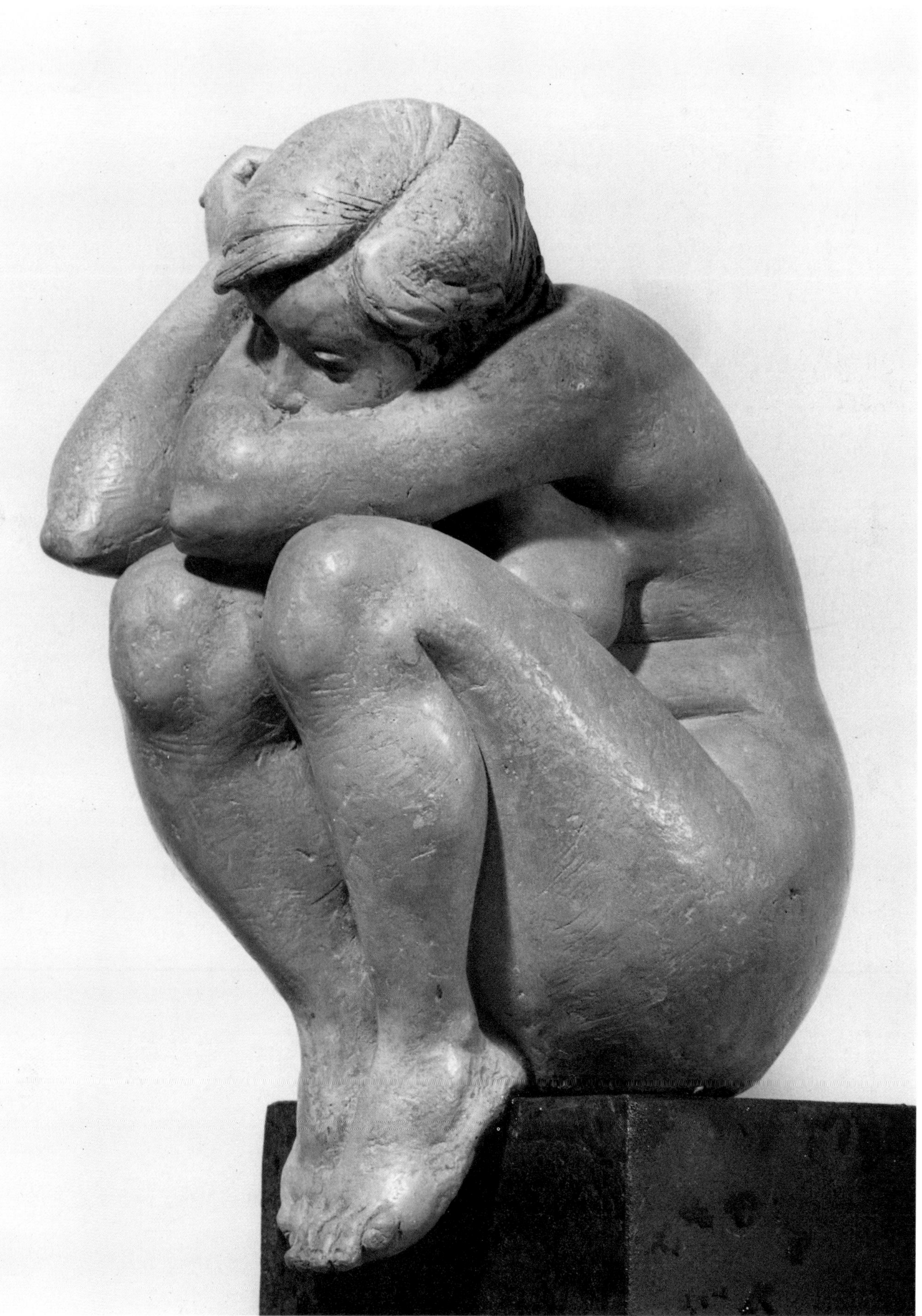

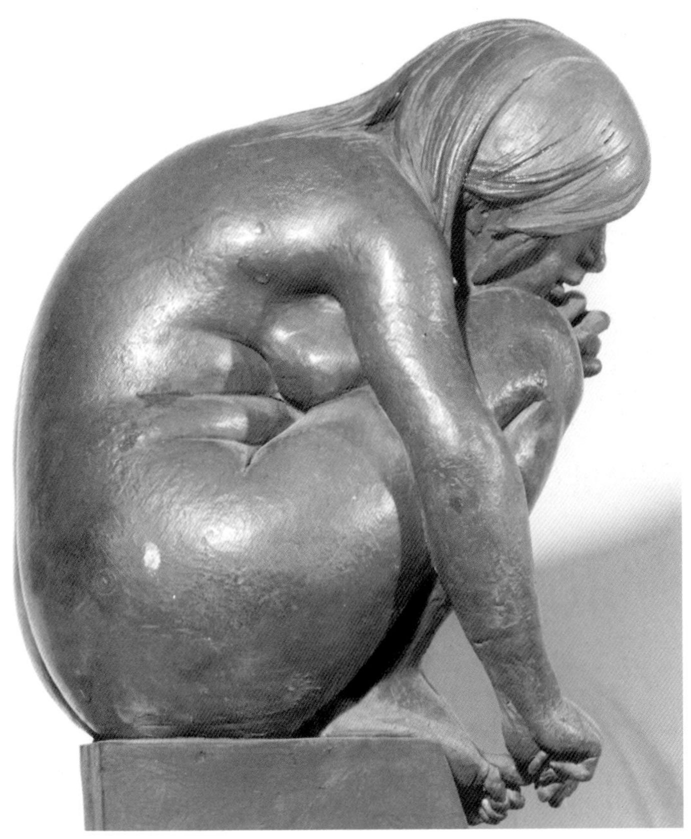

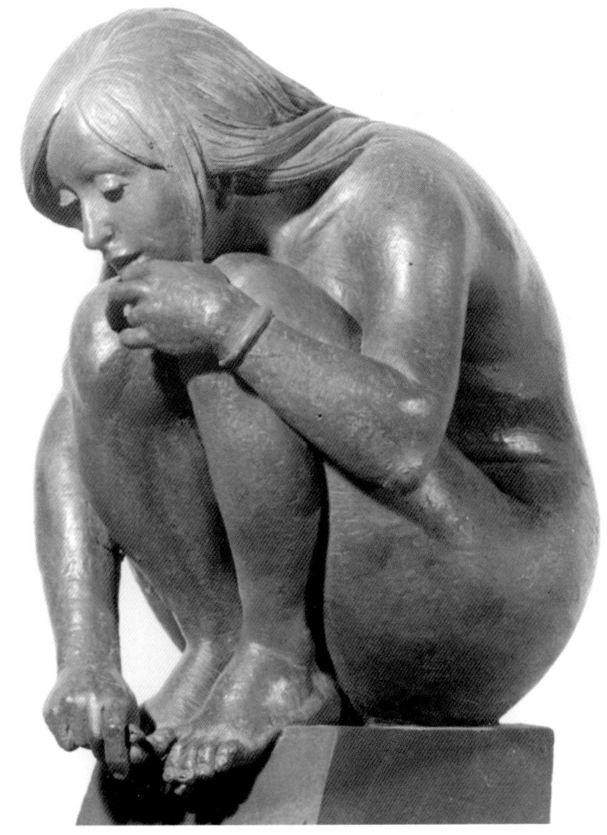

Cutting Toenails, 1981, terra-cotta, 10 inches high. Forum Gallery, New York.

Pensive Woman, 1968, bronze, 12 inches high. Forum Gallery, New York.

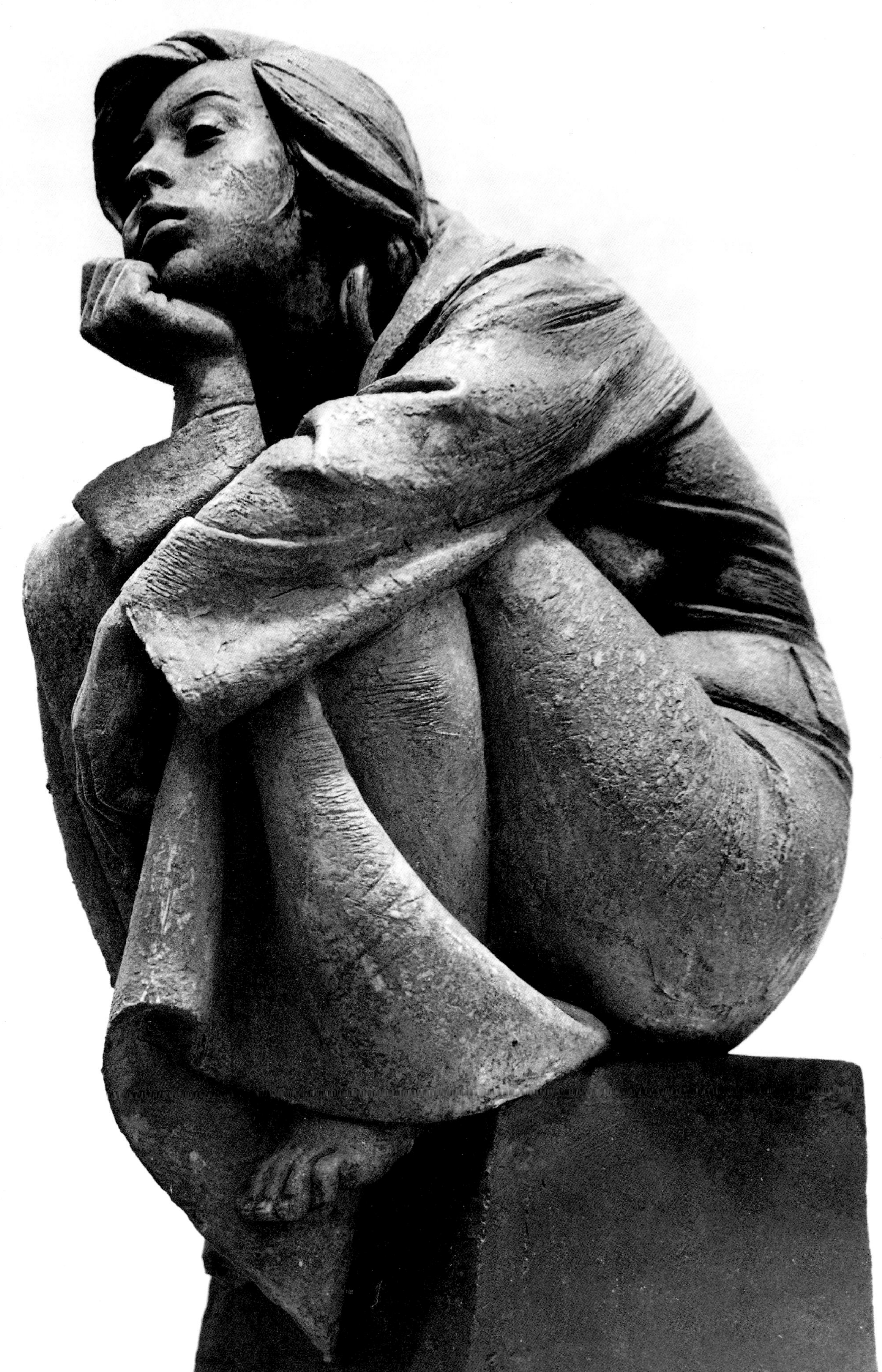

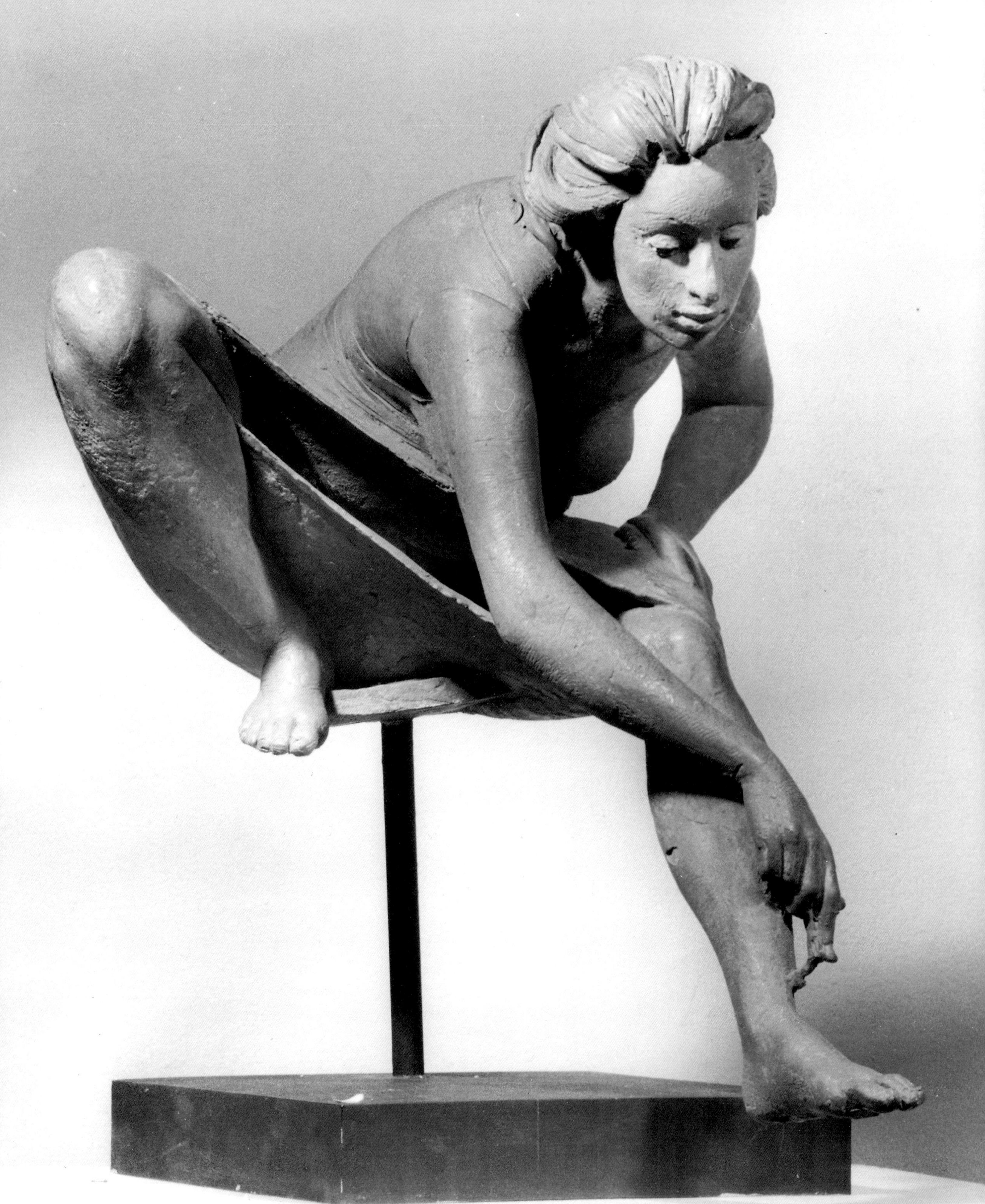

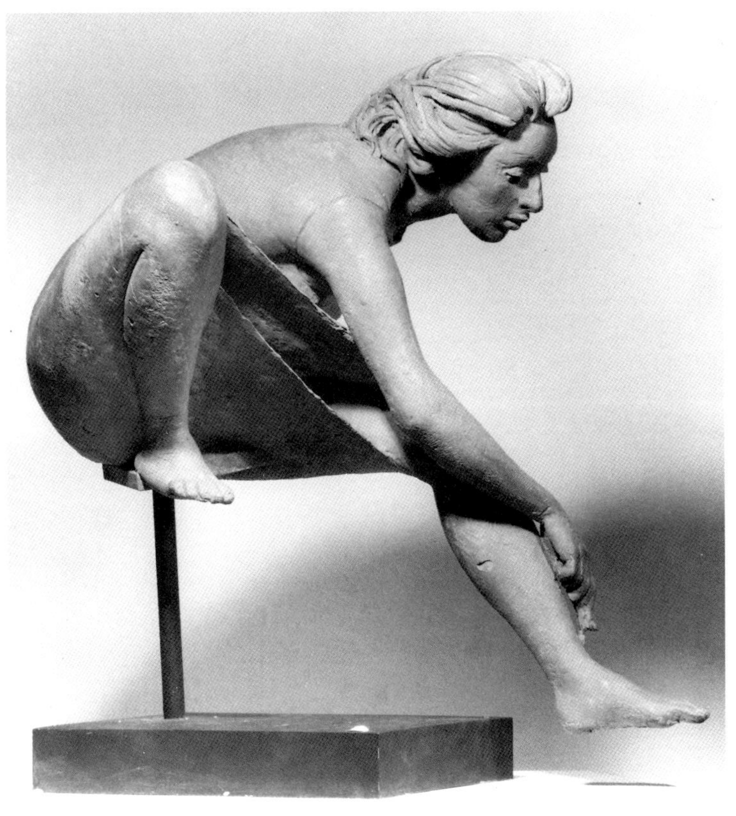

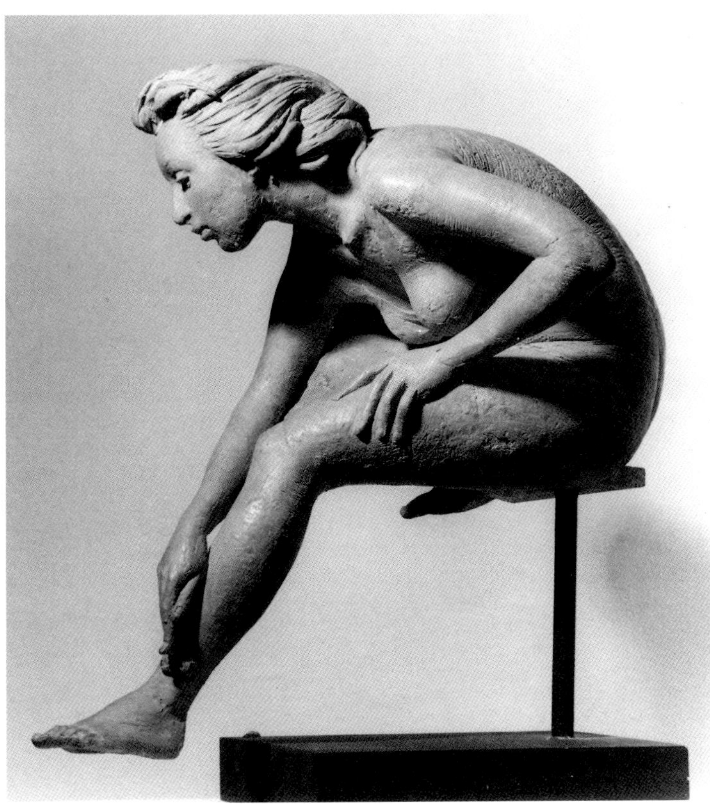

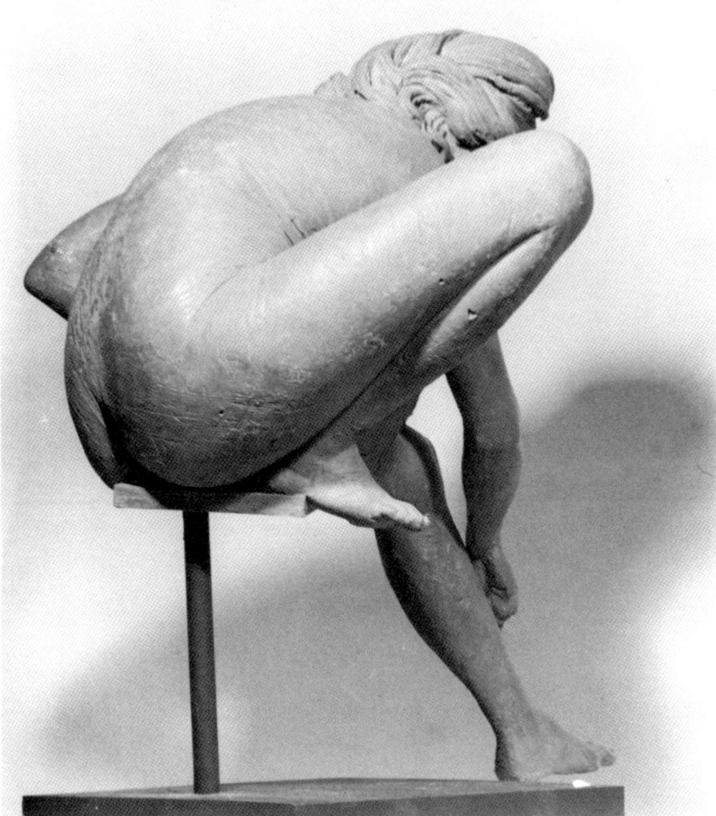

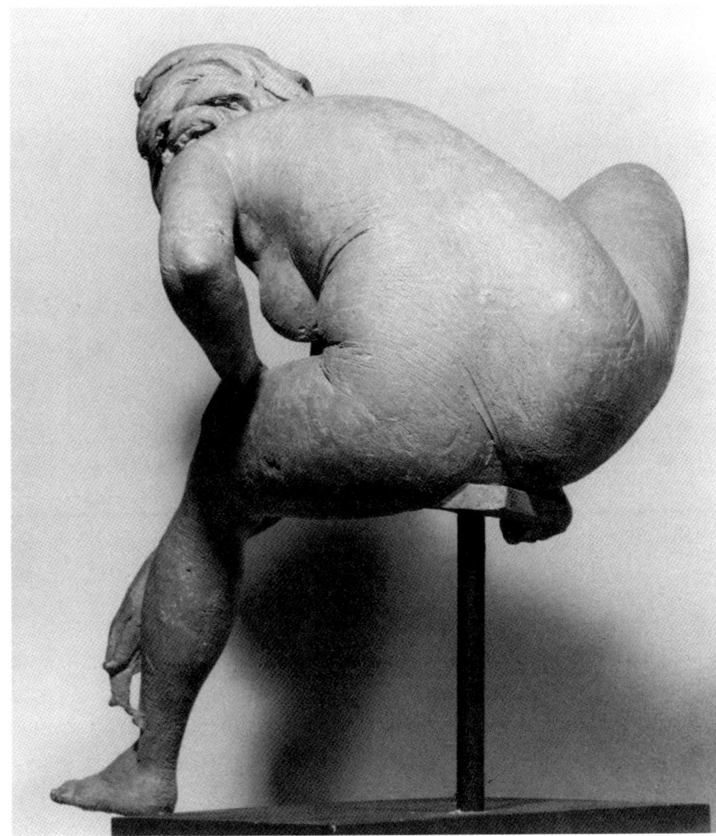

Toilette, 1979, terra-cotta, 16½ x 14½ x 15¼ inches. Forum Gallery, New York. (See also colorplate, page 46.)

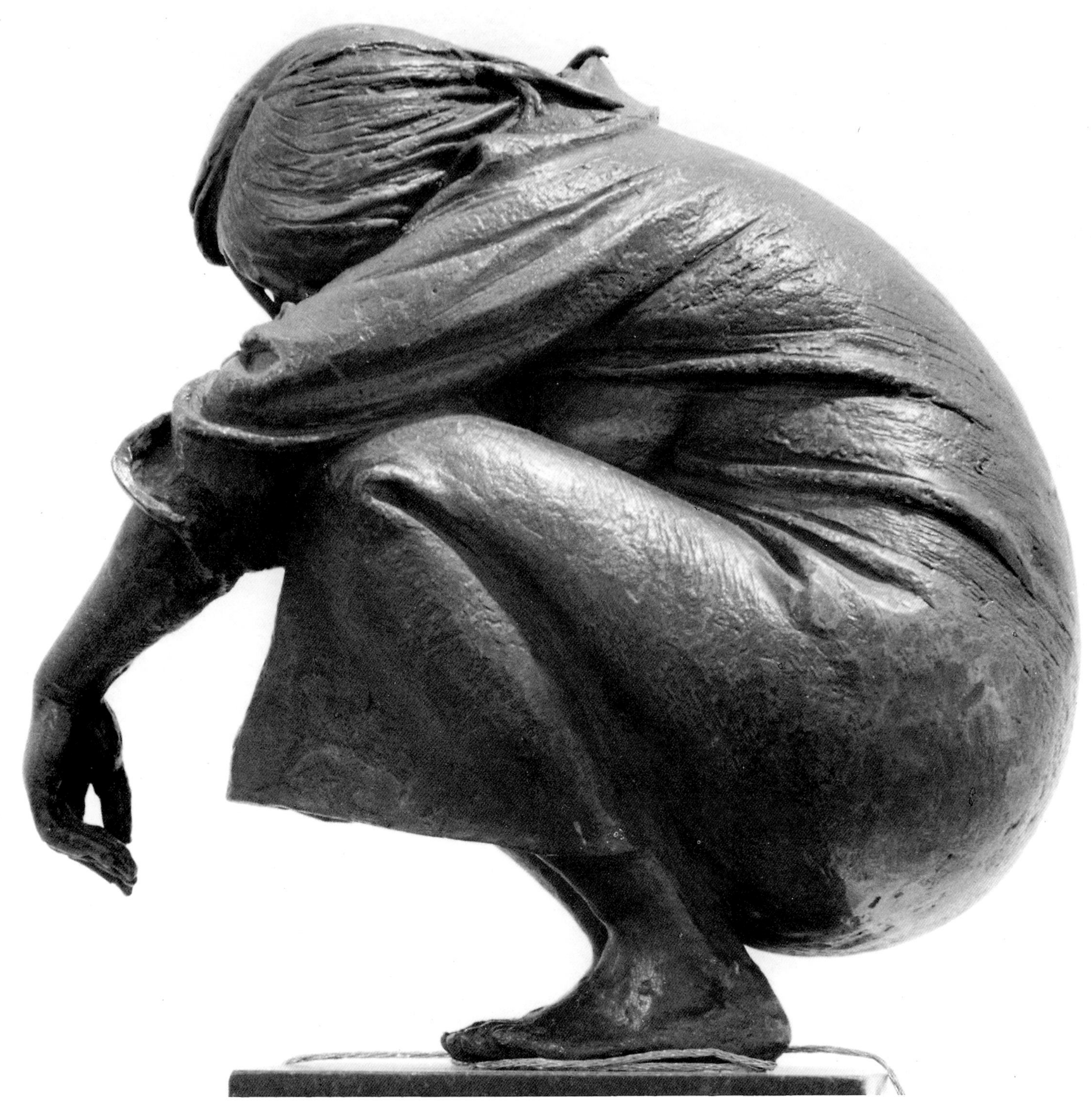

Repose, 1974, bronze, 8 x 8 x 5 inches. Forum Gallery, New York.

Musing, 1985, bronze, 11½ x 6½ x 8½ inches. Private collection.

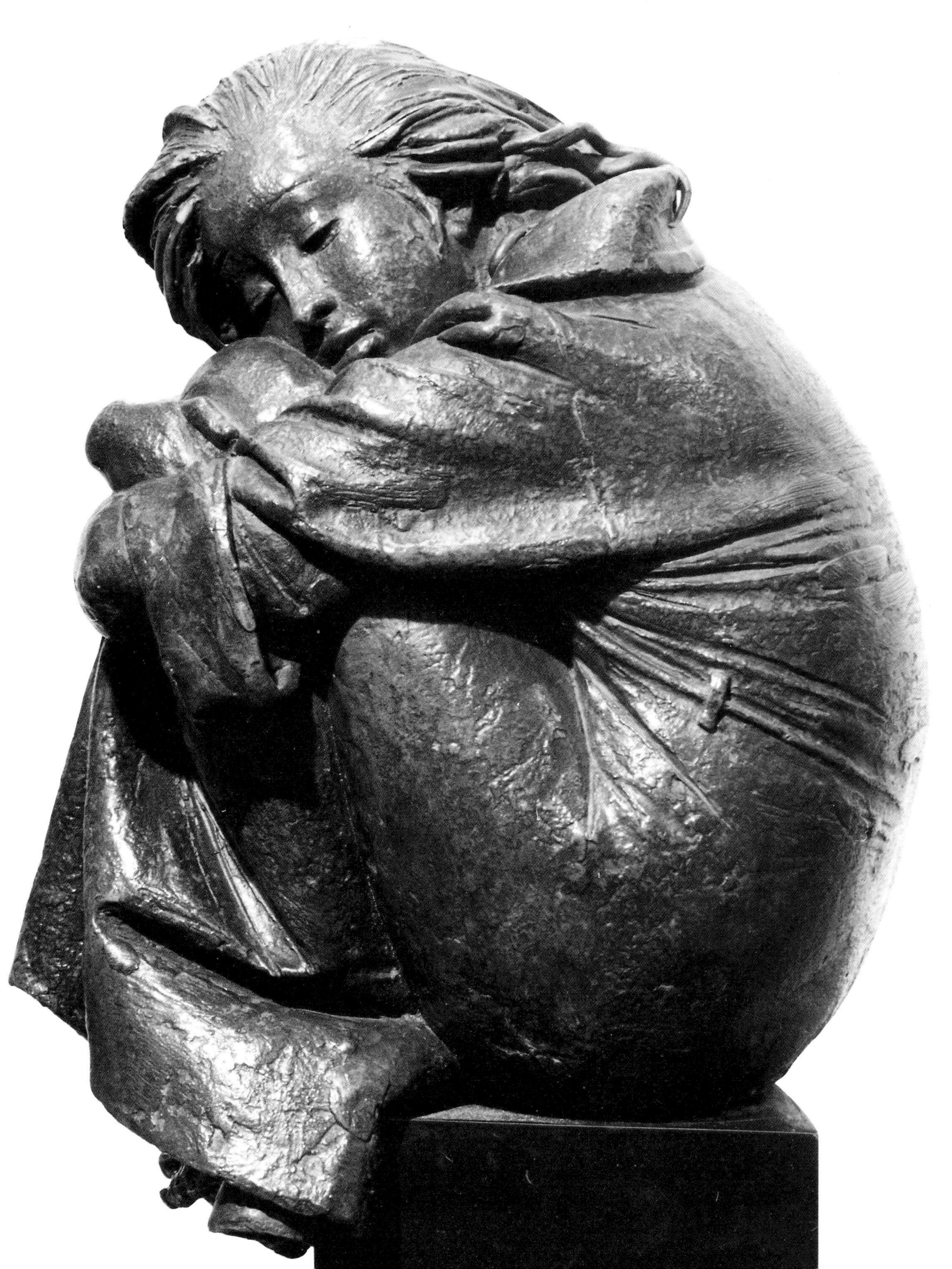

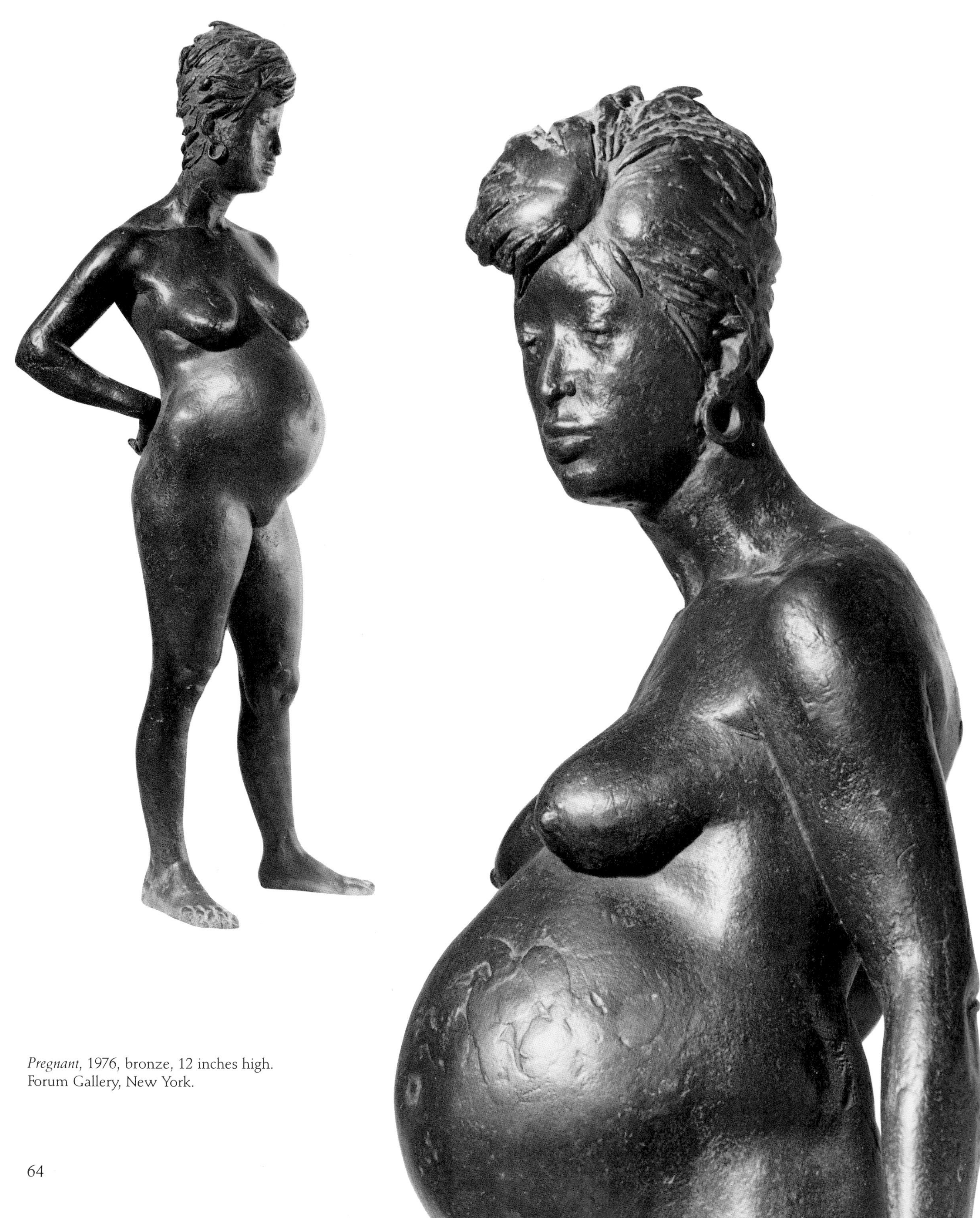

Pregnant, 1976, bronze, 12 inches high.
Forum Gallery, New York.

Study for Fountain, 1978, bronze, 15 inches high. Forum Gallery, New York.

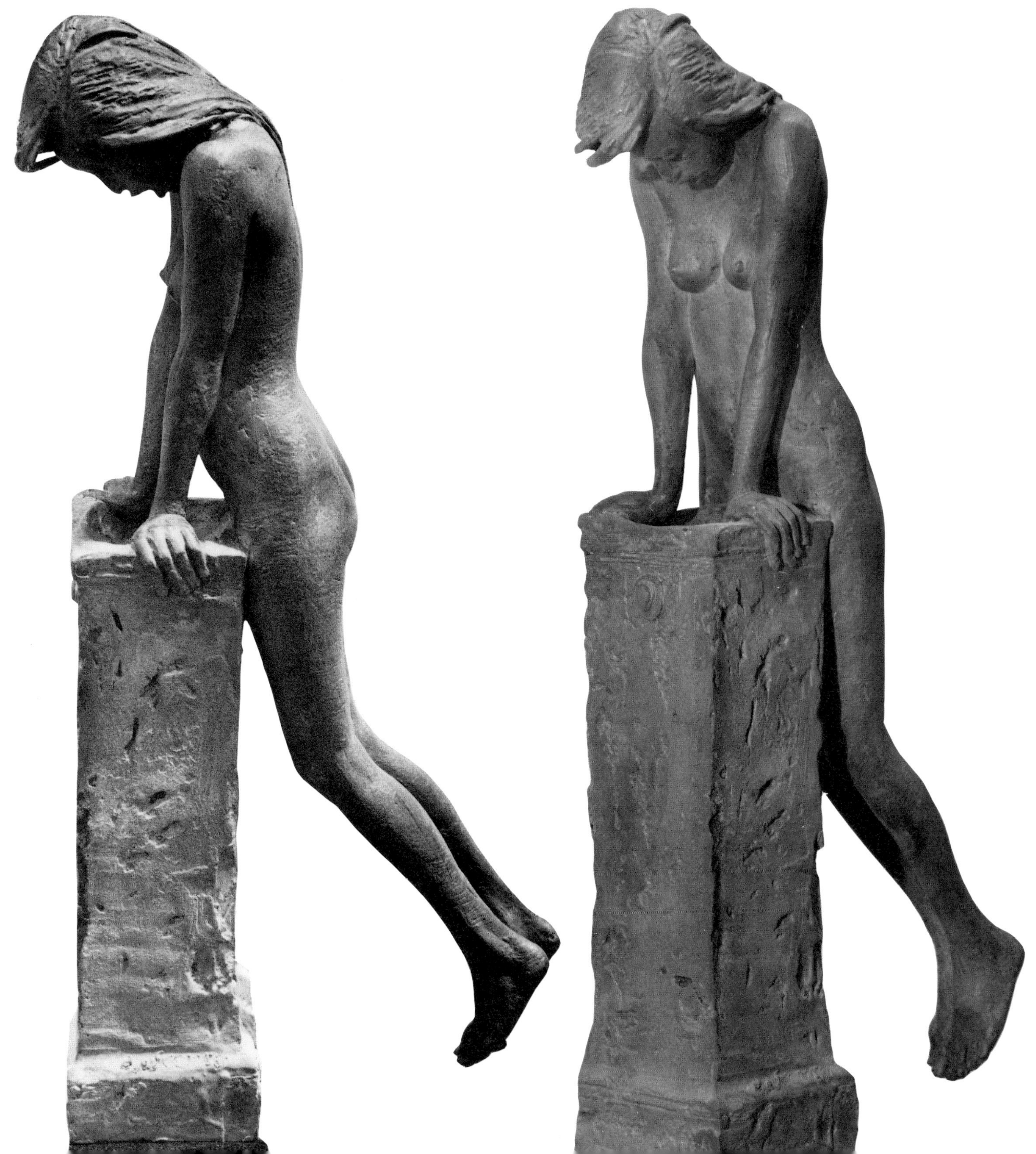

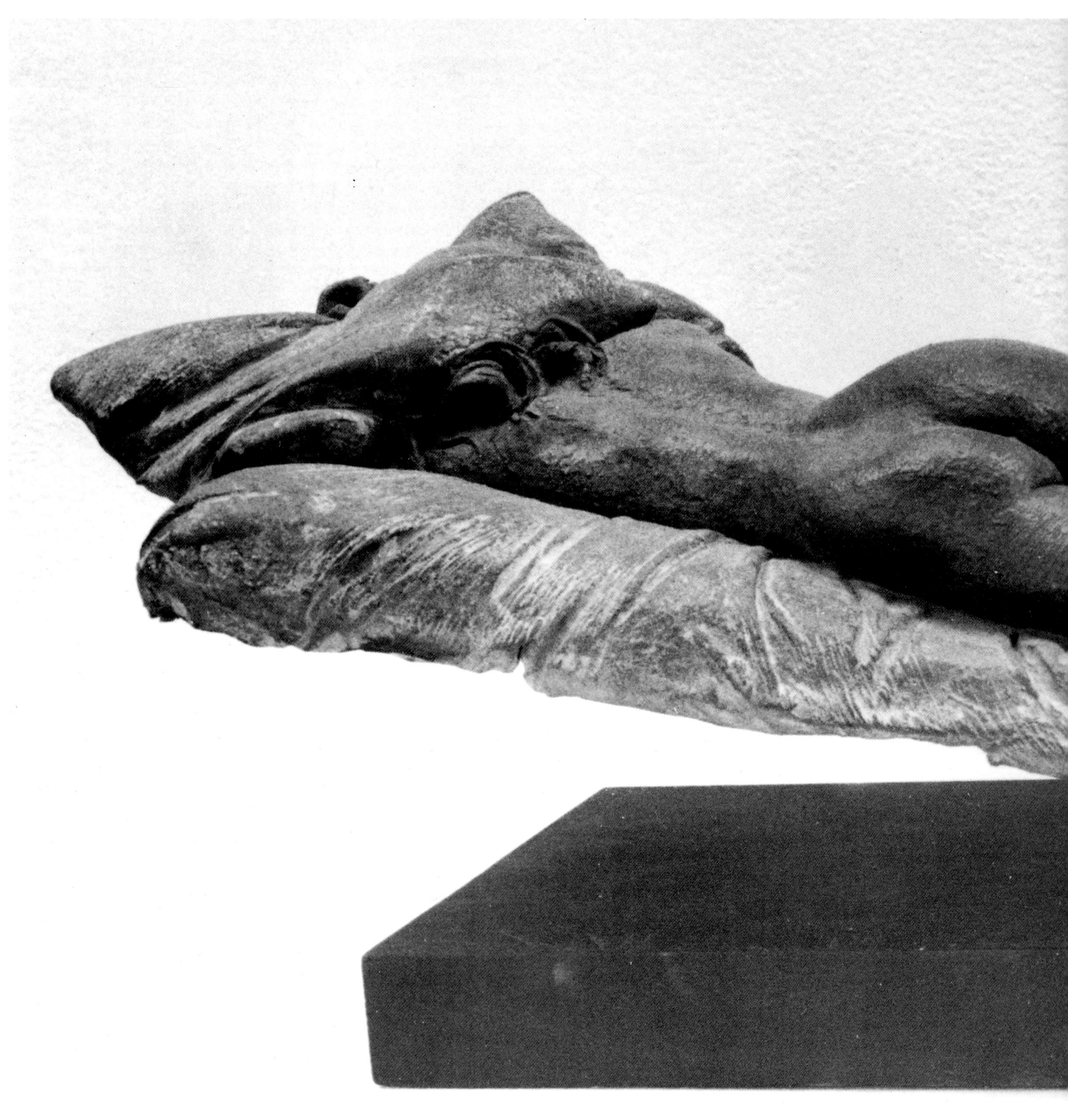

Distraught, 1983, polychrome terra-cotta, 31 x 12 inches. Forum Gallery, New York.

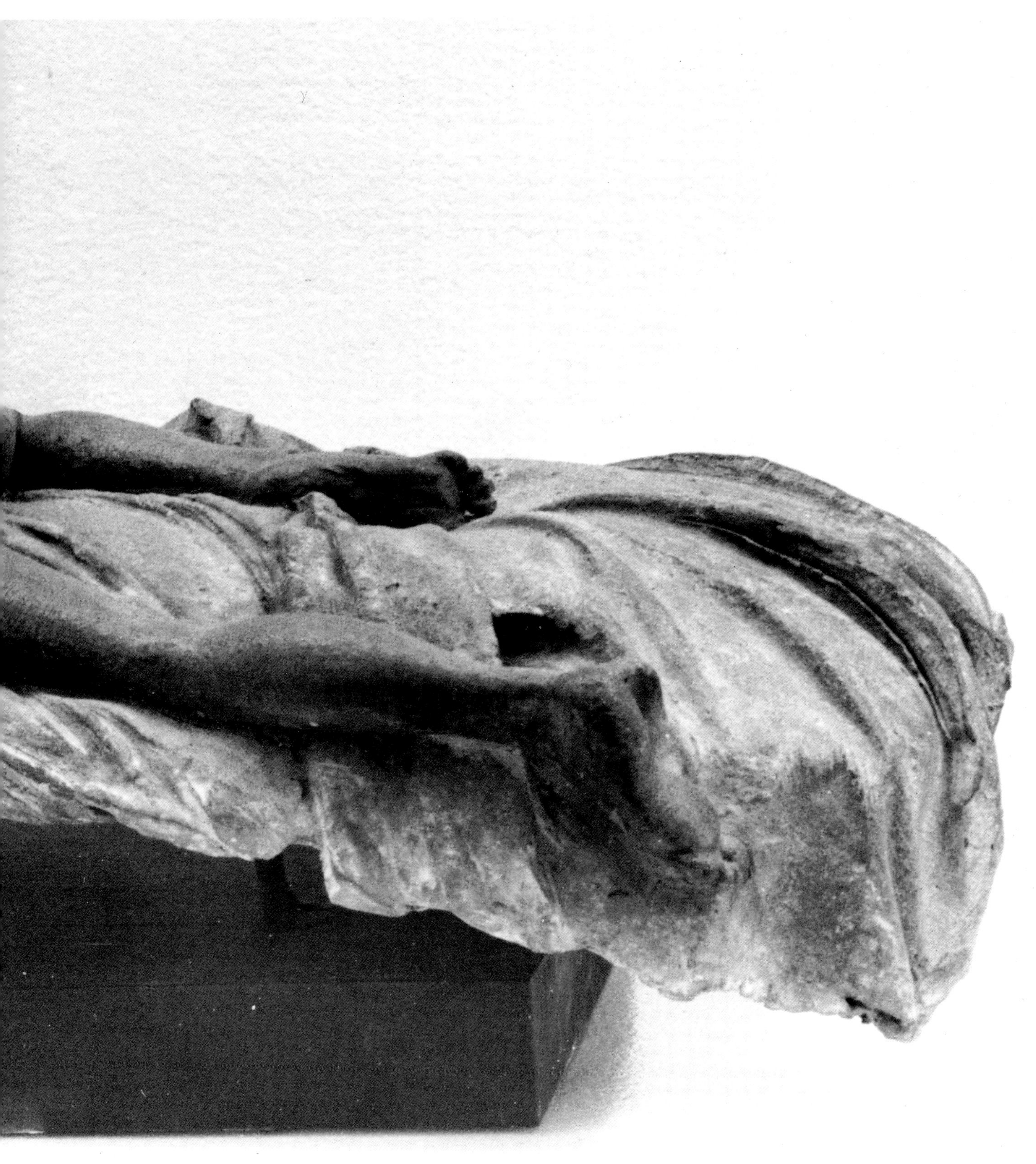

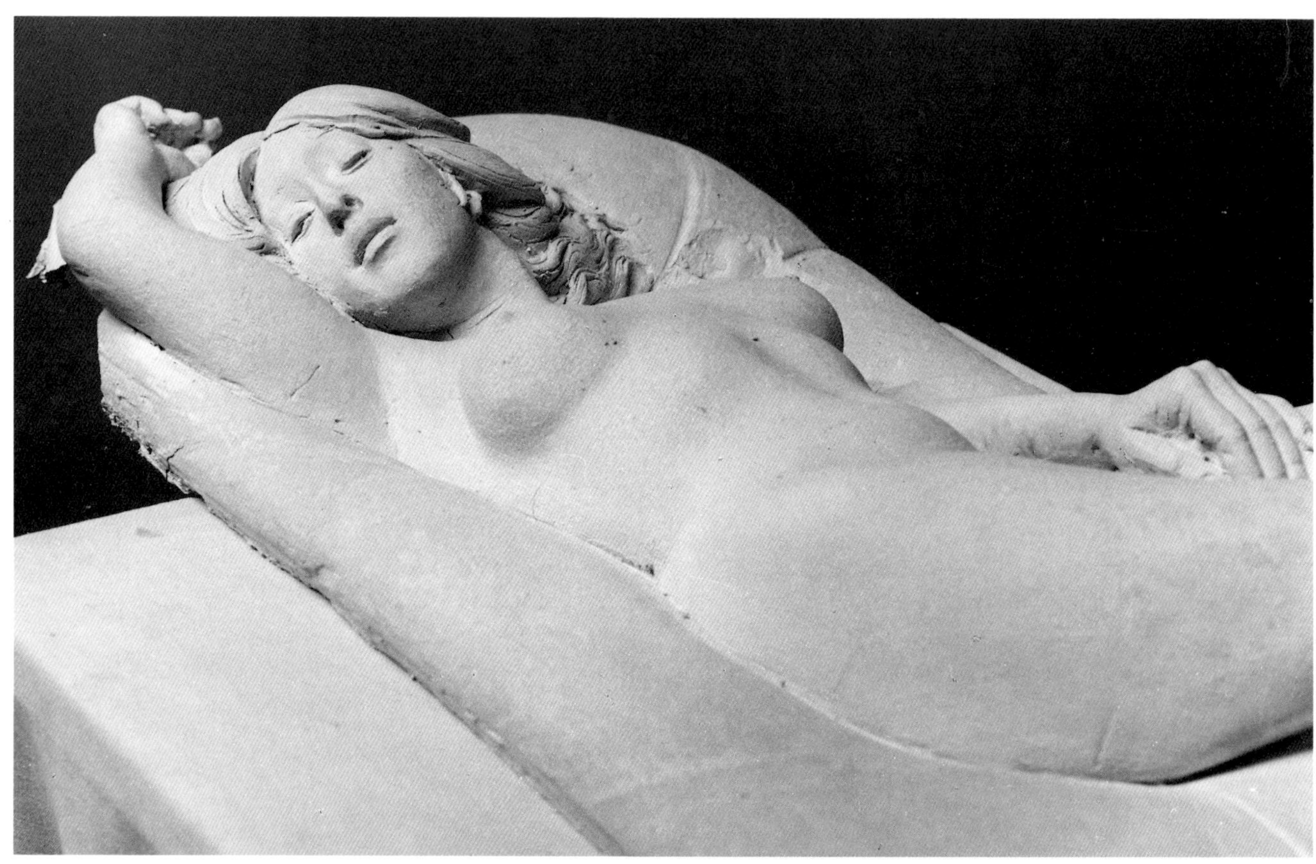

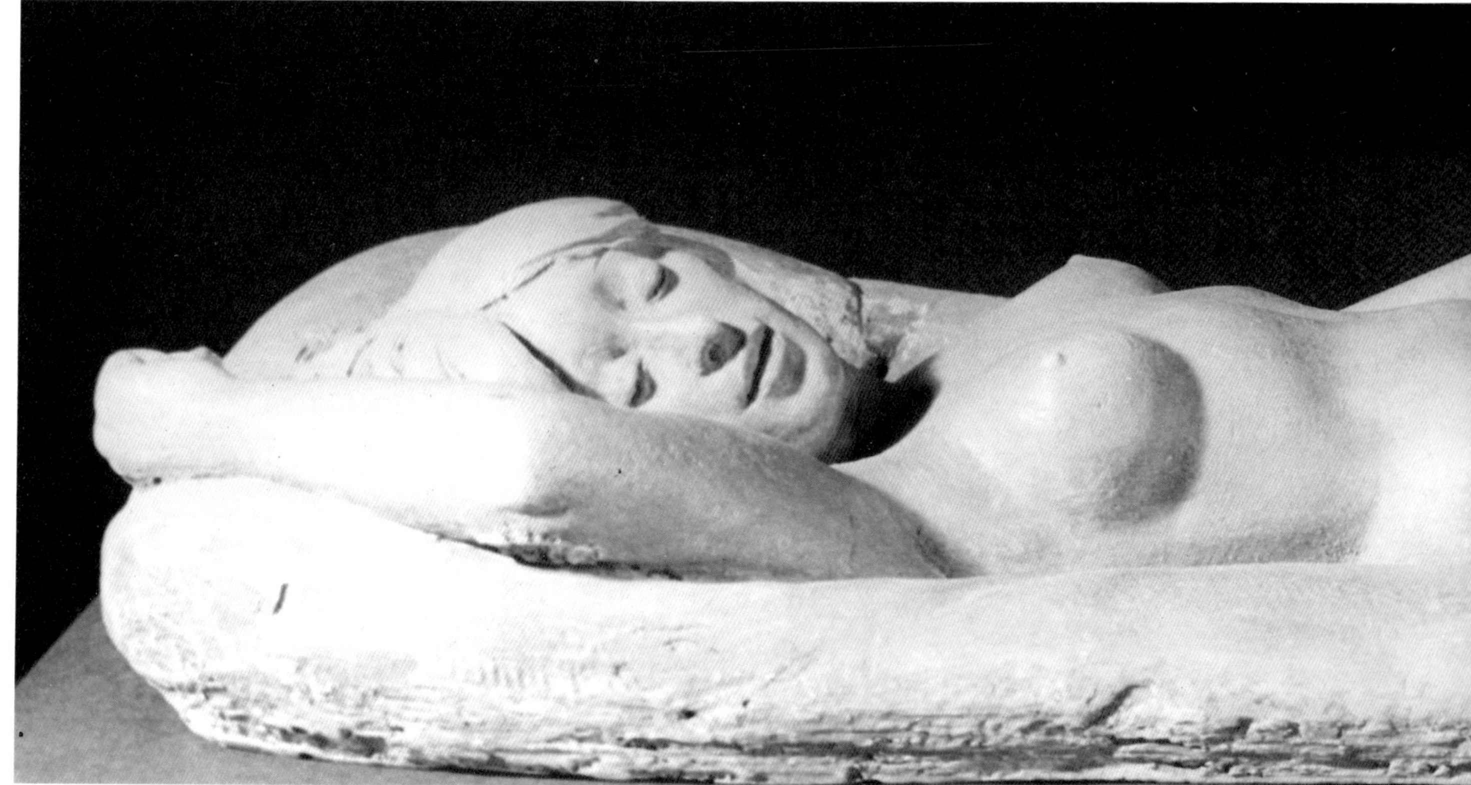

Sleeping Nude, 1983, terra-cotta, 2 x 26 x 12½ inches. Forum Gallery, New York.

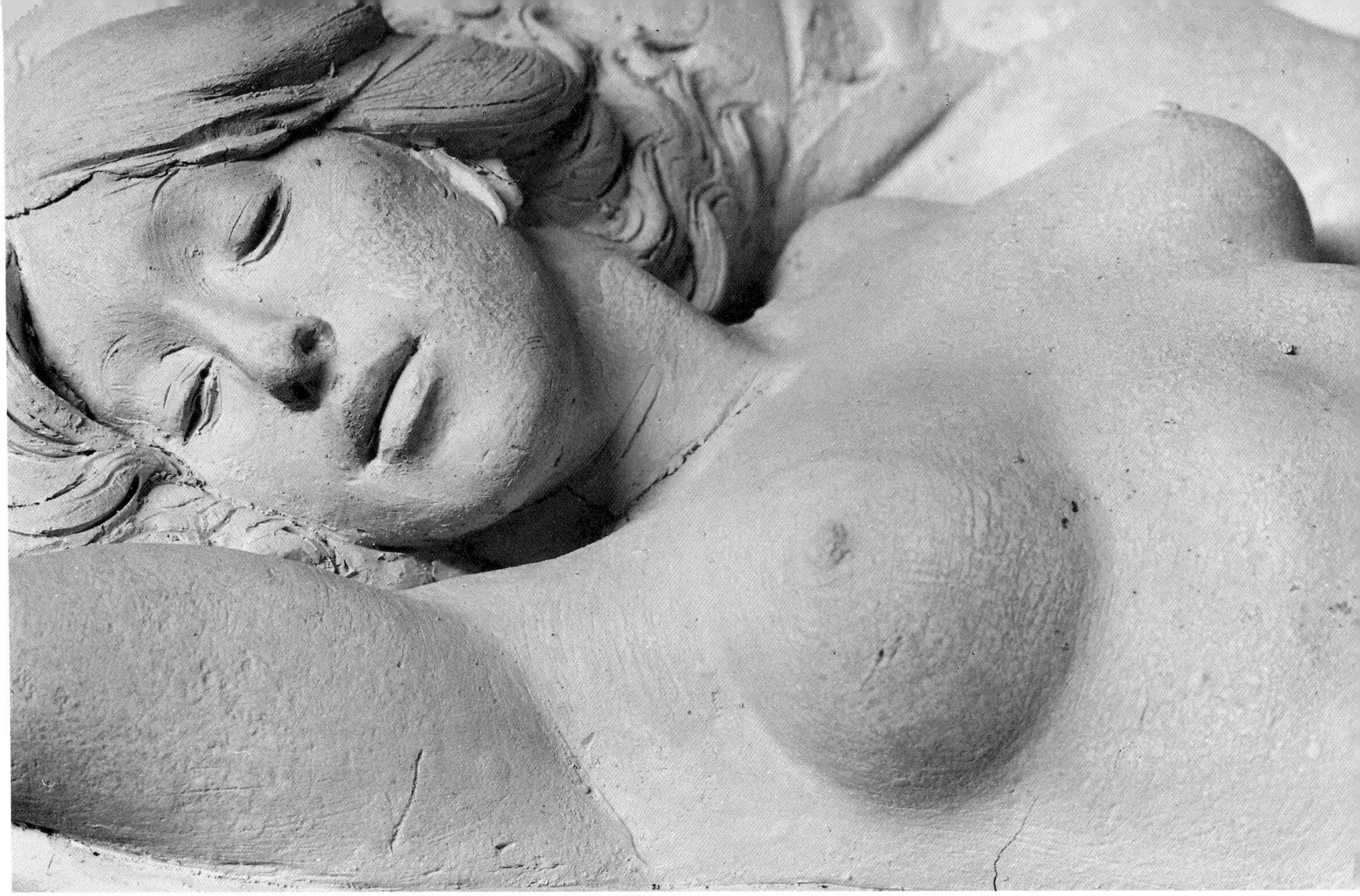

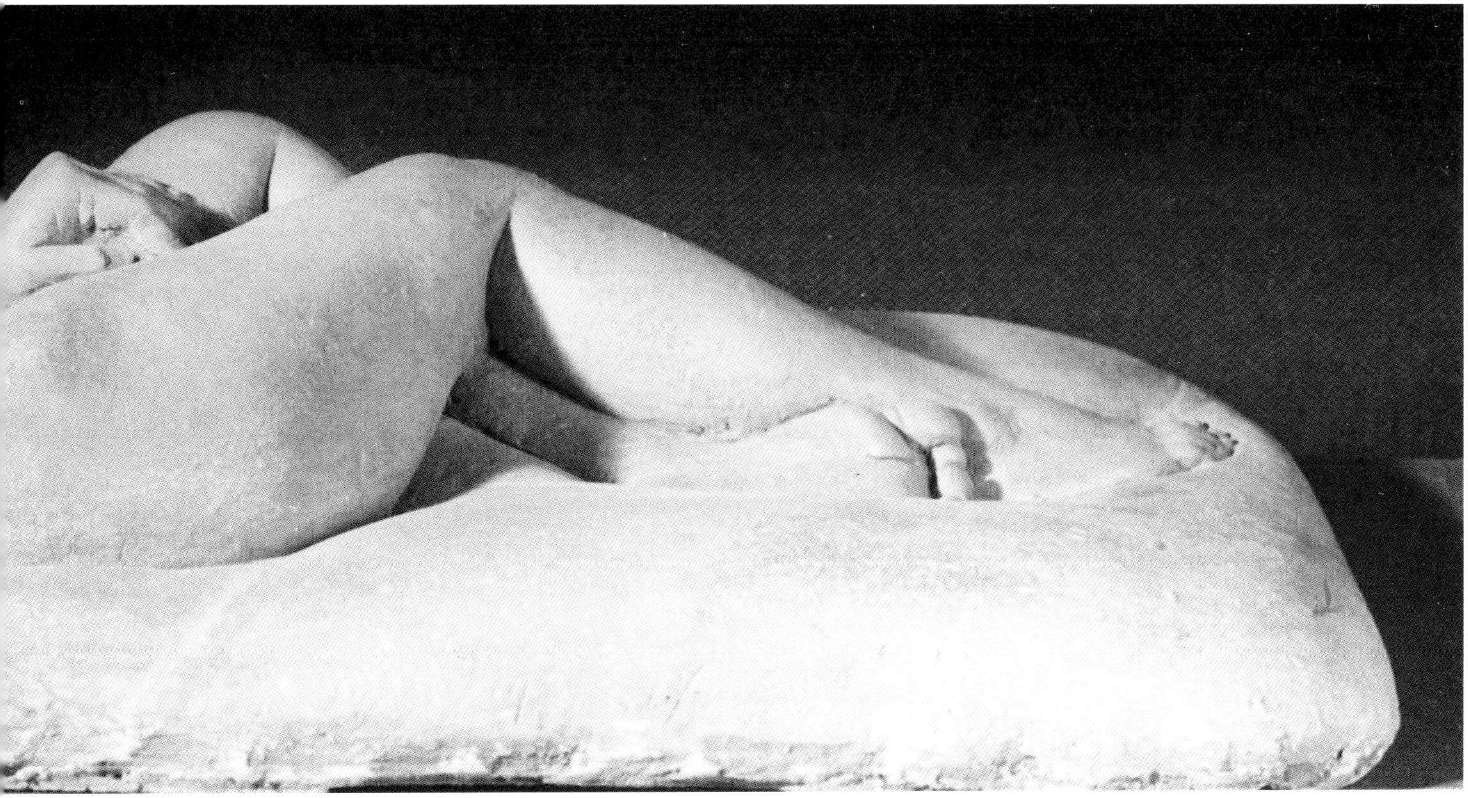

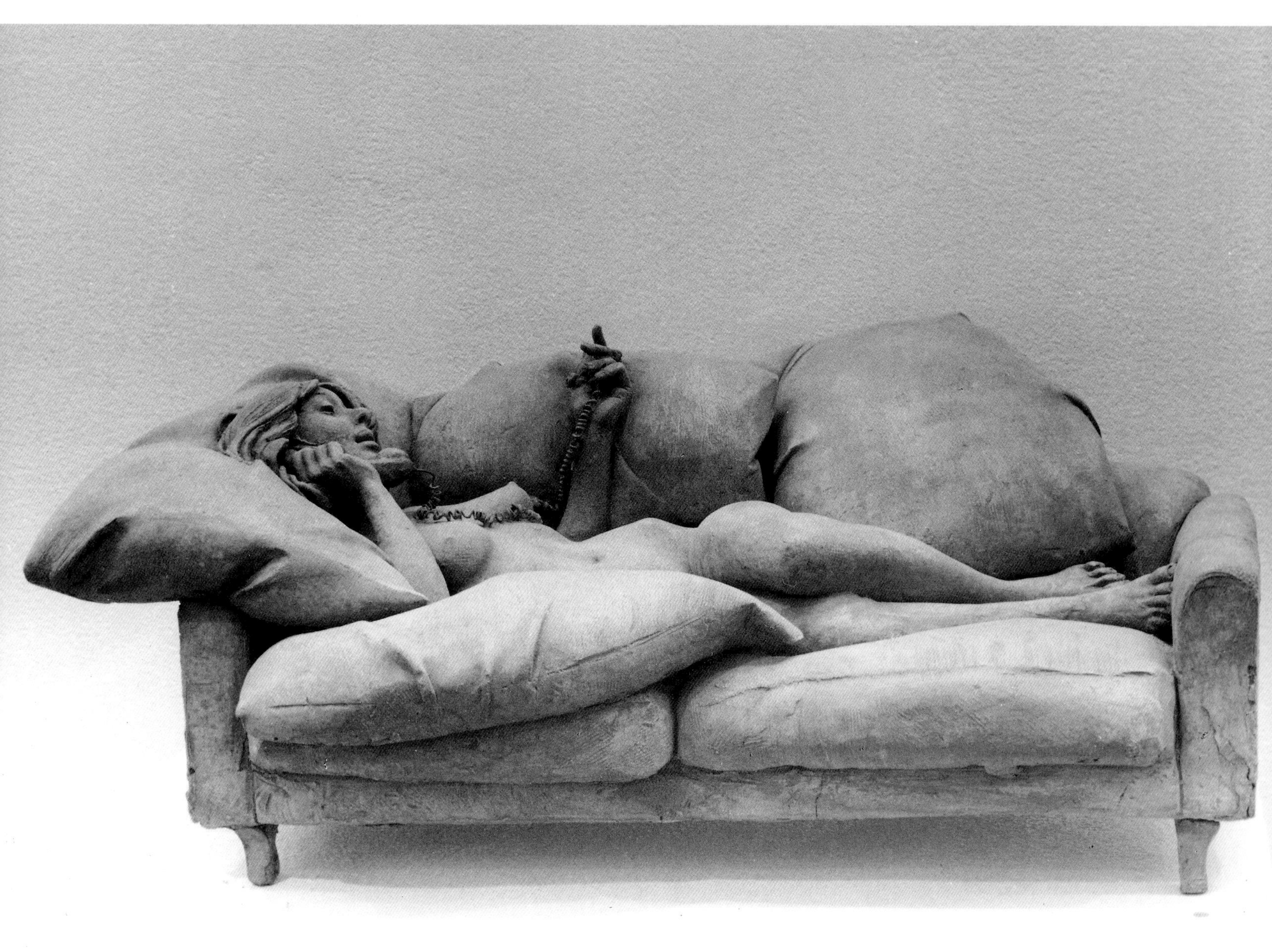

On the Telephone, 1984, polychrome bronze, 20 x 11 x 7 inches. Collection of George Ablah, Wichita, Kansas.

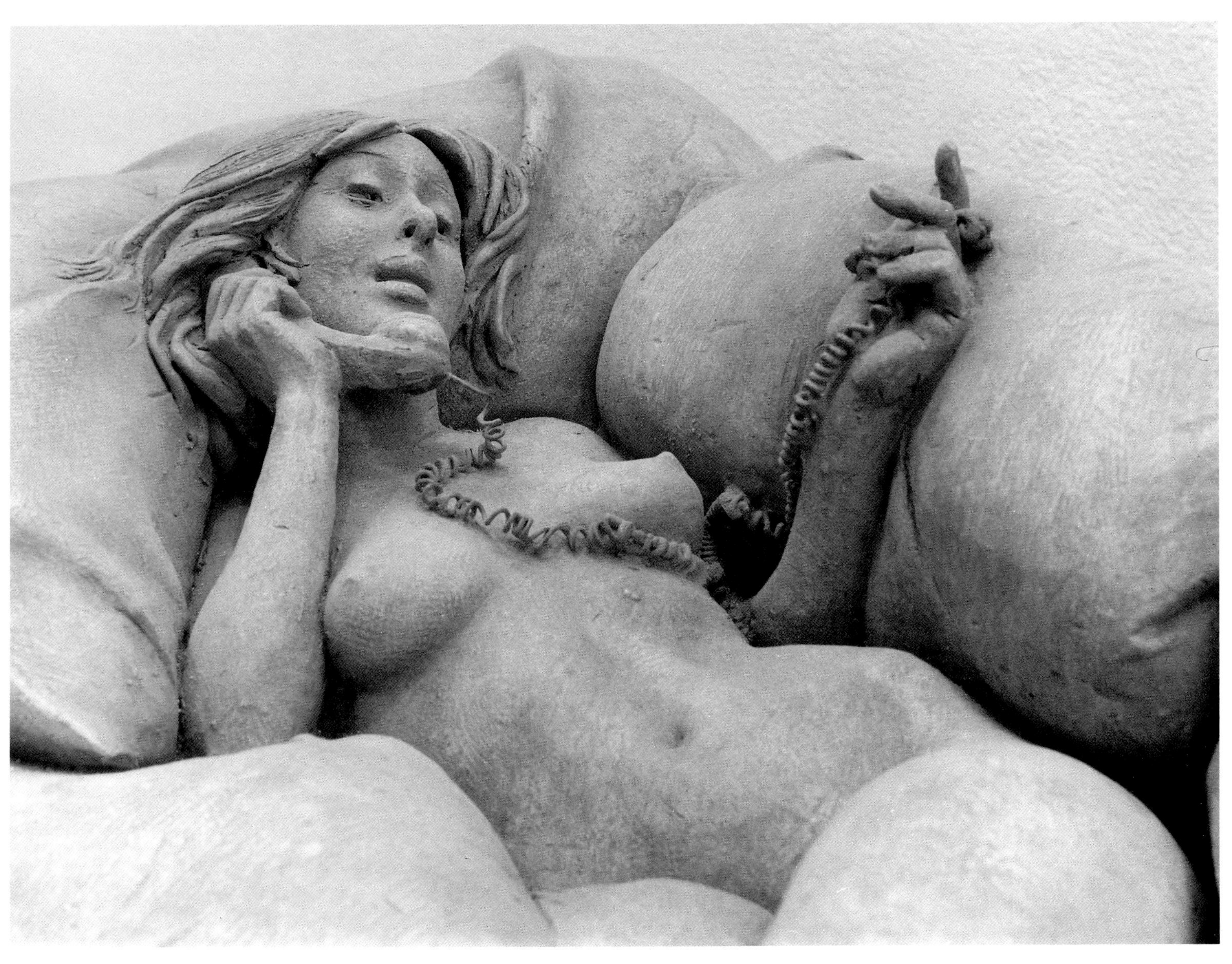

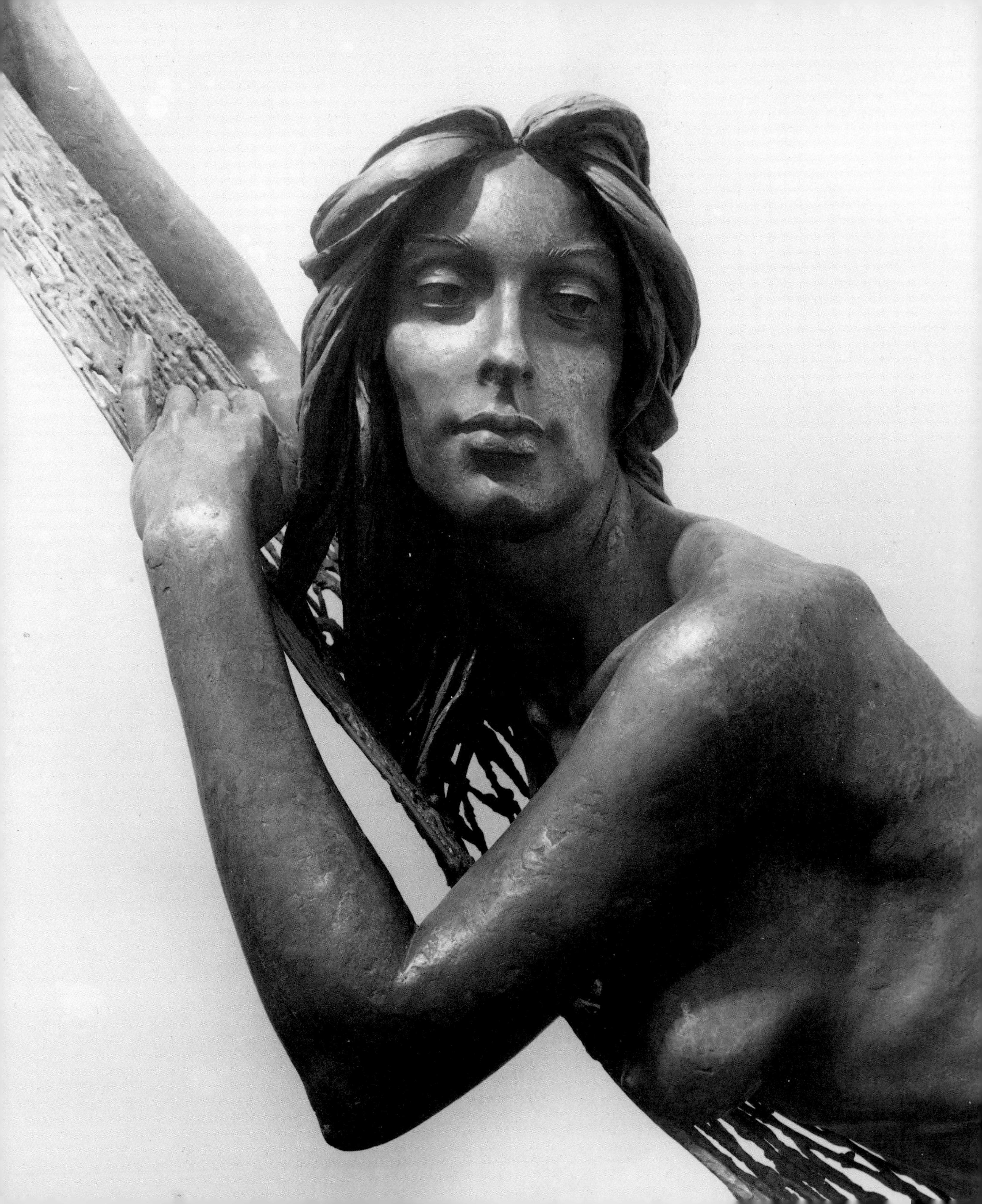

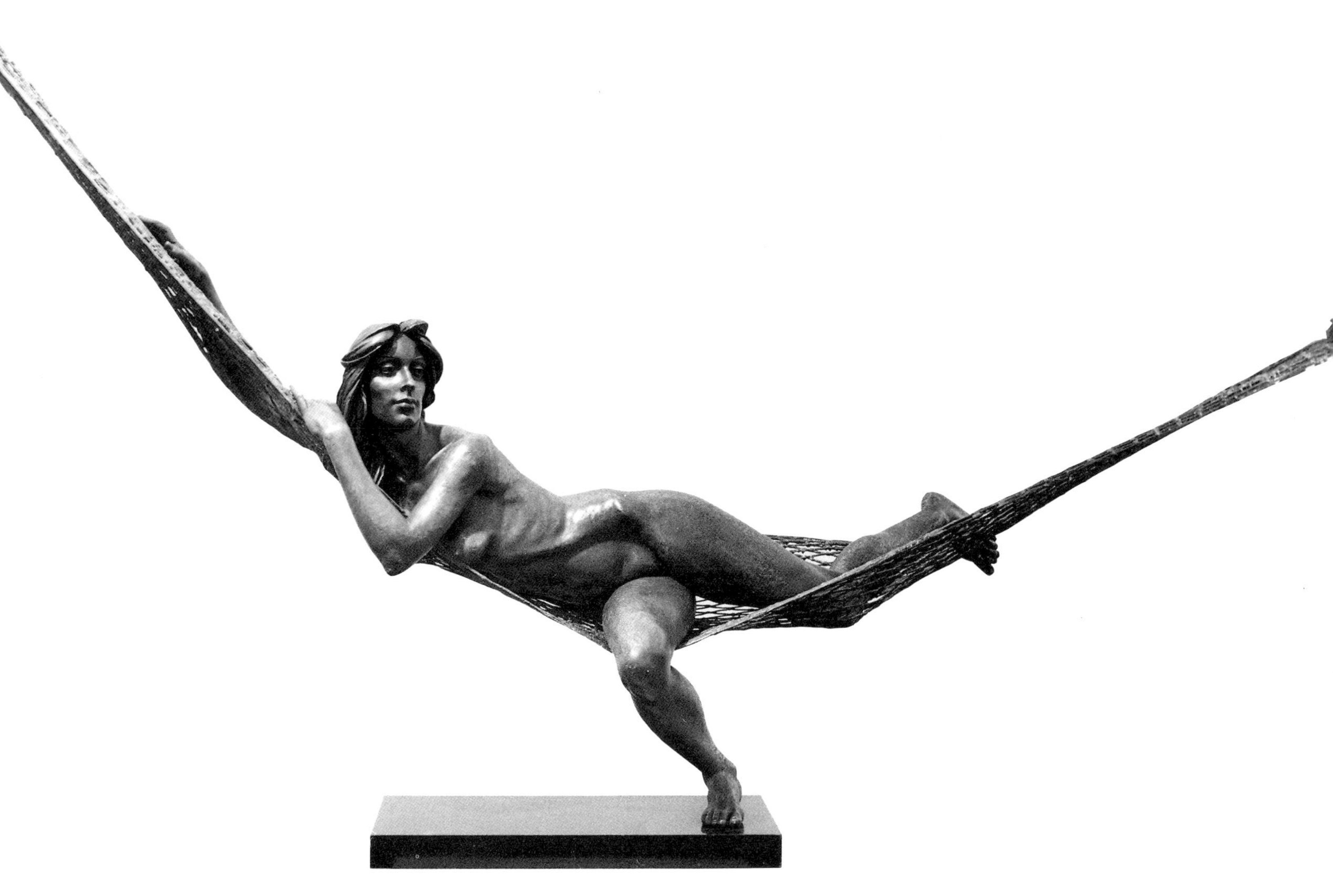

Hammock, 1983, bronze, 60 x 100 x 18 inches. Forum Gallery, New York.

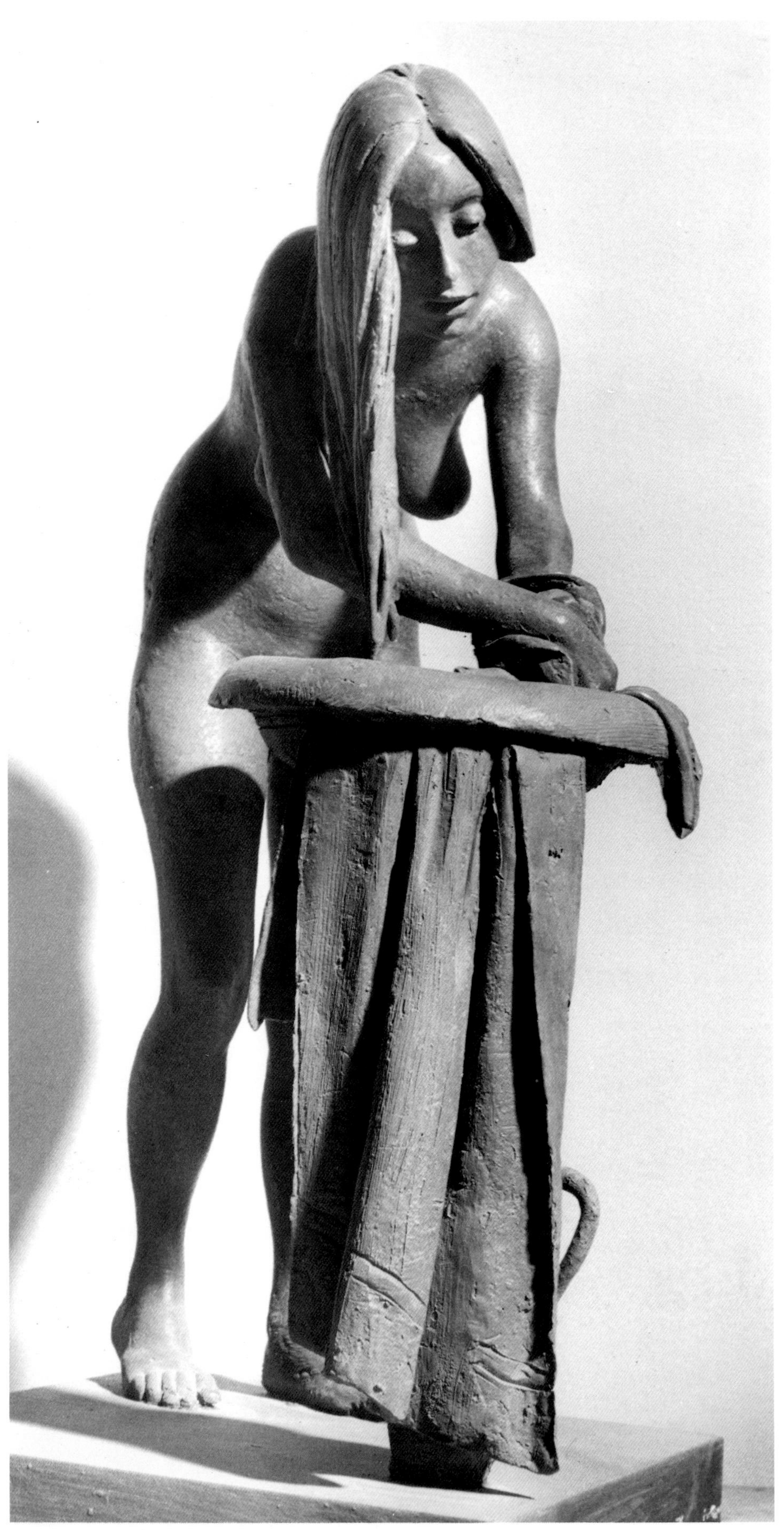

Wash Basin, 1982, terra-cotta, 16 inches high. Forum Gallery, New York.

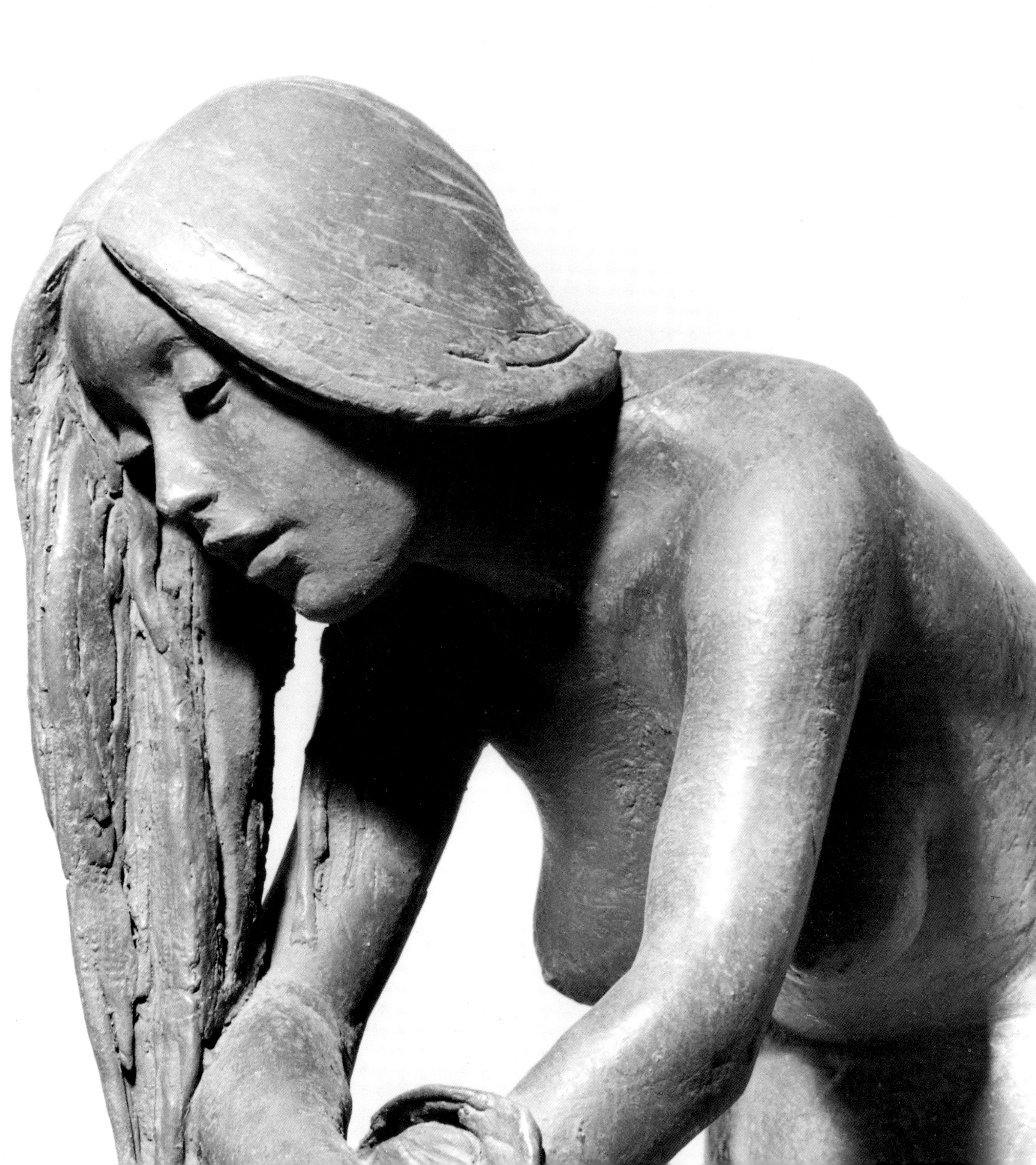

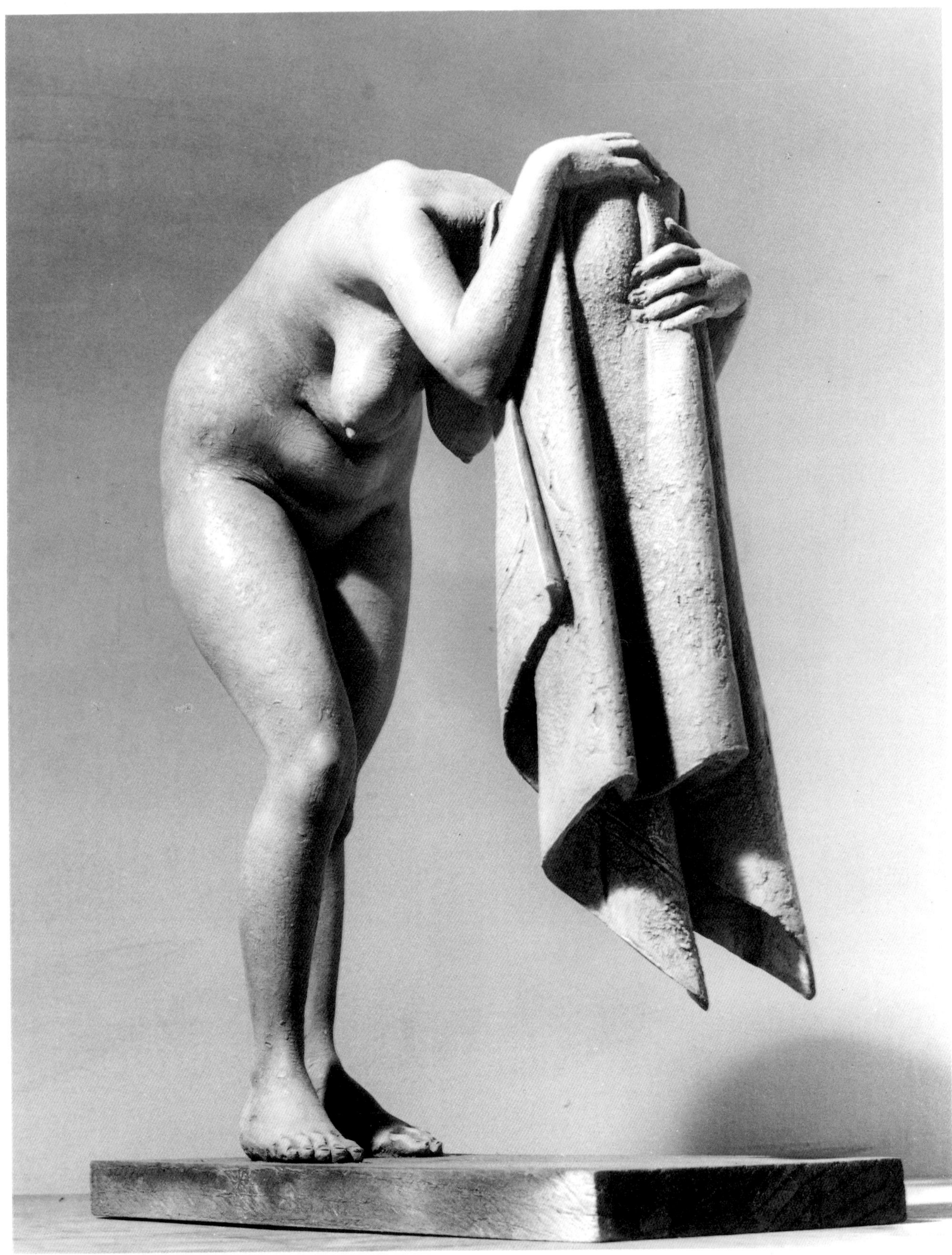

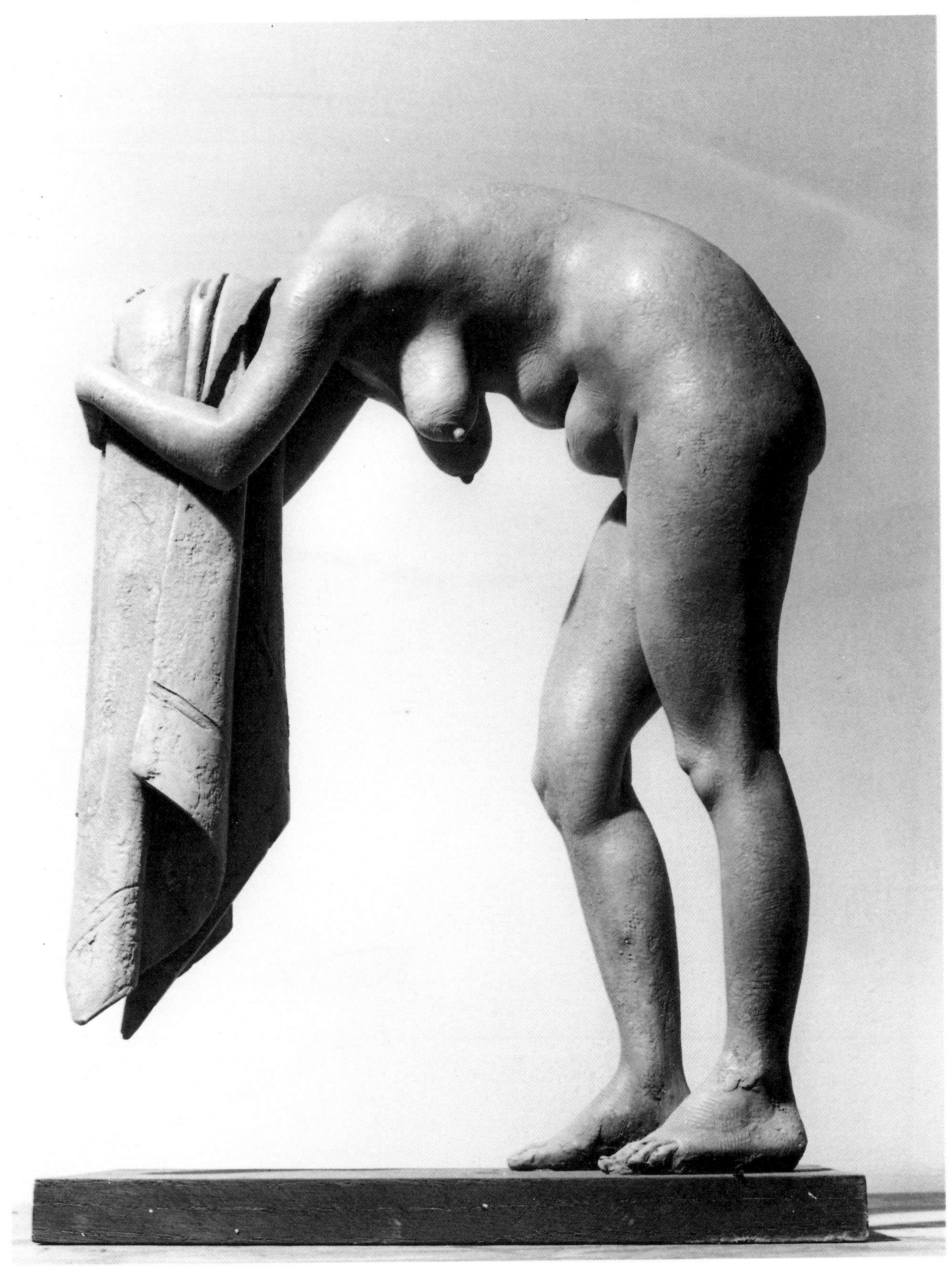

Woman Drying Her Hair, 1987, terra-cotta,
12 inches high. Forum Gallery, New York.

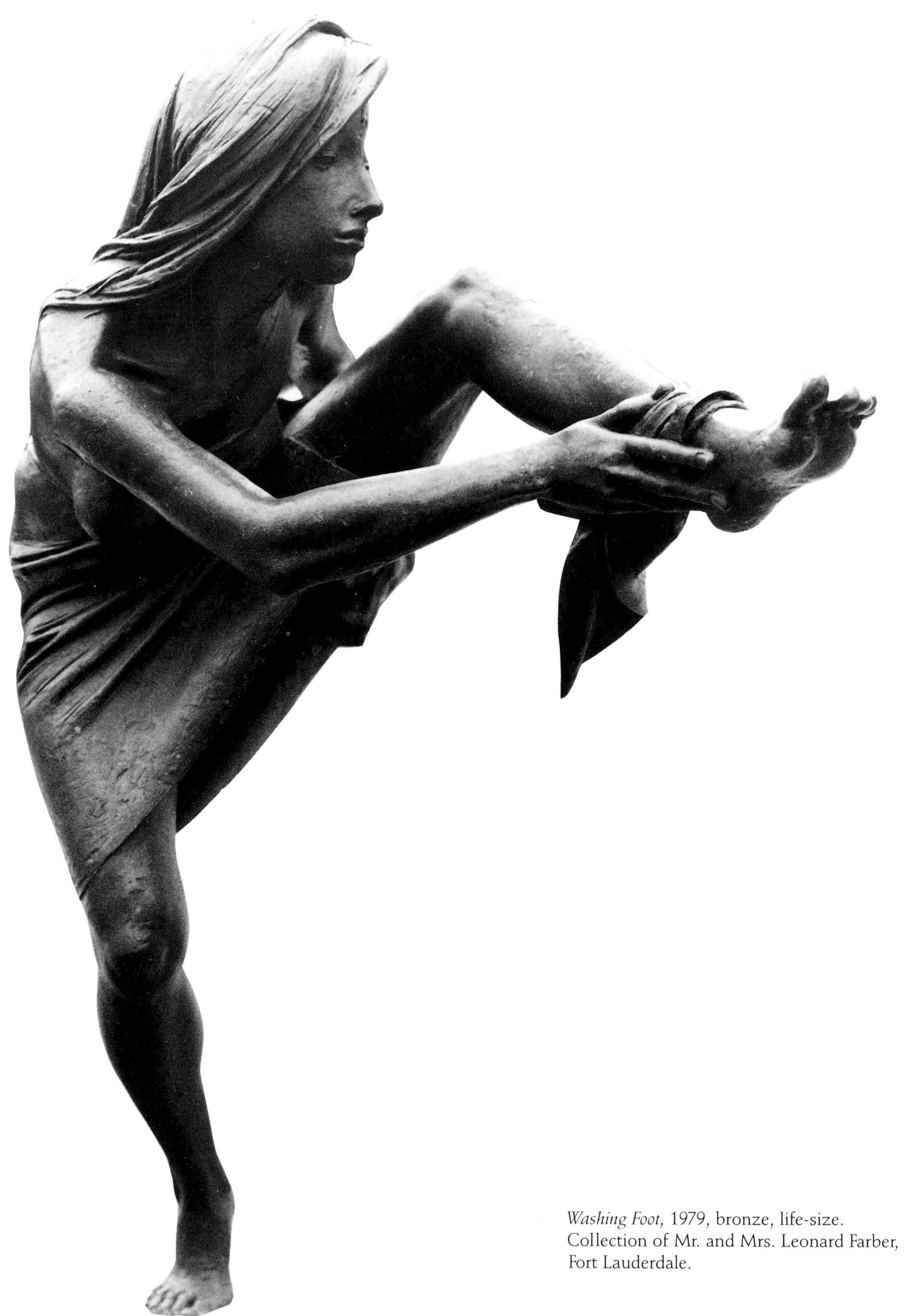

Washing Foot, 1979, bronze, life-size. Collection of Mr. and Mrs. Leonard Farber, Fort Lauderdale.

SCENES OF DAILY LIFE

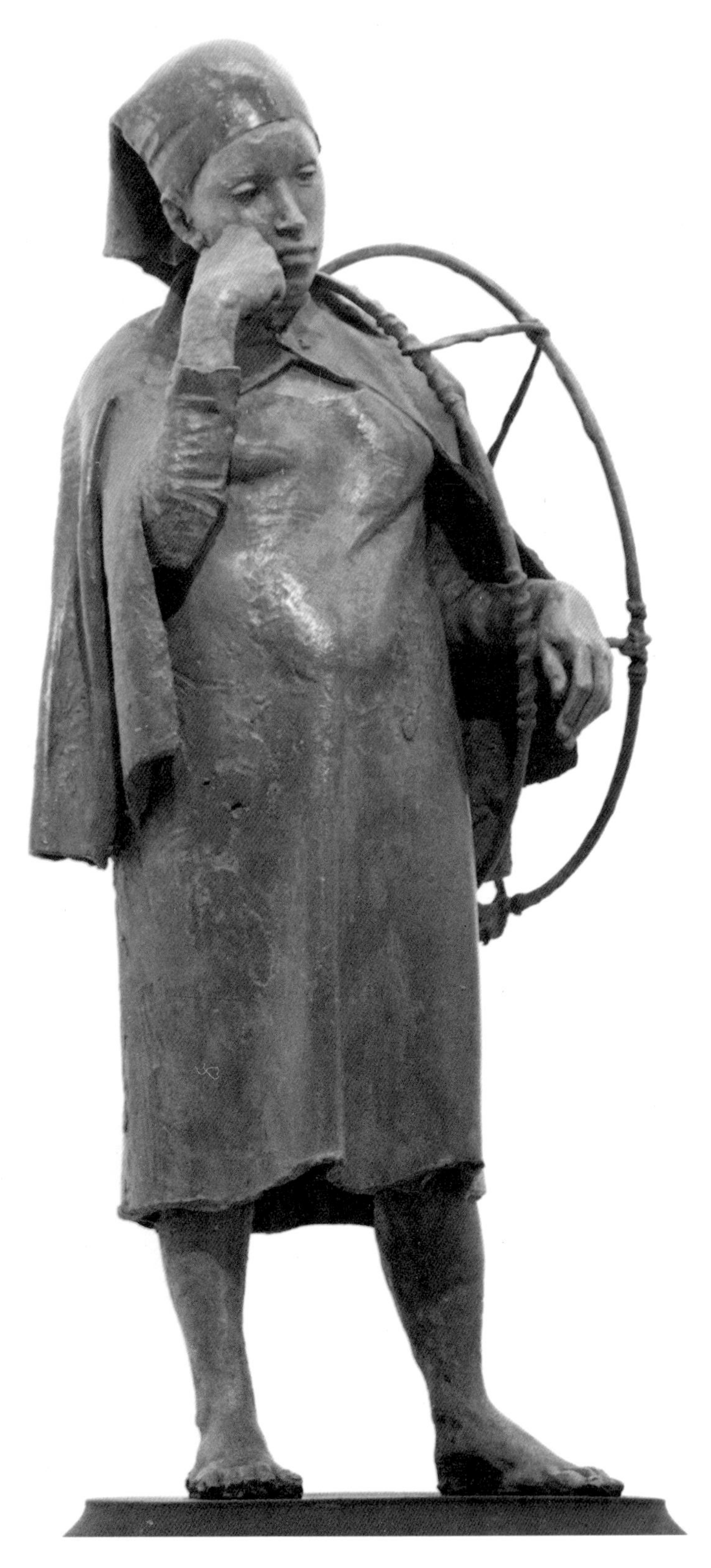

Gathering Hay, 1969, bronze, 8 x 16½ inches. Forum Gallery, New York.

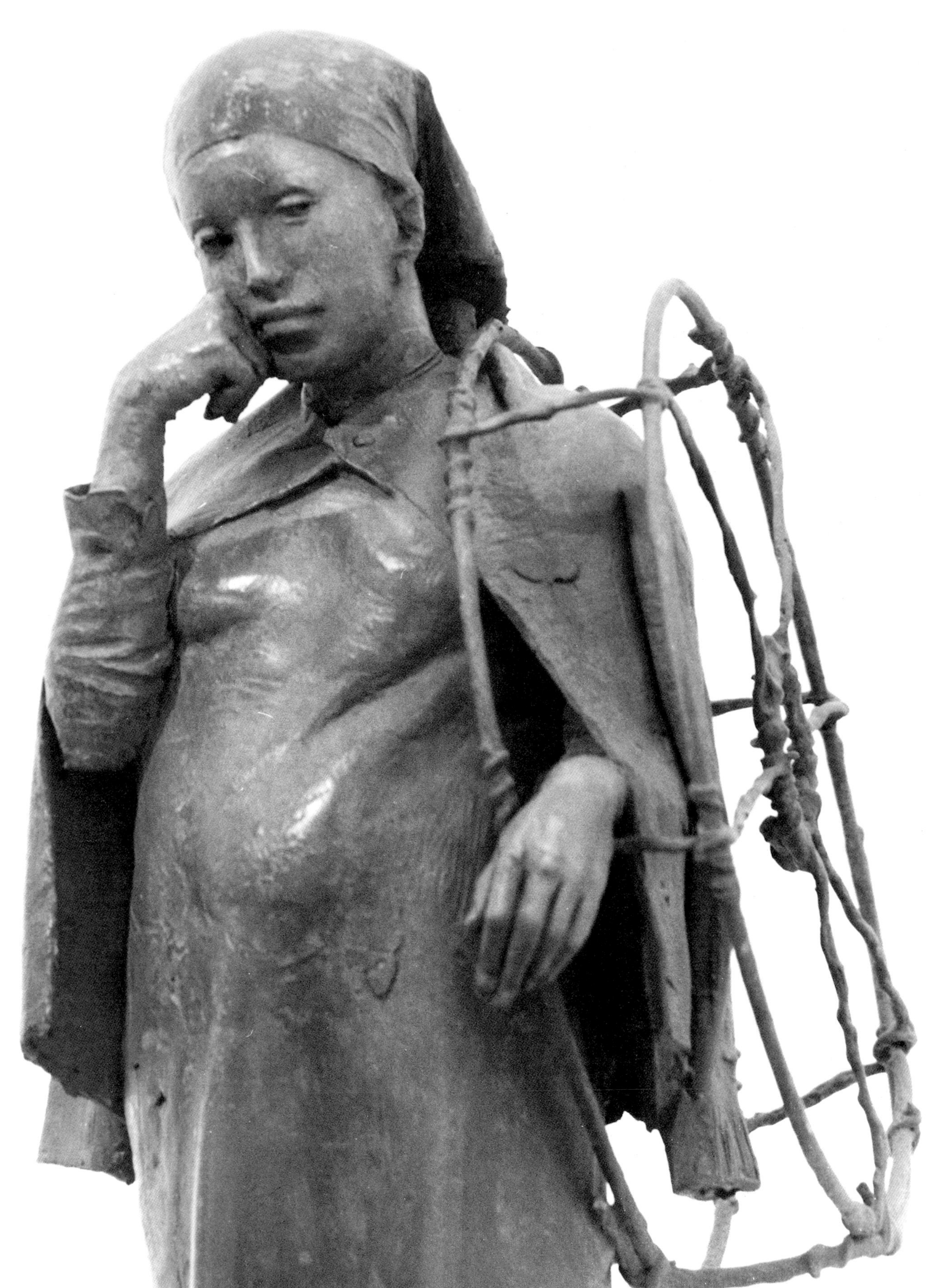

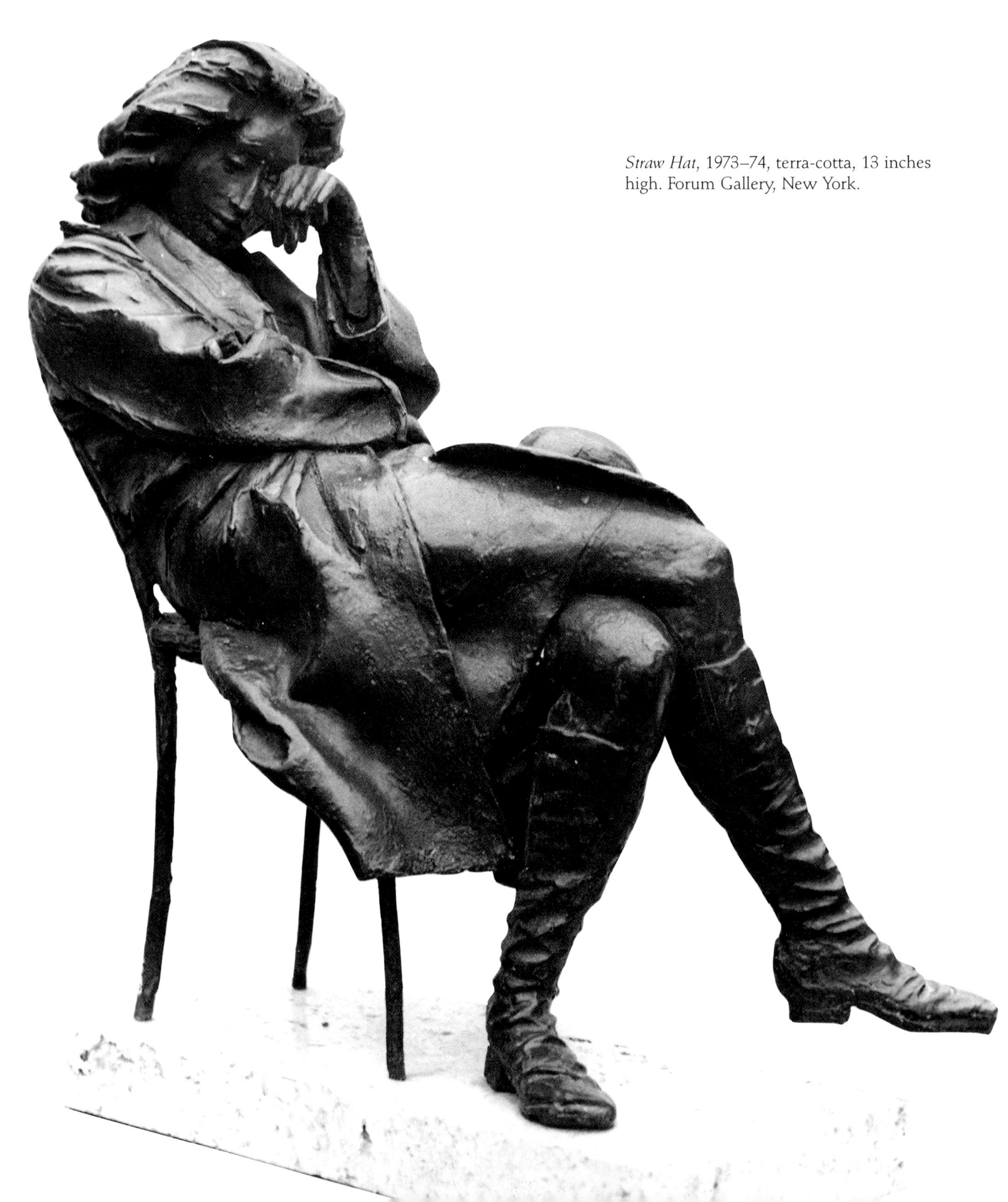

Straw Hat, 1973–74, terra-cotta, 13 inches high. Forum Gallery, New York.

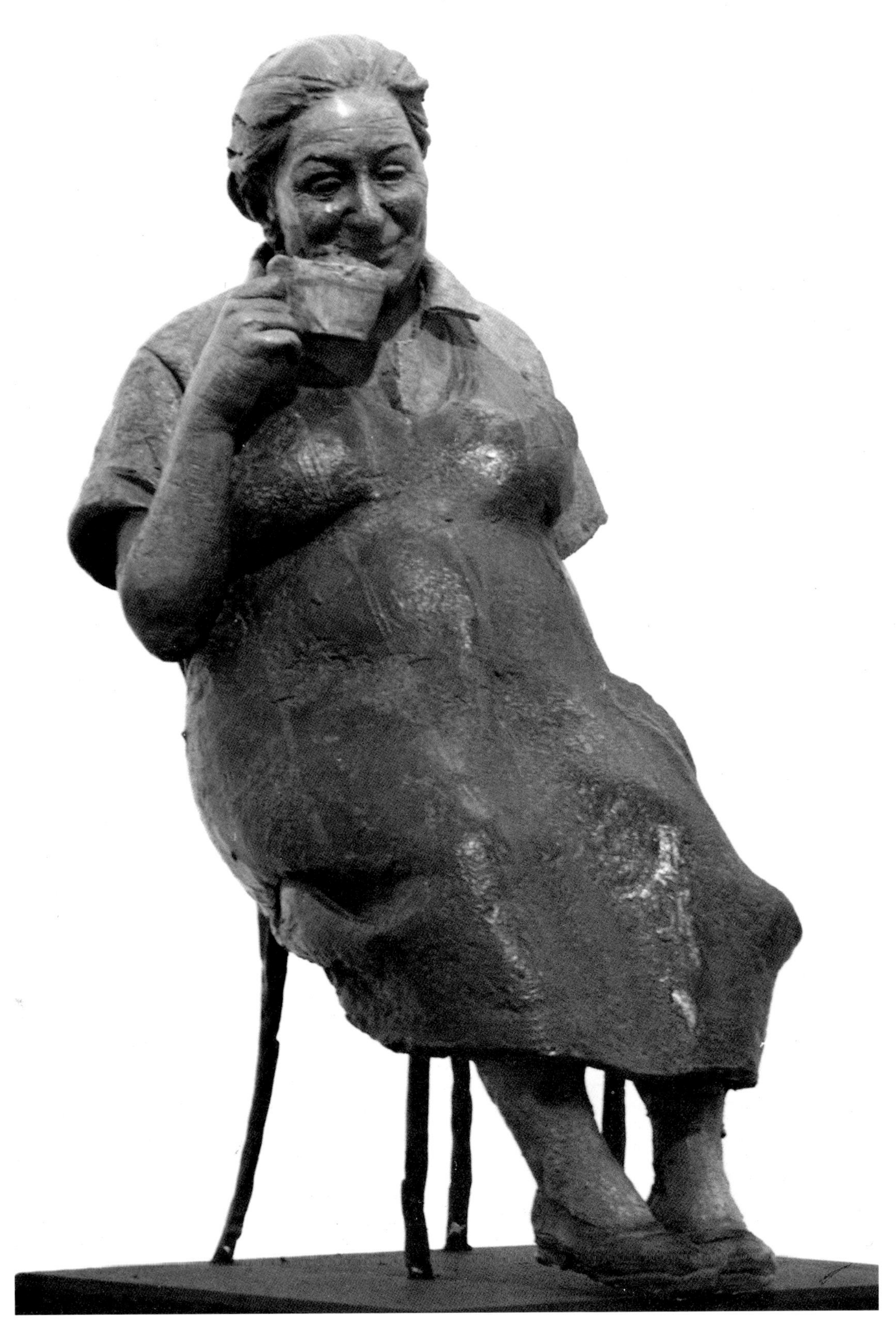

Coffee, 1983, terra-cotta, 15 inches high.
Private collection.

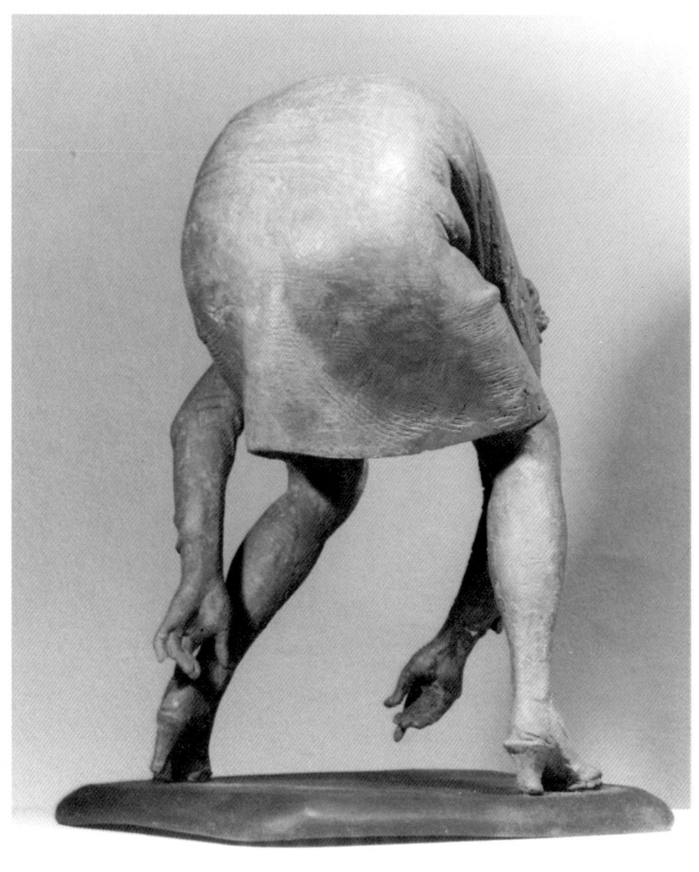

Woman Adjusting Her Shoe, 1979, terracotta, 13 inches high. Forum Gallery, New York. (See also colorplate, page 47.)

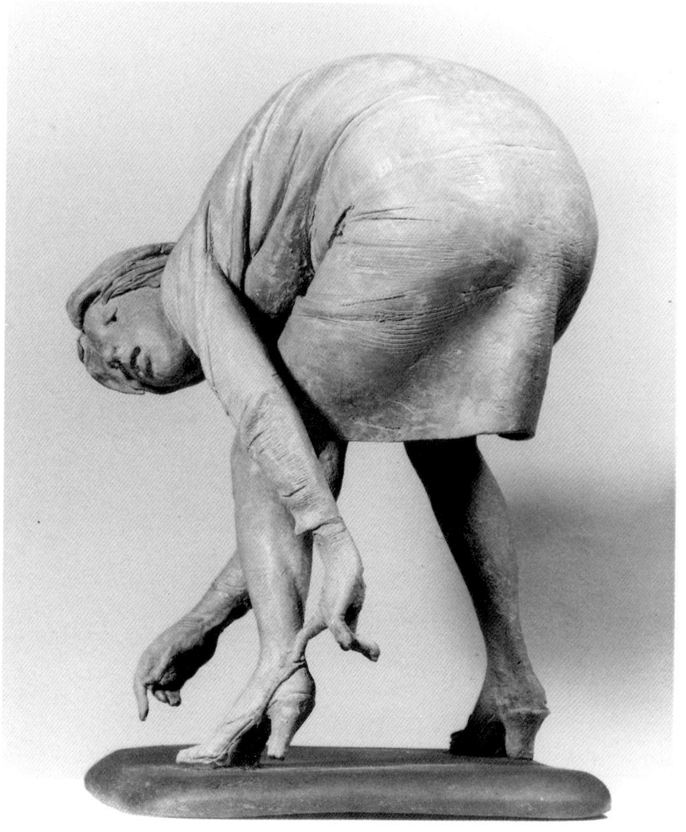

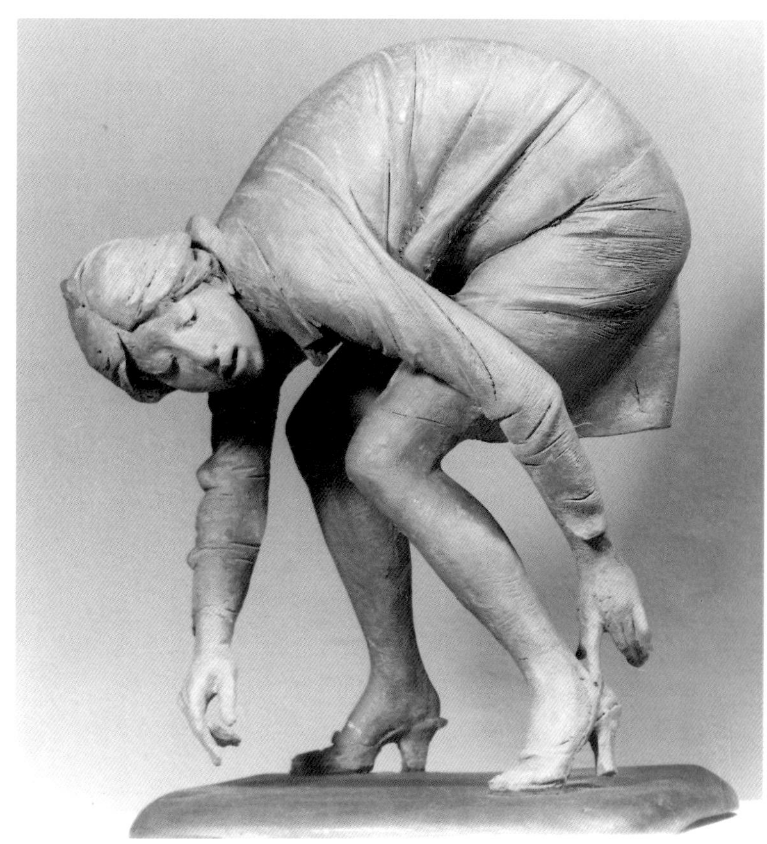

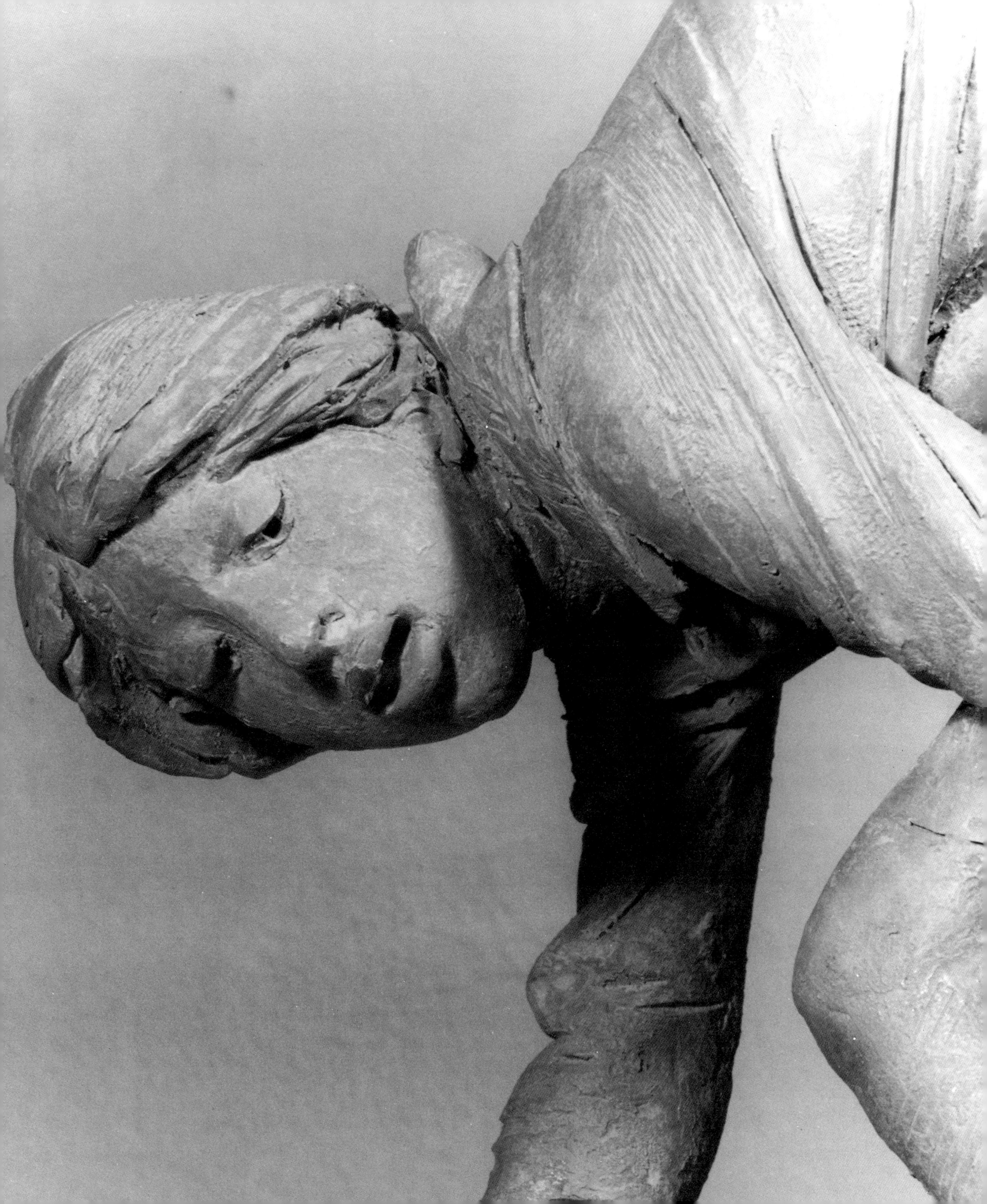

Woman in Thought, 1982, bronze, 20½ x 18 x 8 inches. Collection of Mr. and Mrs. Norman Segal, New York.

Barre, 1982, polychrome terra-cotta, 18 inches high. Forum Gallery, New York.

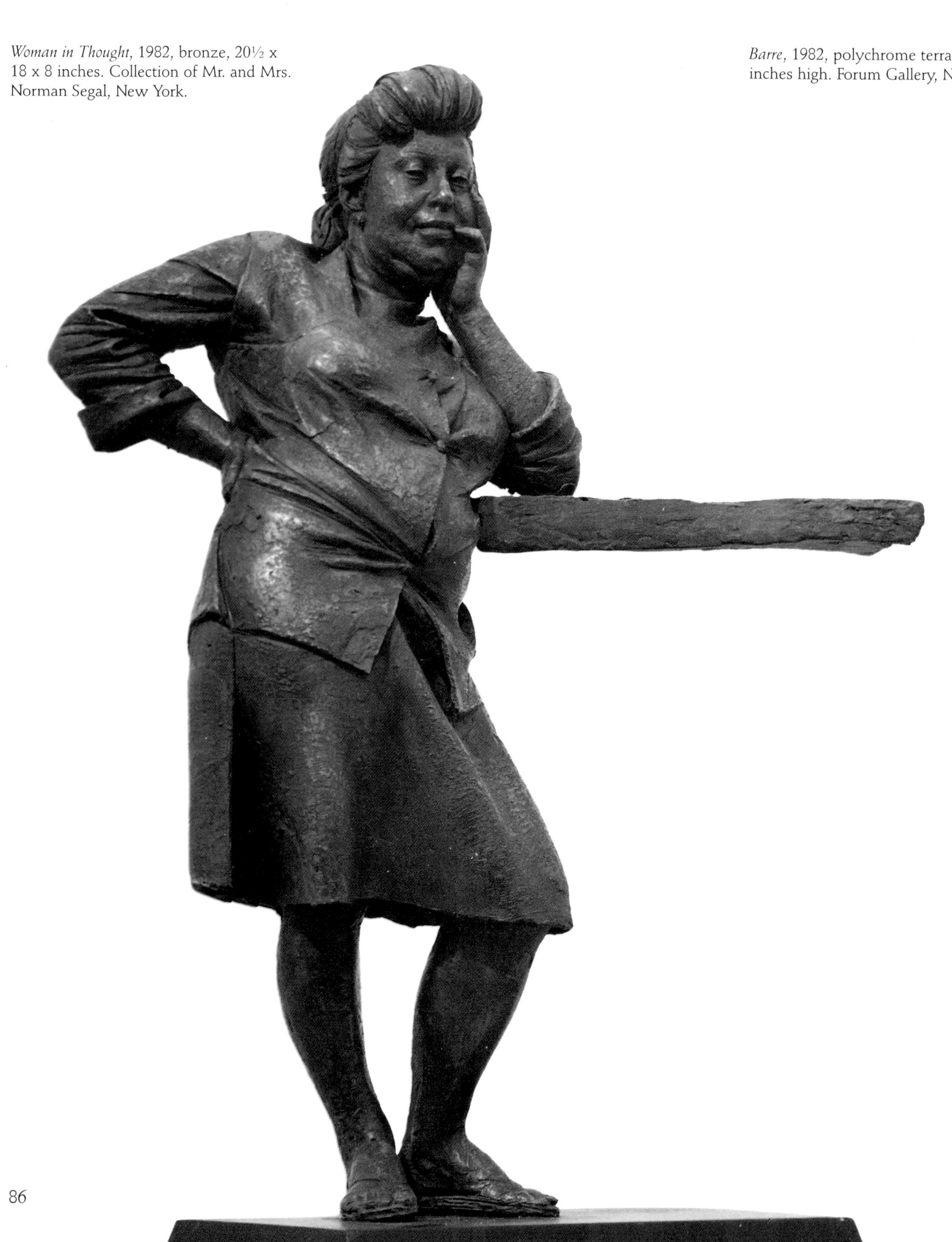

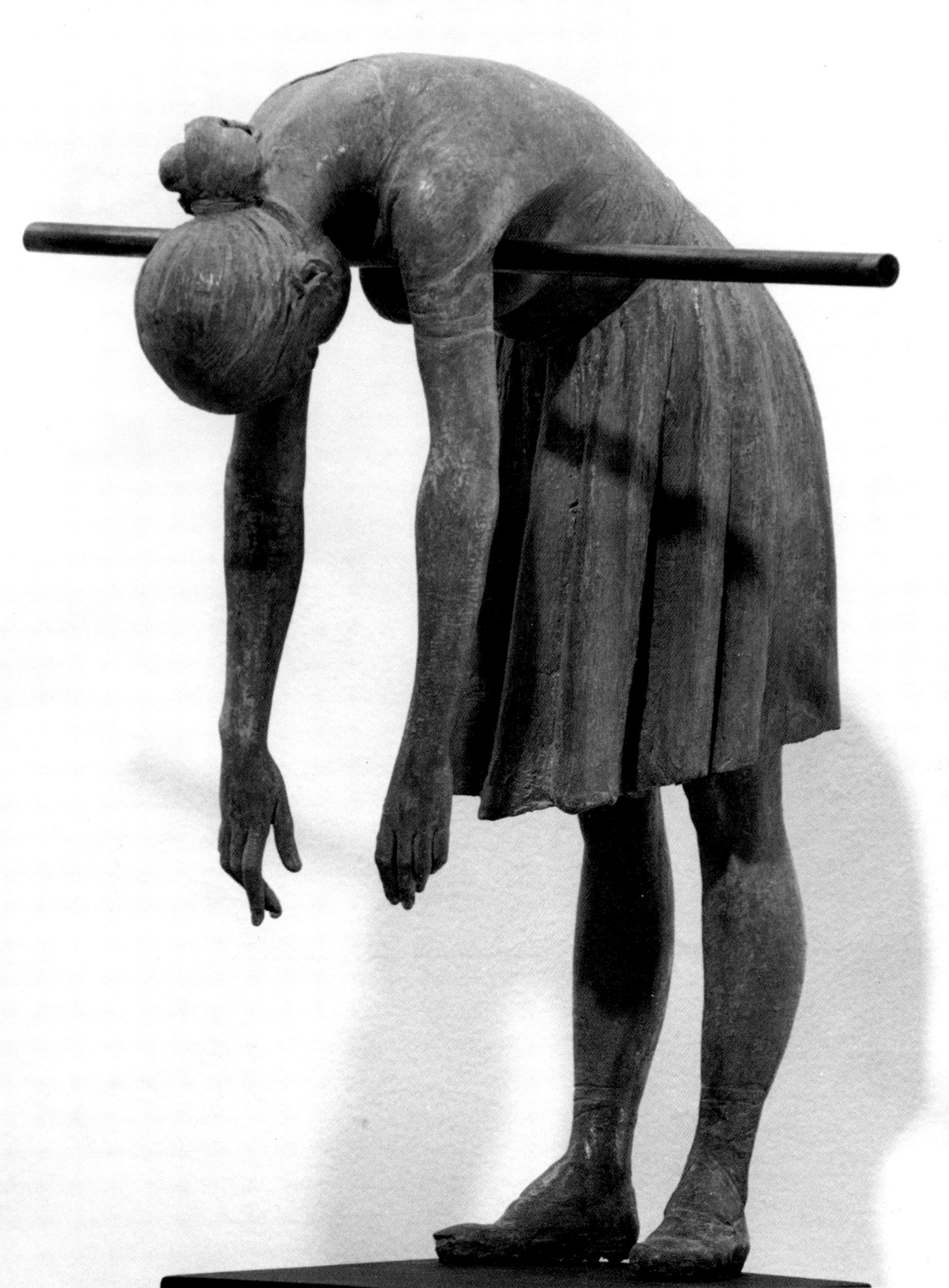

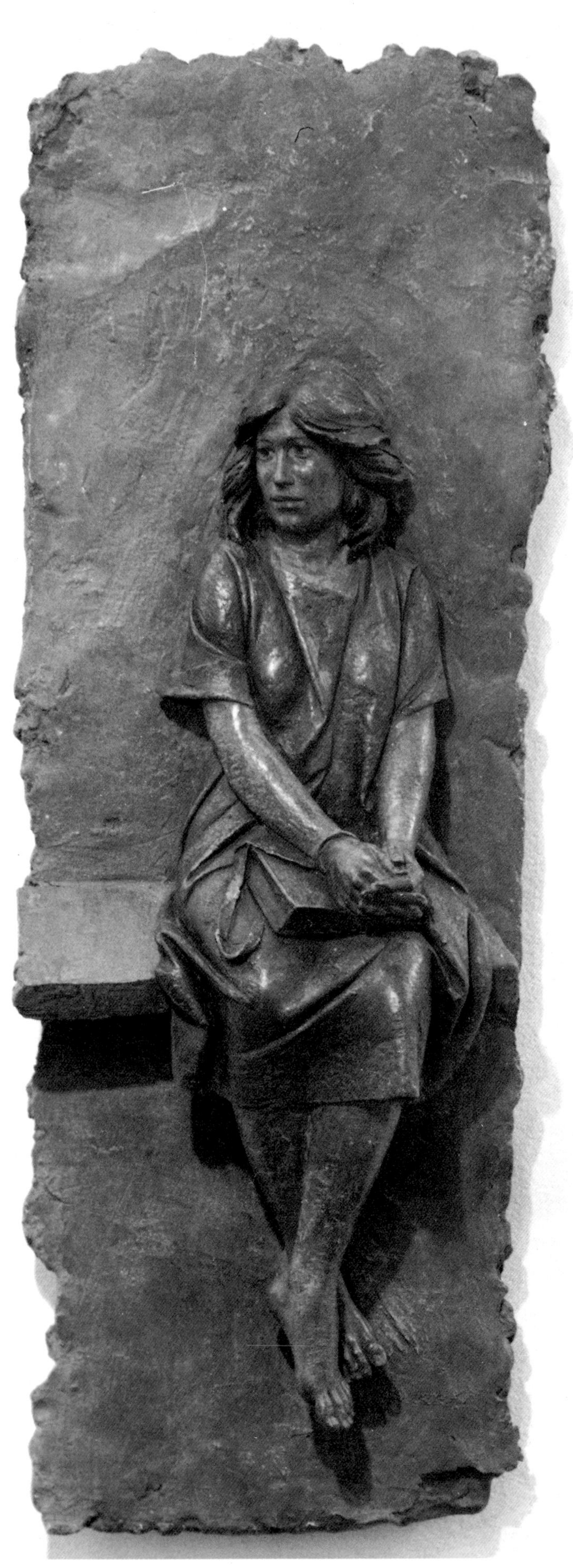

Waiting, 1983, terra-cotta relief, 13 x 17 inches. Forum Gallery, New York.

Telephone (No Answer), 1984–85, bronze, 29 x 7½ x 7 inches. Forum Gallery, New York.

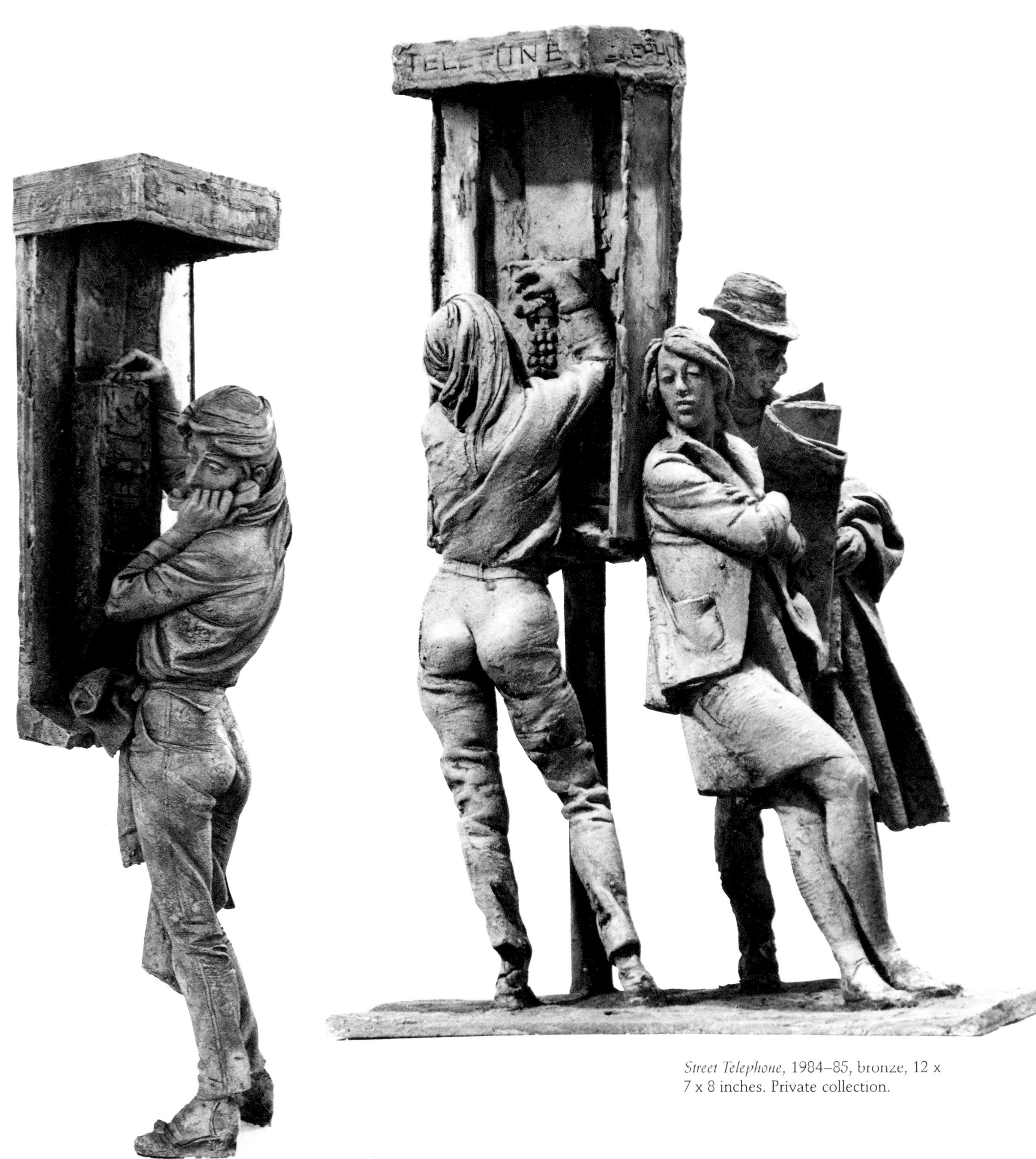

Street Telephone, 1984–85, bronze, 12 x 7 x 8 inches. Private collection.

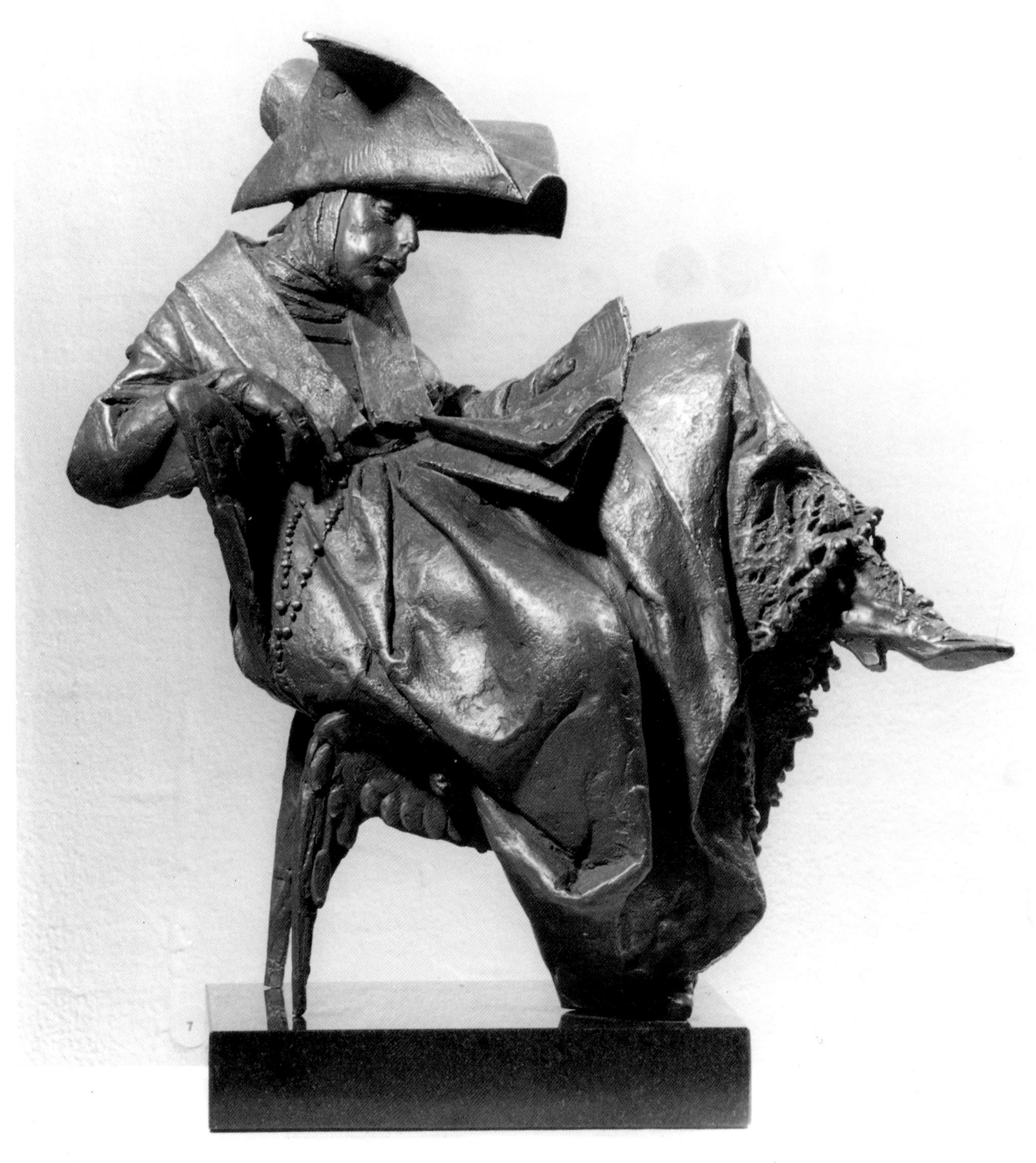

Nun of Monza, 1987, bronze, 13 inches high. Collection of Mr. and Mrs. Harold Kozupsky, Conway, Massachusetts.

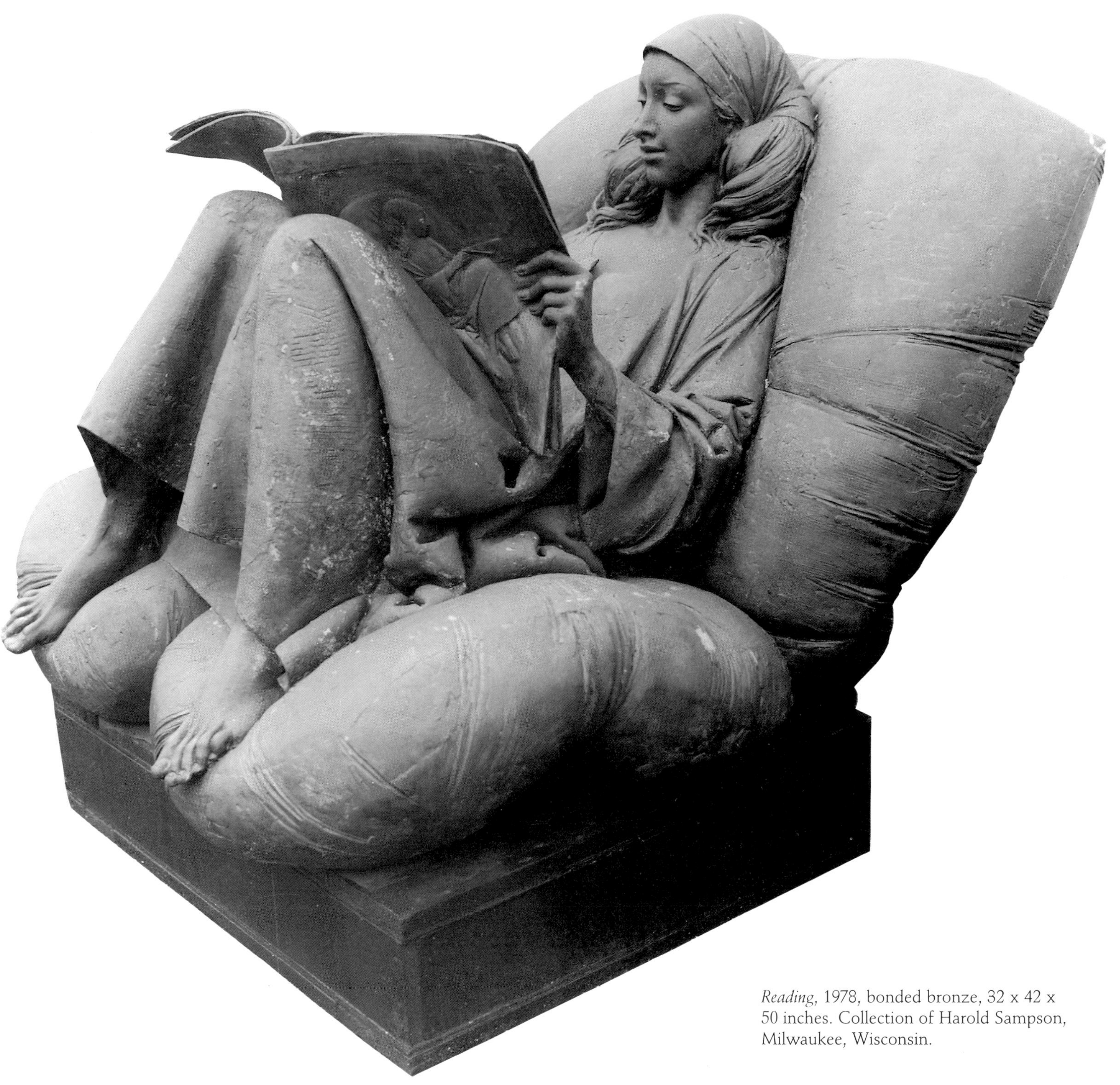

Reading, 1978, bonded bronze, 32 x 42 x 50 inches. Collection of Harold Sampson, Milwaukee, Wisconsin.

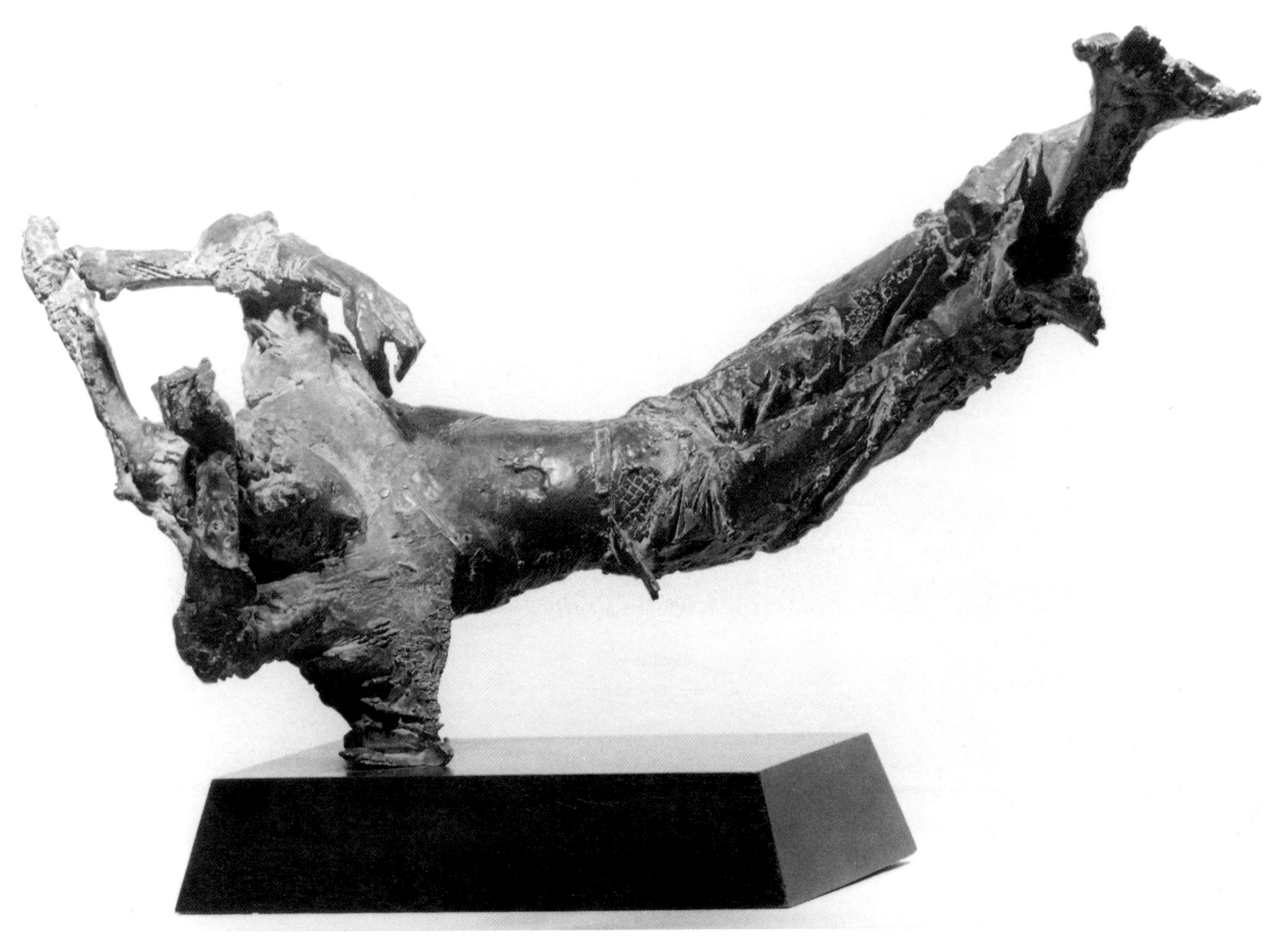

Demonstrator, 1965–67, bronze, 18 inches high. Collection of Joan R. Sovern, New York.

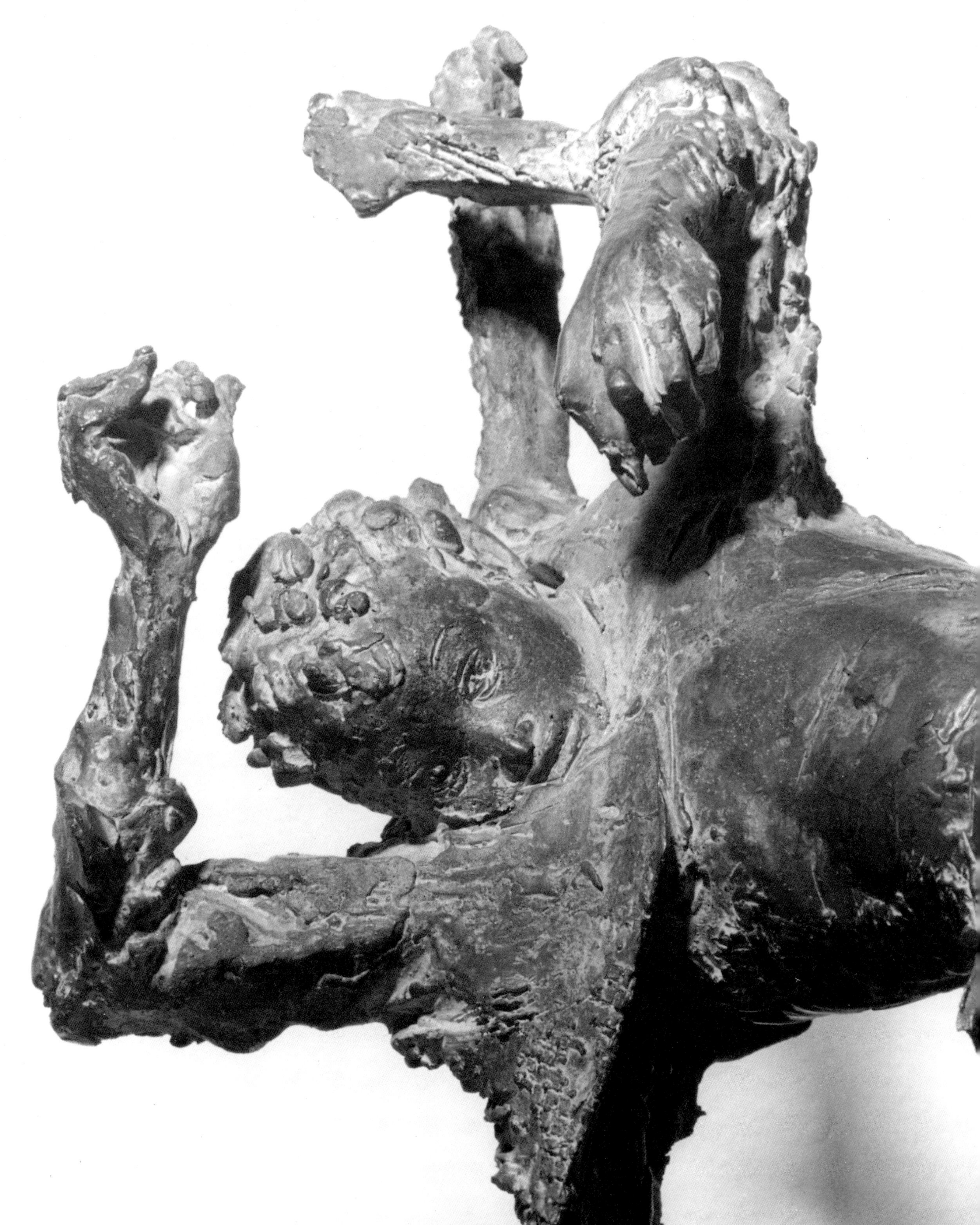

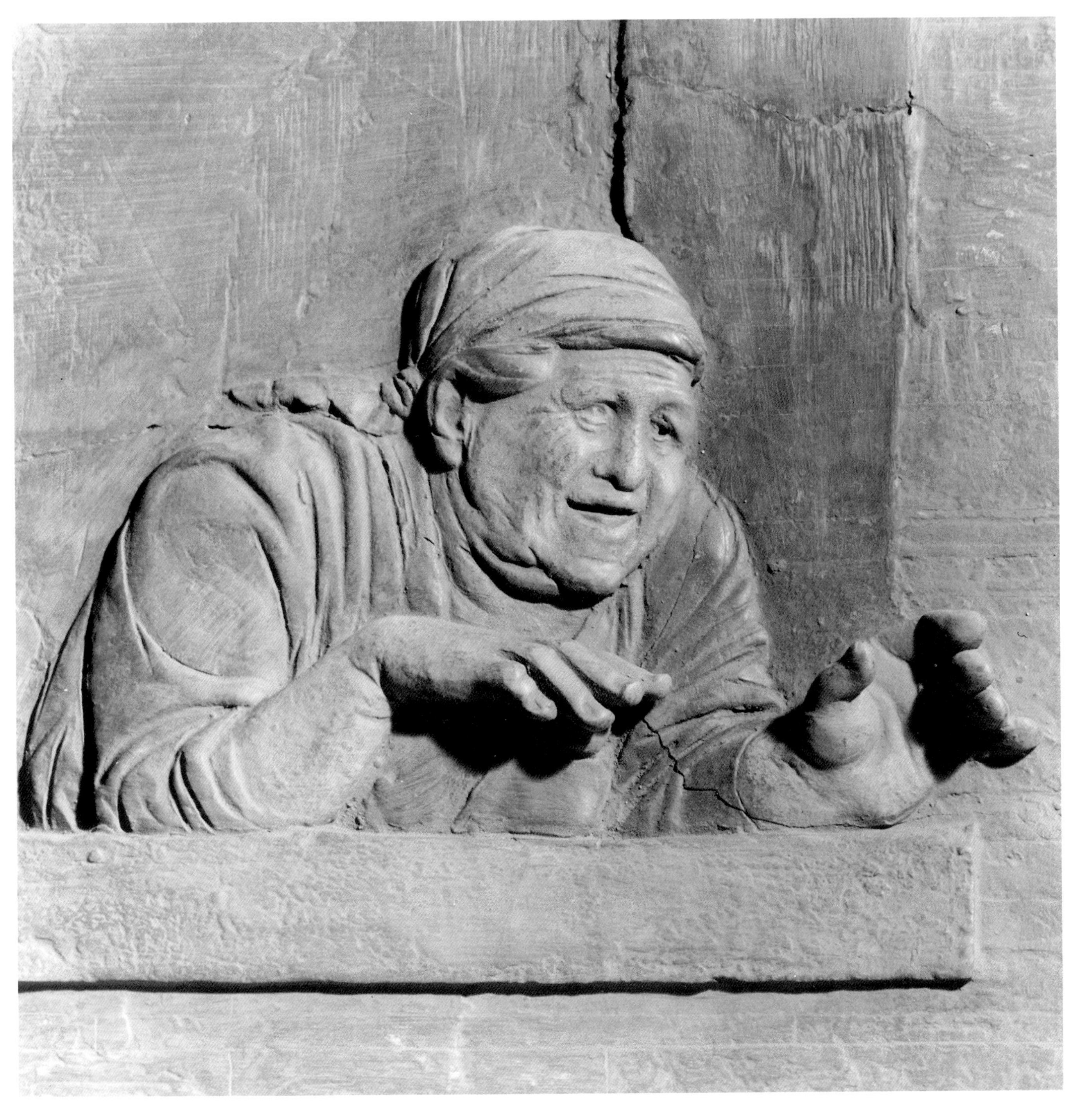

Conversation, 1974, terra-cotta relief, 31 x 16 inches. Forum Gallery, New York.

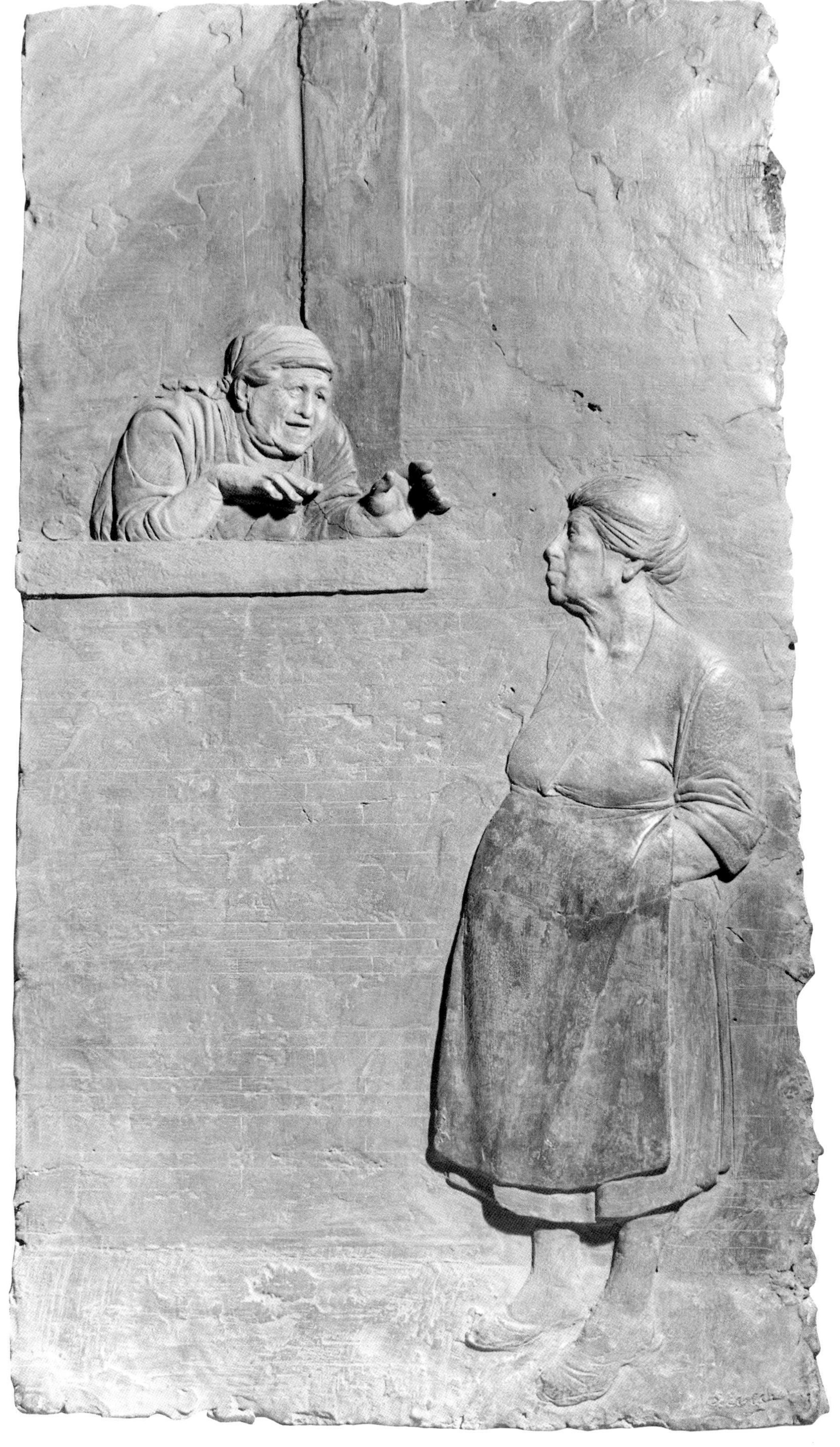

Market Place, 1975–76, bronze, 20 x 10 inches. Forum Gallery, New York.

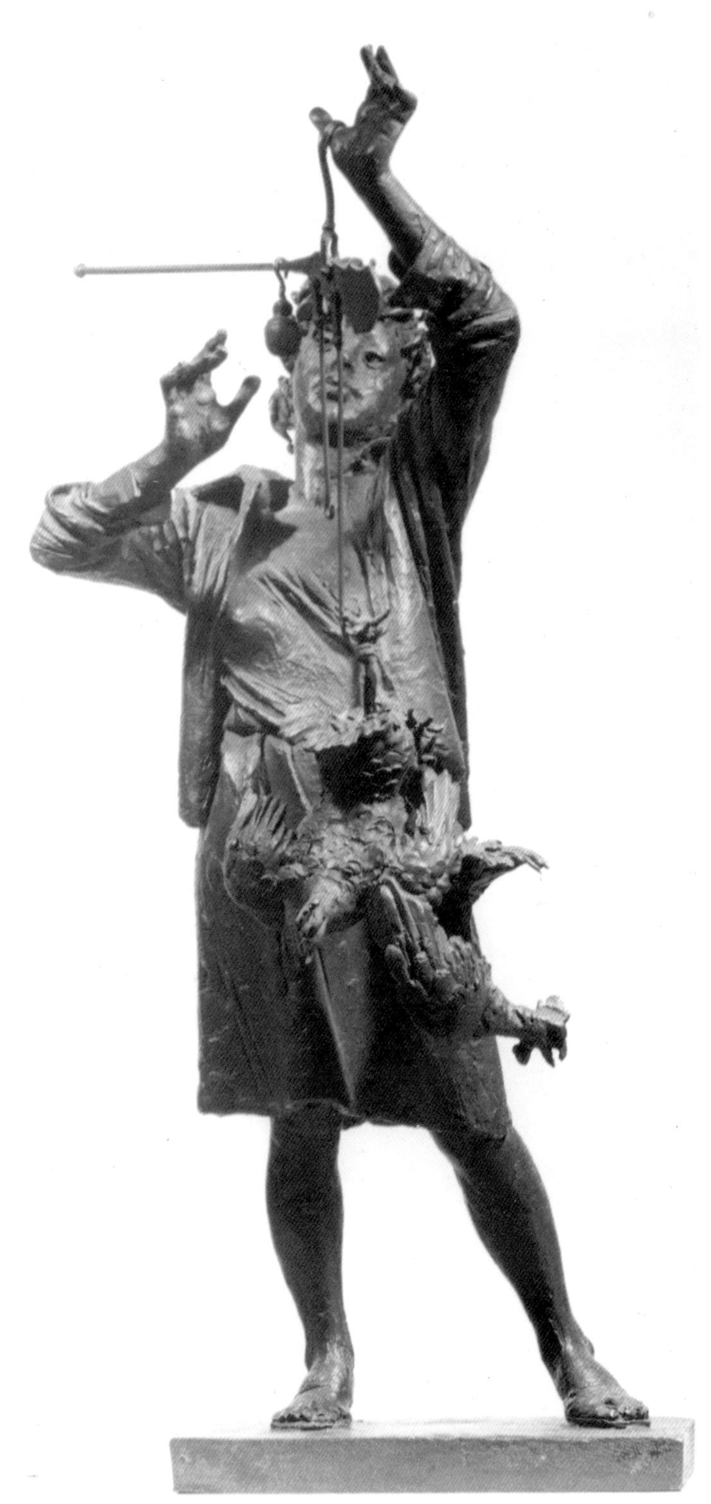

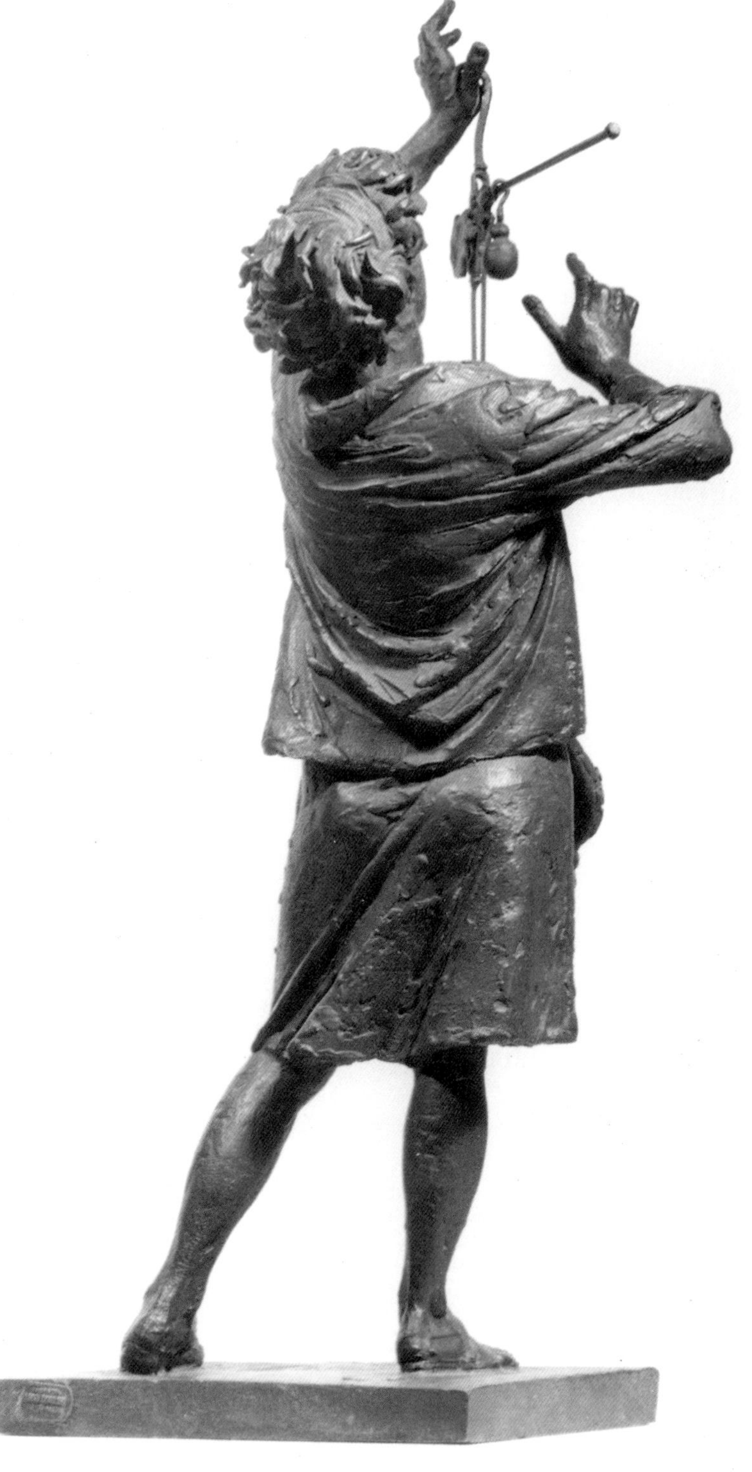

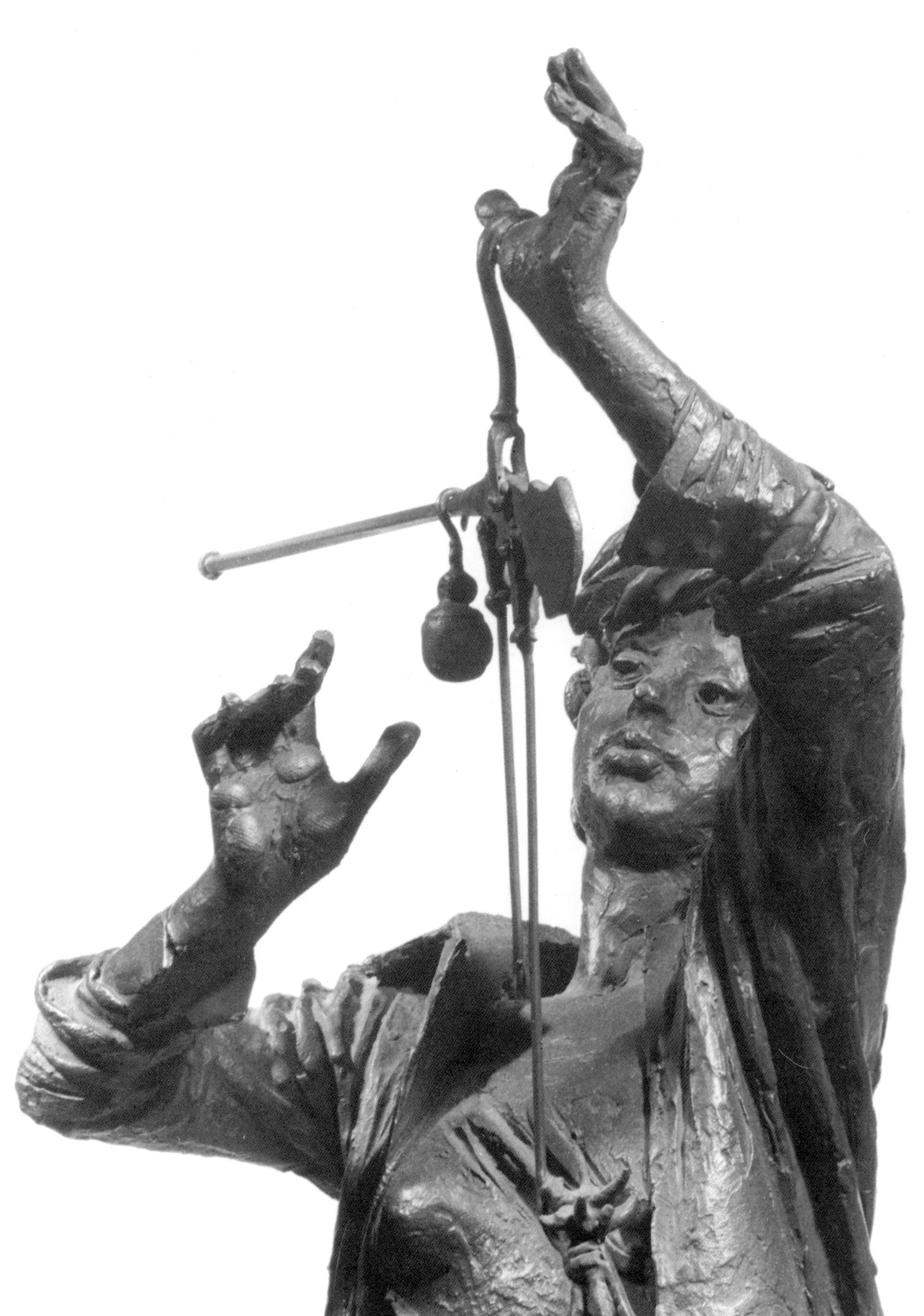

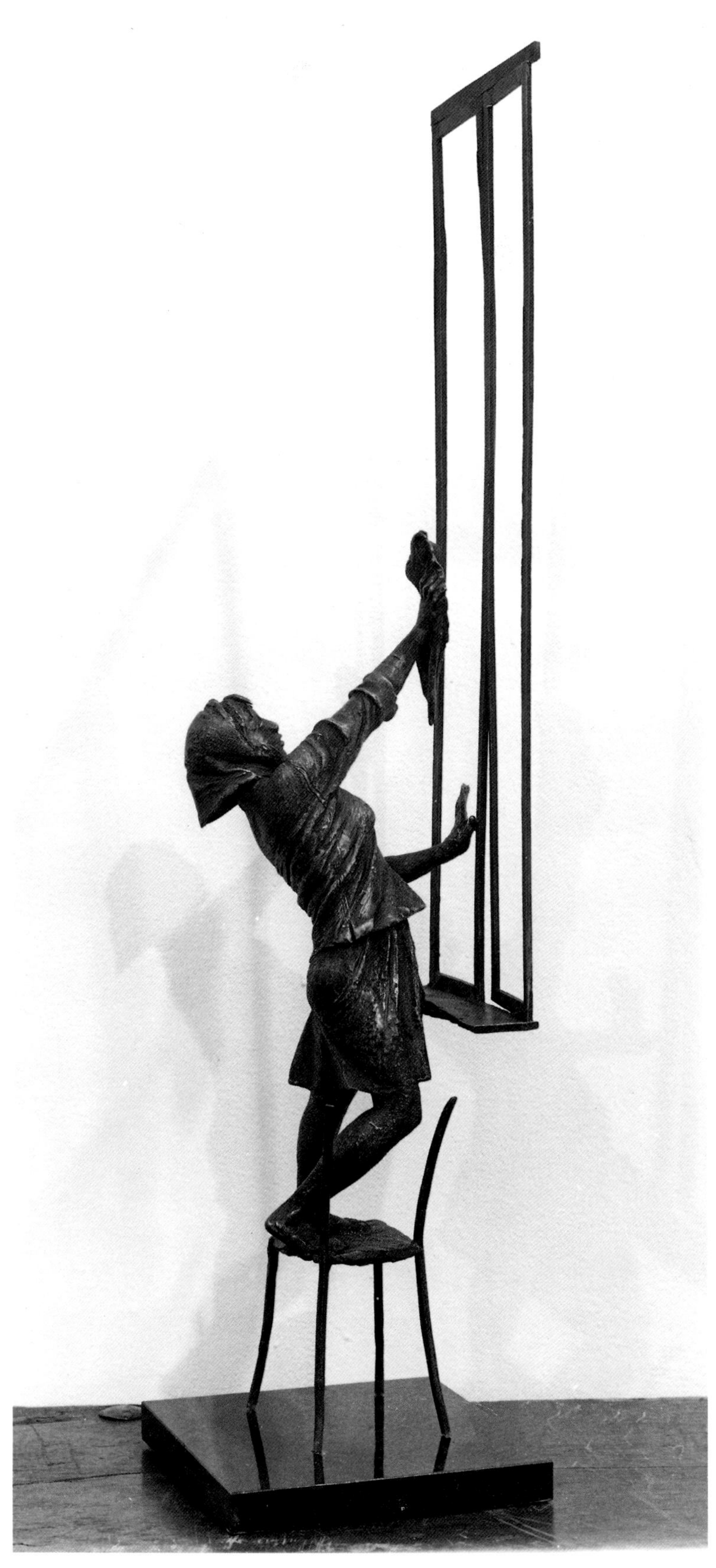

Window Washer, c. 1982, bronze, 26½ x 5½ x 5 inches. Private collection.

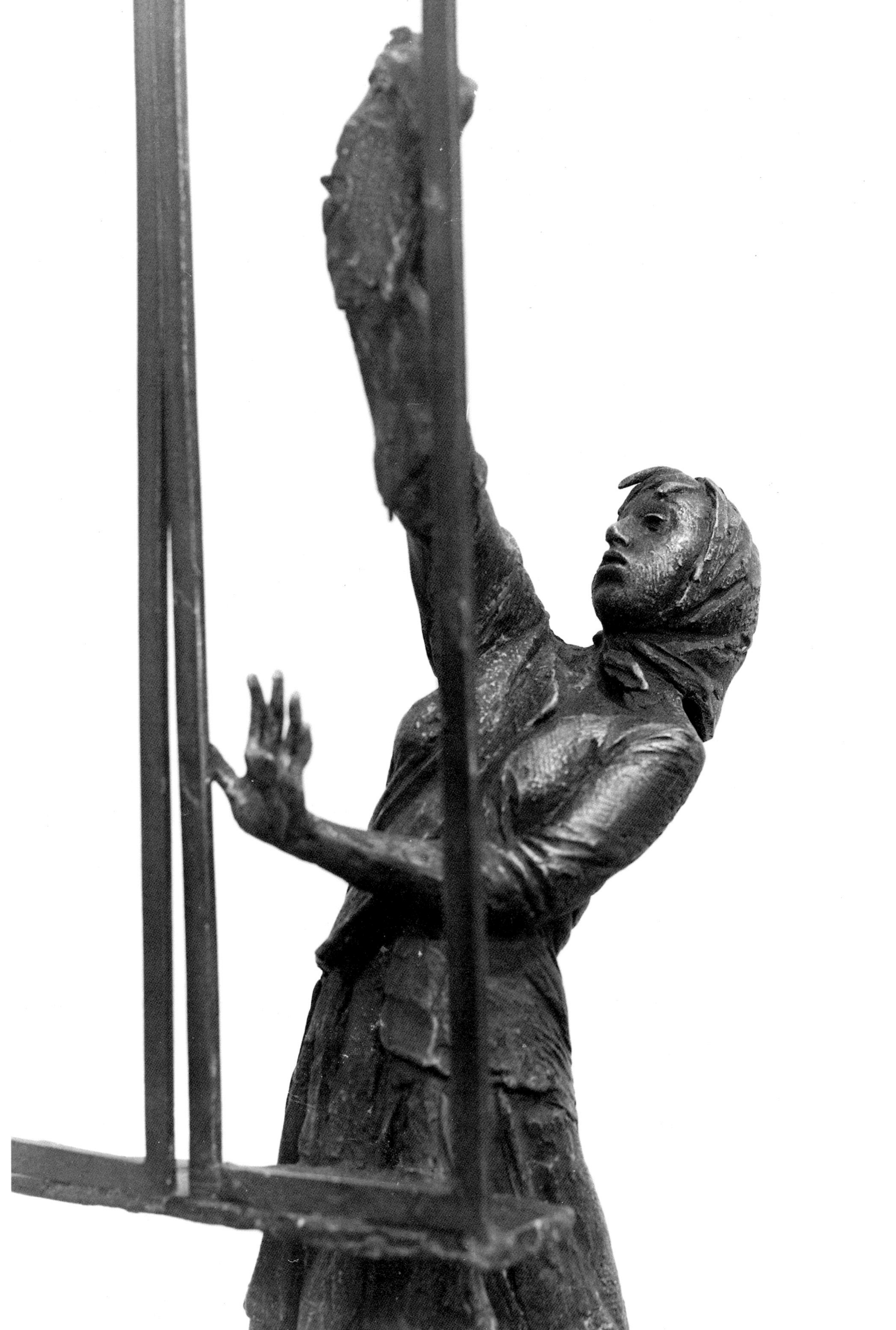

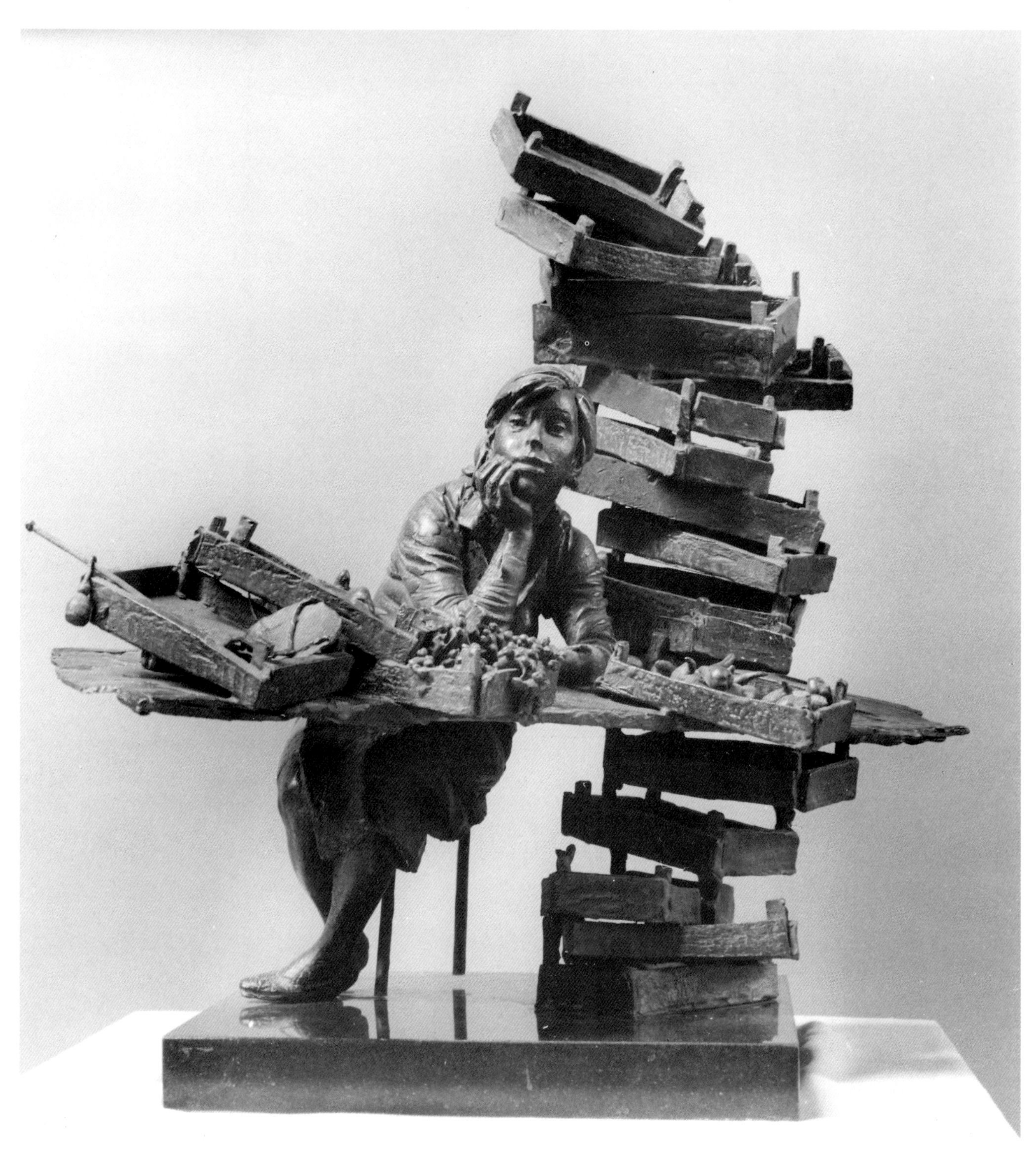

Vendor, 1984–85, bronze, 13 x 19 x 7 inches. Forum Gallery, New York.

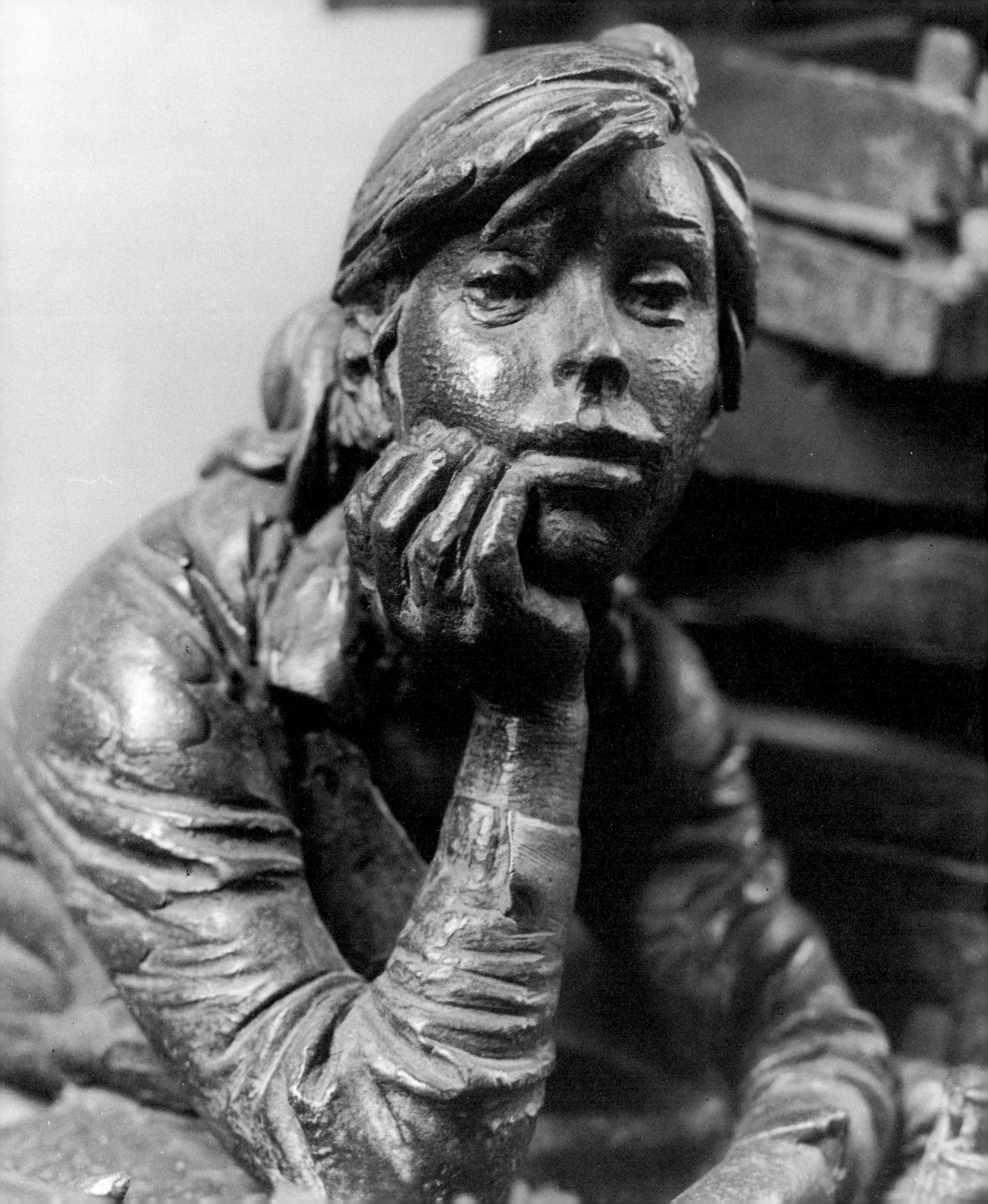

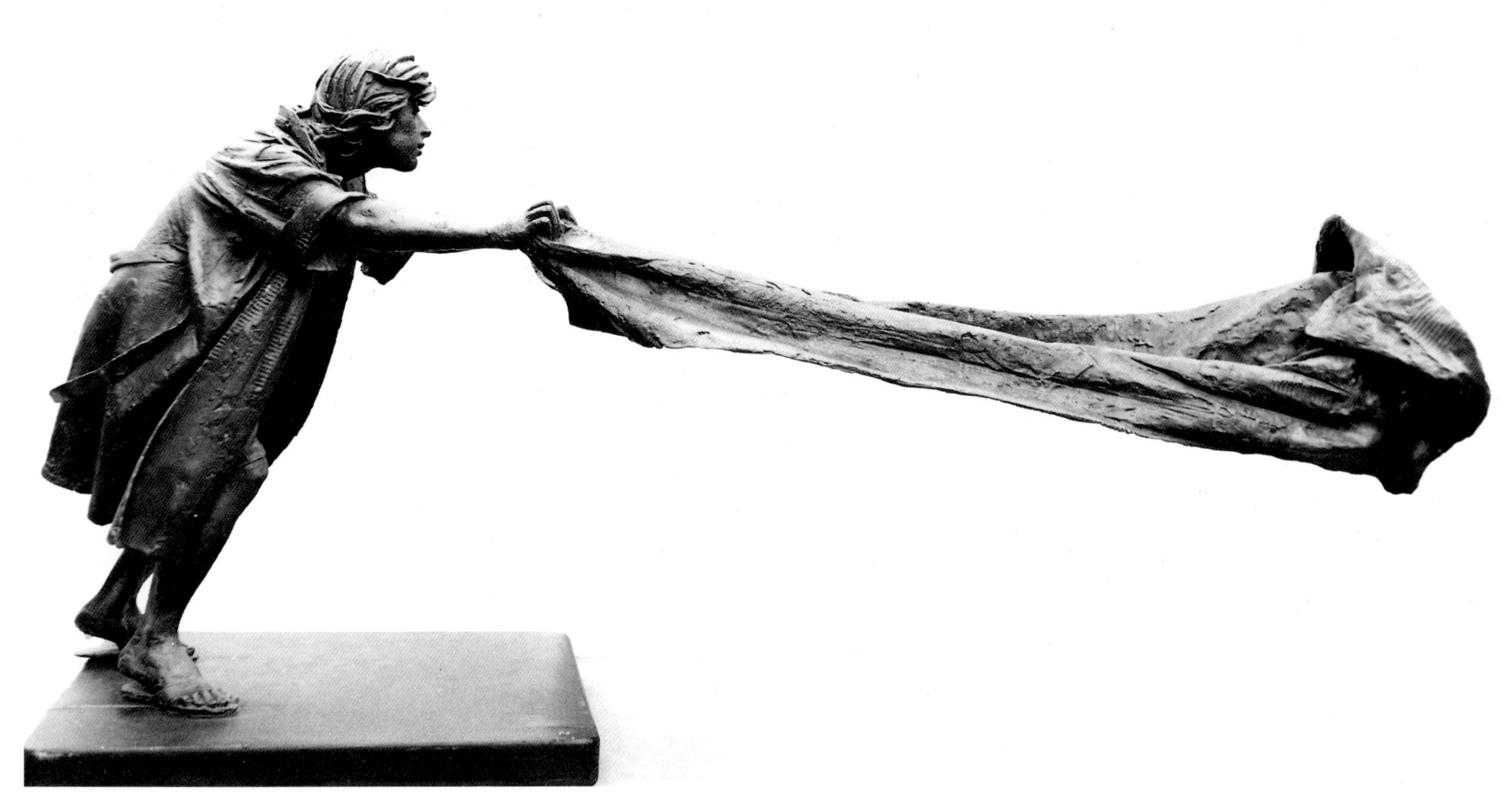

Spring Cleaning, 1976, bronze, 14½ x 26 inches. Private collection.

Tailor, 1984–85, terra-cotta, 18 x 9 x 7 inches. Forum Gallery, New York.

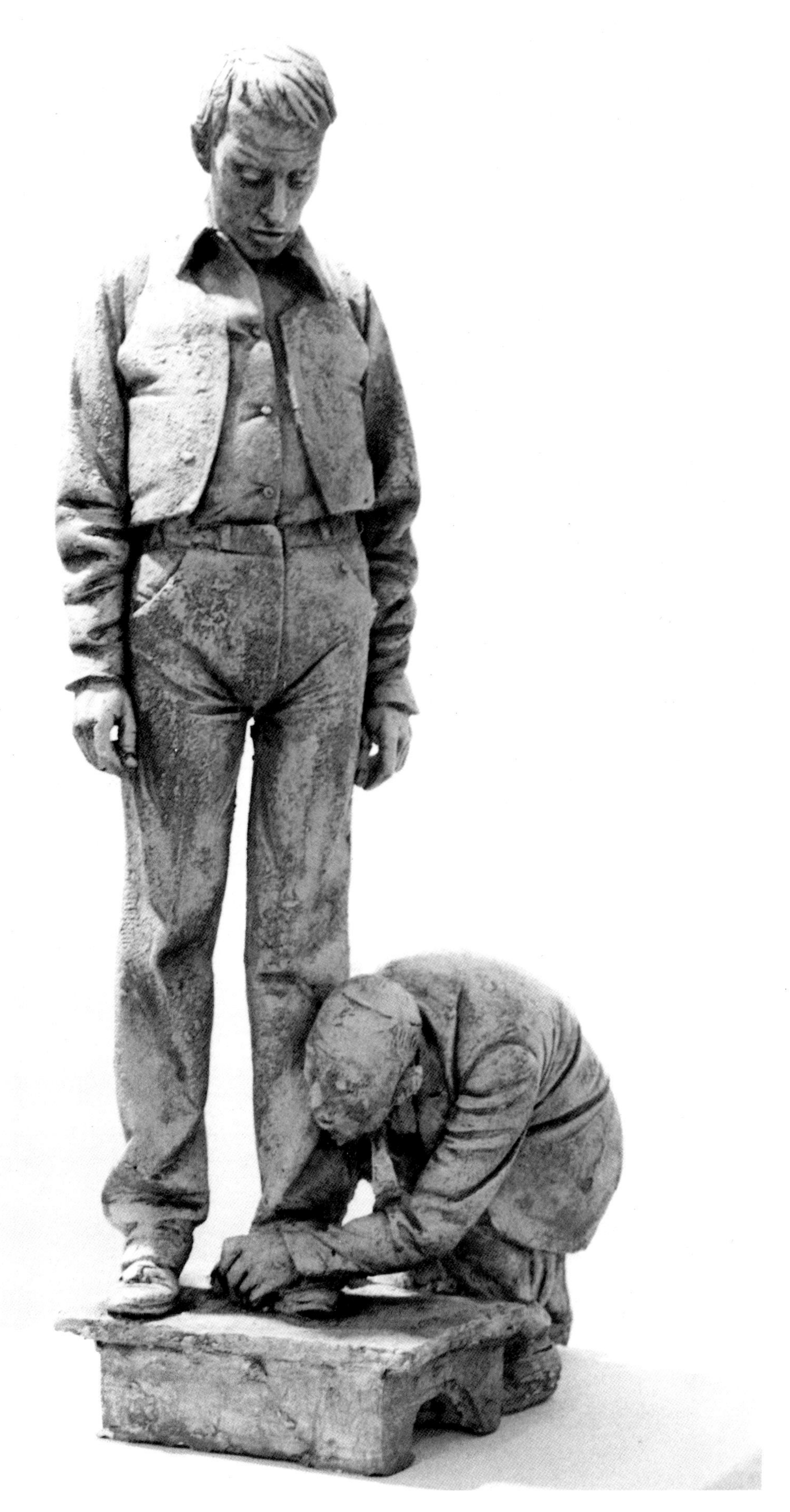

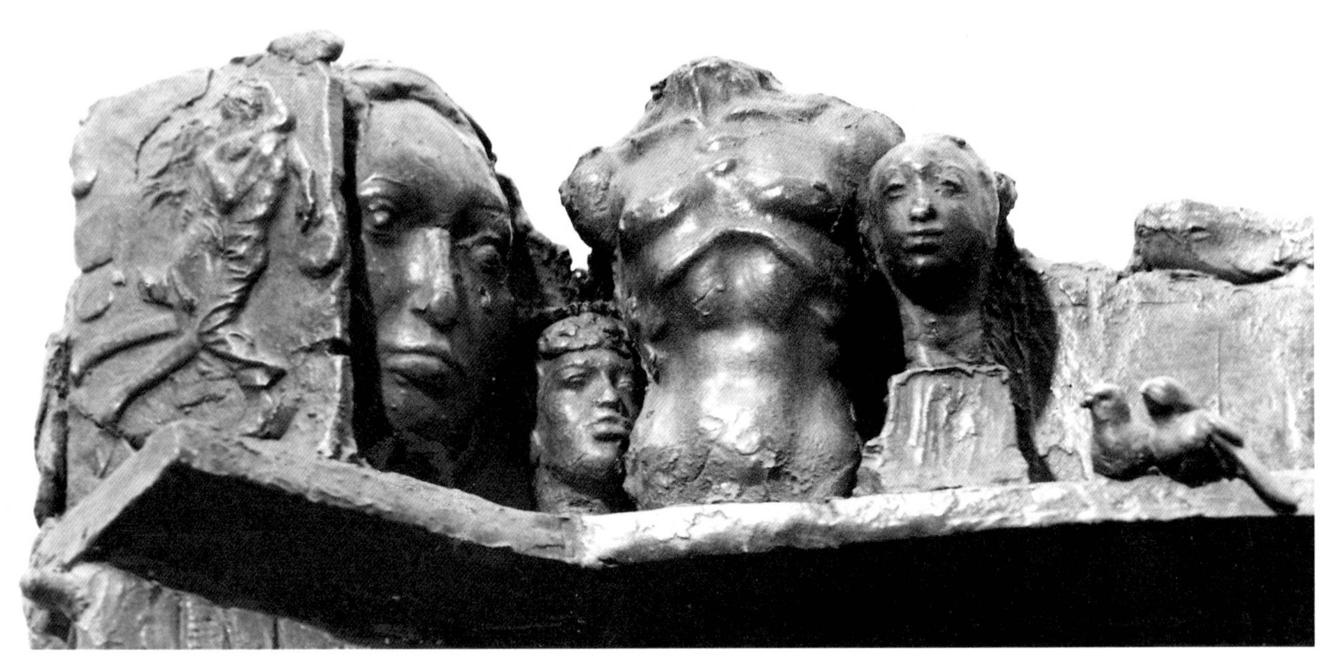

Sculptor's Studio, 1982, terra-cotta relief,
25 x 17 inches. Forum Gallery, New York.

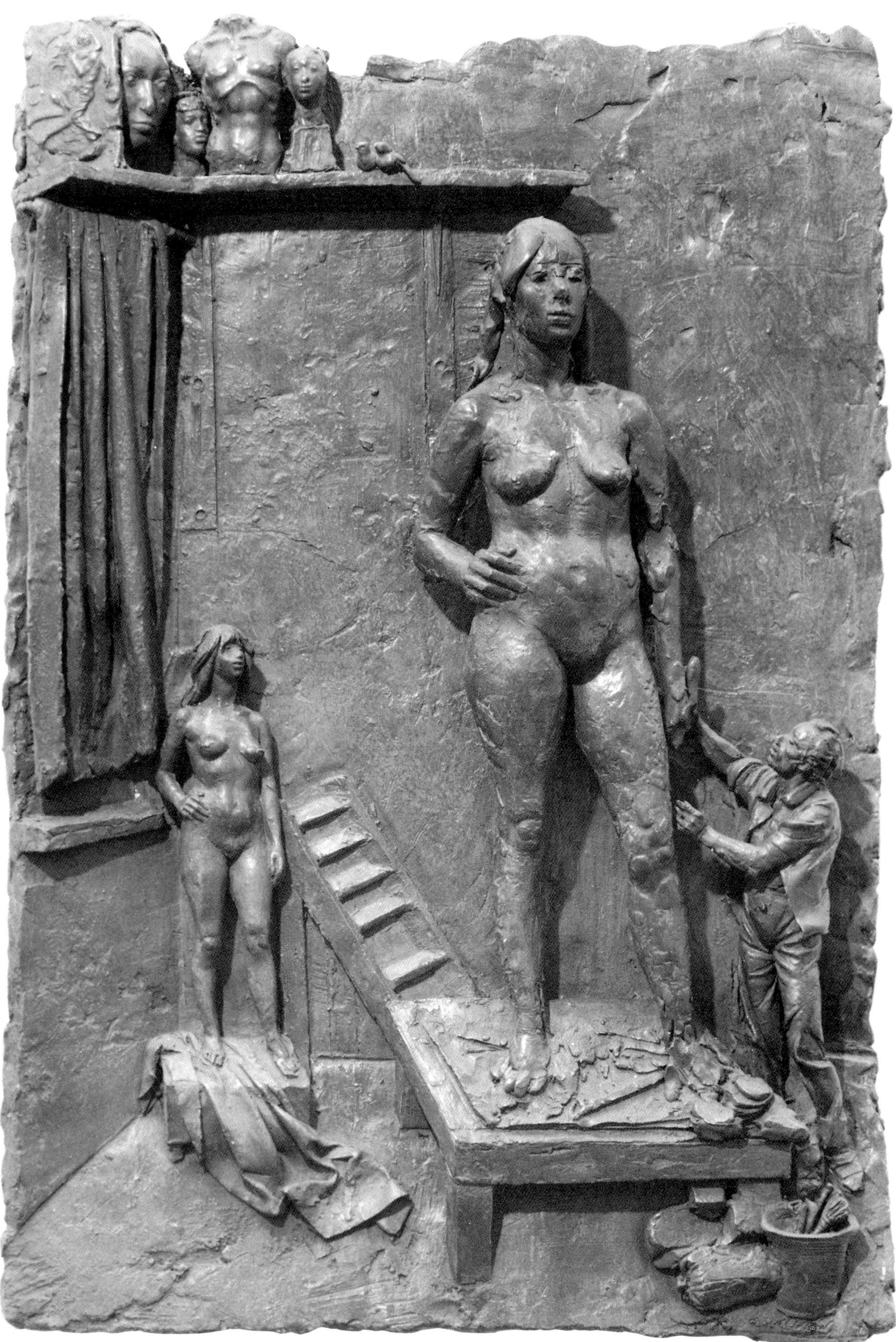

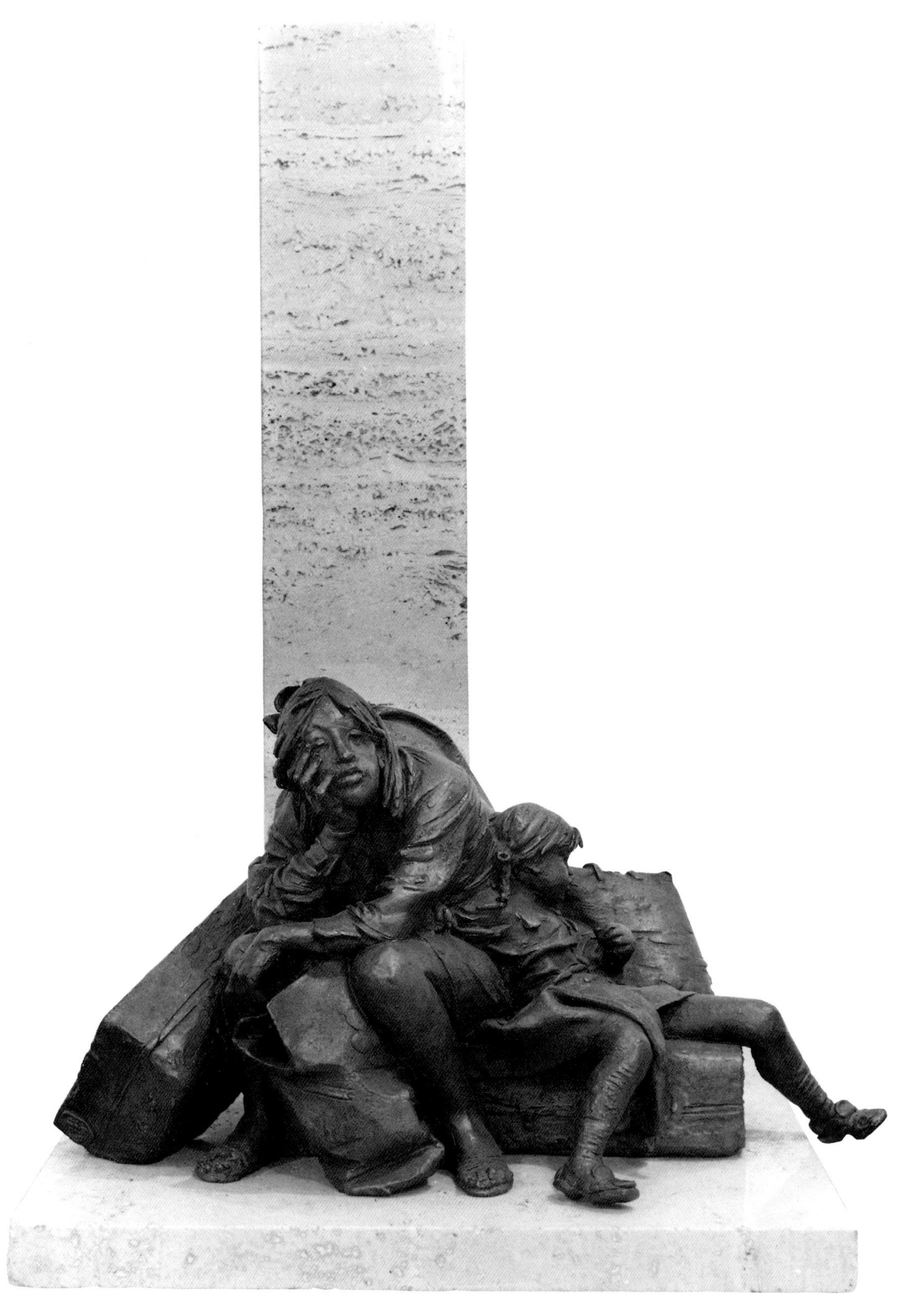

Waiting #2, 1976, bronze and marble, 24 x 17 inches. Forum Gallery, New York.

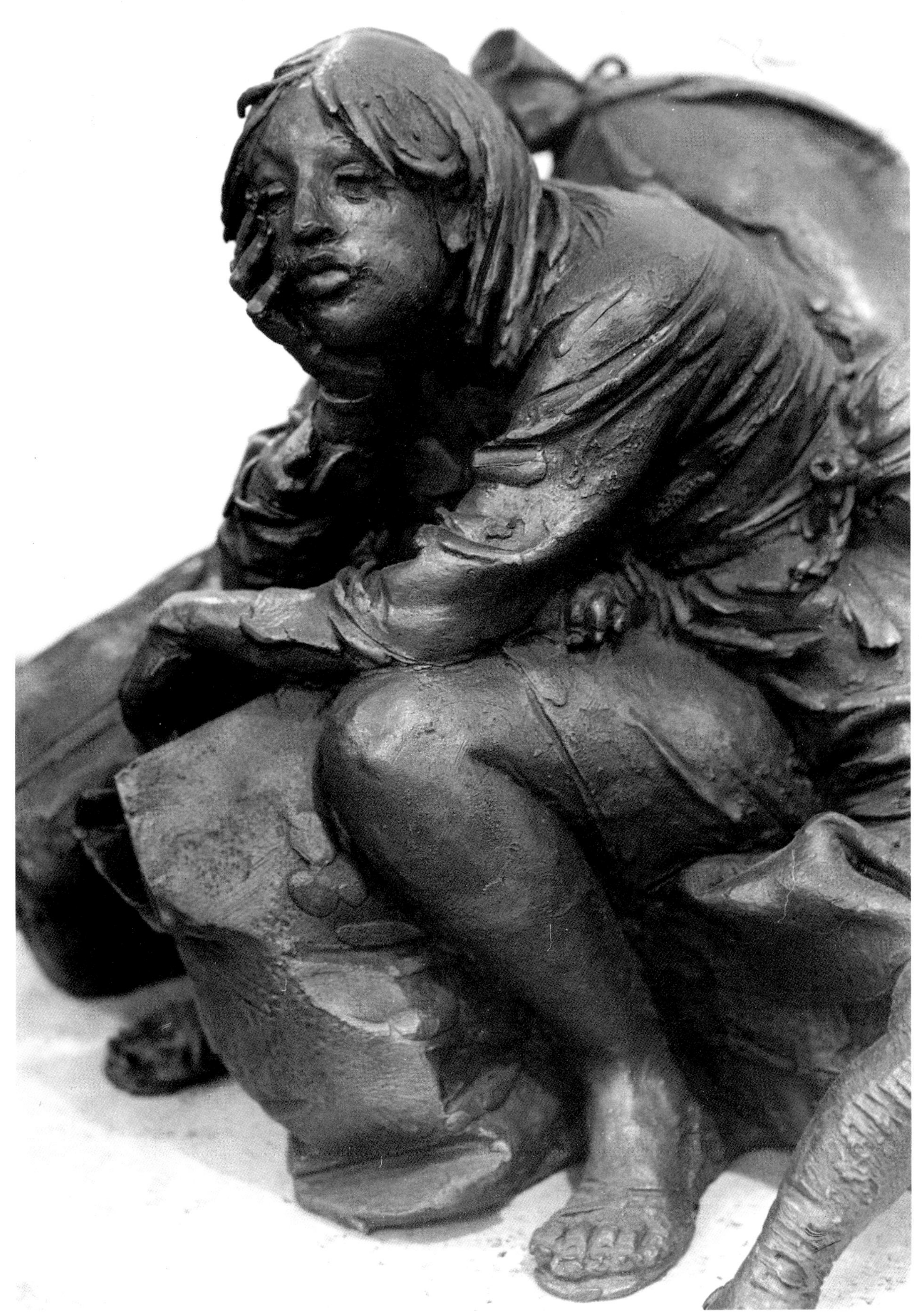

Mother and Daughter, 1983, polychrome terra-cotta, 12 x 22 x 10 inches. Forum Gallery, New York.

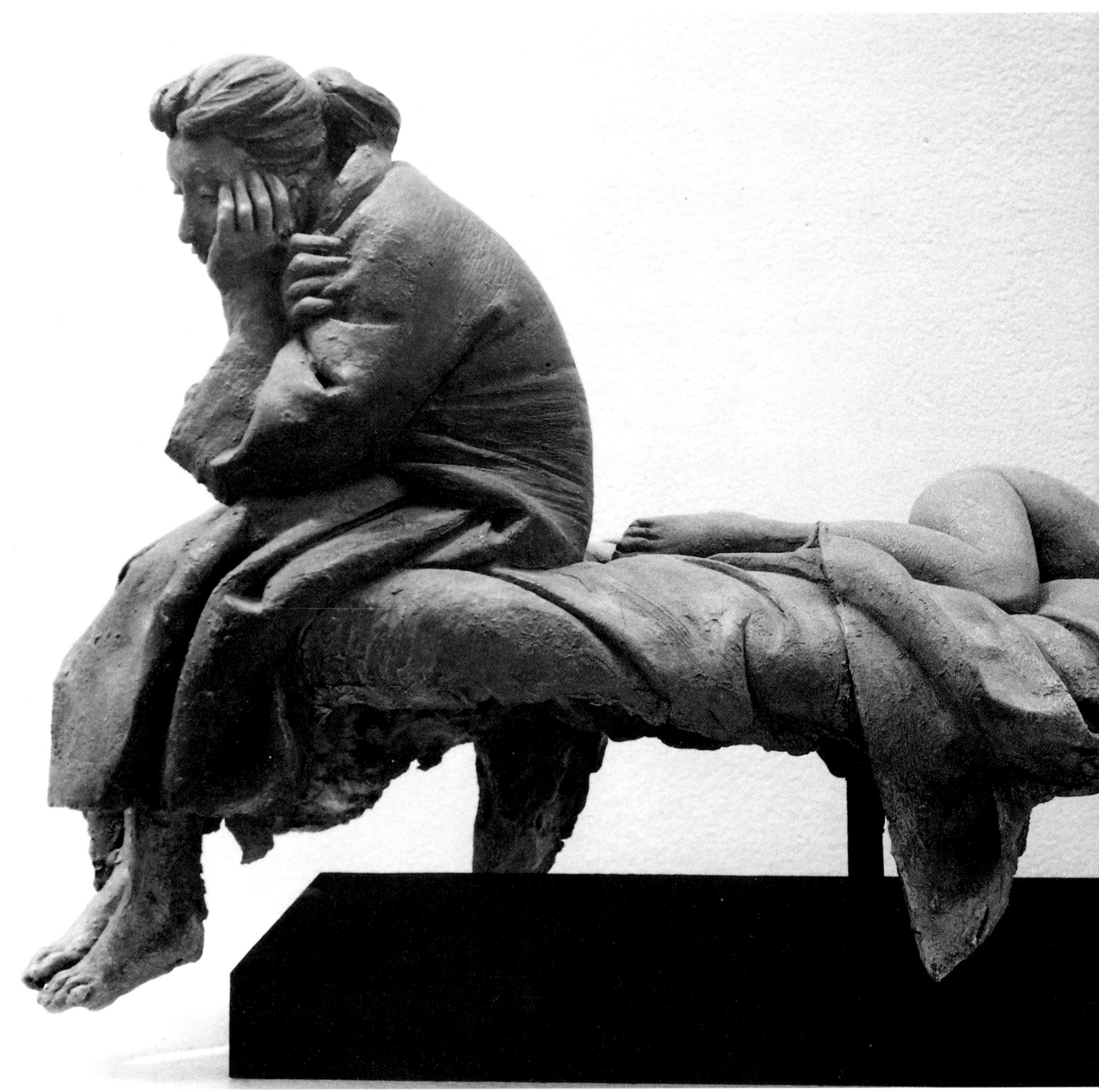

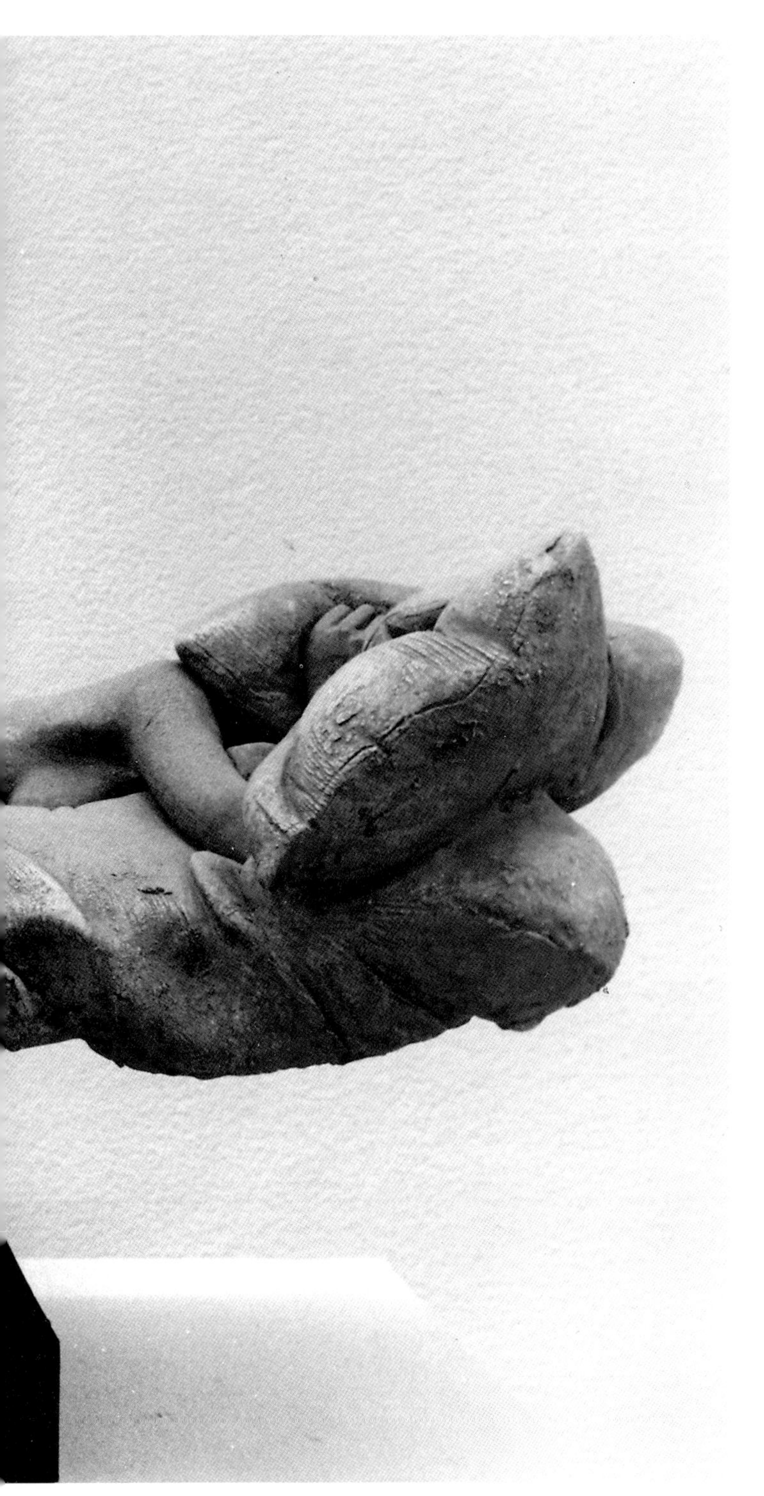

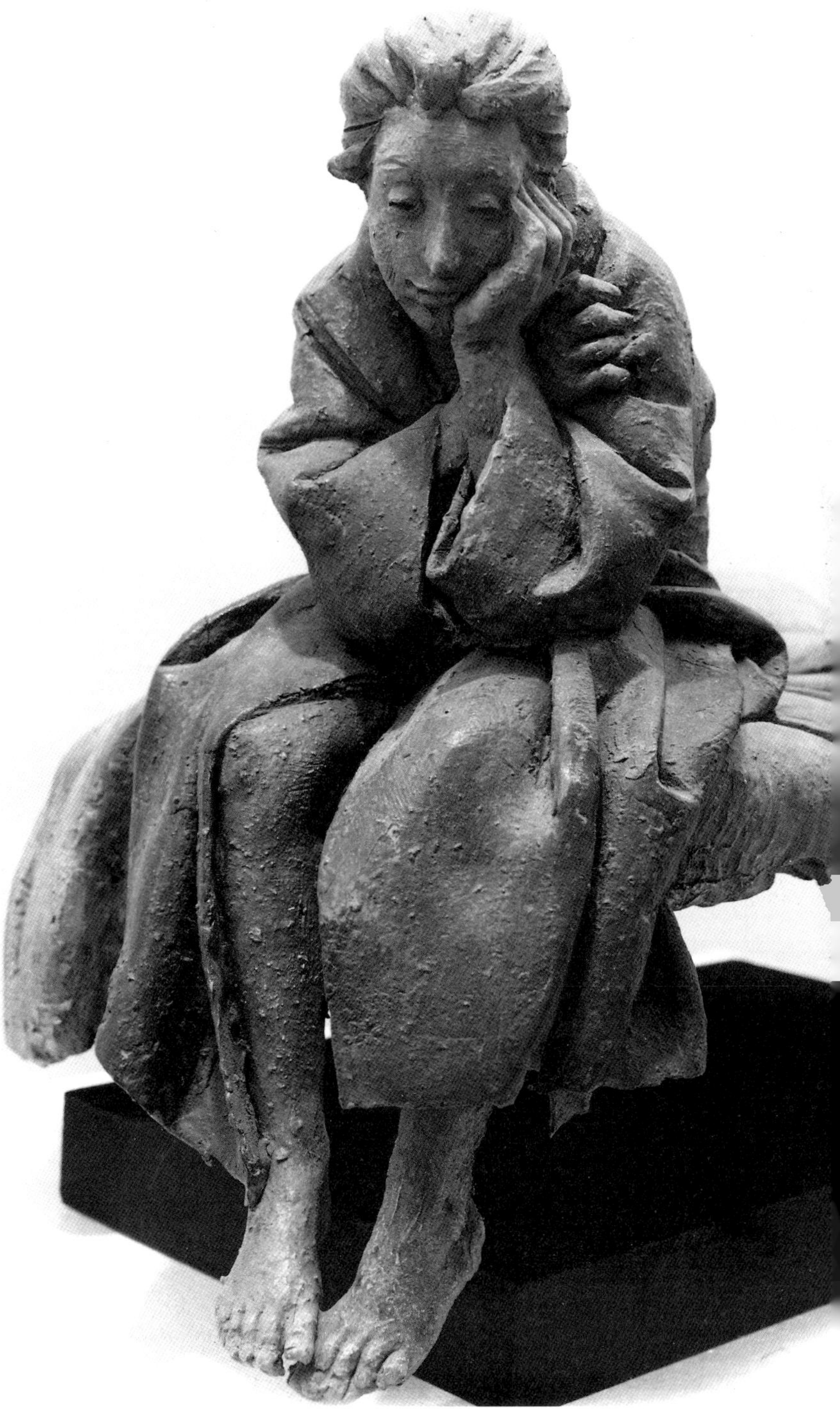

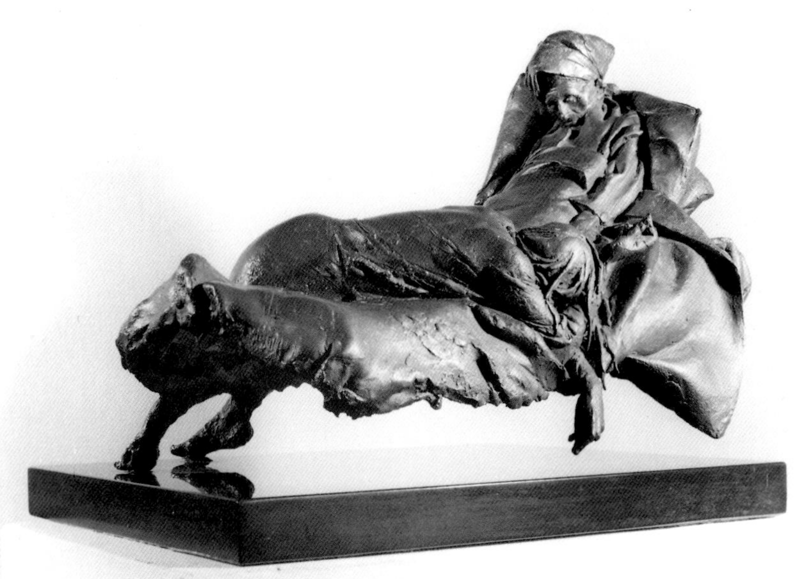

Pietà, 1970, bronze, 11 x 18½ inches.
Private collection.

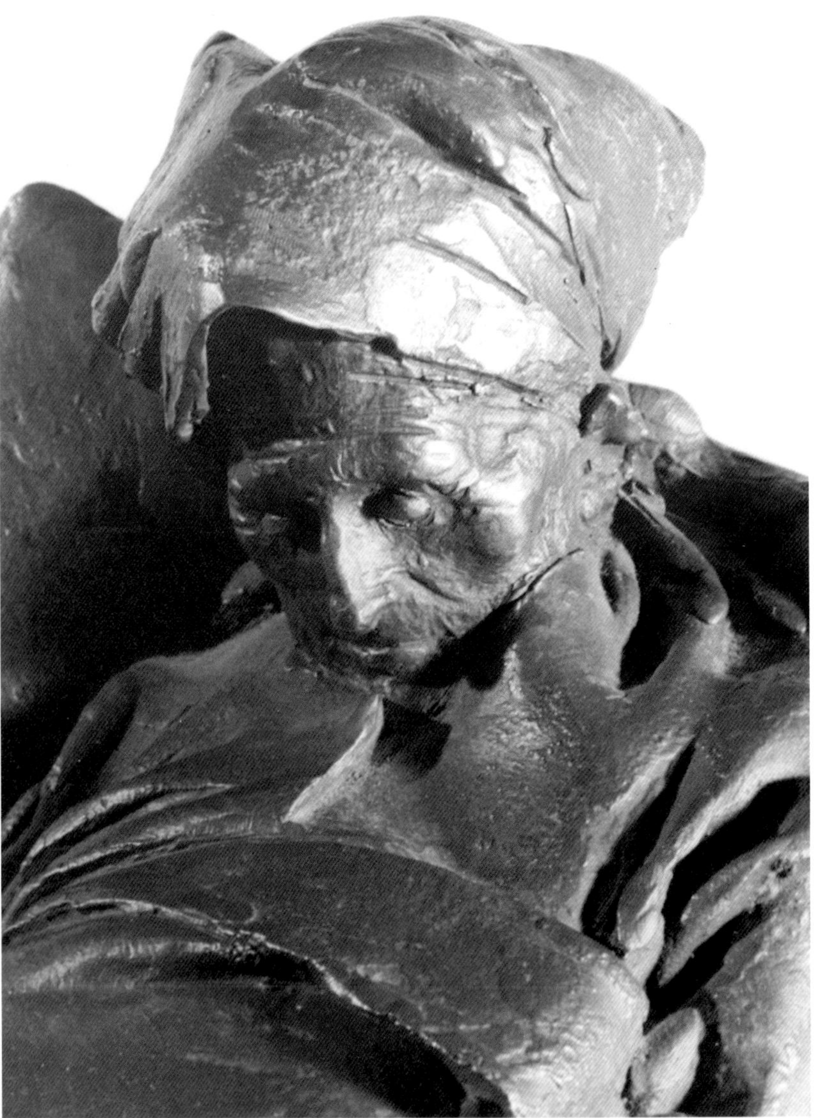

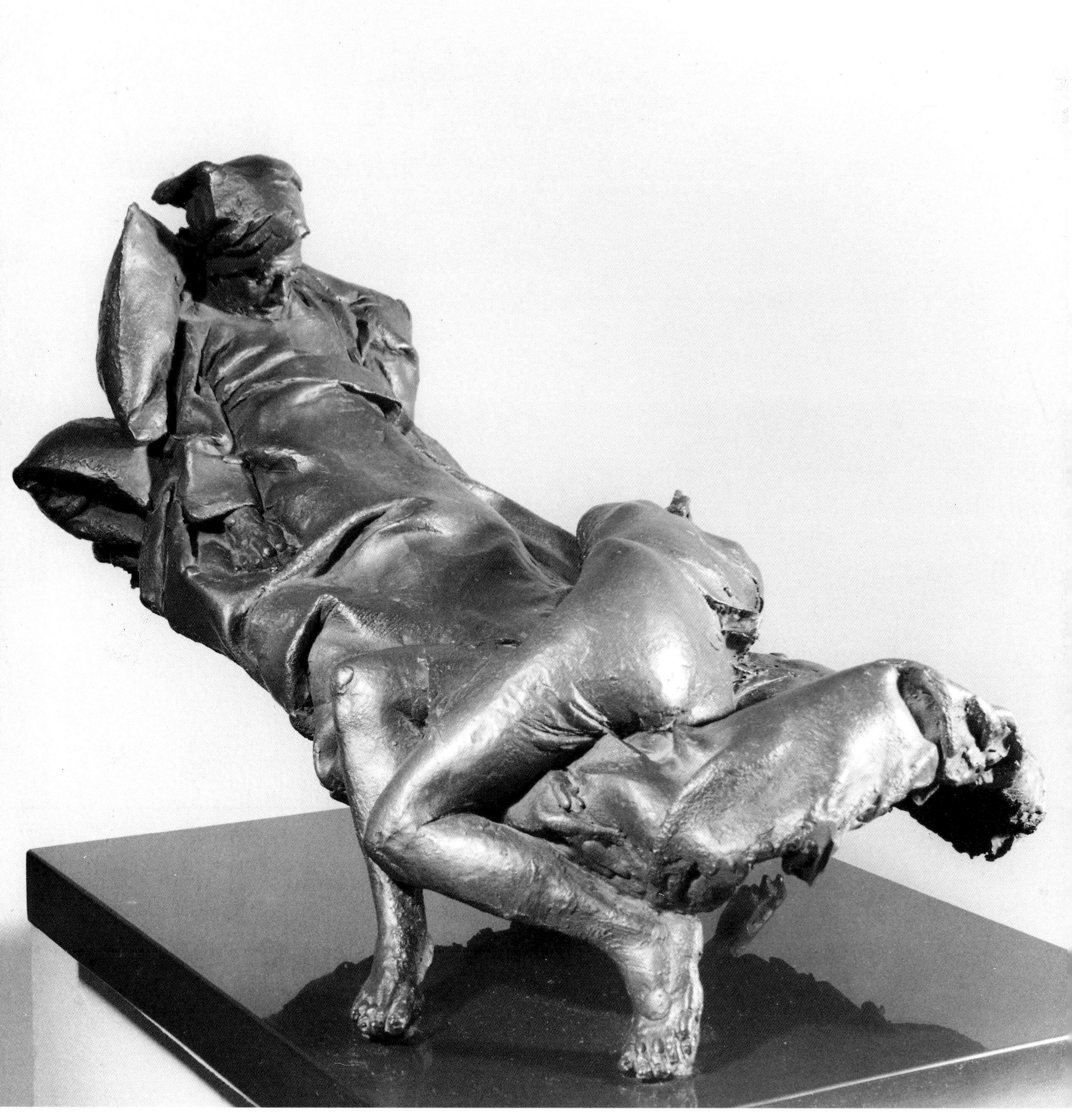

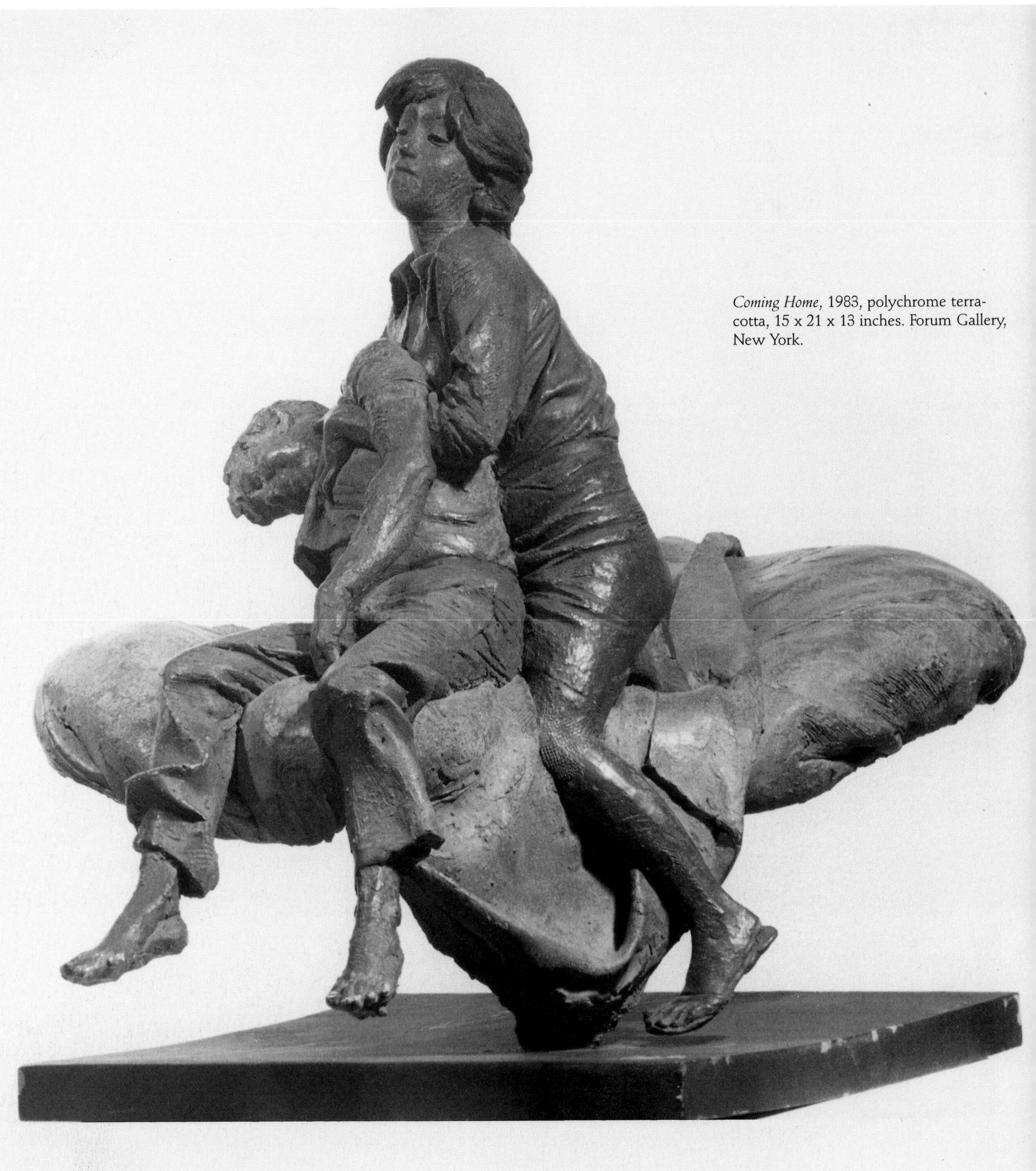

Coming Home, 1983, polychrome terra-cotta, 15 x 21 x 13 inches. Forum Gallery, New York.

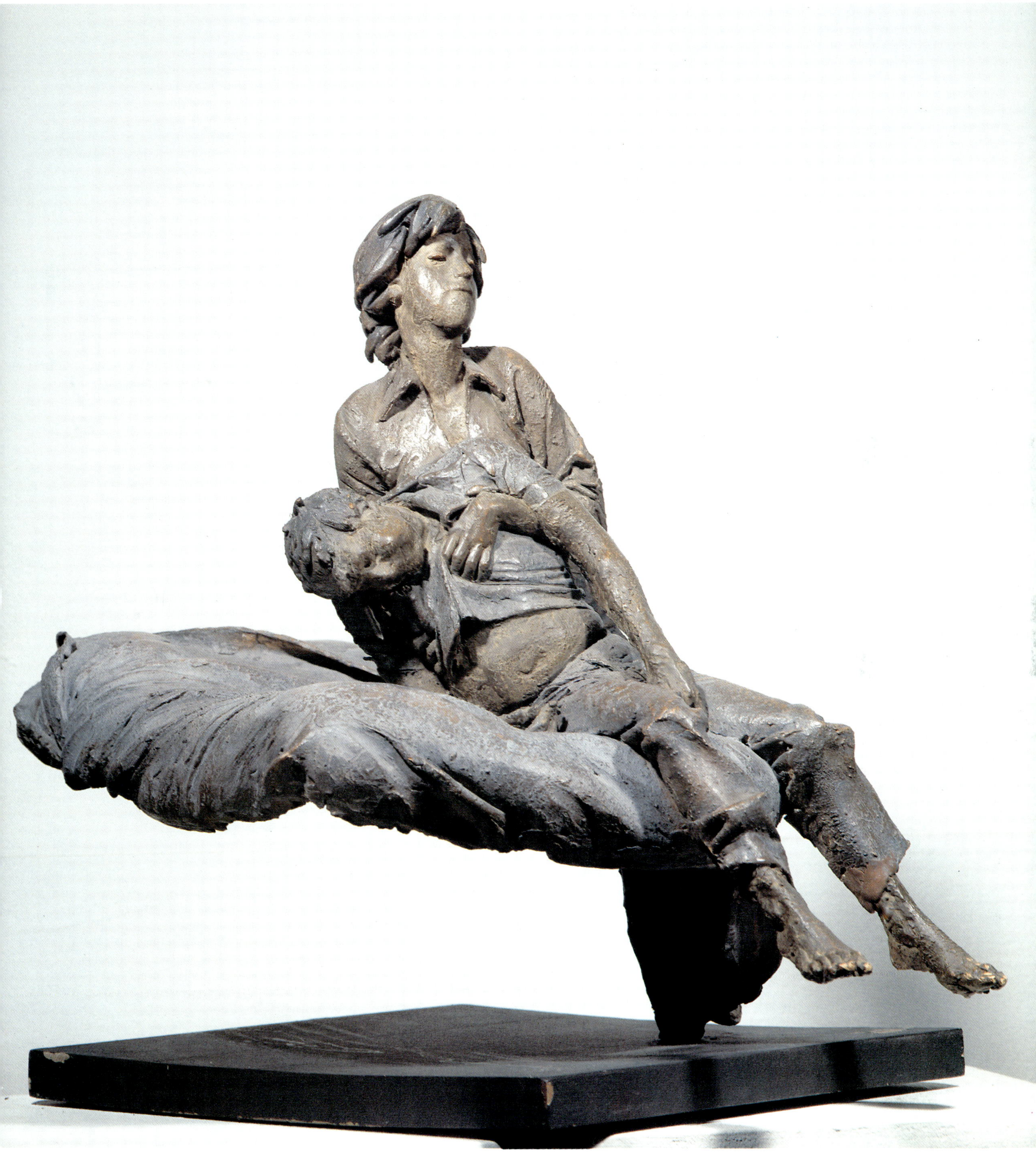

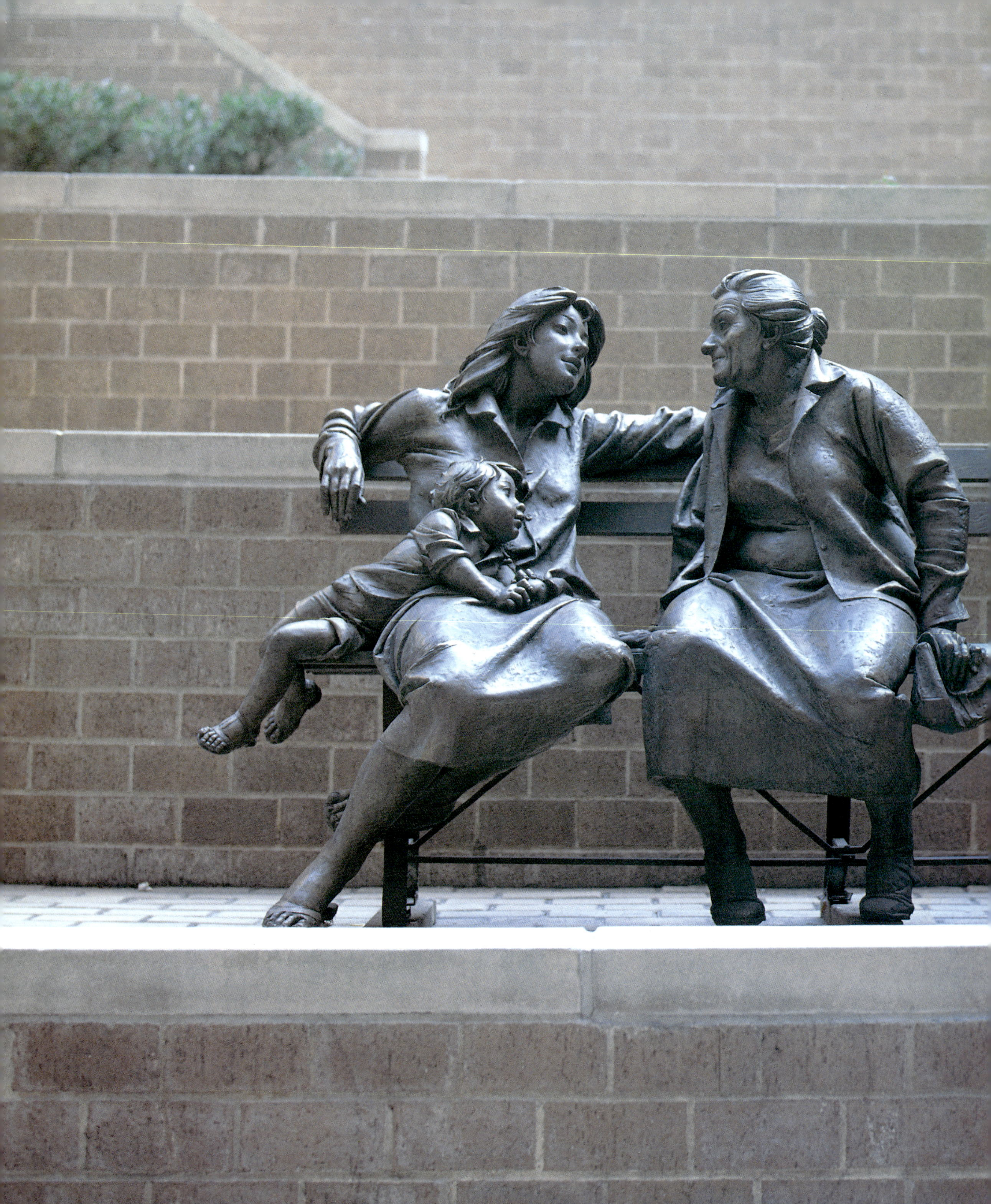

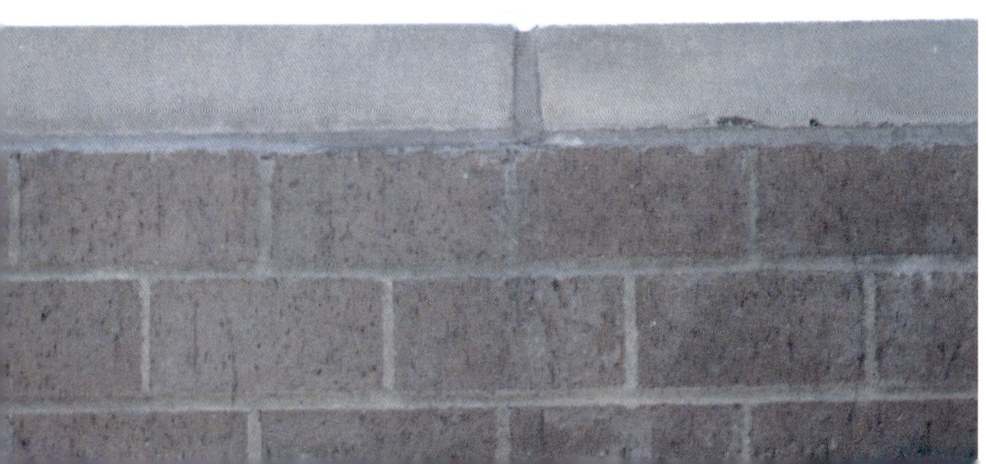

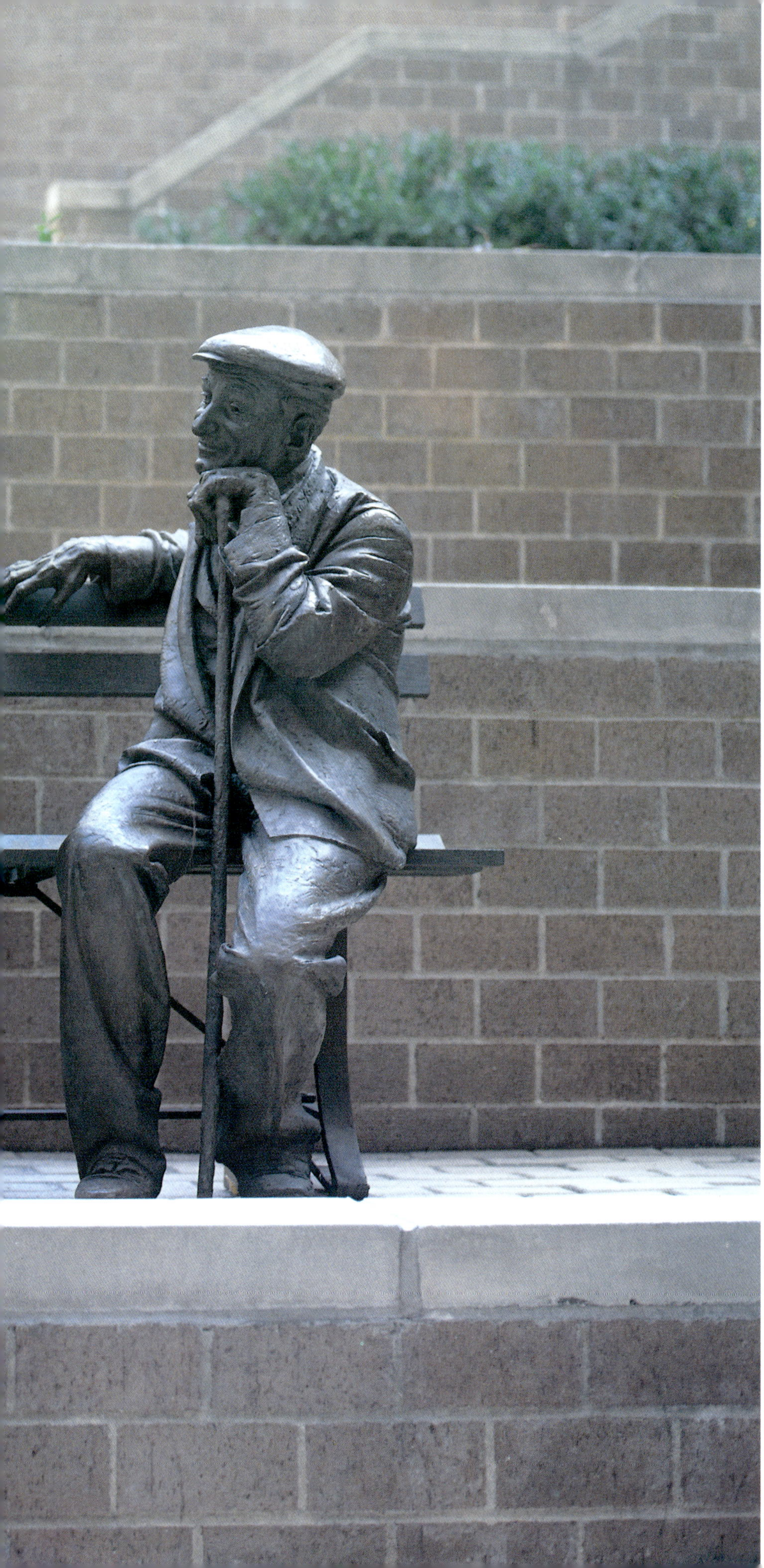

Park Bench, 1985, bronze, life-size. Montana Building, New York. (See also black-and-white illustration, page 117.)

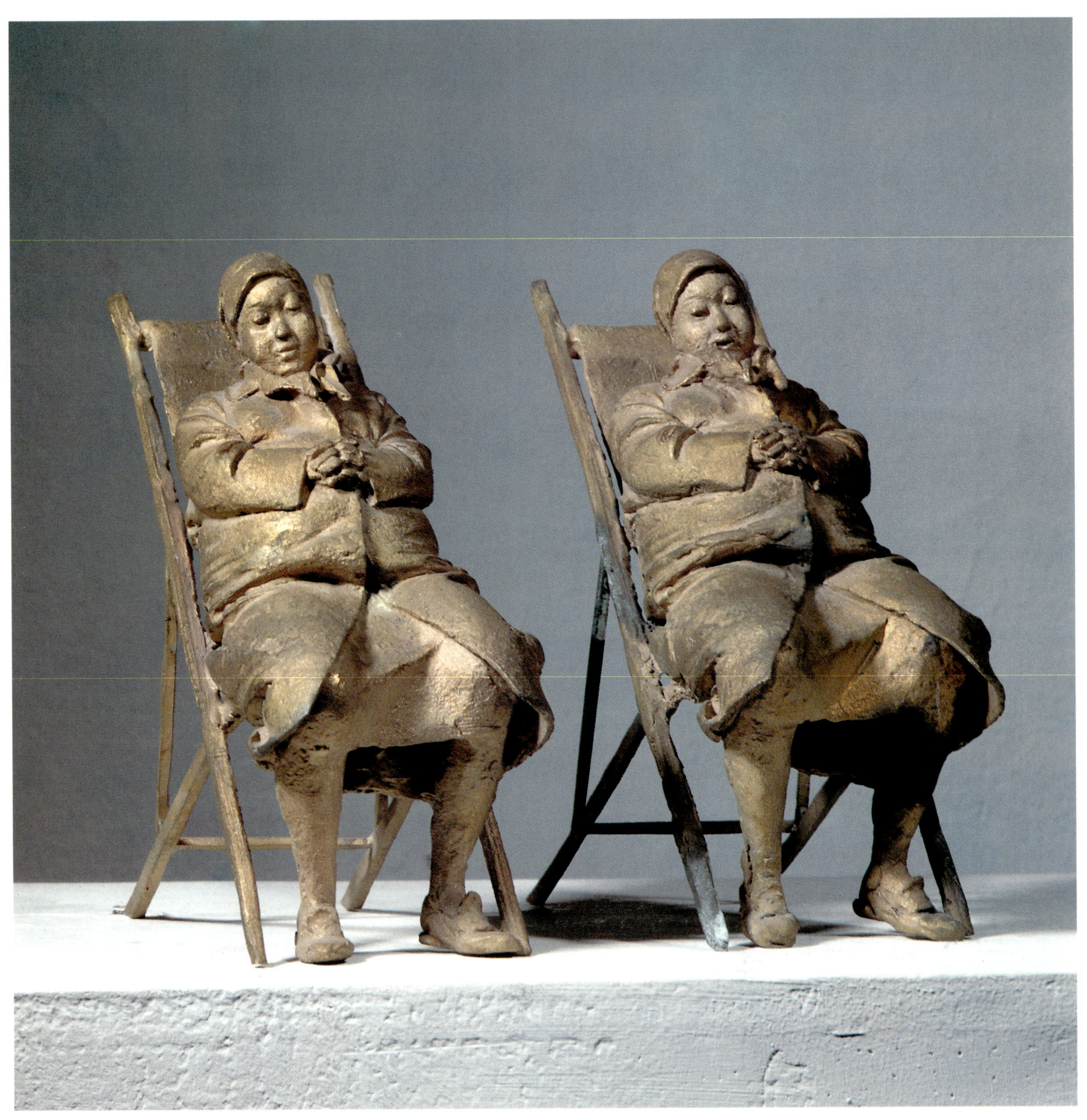

Woman in Lawn Chair (two casts), 1986, bronze, 9 x 9 inches. Forum Gallery, New York.

Park Bench (detail), 1985, bronze, life-size. Montana Building, New York. (See also colorplate, pages 114–15.)

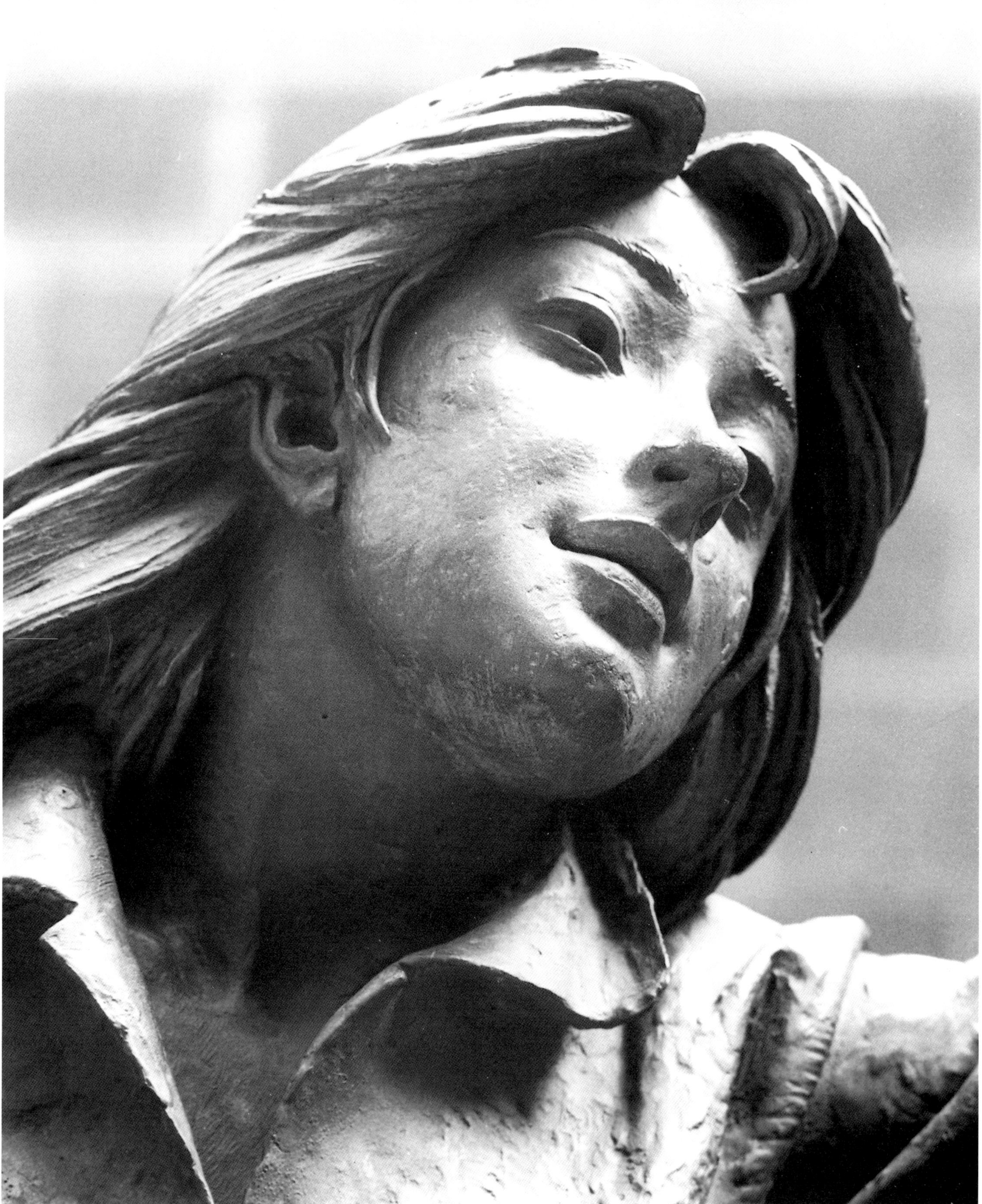

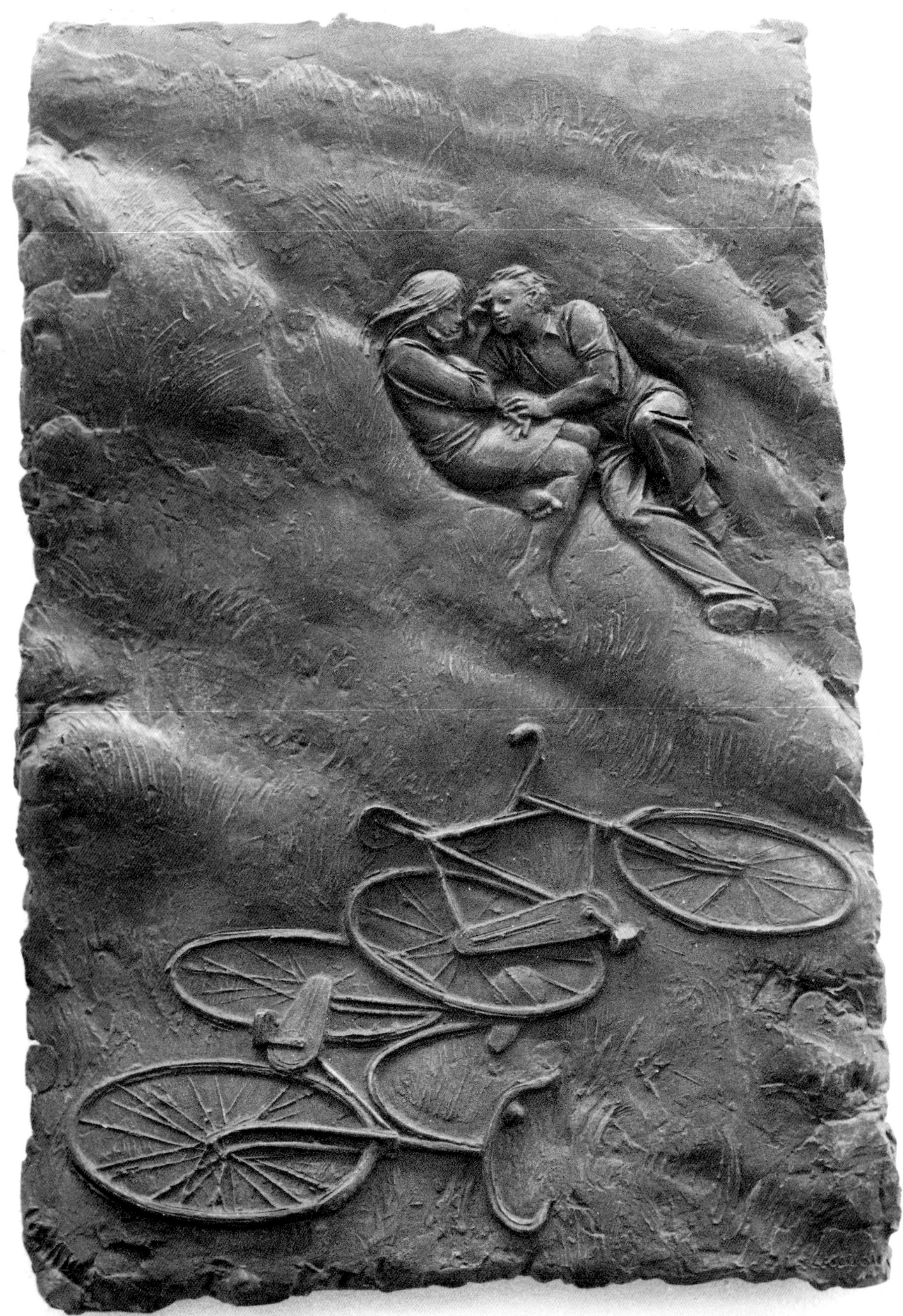

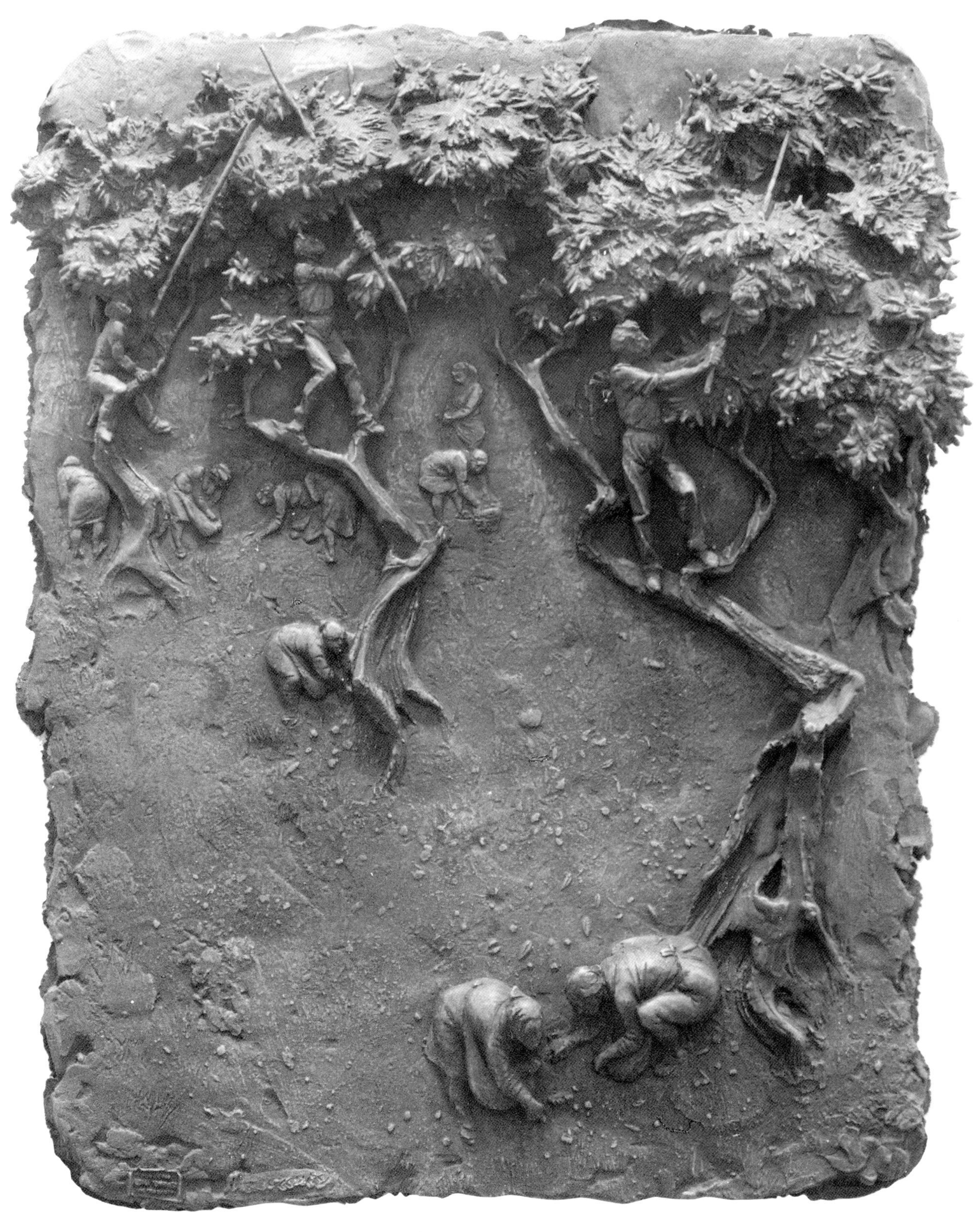

Olive Pickers, 1983, bronze relief, 18 x 14½ inches. Collection of Mr. and Mrs. Harvey Gladstein, Salisbury, Connecticut.

In the Park, 1977, terra-cotta relief, 25 x 18 inches. Forum Gallery, New York.

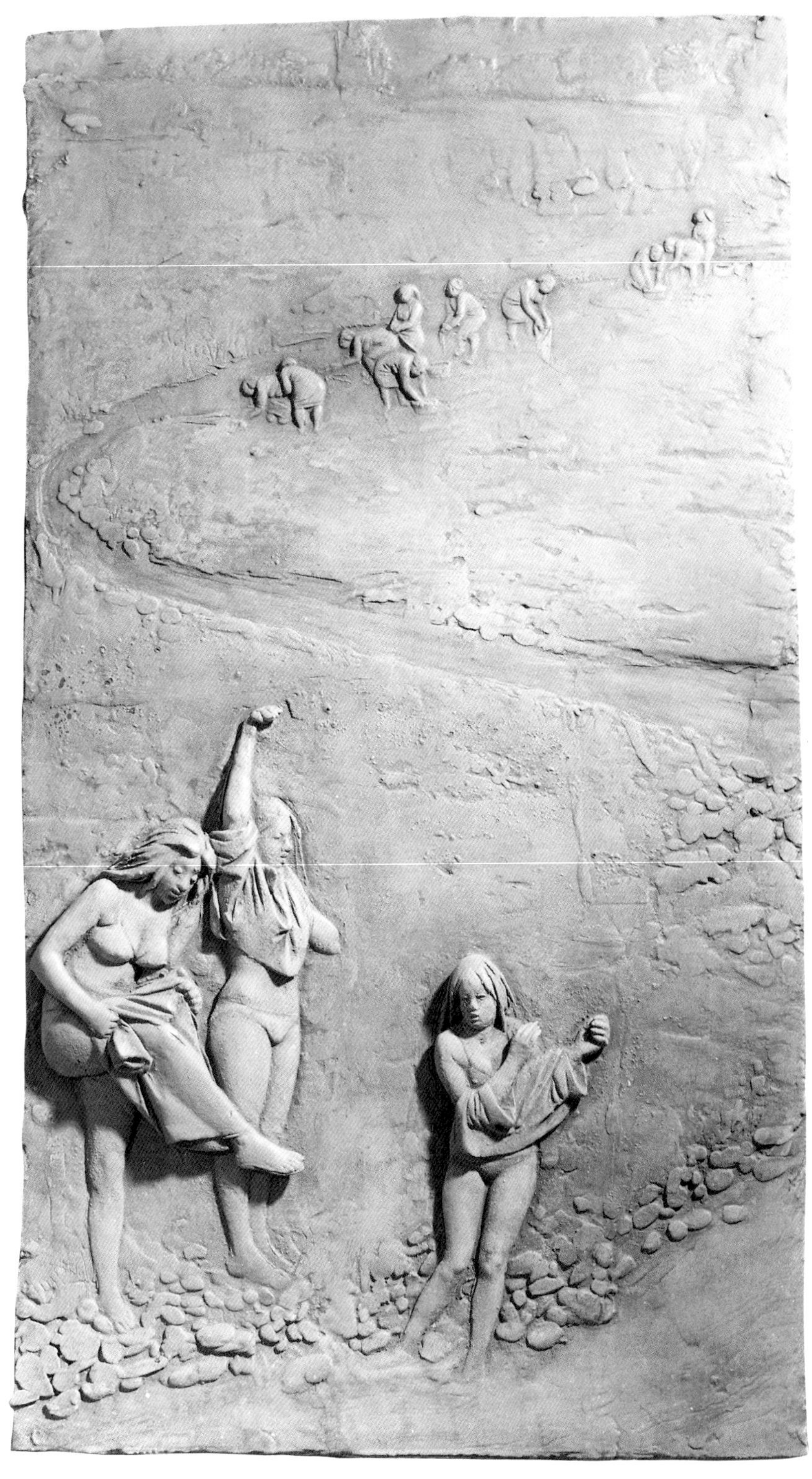

The Stream, 1979, terra-cotta relief, 31 x 16 inches. Forum Gallery, New York.

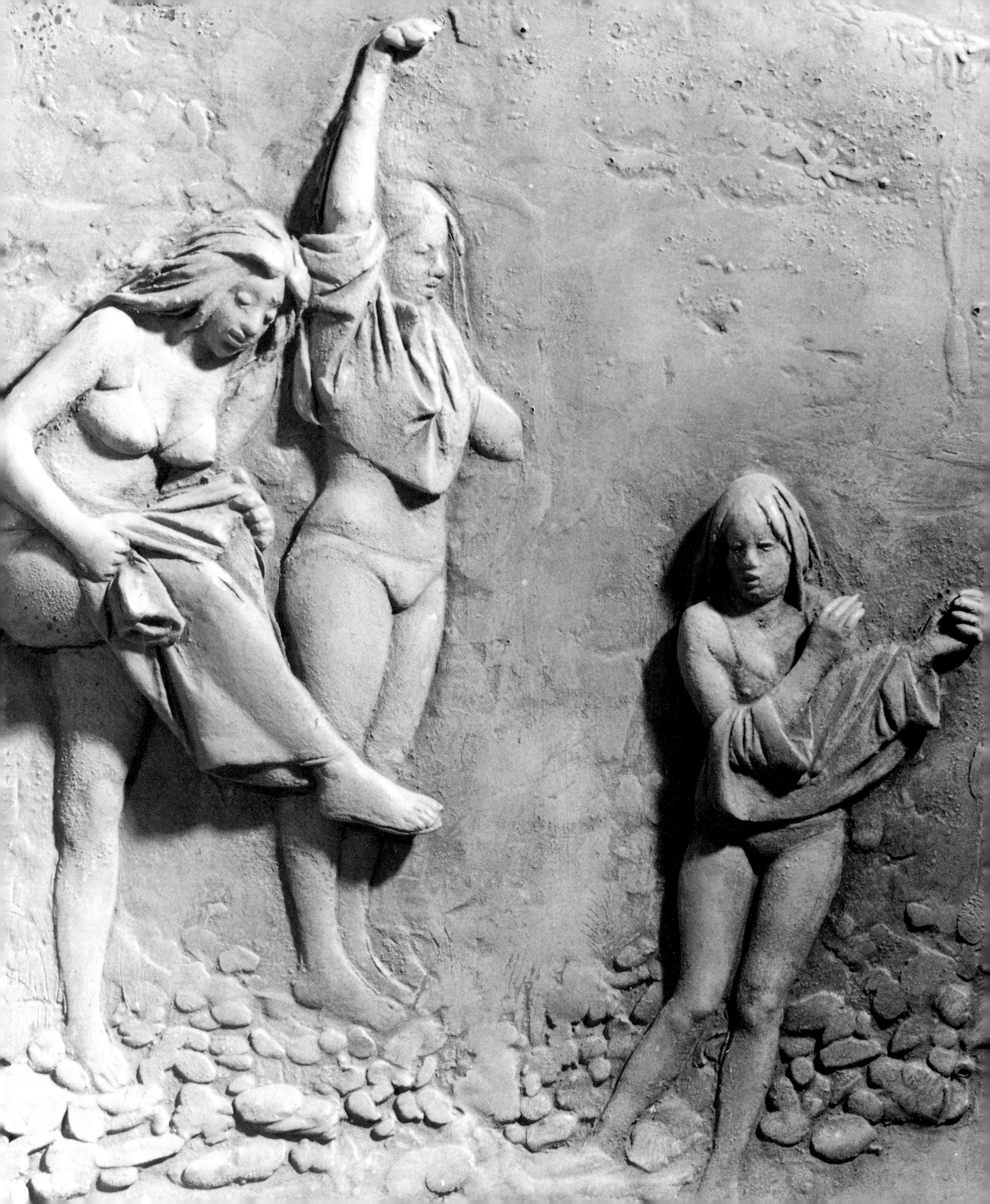

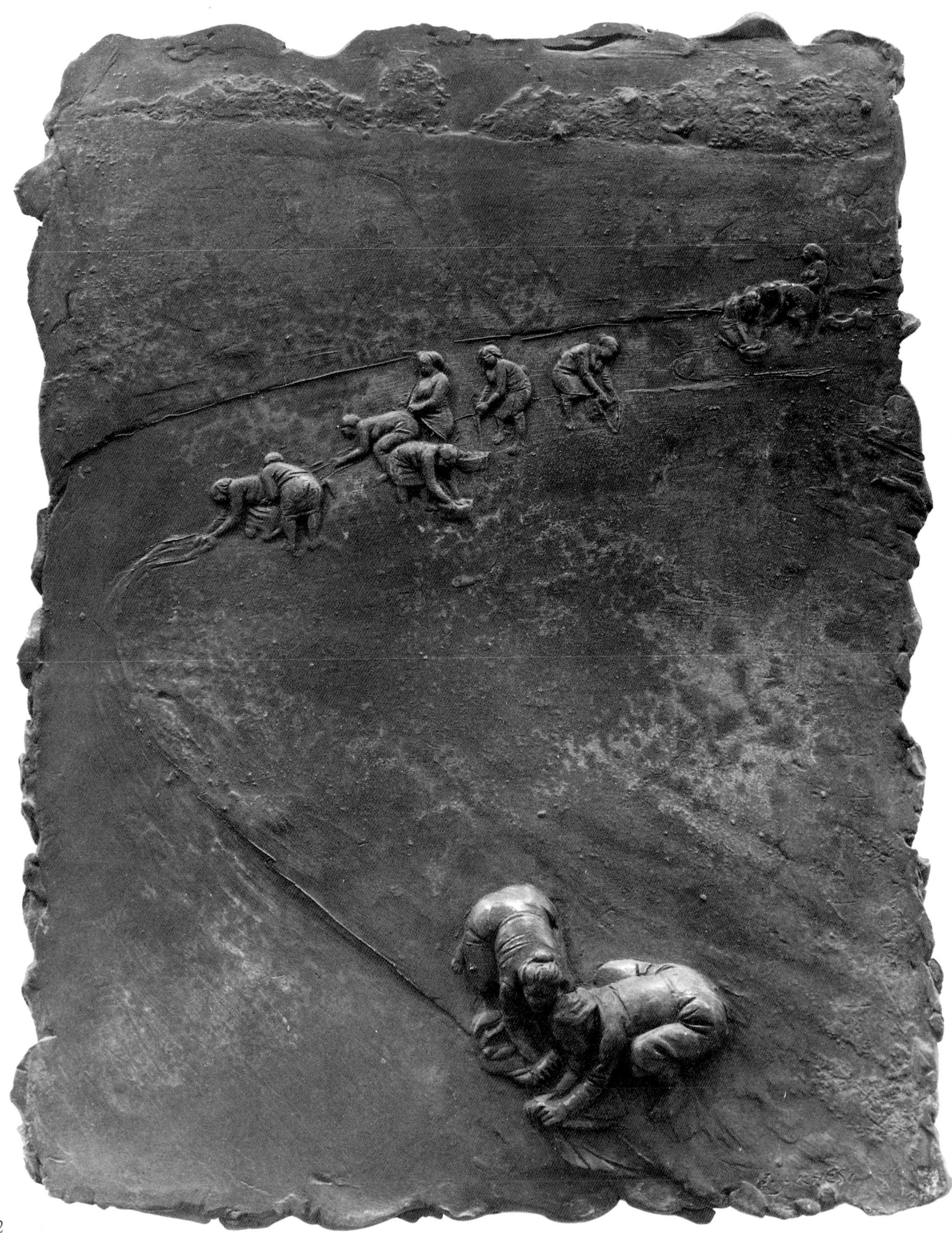

Washing, 1982, terra-cotta relief, 17 x 12½ inches. Forum Gallery, New York.

Shoppers, 1984, bronze, 12 x 20 inches. Forum Gallery, New York.

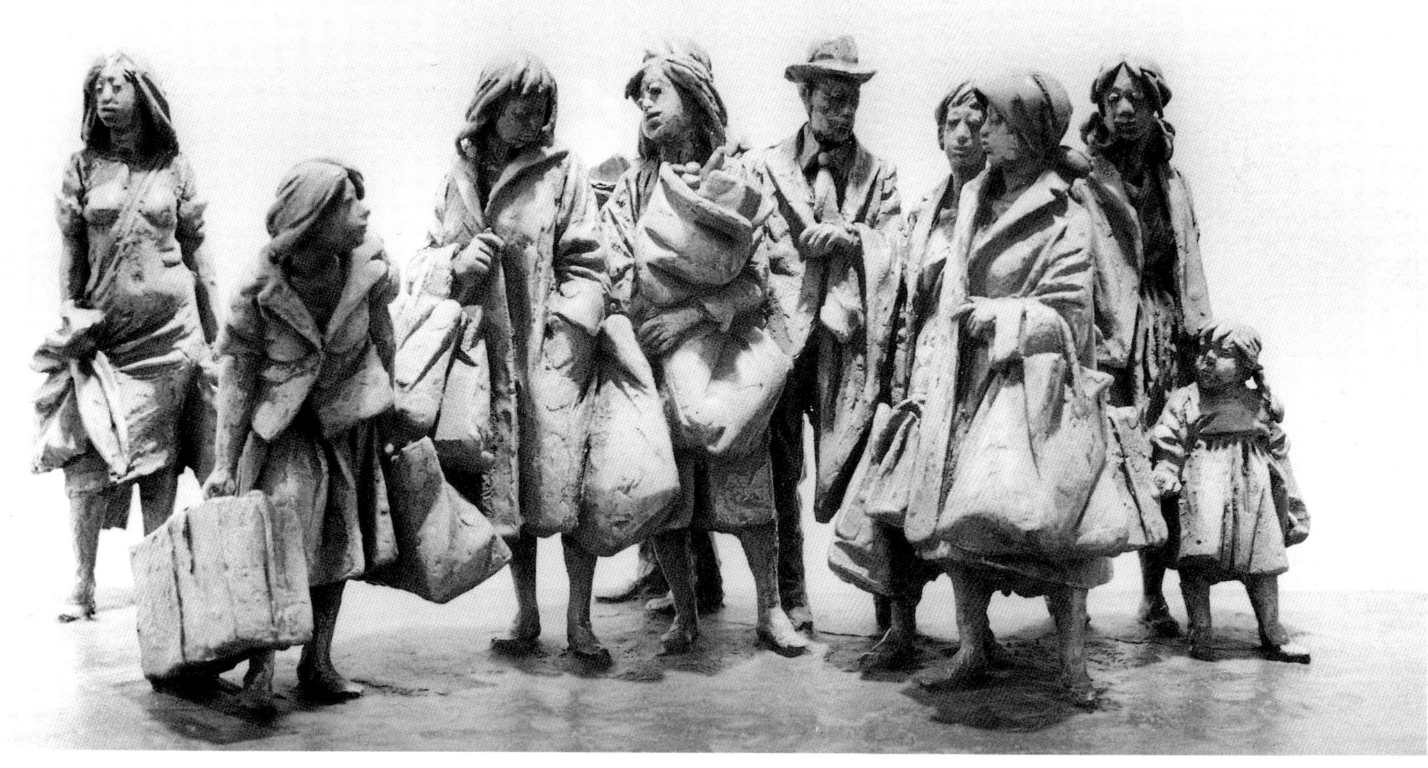

Tradespeople, 1963, bronze, 13 feet wide. National Westminster Bank USA, New York.

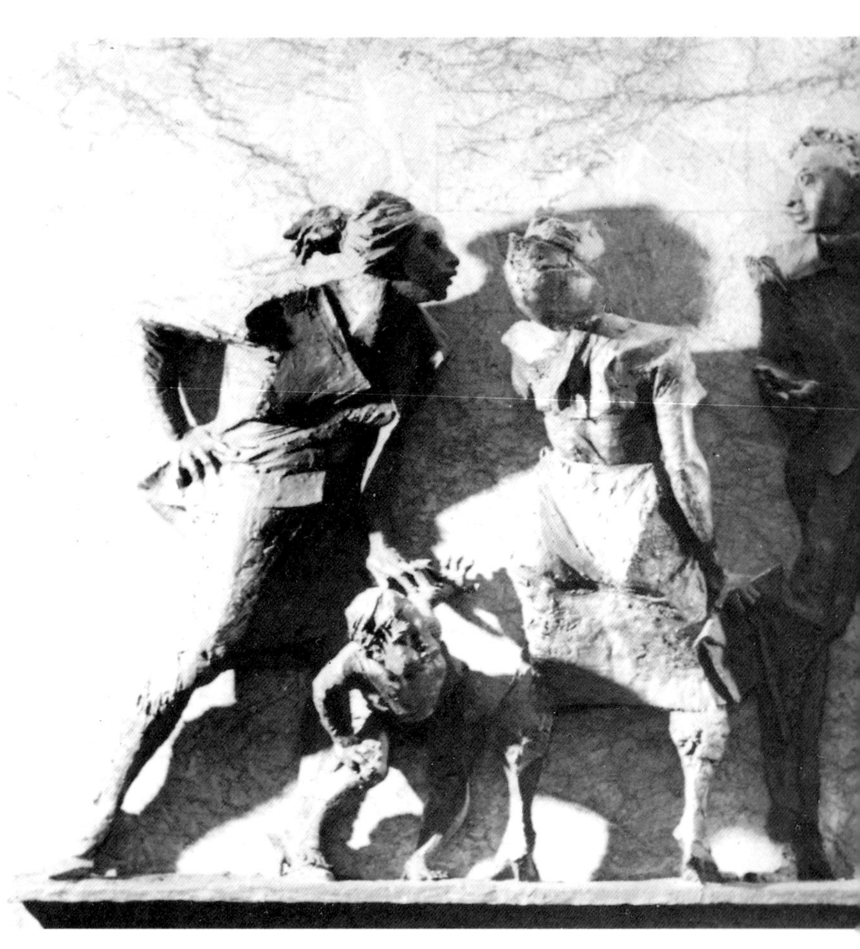

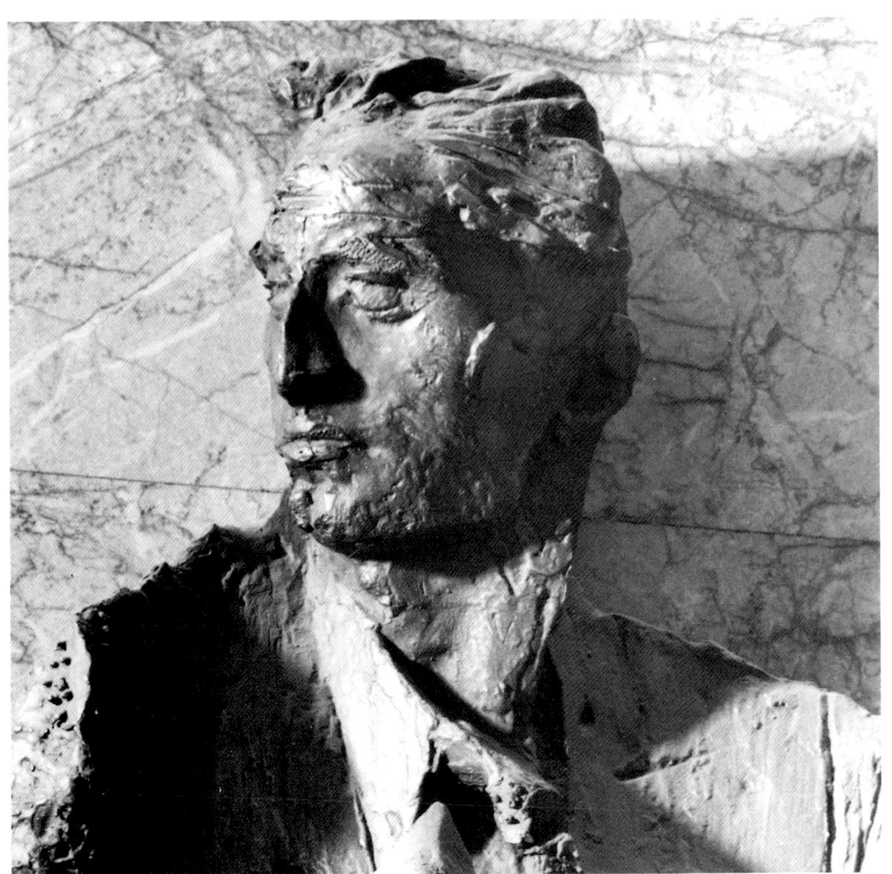

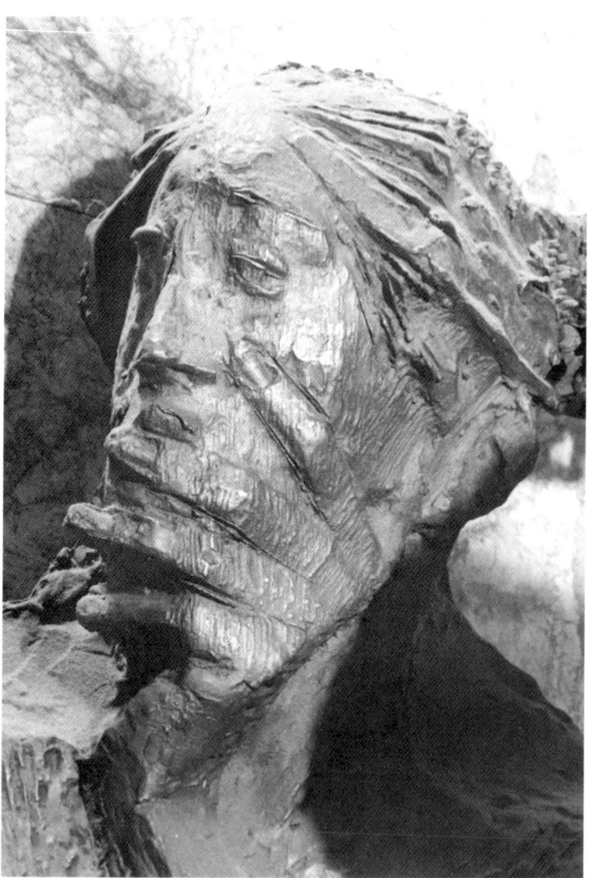

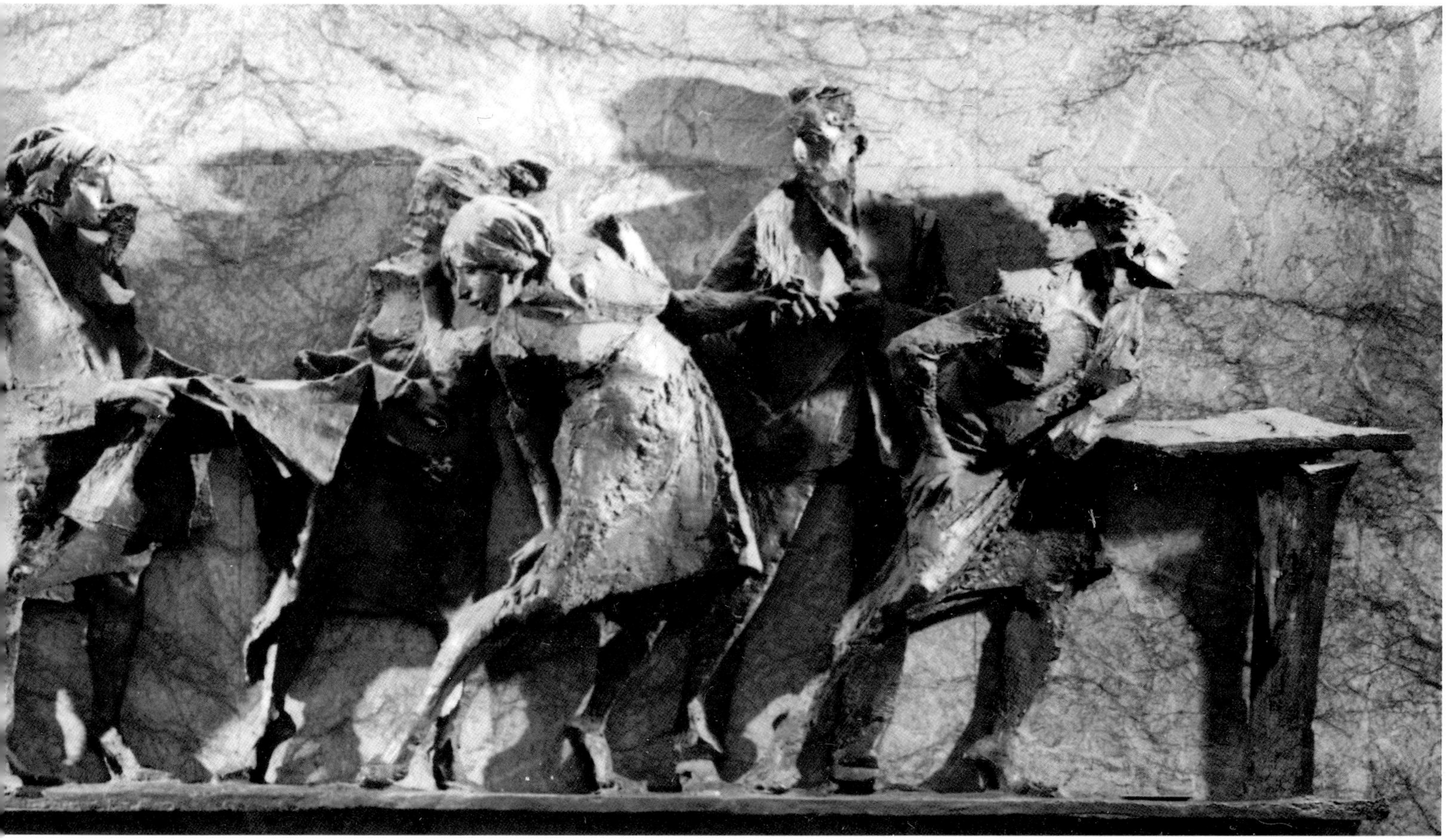

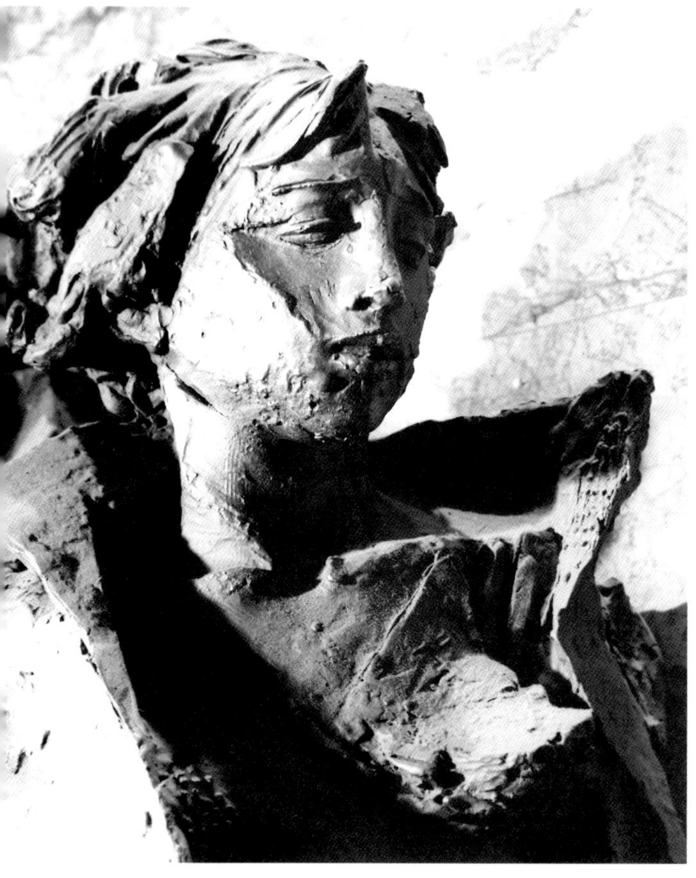

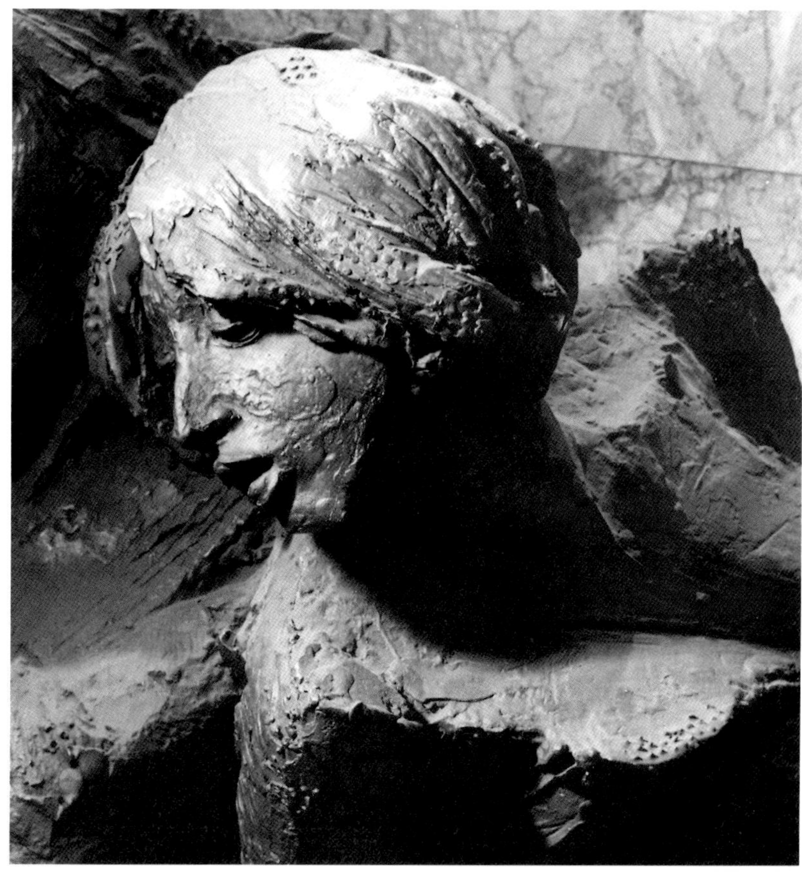

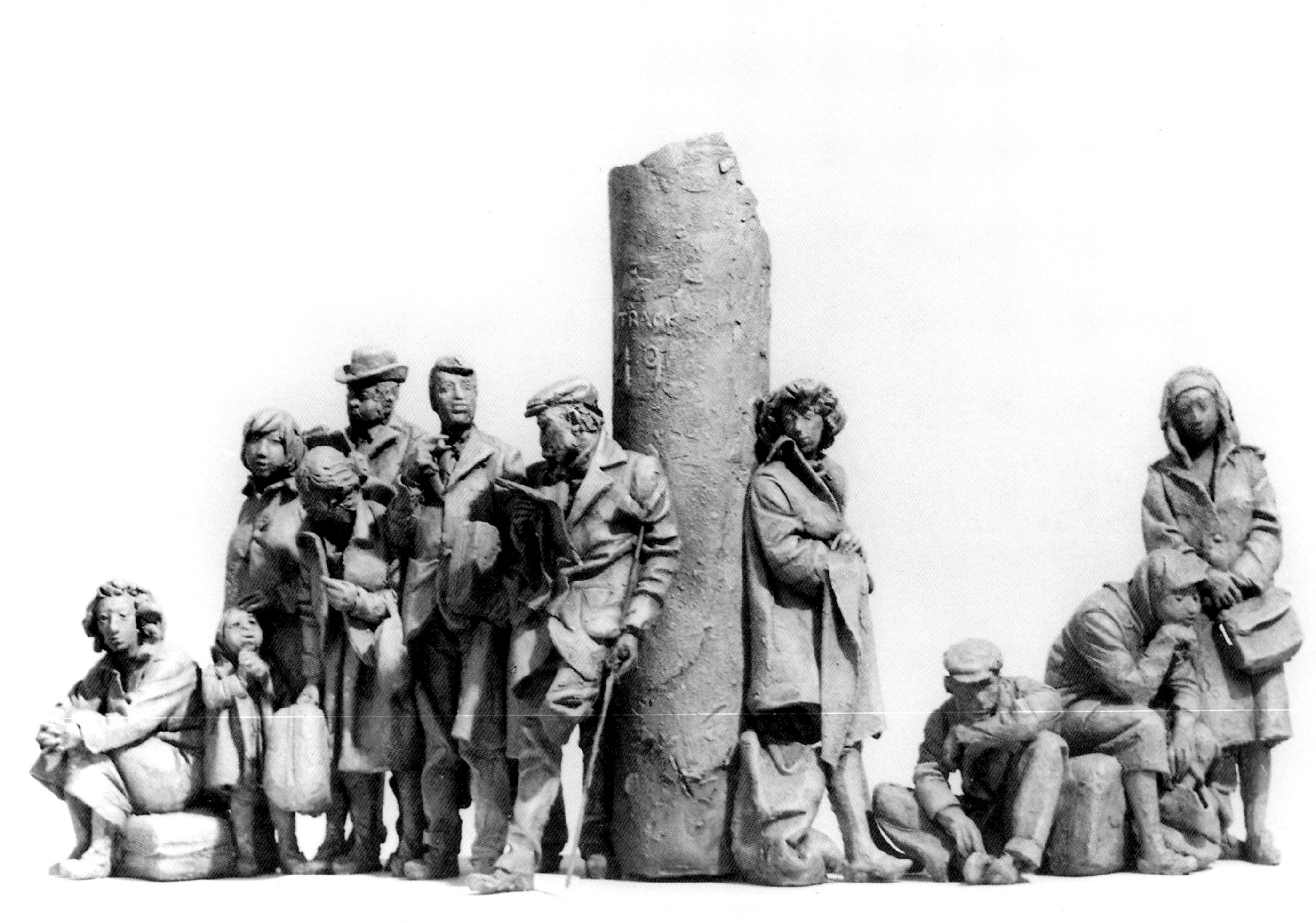

Track 19, 1984–85, terra-cotta, 12 x 22 x 8½ inches. Forum Gallery, New York.

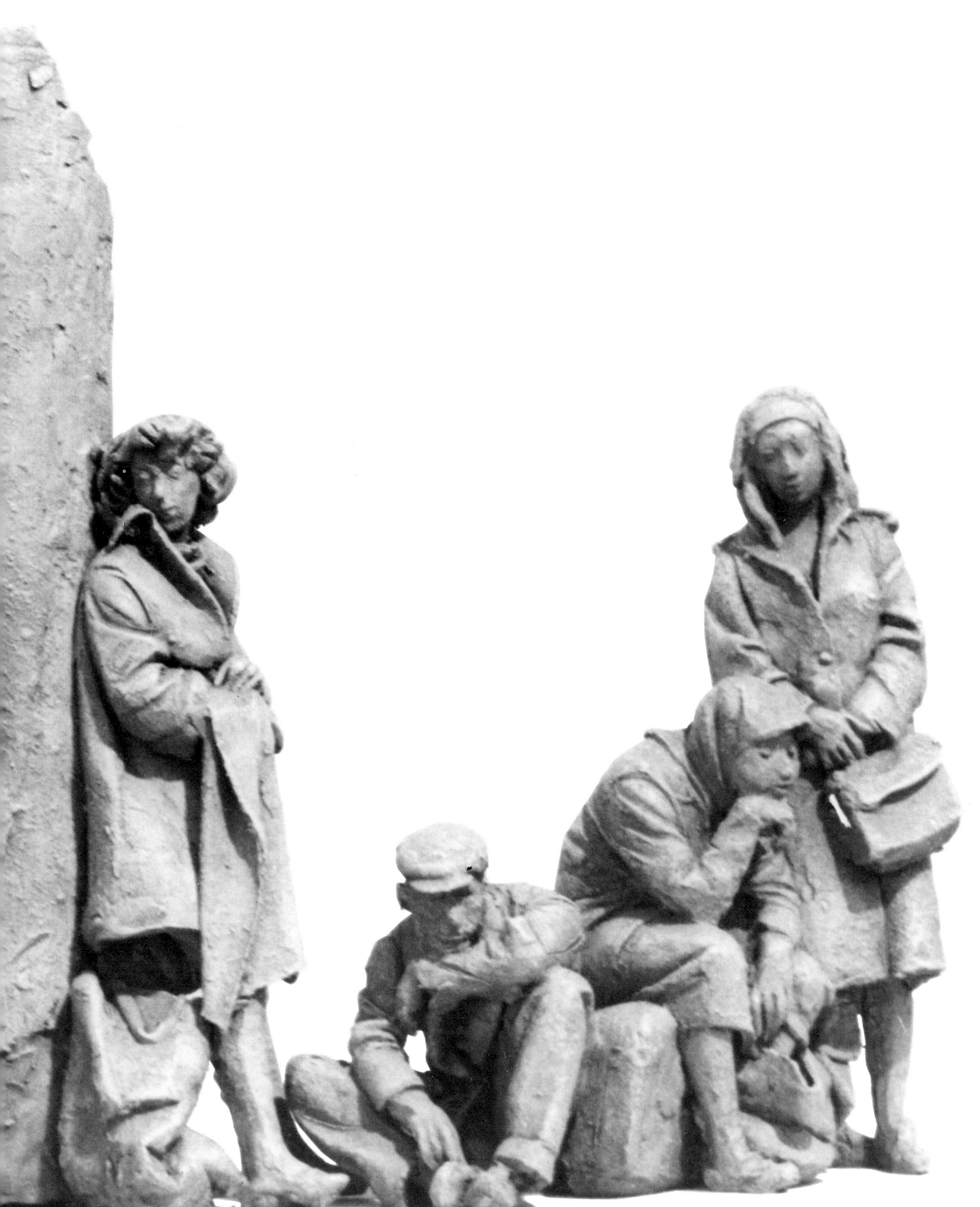

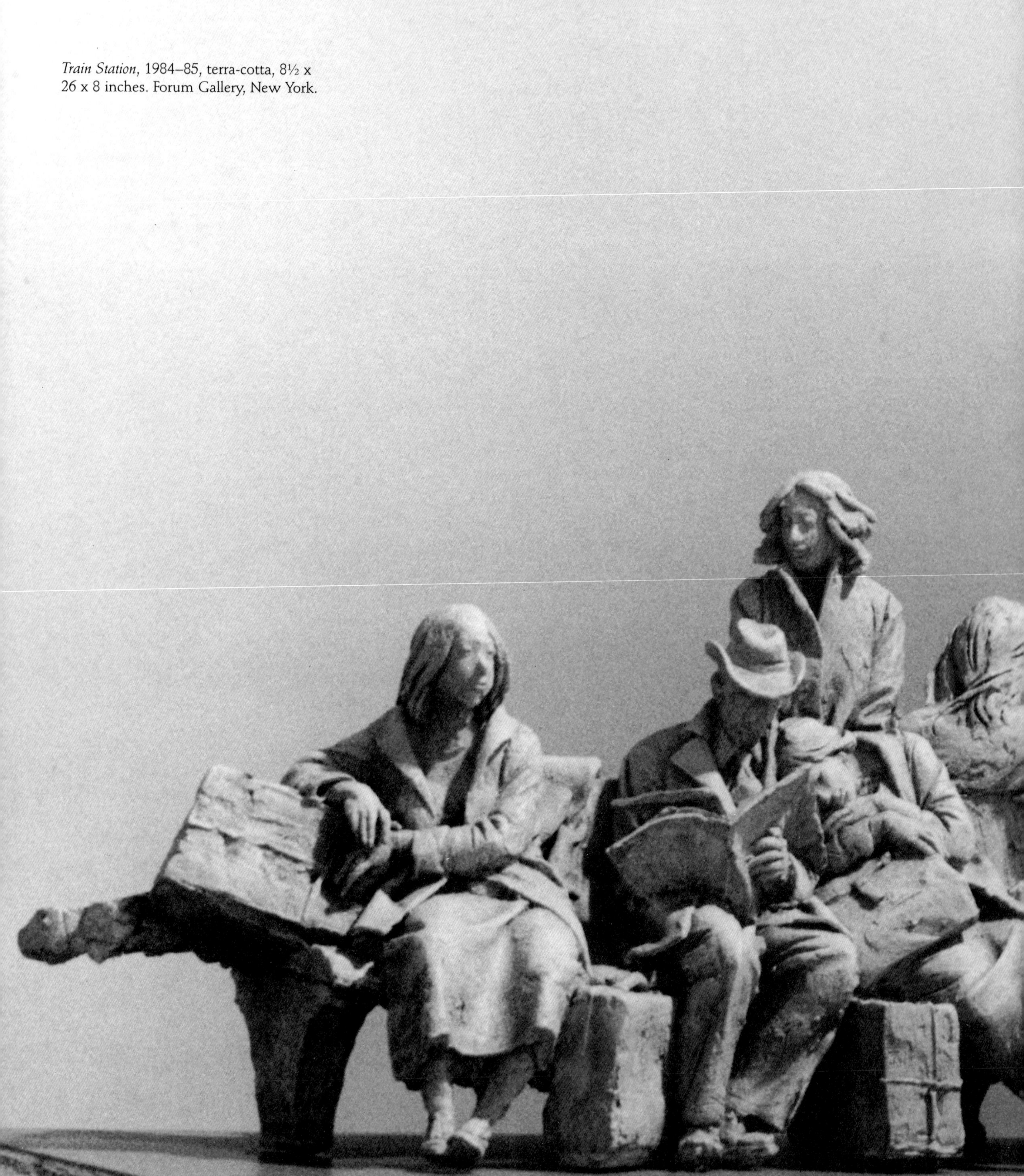

Train Station, 1984–85, terra-cotta, 8½ x 26 x 8 inches. Forum Gallery, New York.

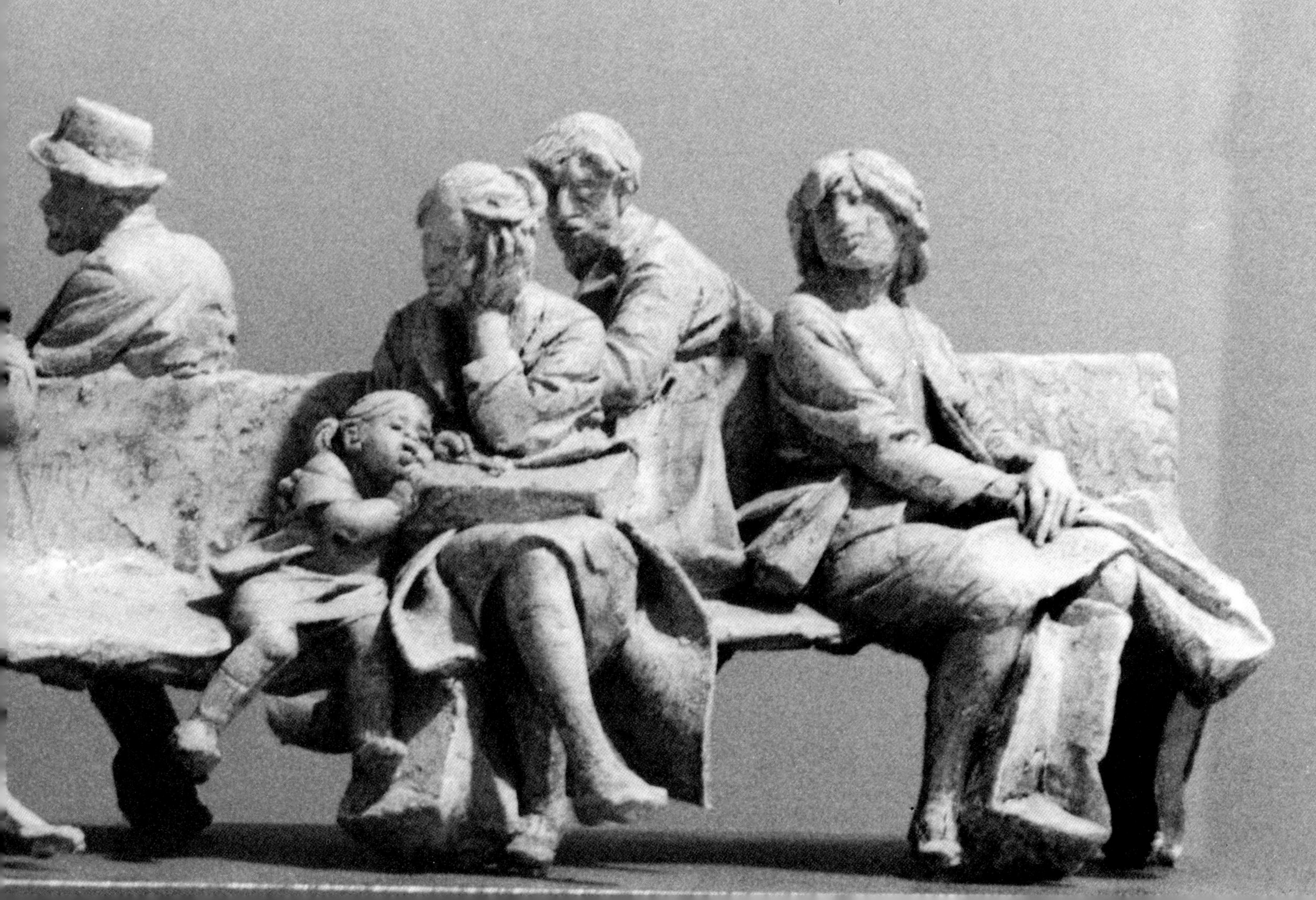

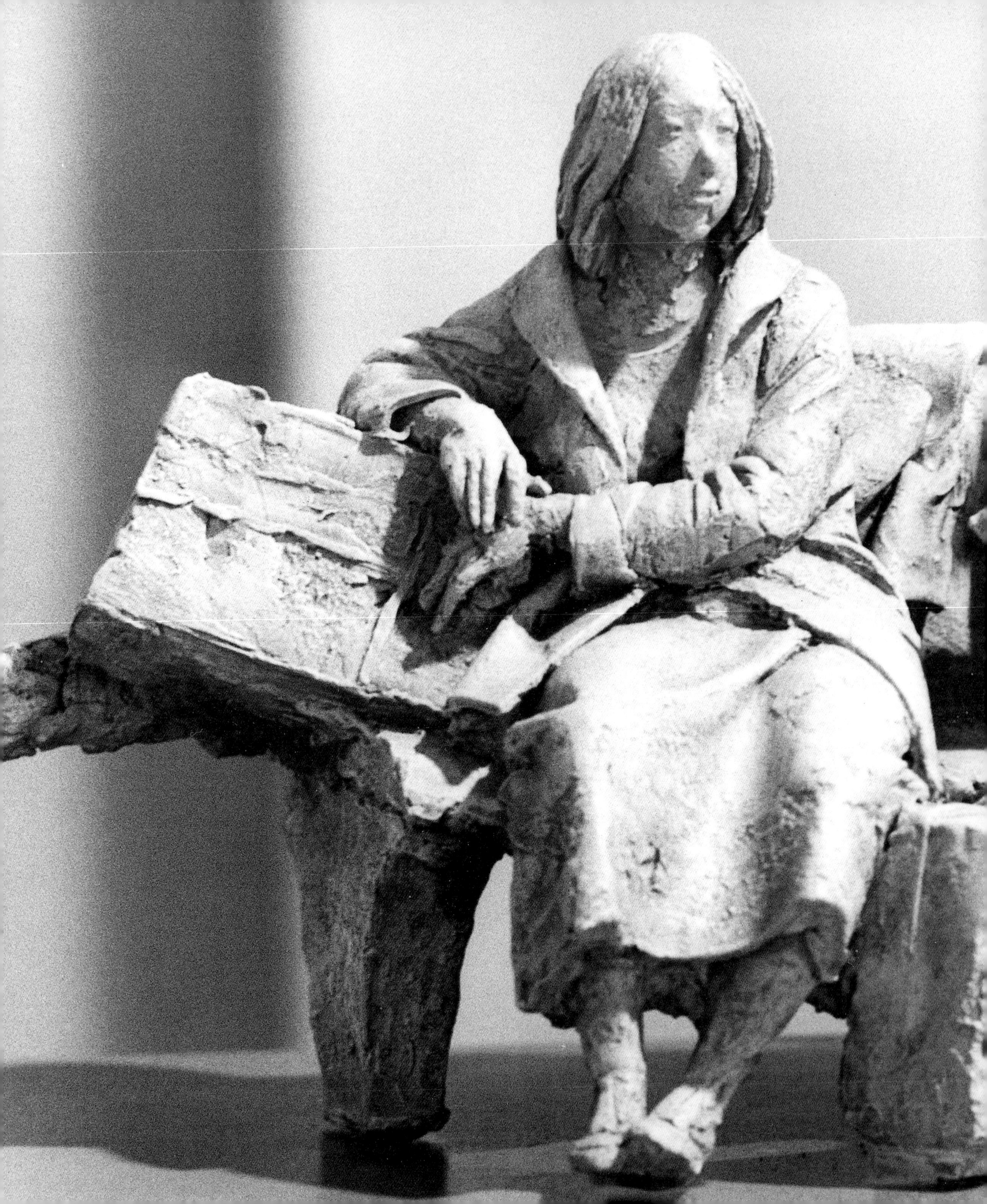

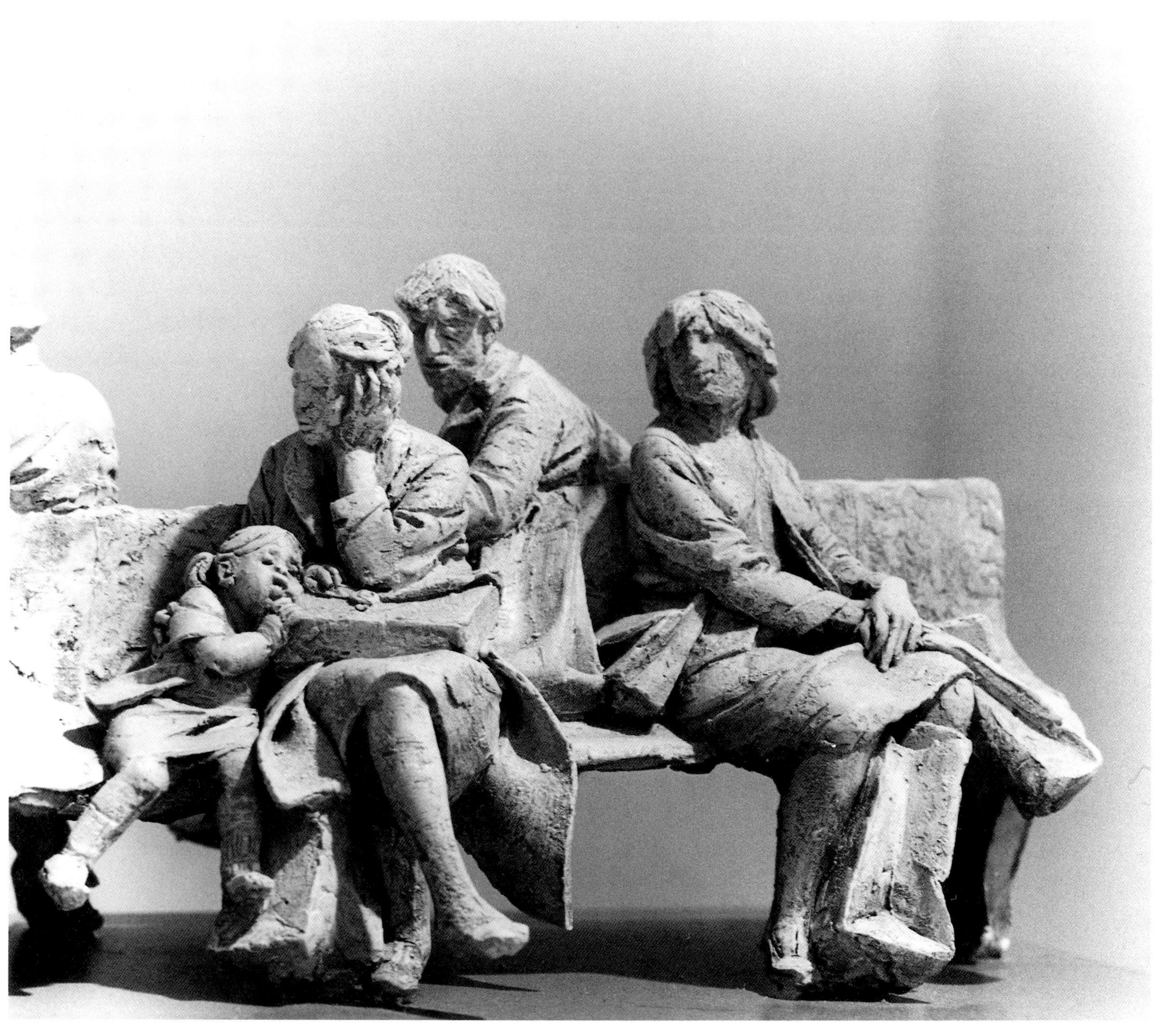

Train Station (details)

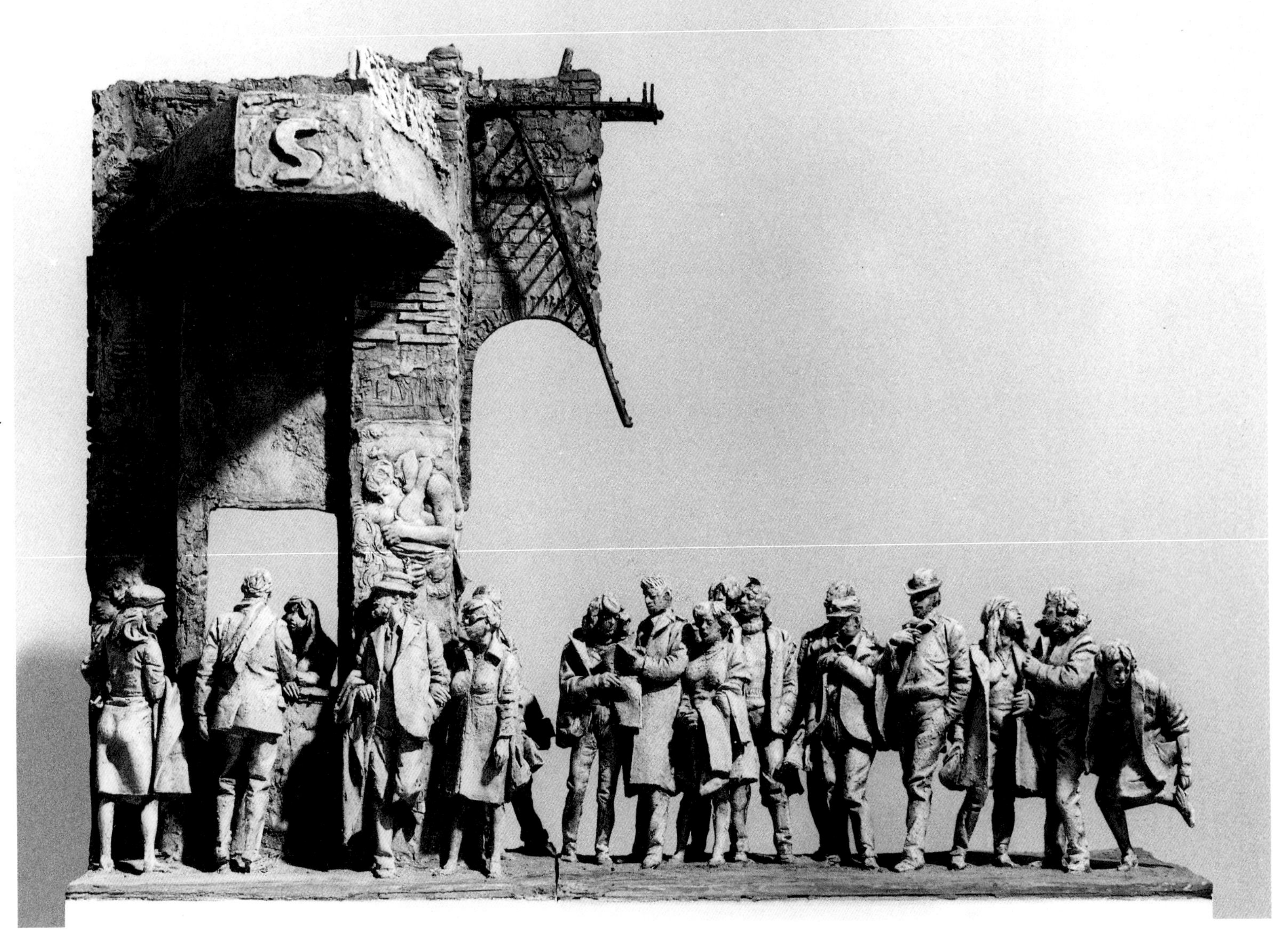

Saint Mark's Theater, 1984–85, terra-cotta, 26 x 33 x 14 inches. Forum Gallery, New York.

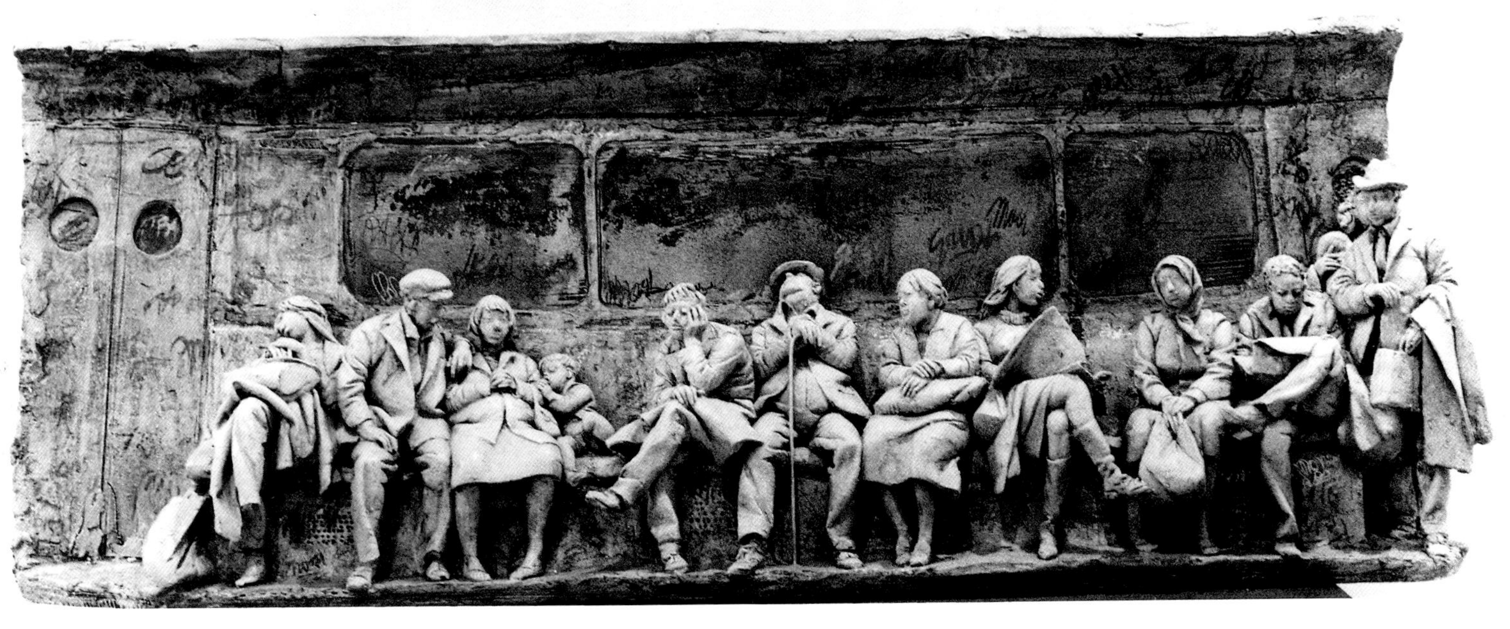

Subway #1, 1984–85, terra-cotta relief, 13½ x 34 inches. Forum Gallery, New York.

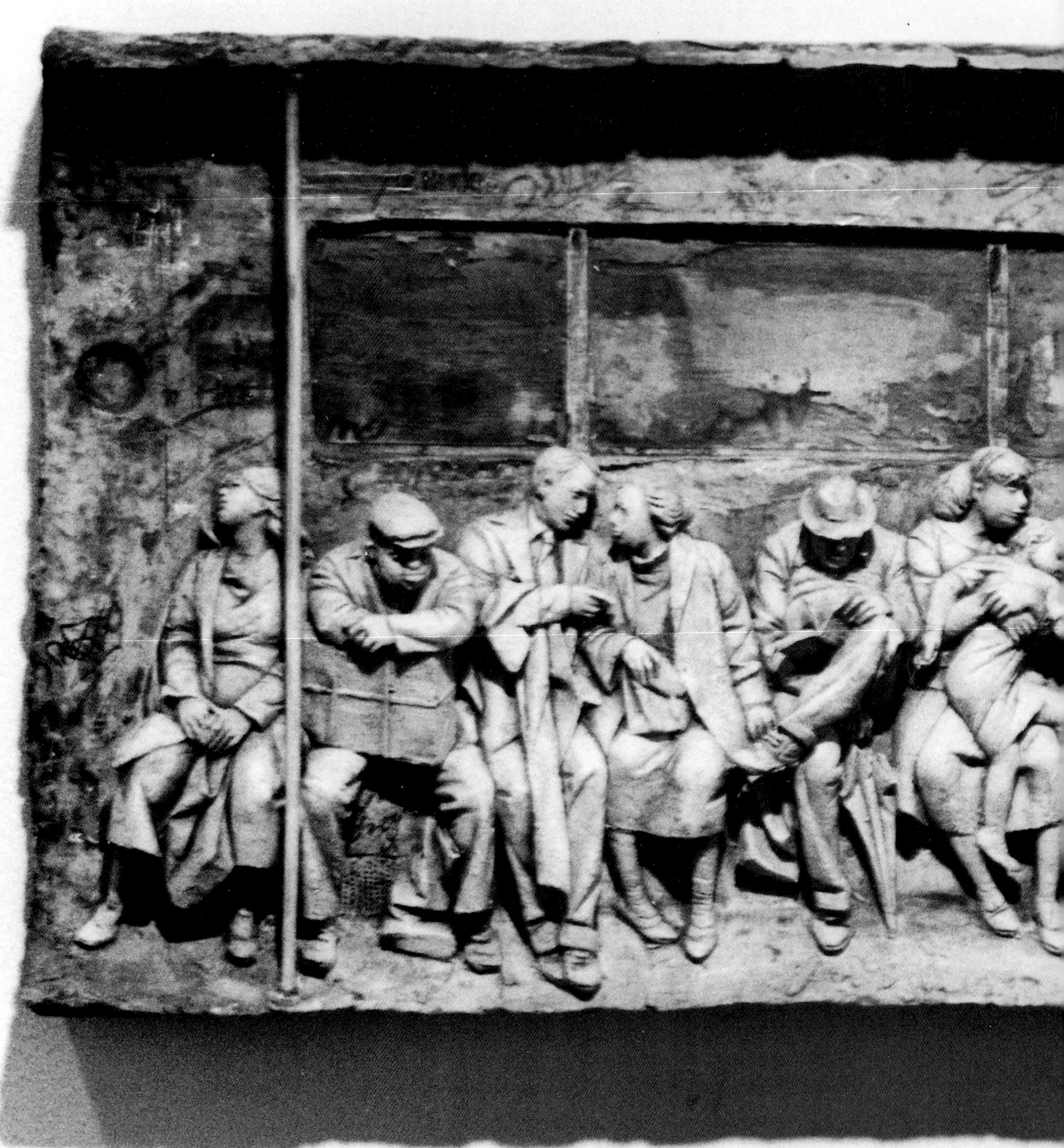

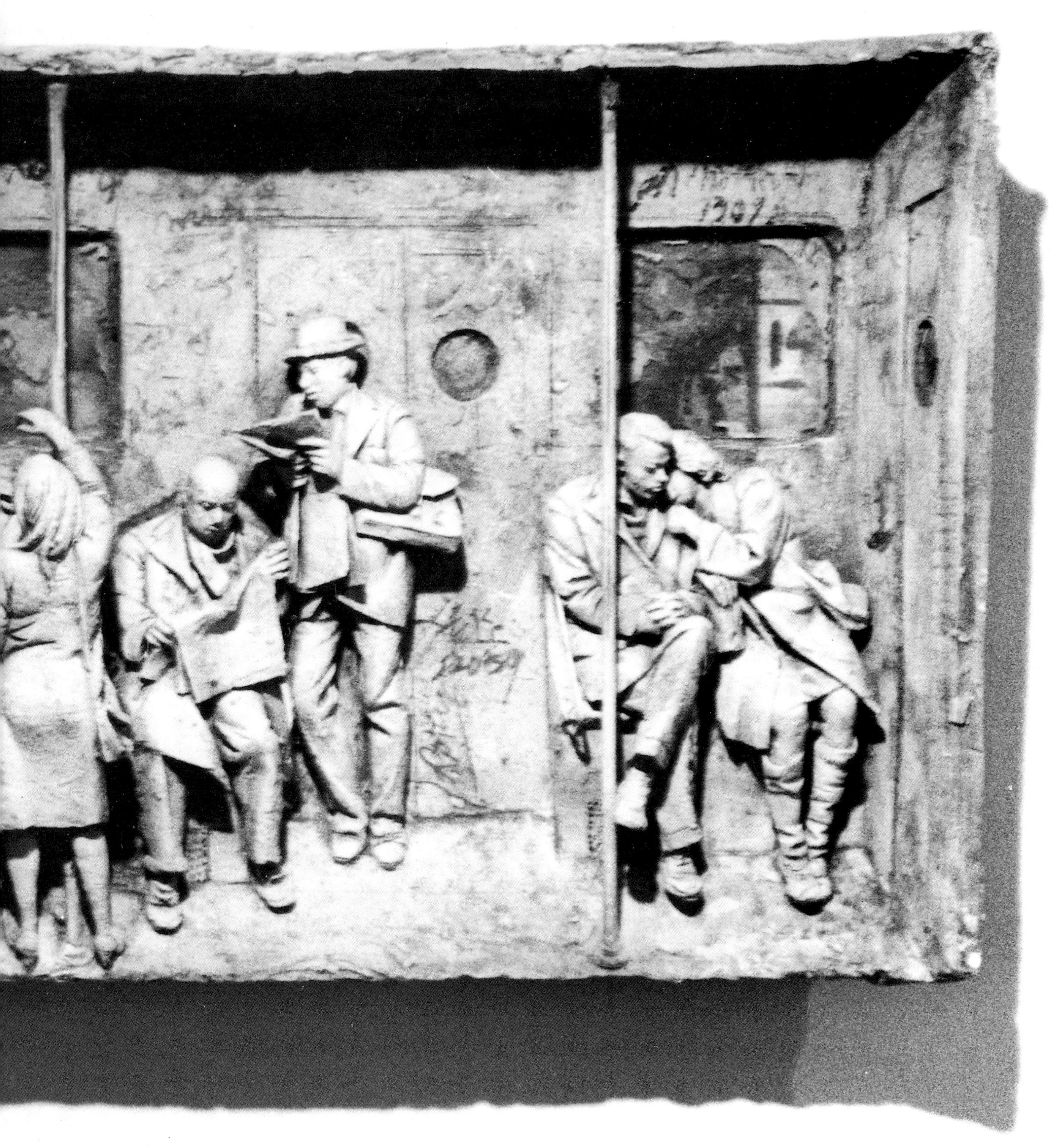

Subway #2, 1984–85, terra-cotta relief, 16 x 37 inches. Forum Gallery, New York.

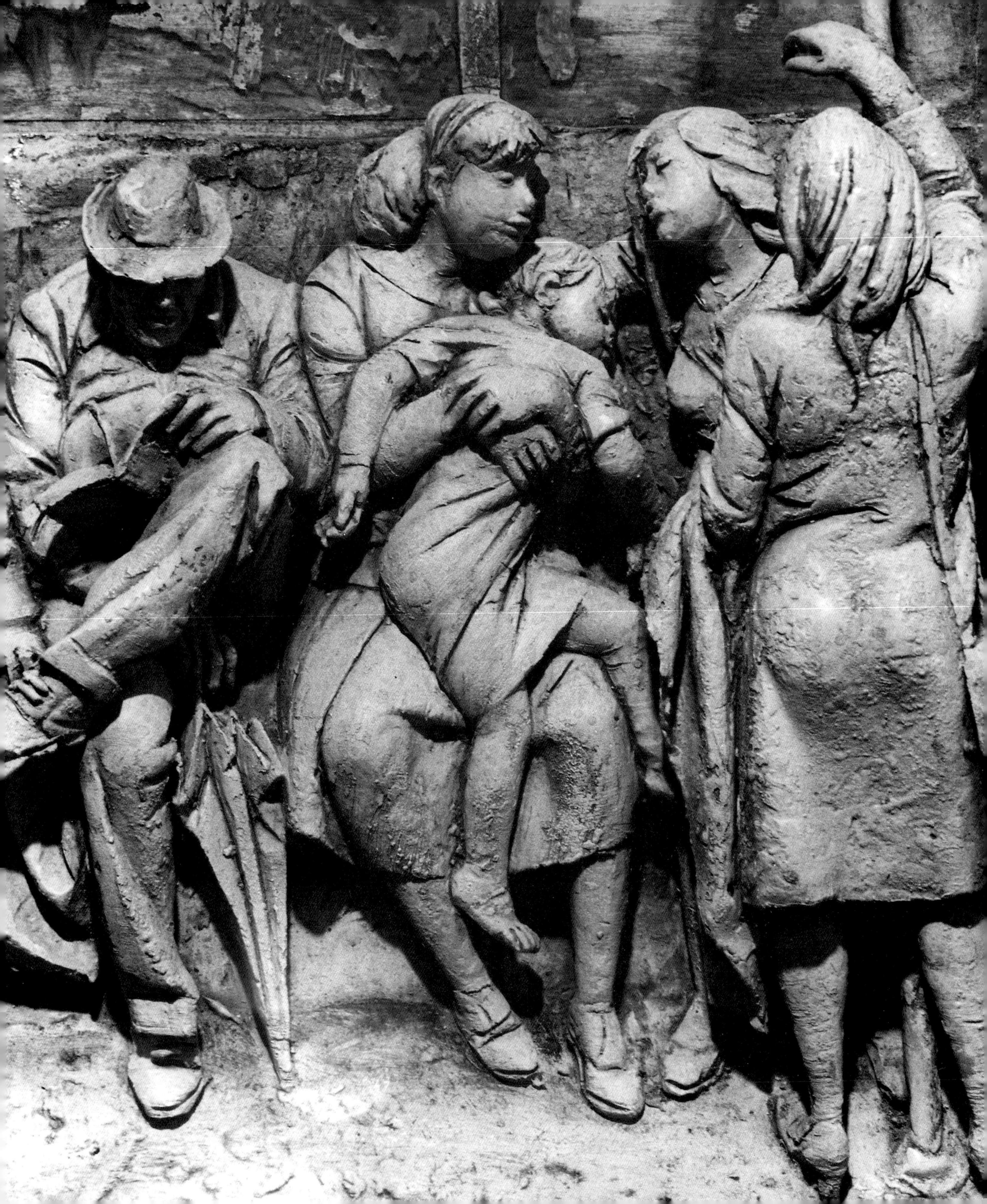

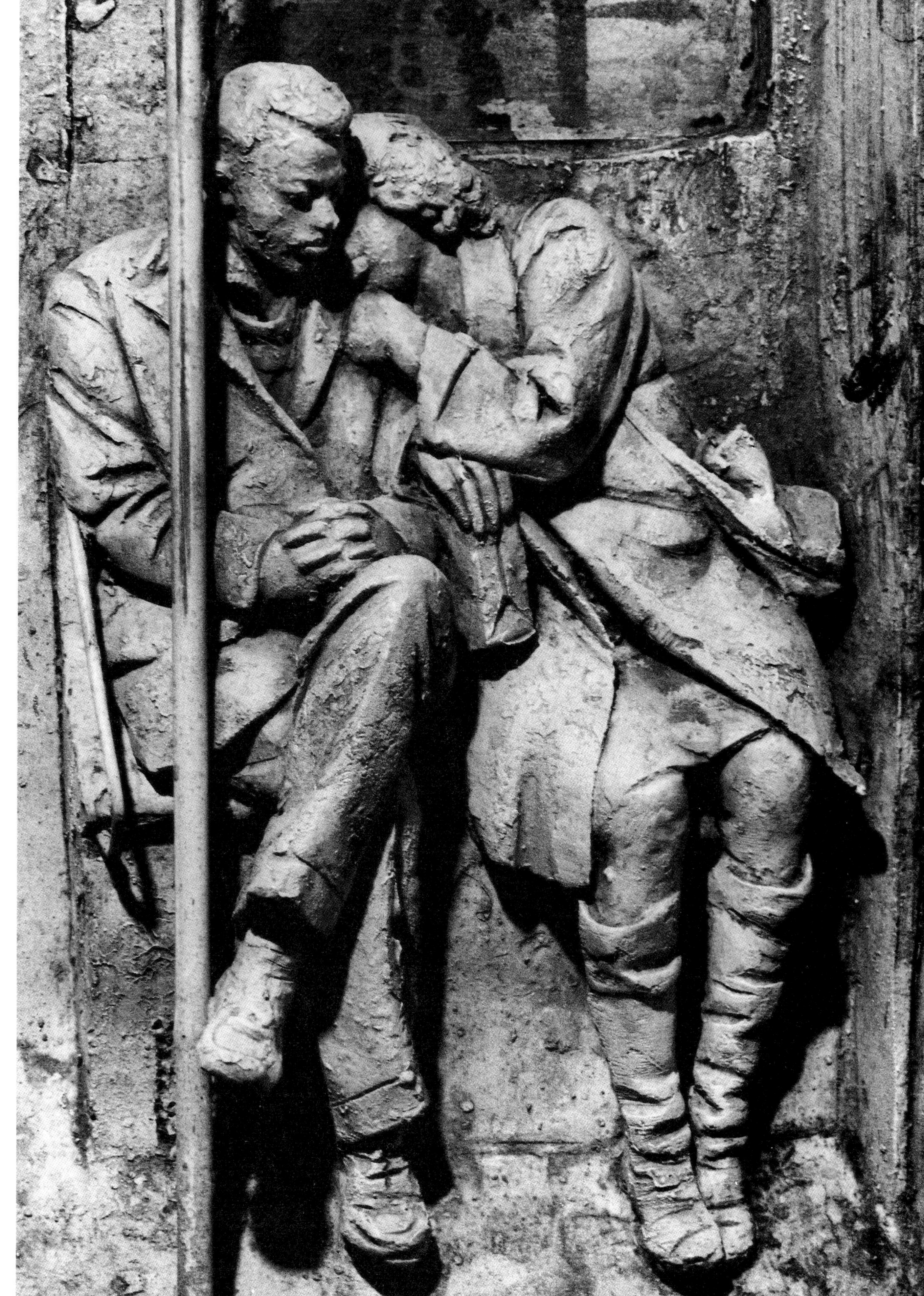

Subway #2
(details)

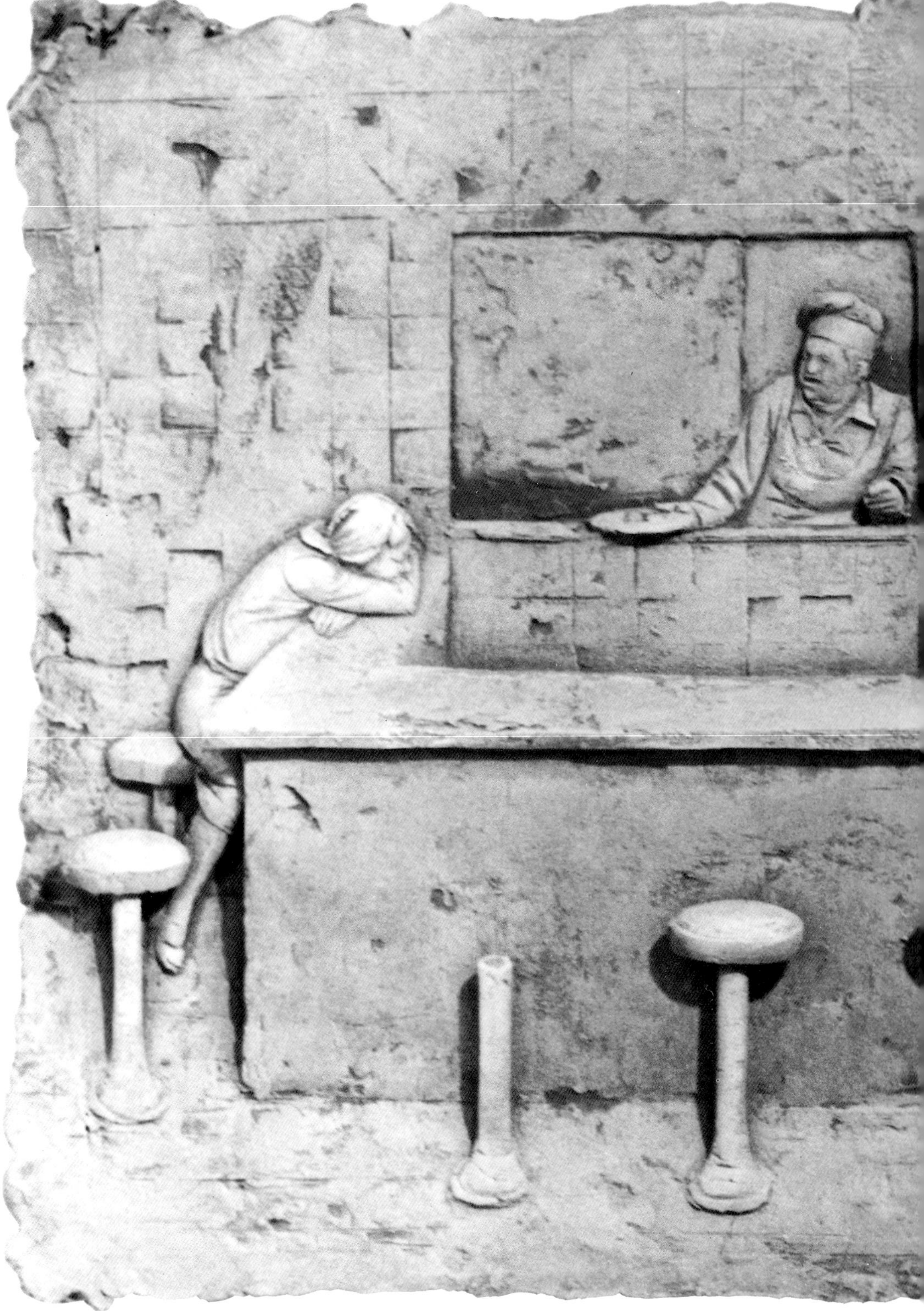

Diner, 1984–85, terra-cotta relief, 17 x 30 inches. Forum Gallery, New York.

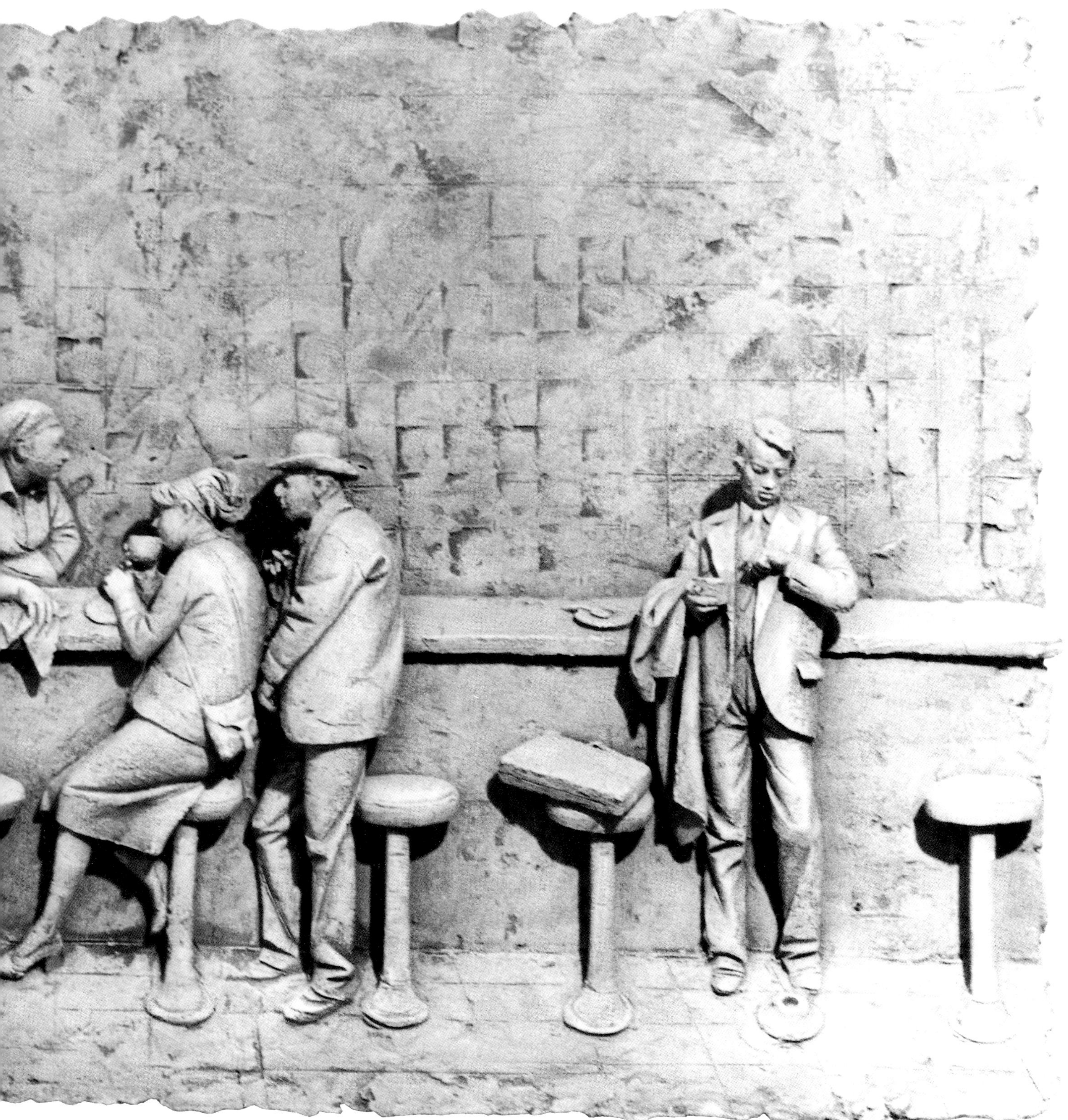

Turkish Bath, 1984–85, terra-cotta, 11 x 34 x 9 inches. Forum Gallery, New York.

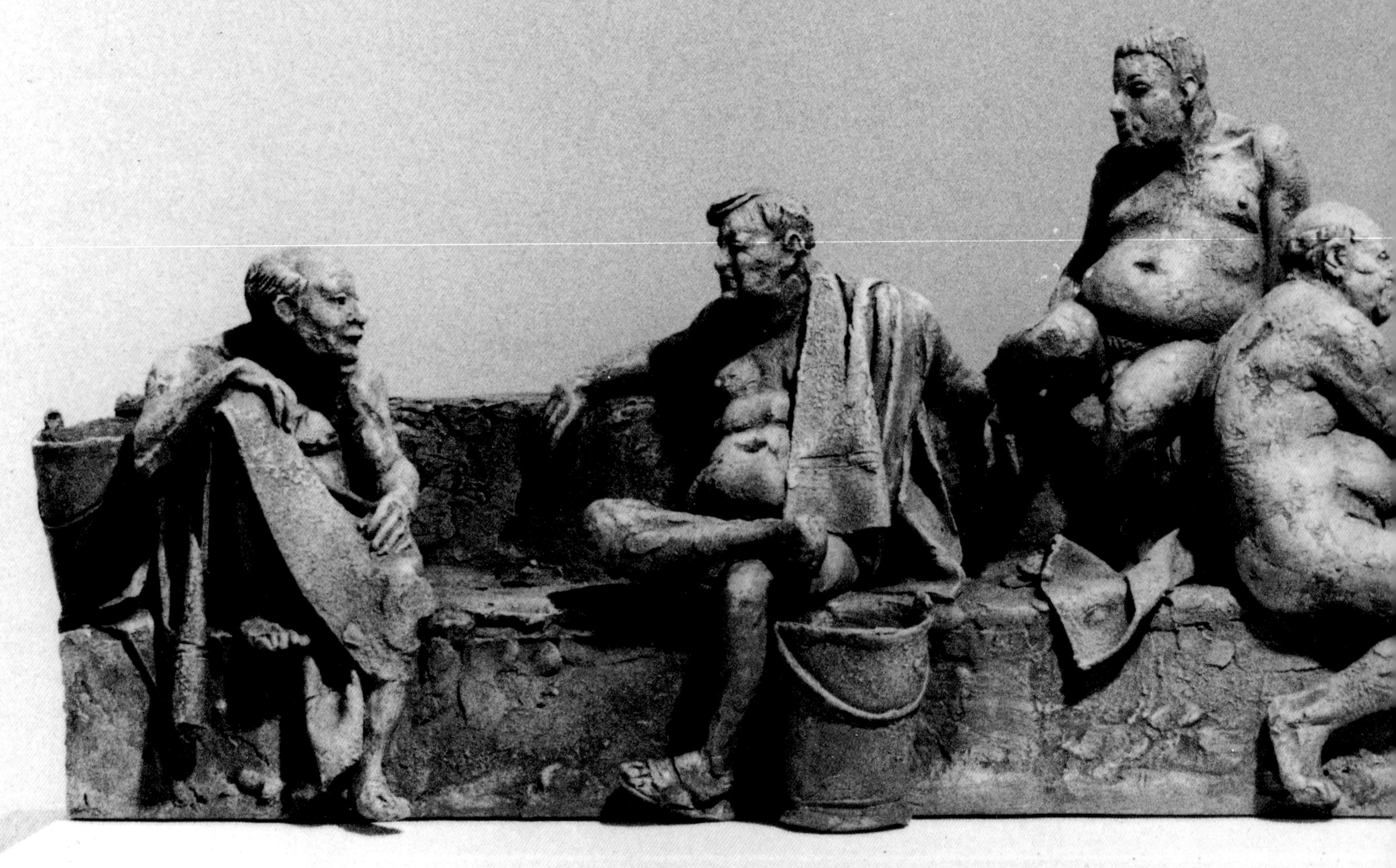

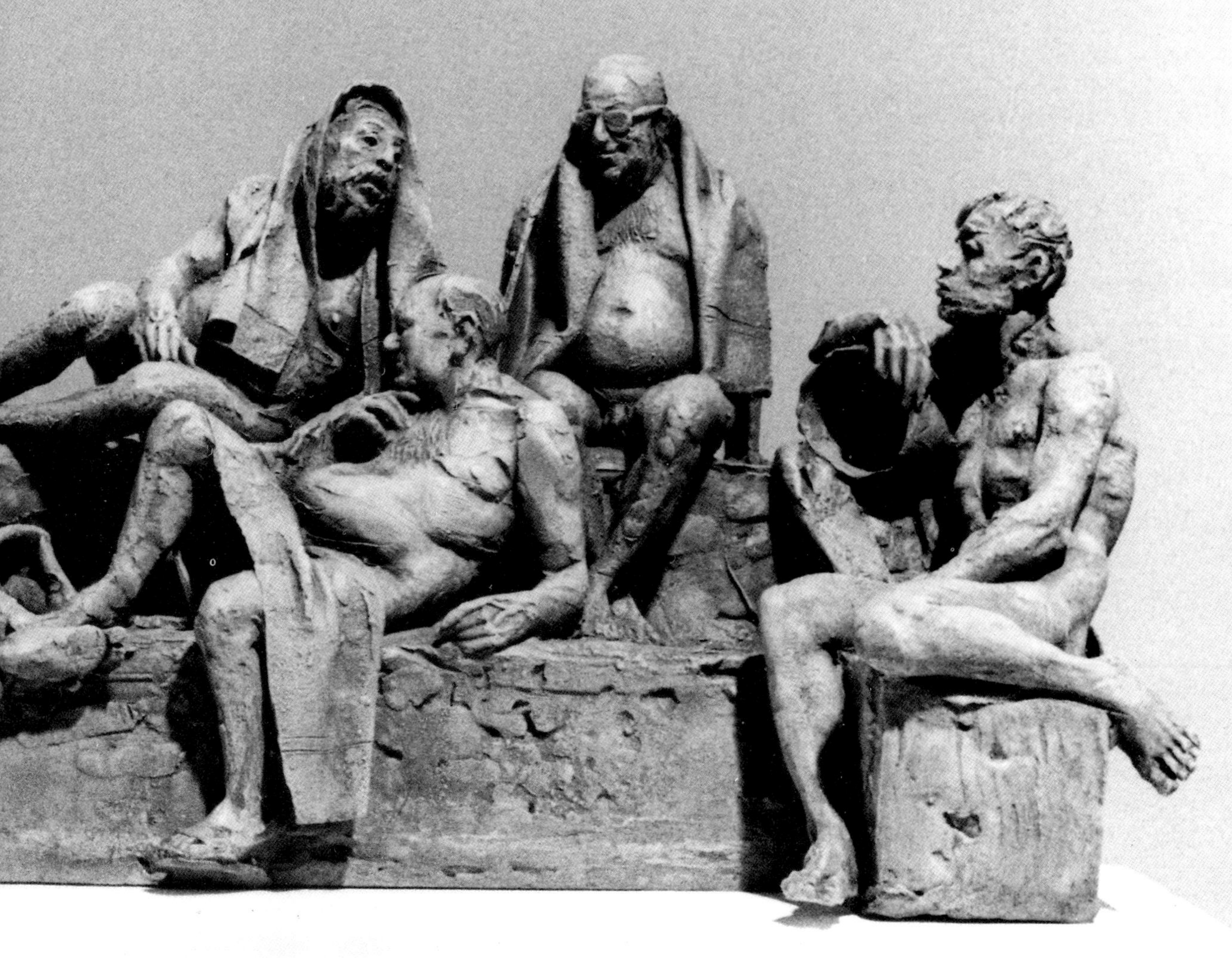

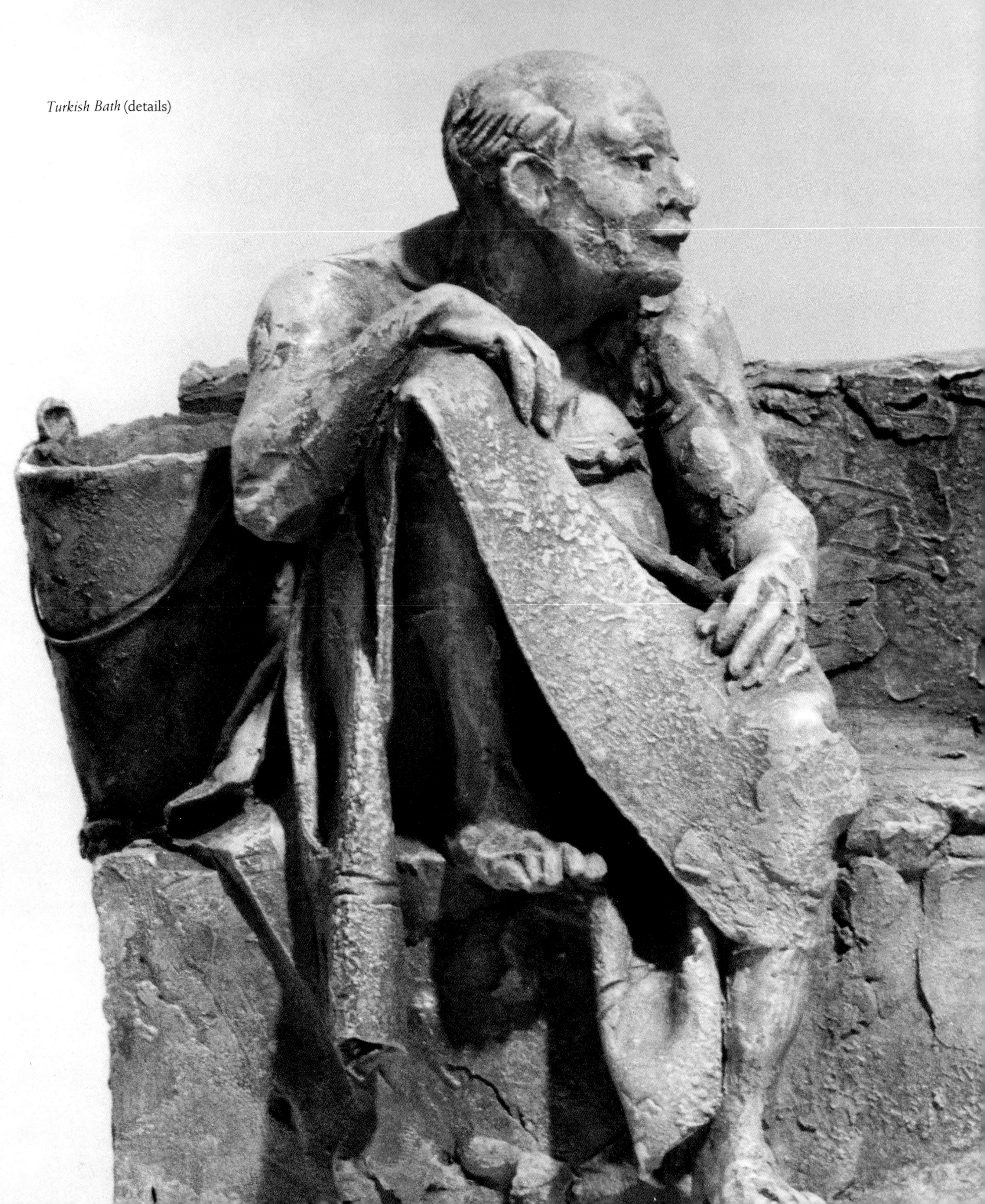

Turkish Bath (details)

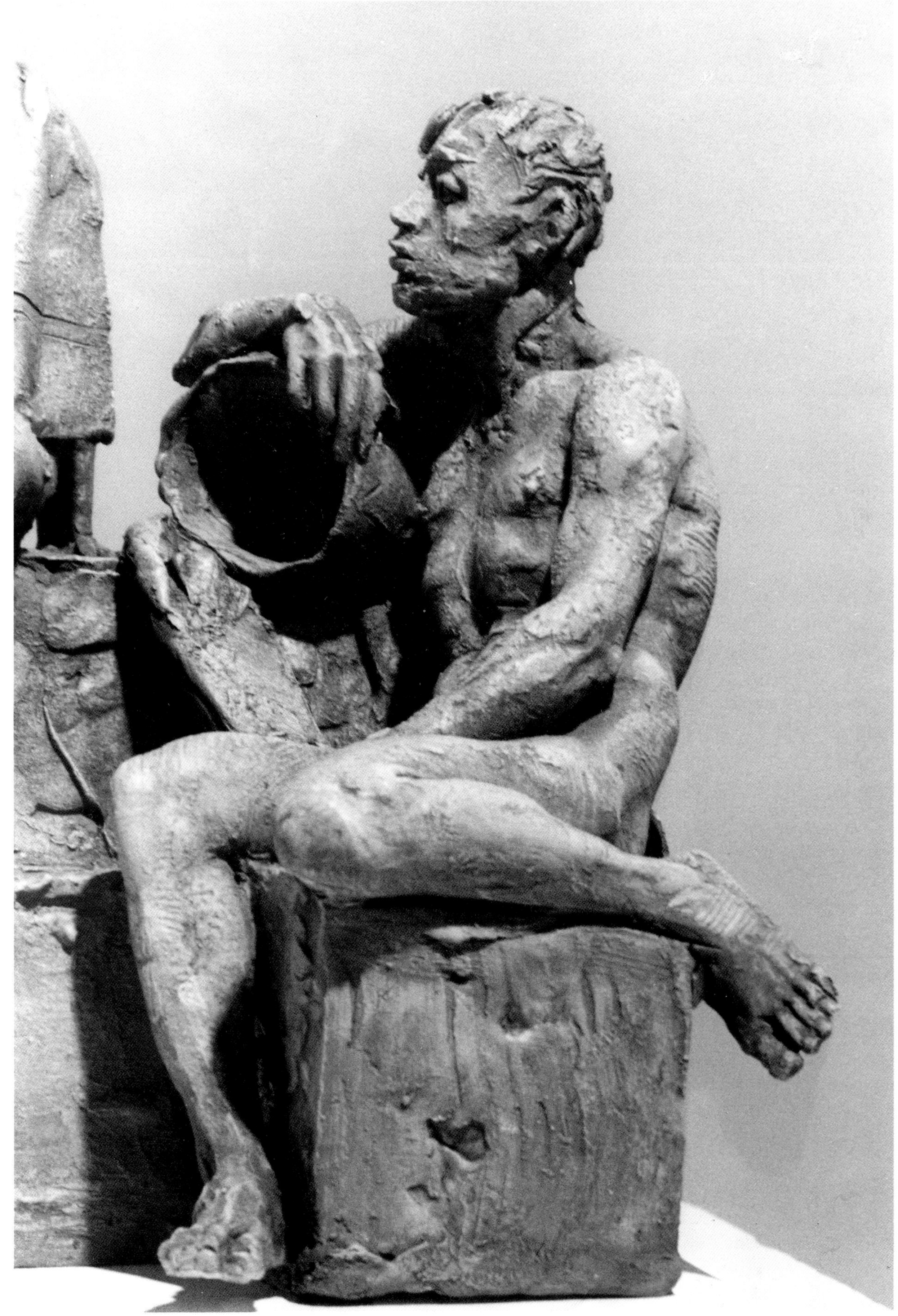

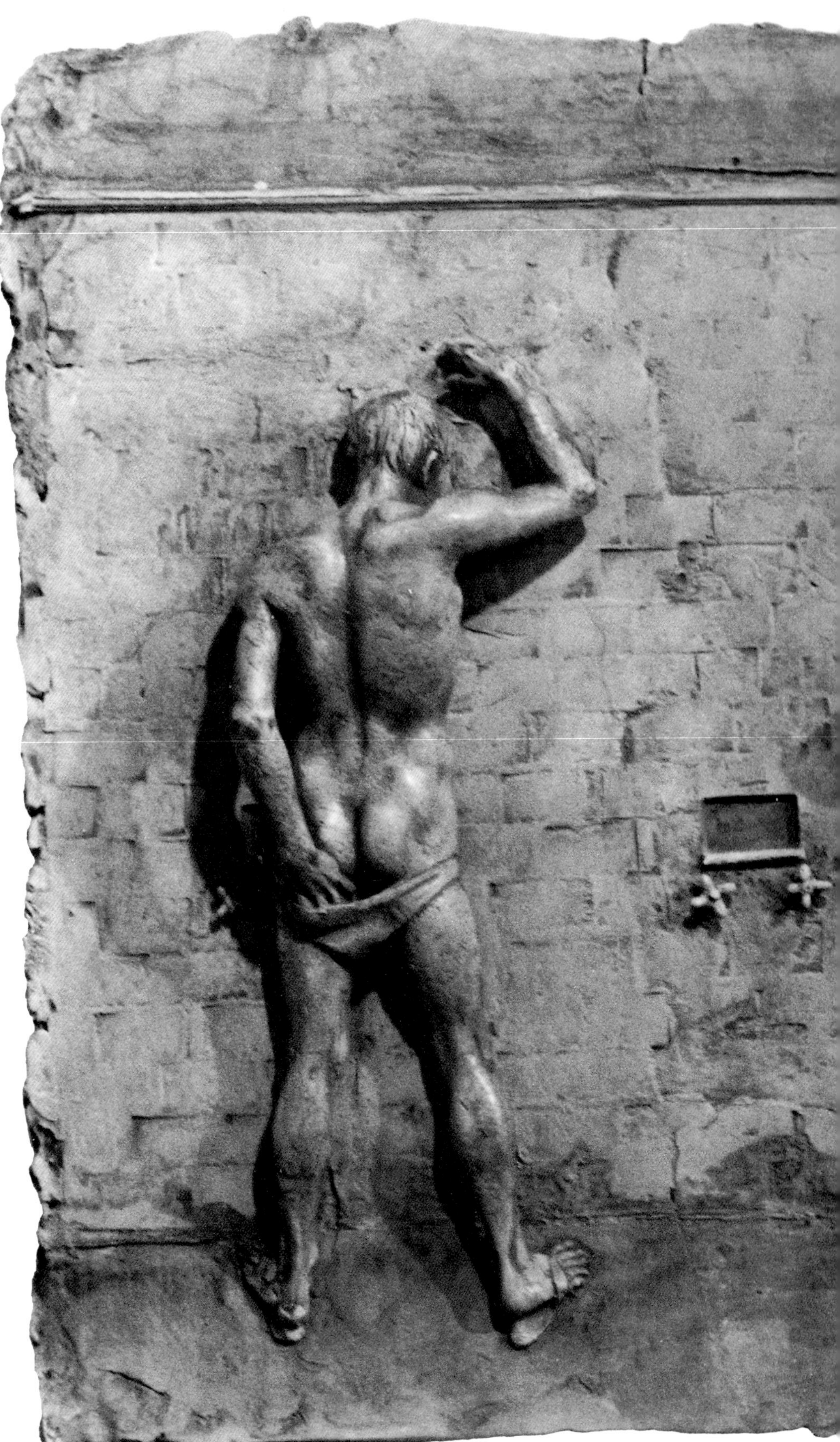

Shower, 1984–85, terra-cotta relief, 22 x 35 inches. Forum Gallery, New York.

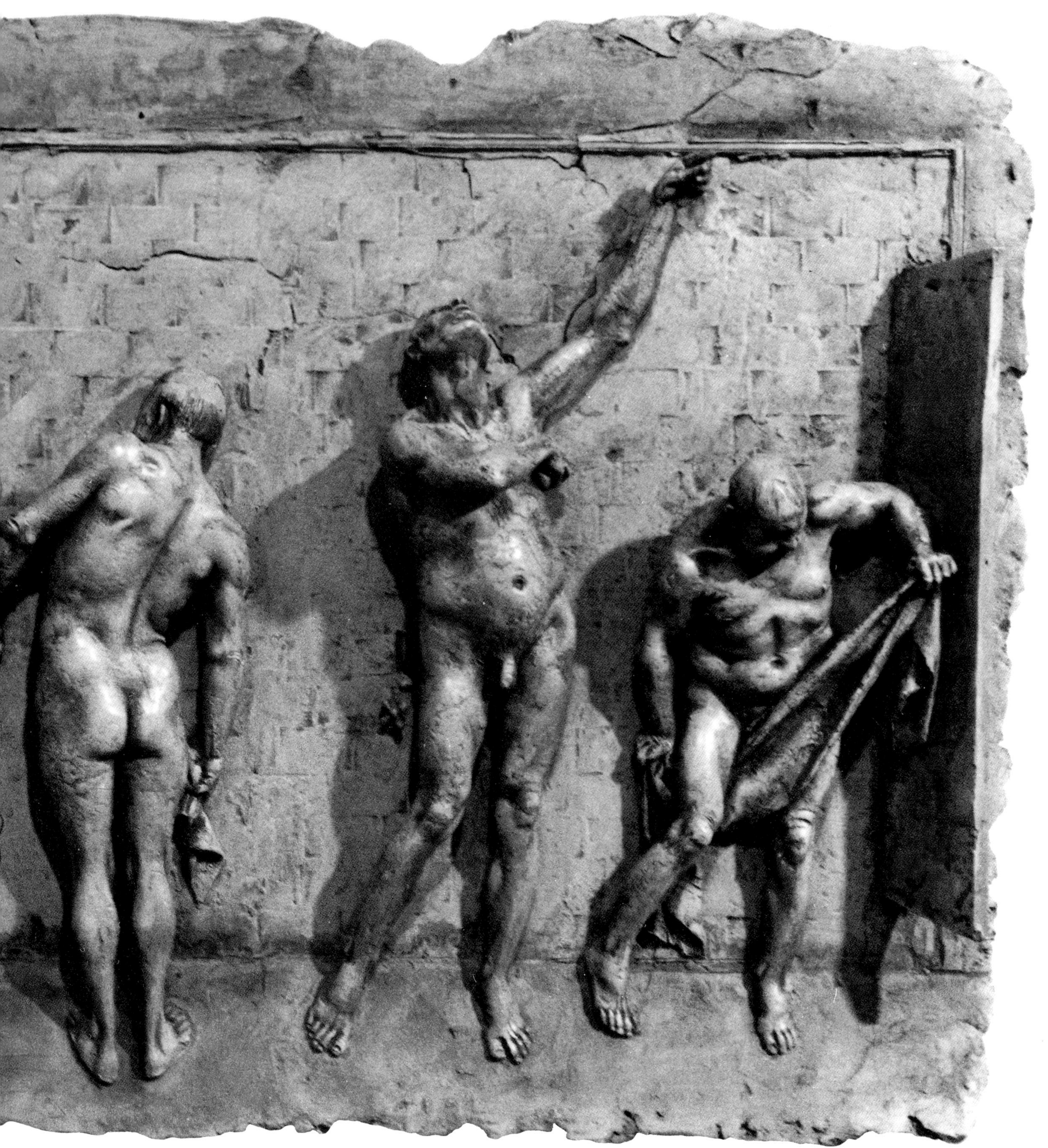

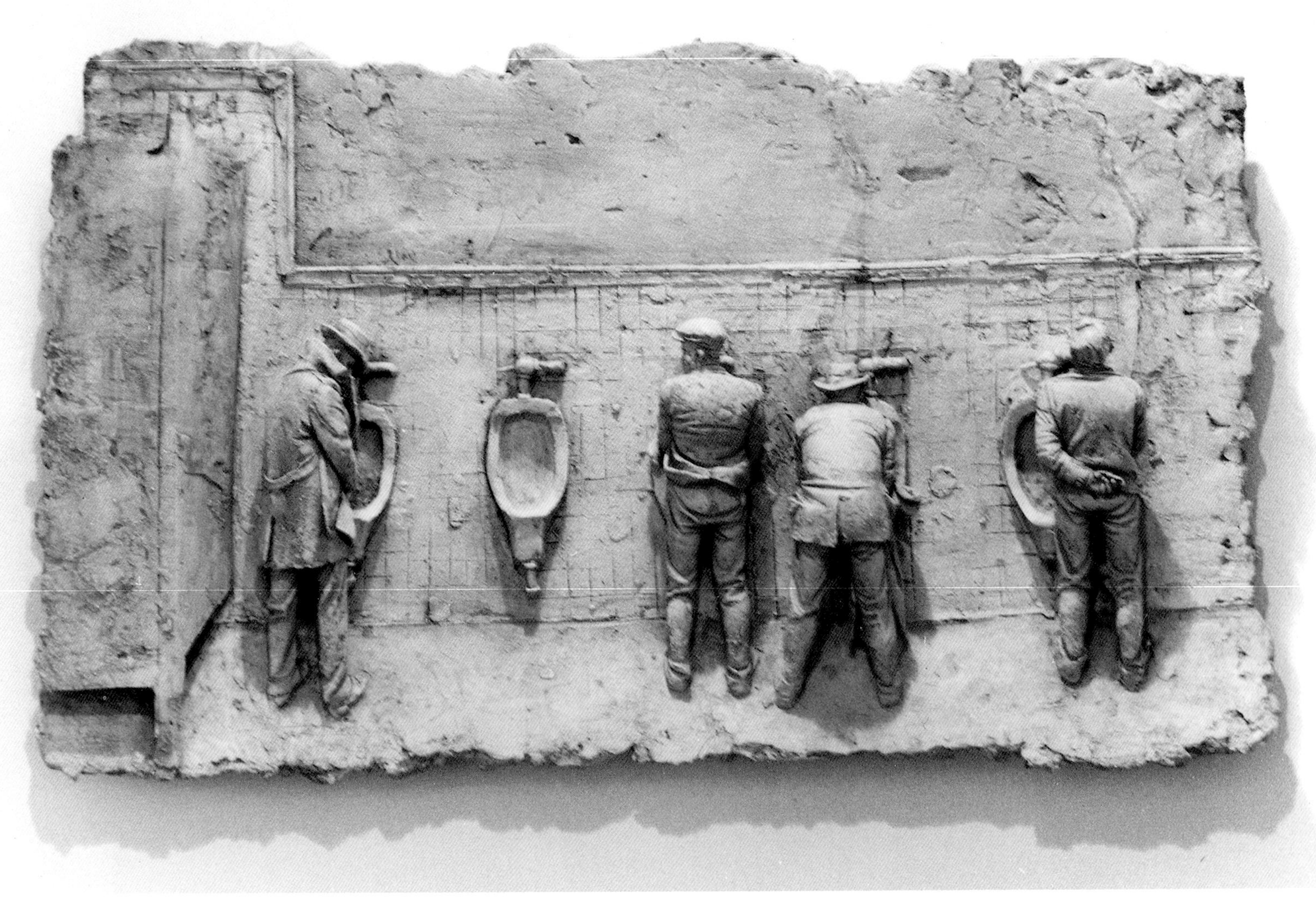

Men's Room, 1984–85, terra-cotta relief,
7 x 29 inches. Forum Gallery, New York.

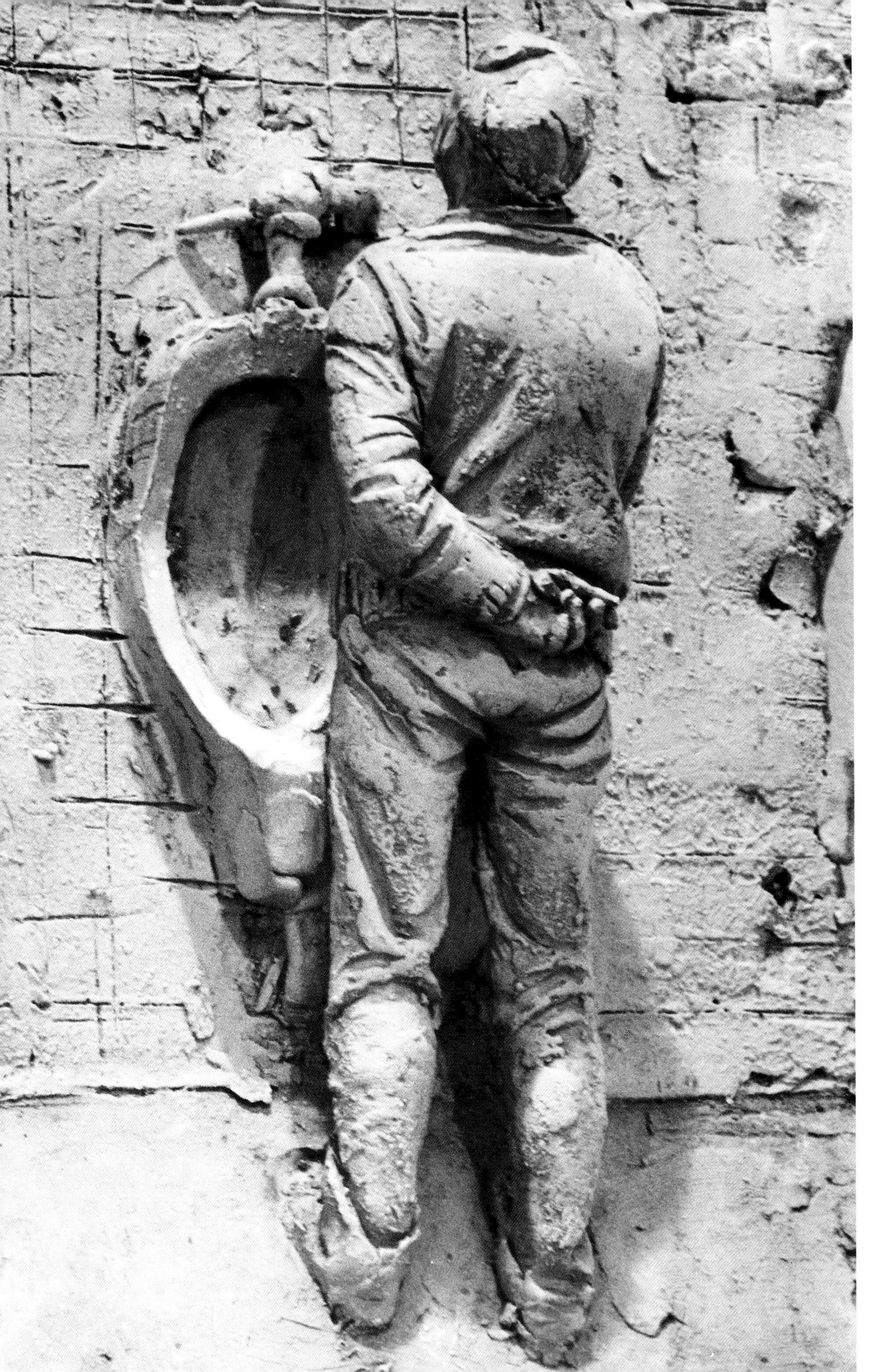

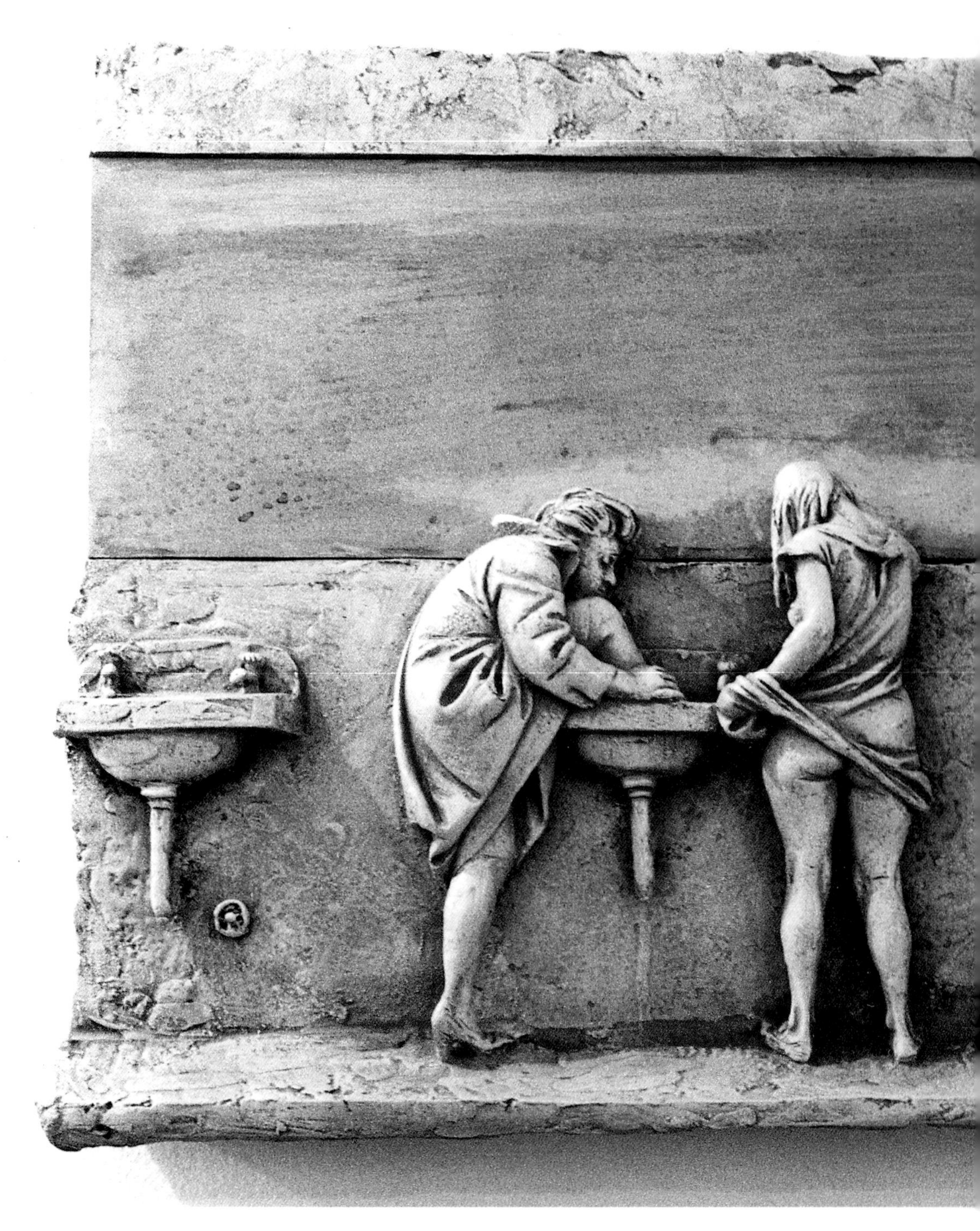

Women's Rest Room, 1984–85, bronze relief, 15½ x 27 inches. Collection of Judith Peck, Mahwah, New Jersey.

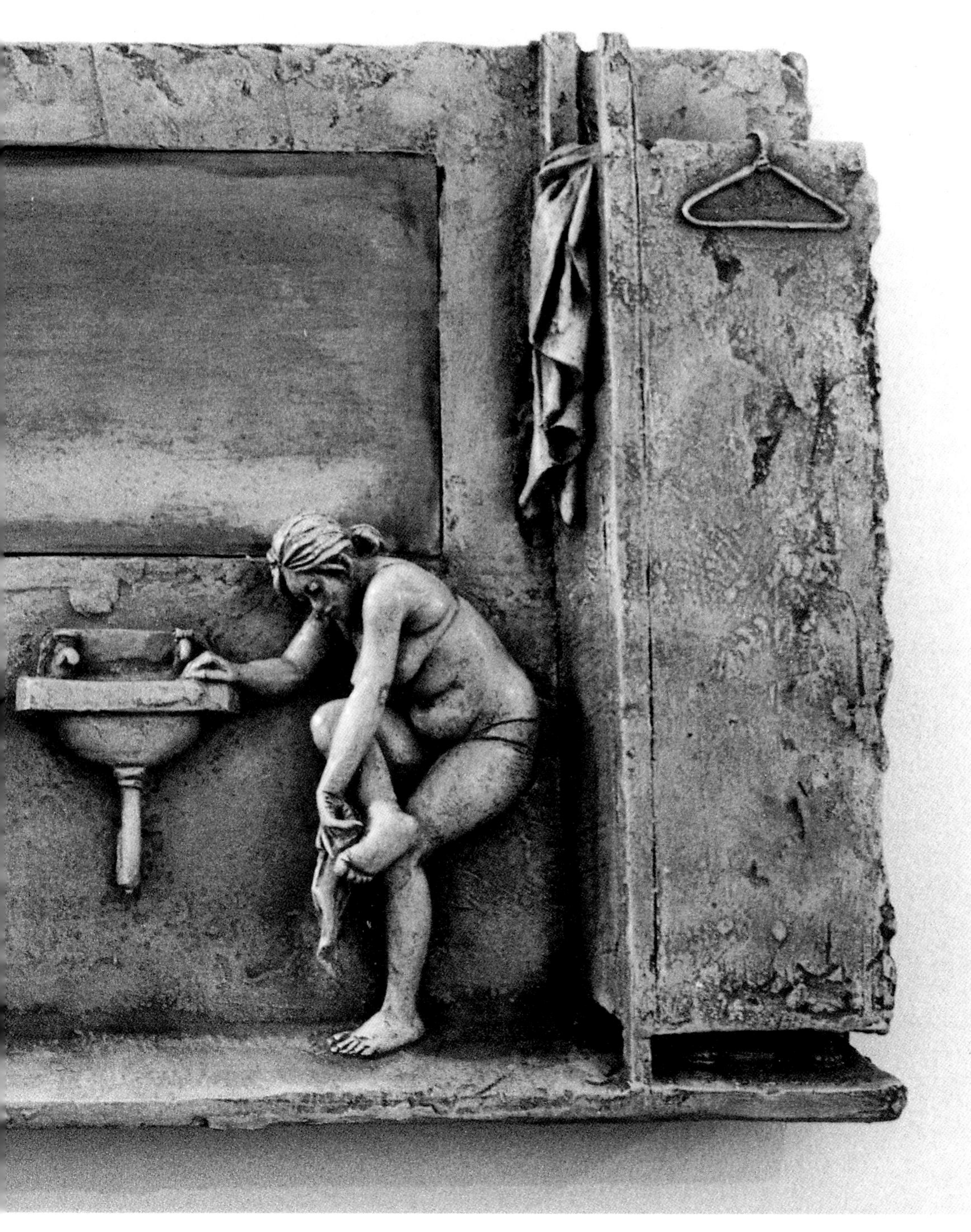

Women's Rest Room (details) ▸

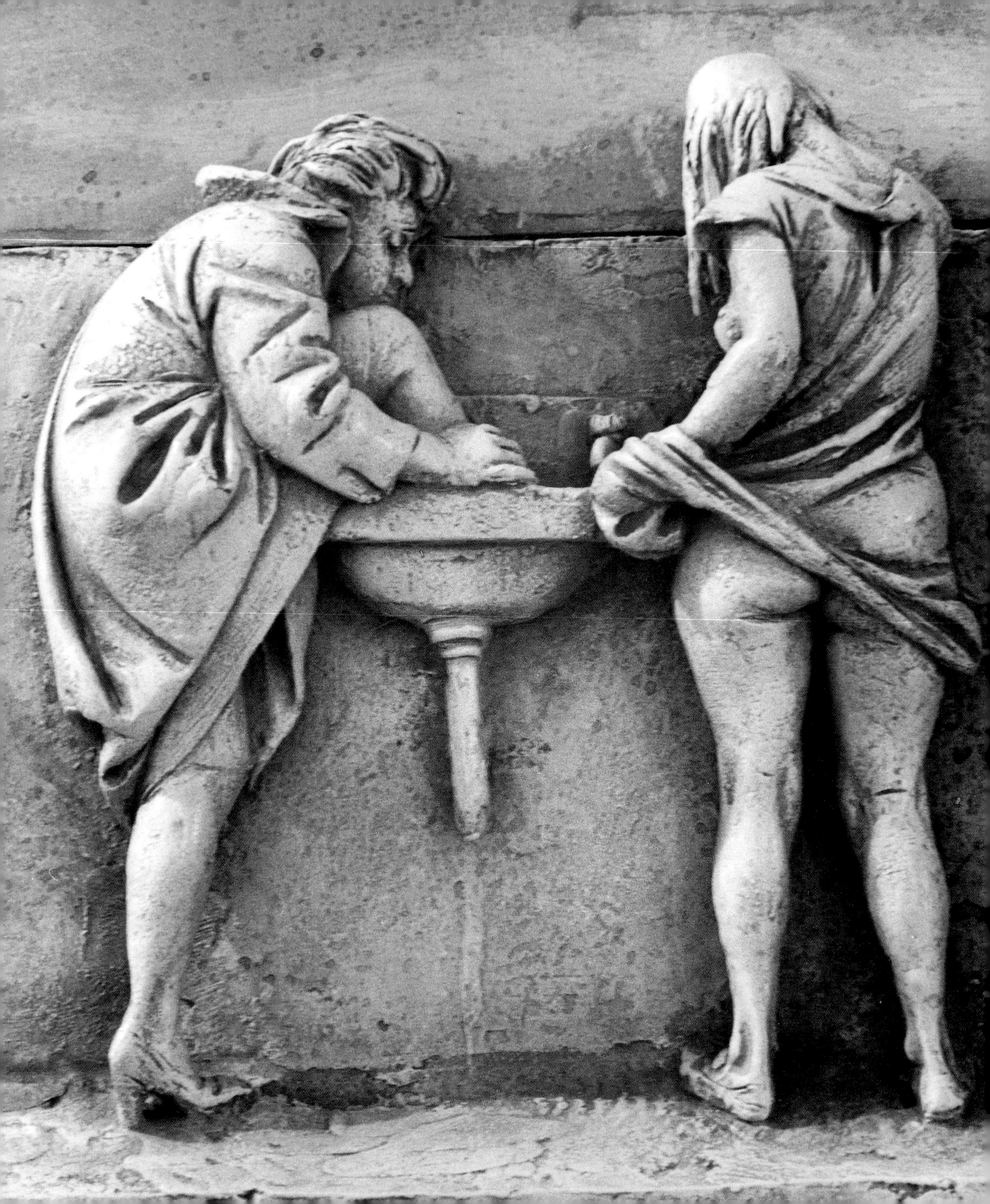

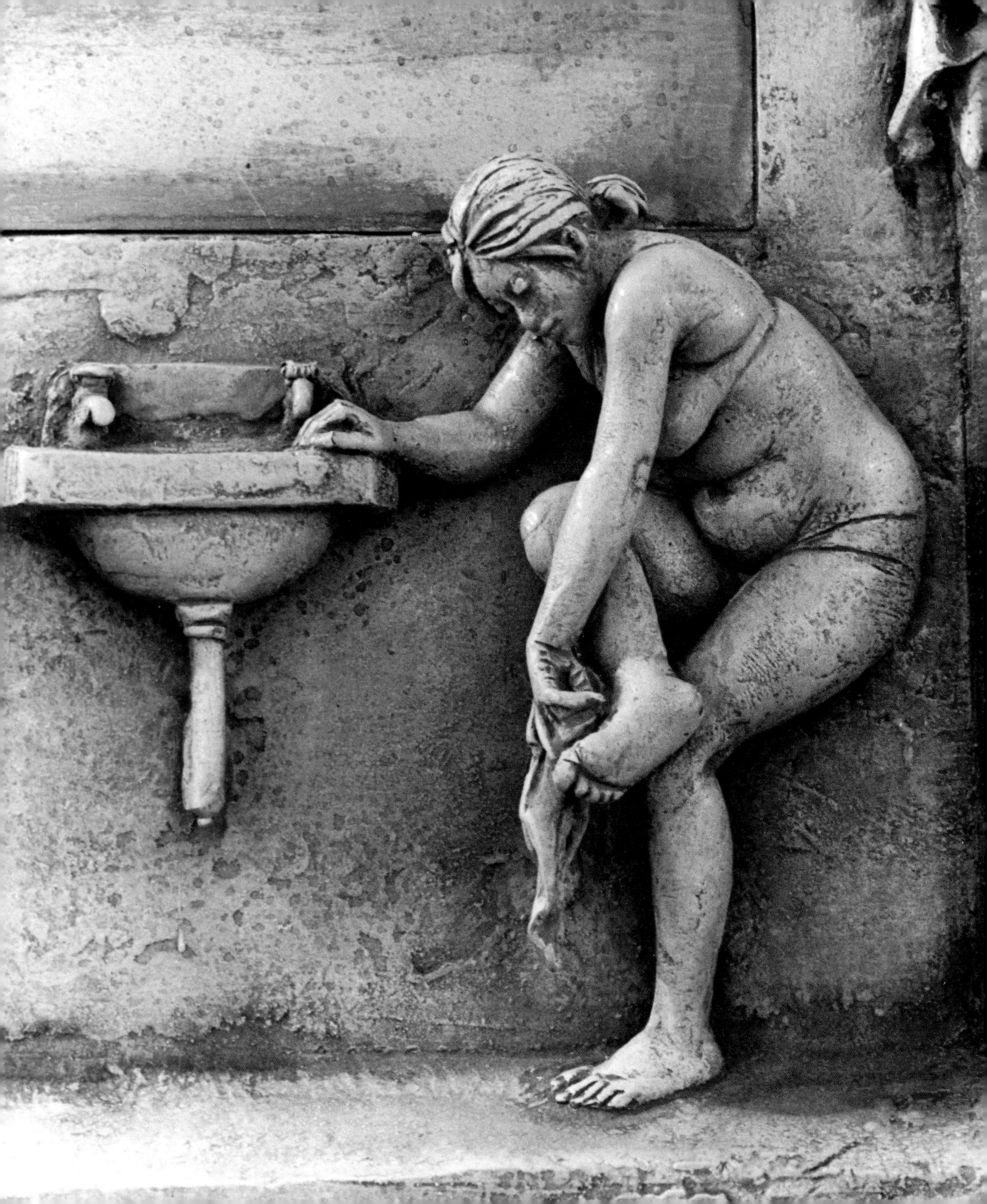

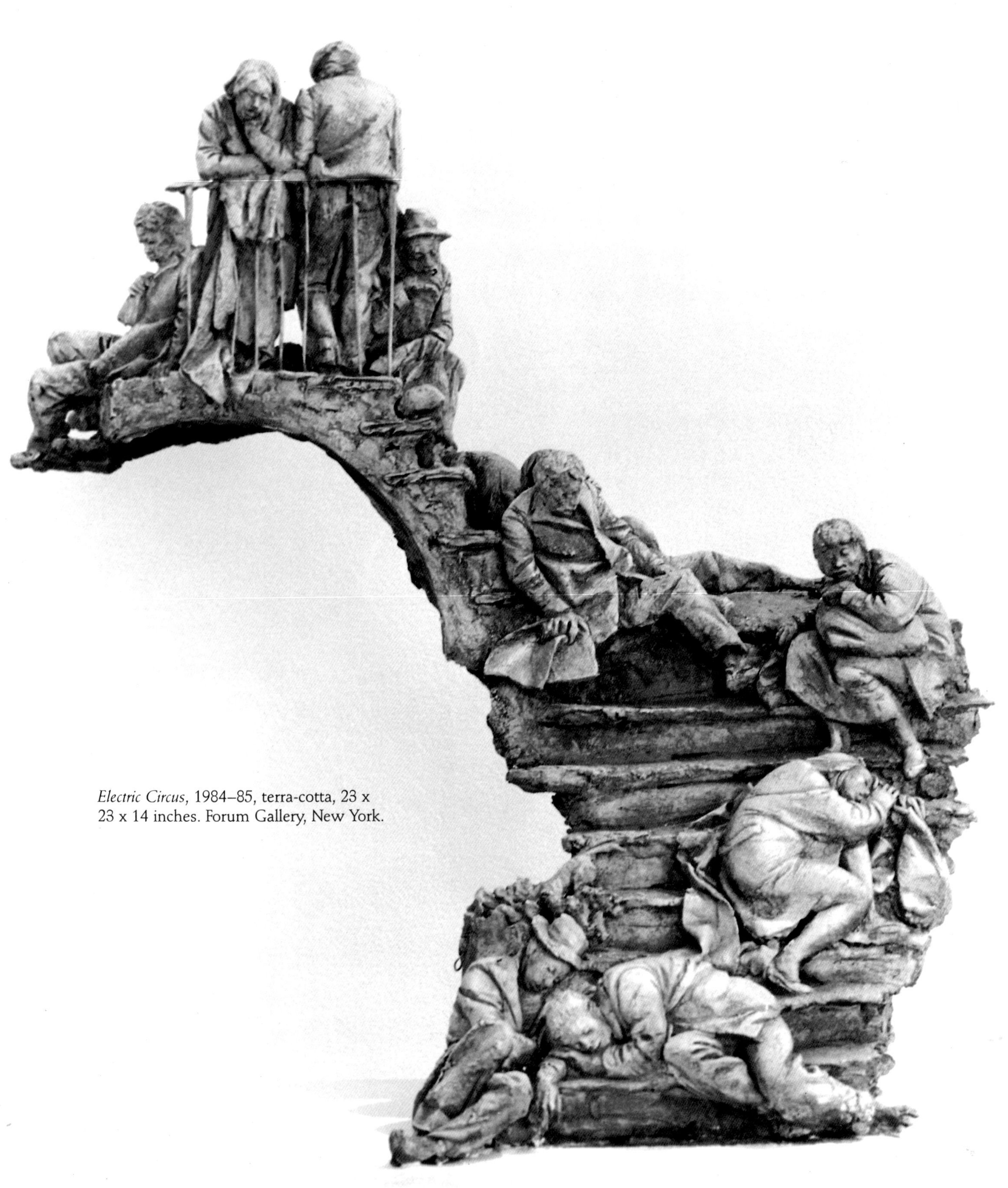

Electric Circus, 1984–85, terra-cotta, 23 x 23 x 14 inches. Forum Gallery, New York.

CLASSICAL AND RELIGIOUS THEMES

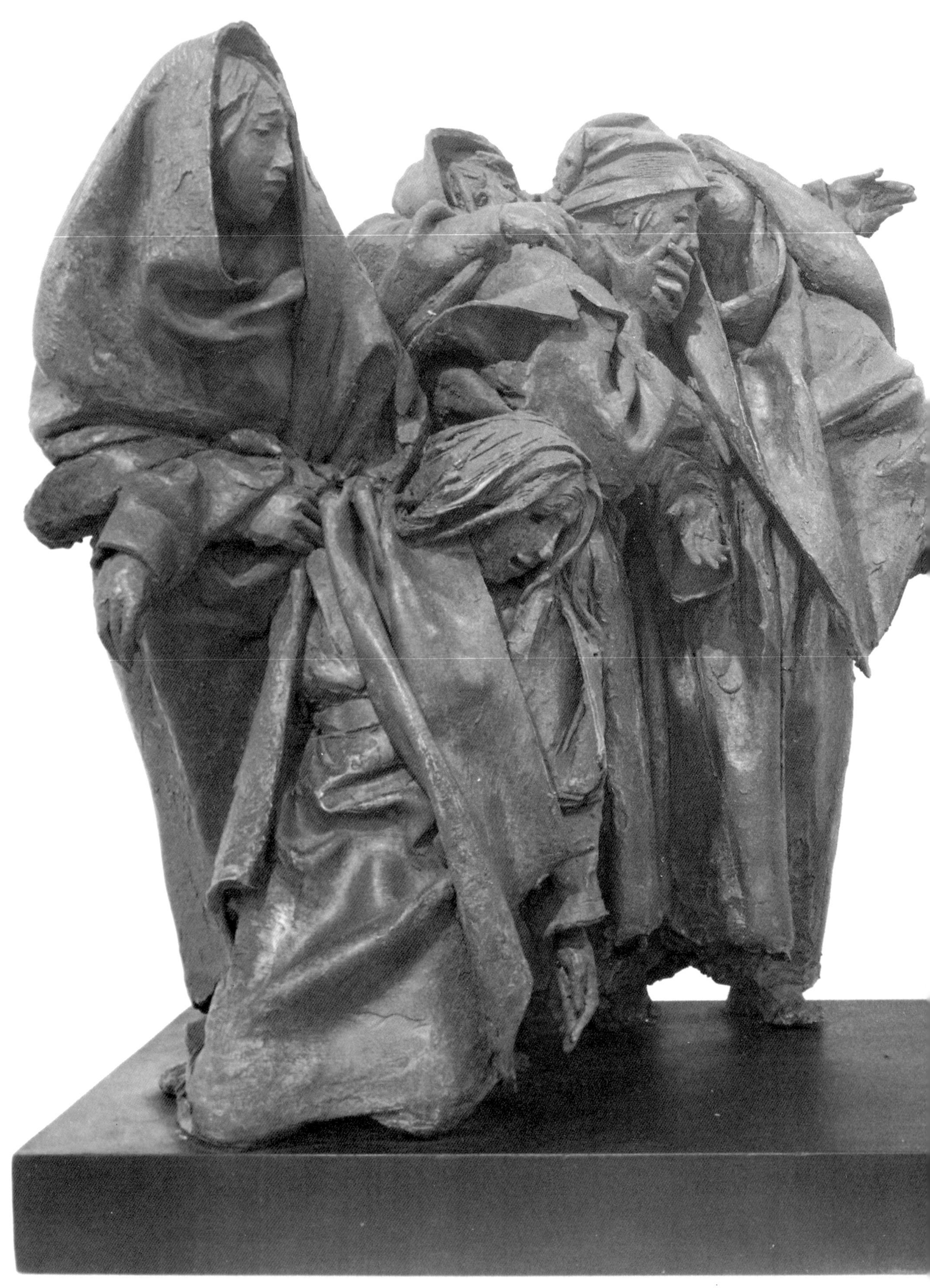

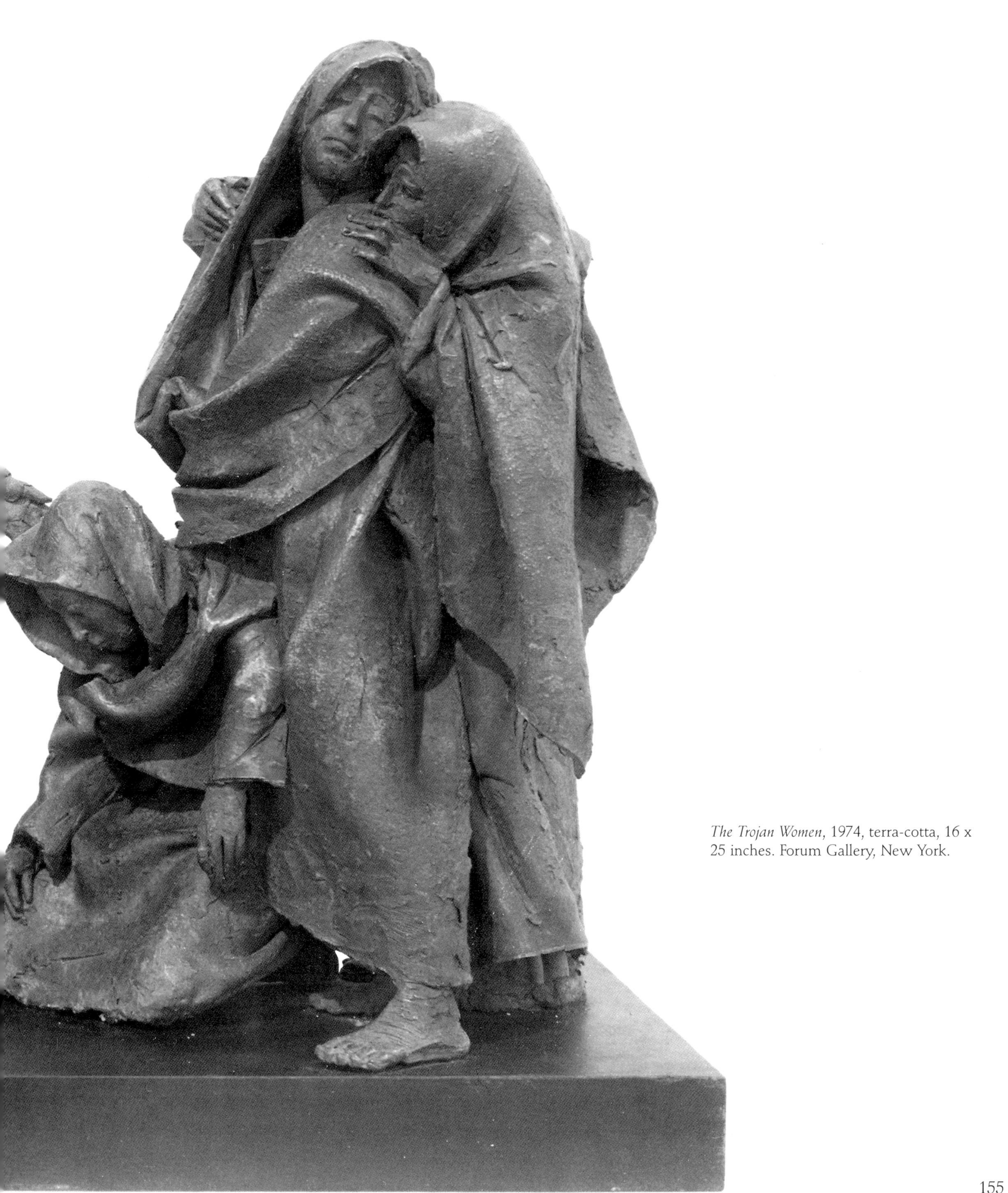

The Trojan Women, 1974, terra-cotta, 16 x 25 inches. Forum Gallery, New York.

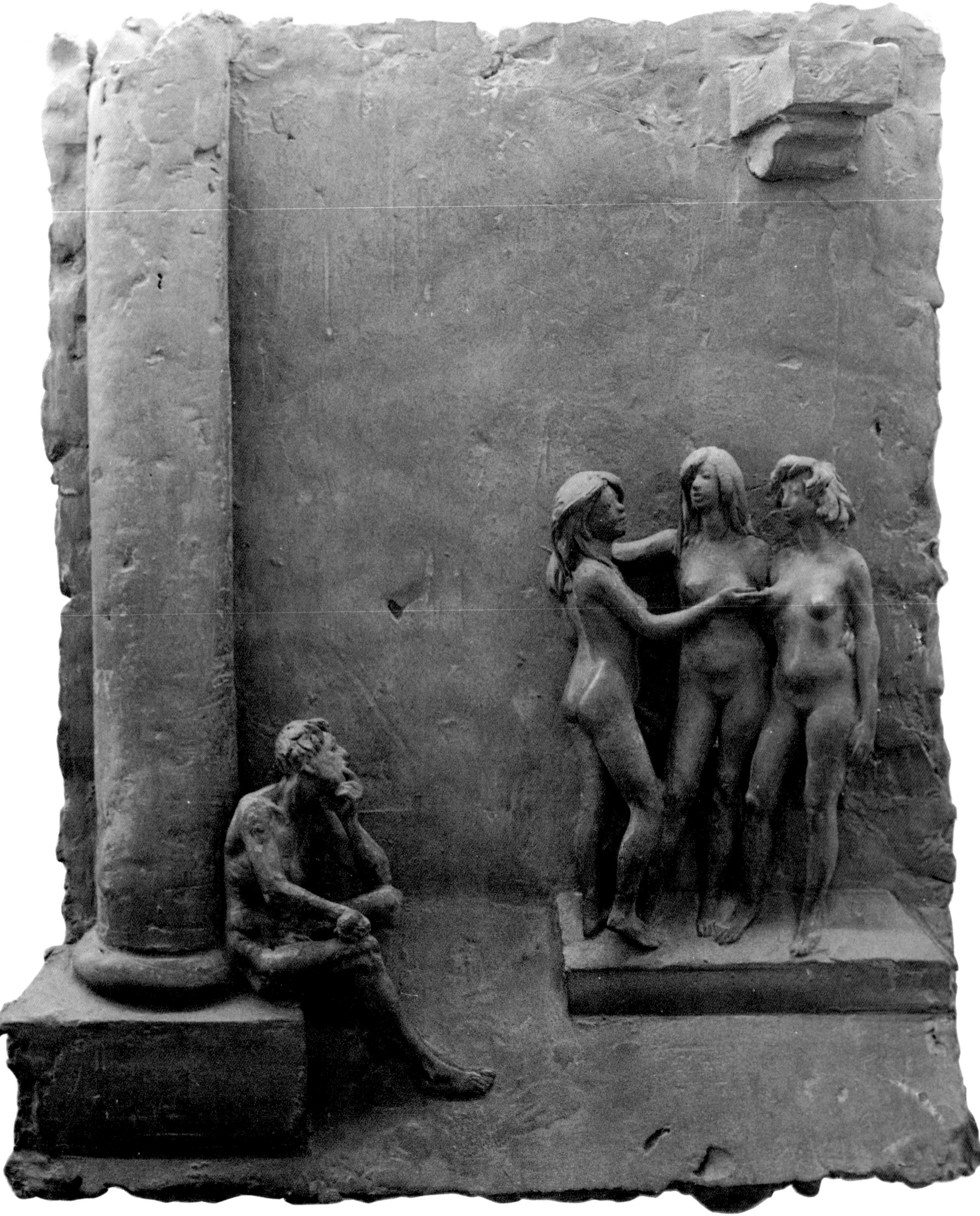

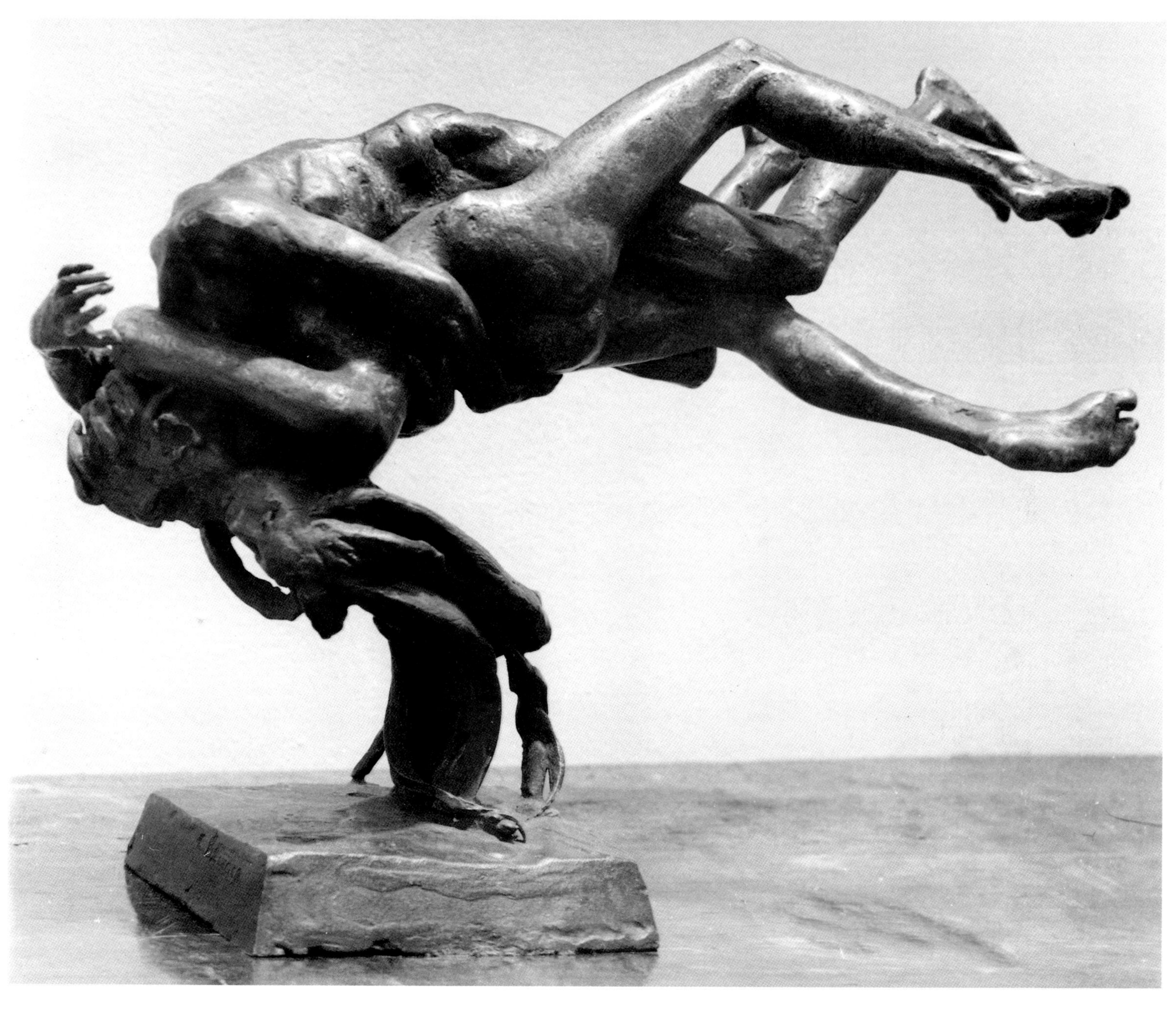

Paolo and Francesca, 1983, bronze, 10 x 13 x 7 inches. Forum Gallery, New York.

Judgment of Paris, 1982, terra-cotta relief, 25 x 18 inches. Collection of Laura and David Finn, New York.

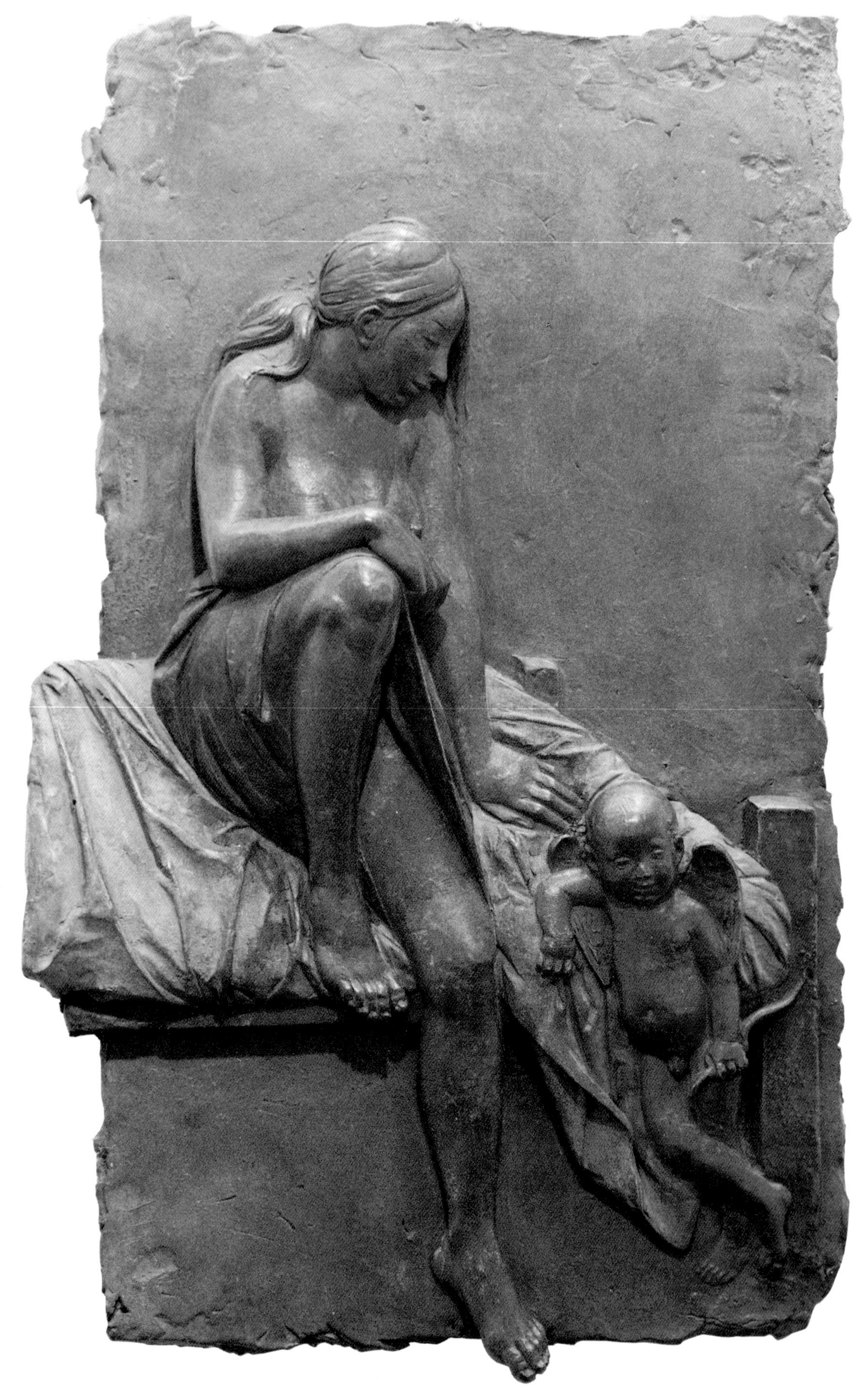

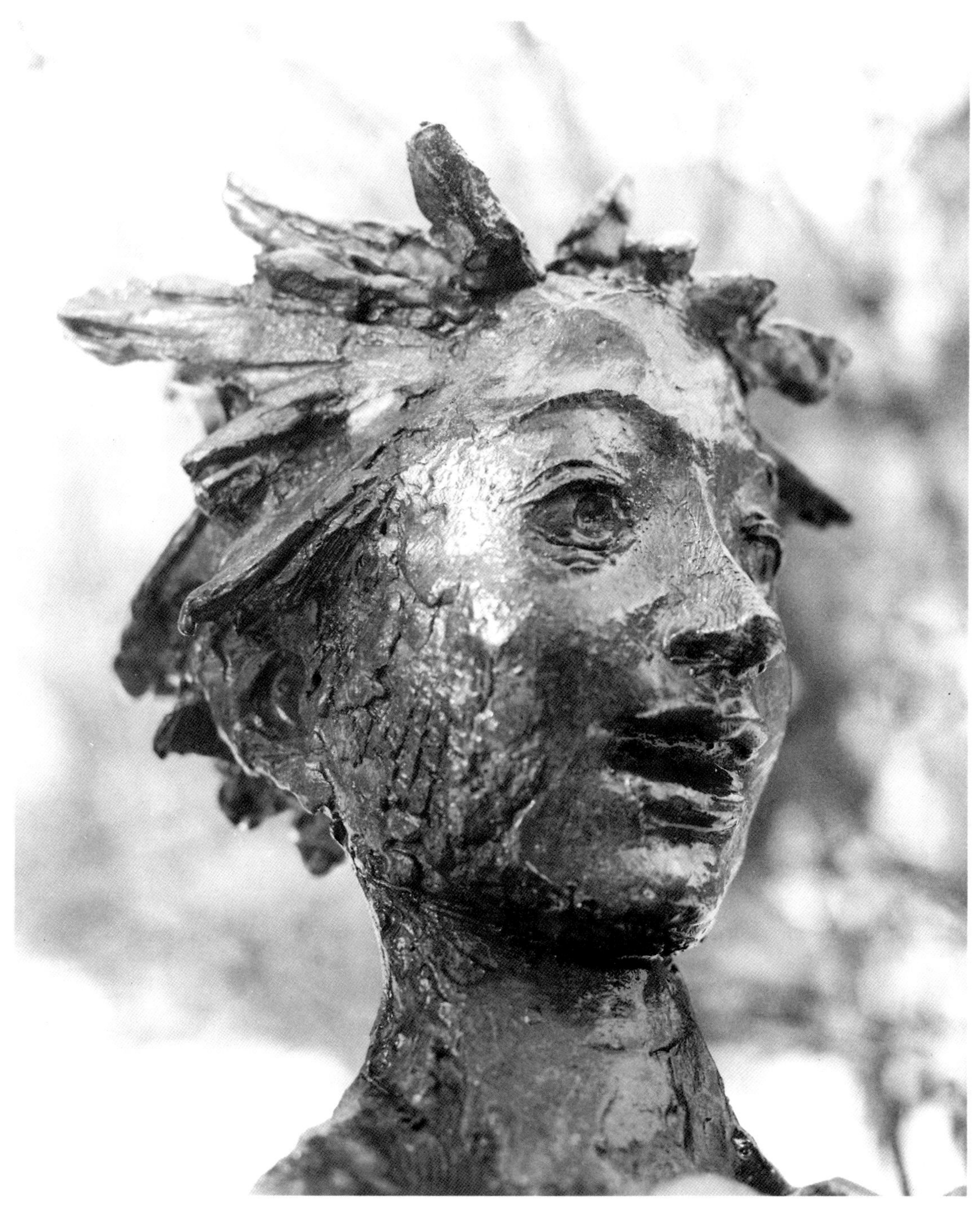

Boy with Goat (detail), 1961, bronze, 5 feet high. Collection of Laura and David Finn, New York.

Valentine's Day, 1983, terra-cotta relief, 24 x 17 inches. Forum Gallery, New York.

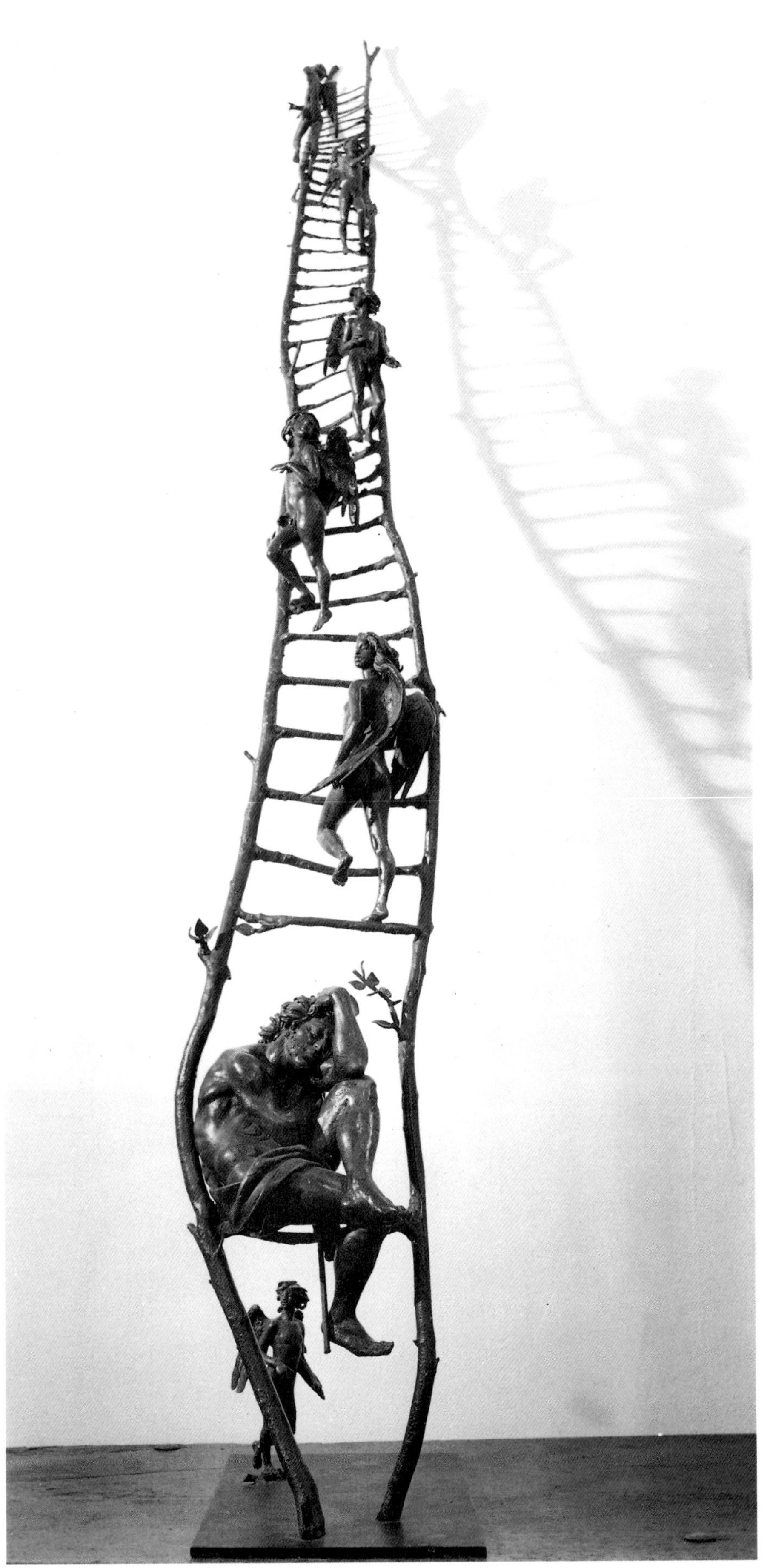

Jacob's Ladder, 1978, bronze, 85 inches high (including base). Forum Gallery, New York.

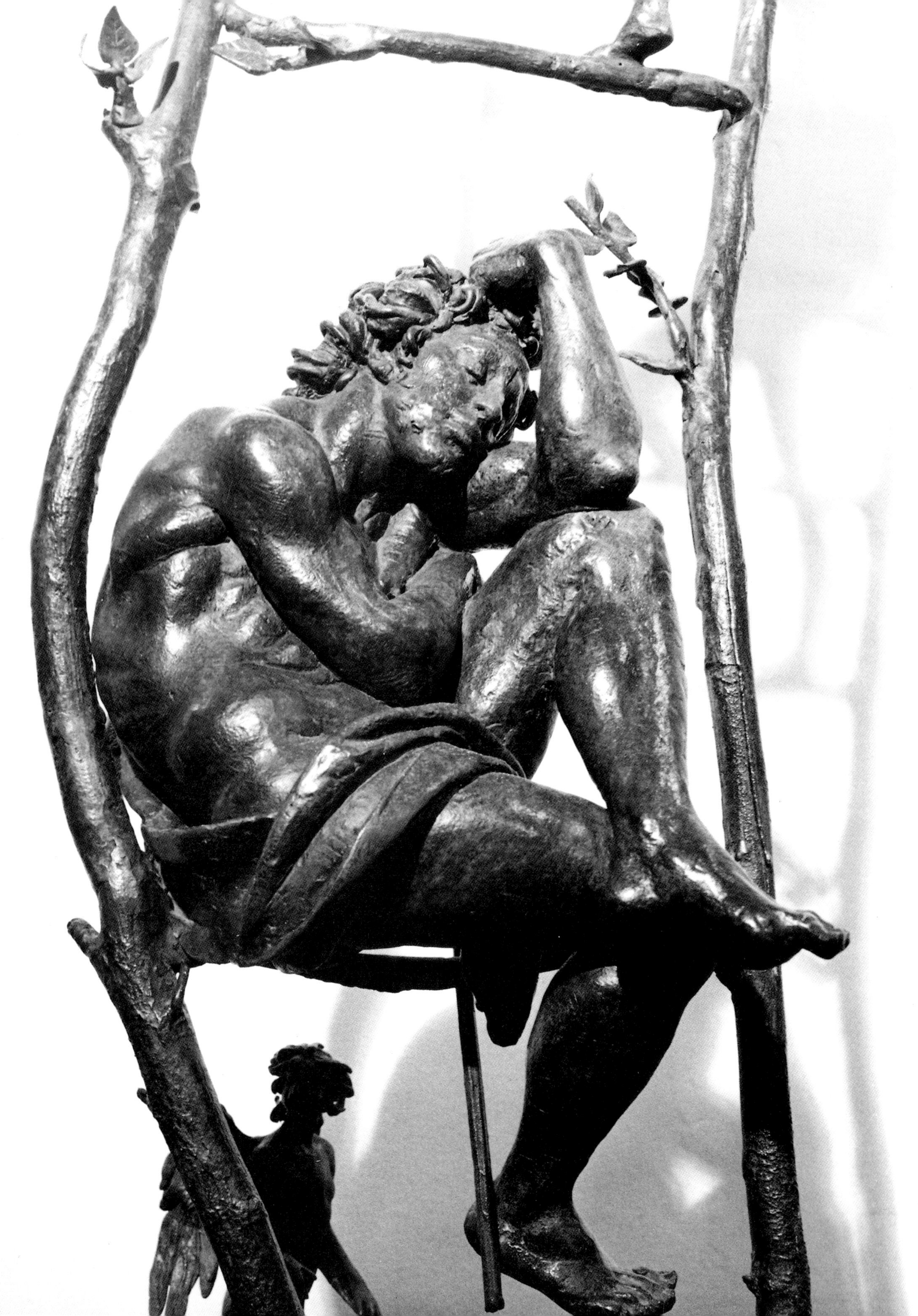

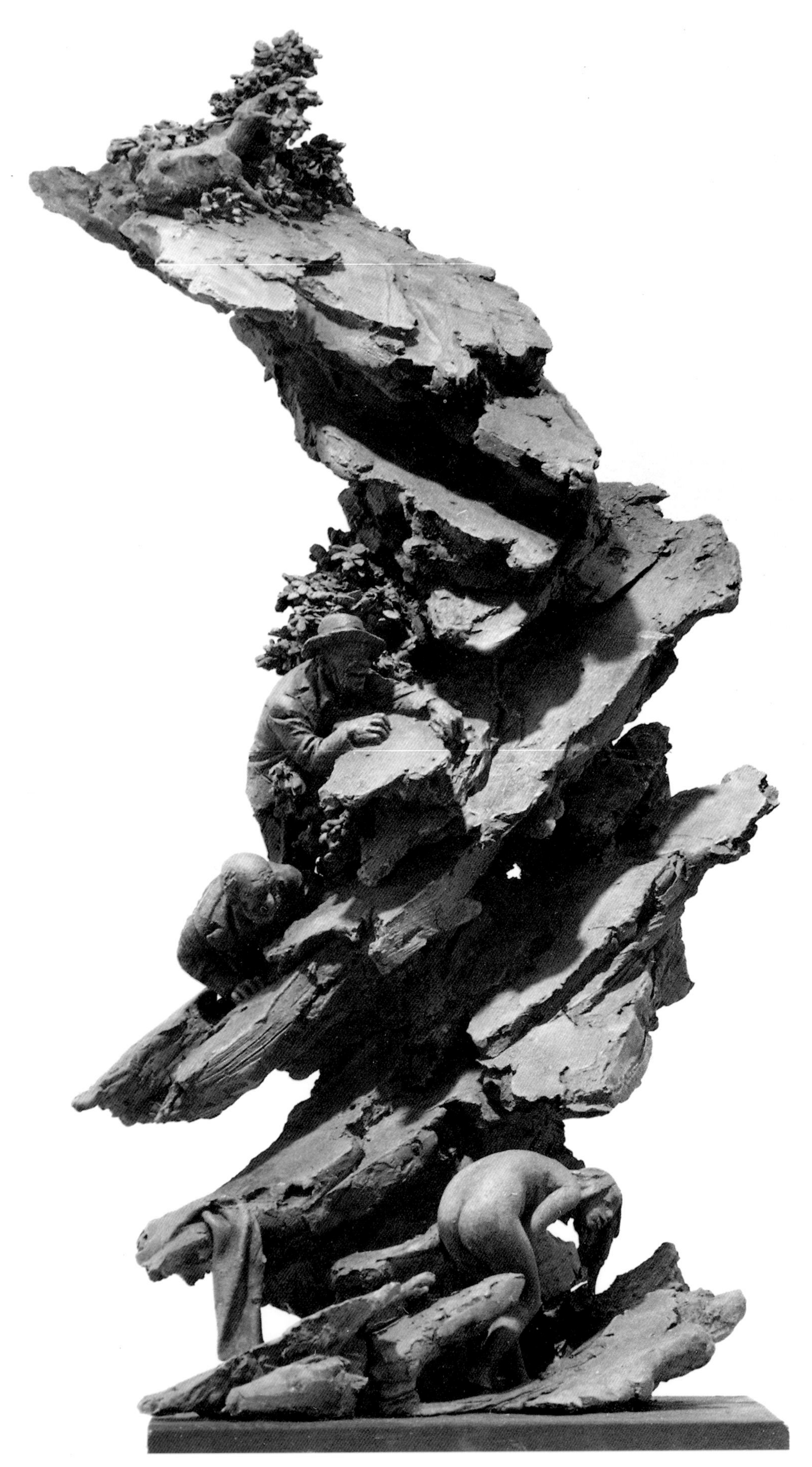

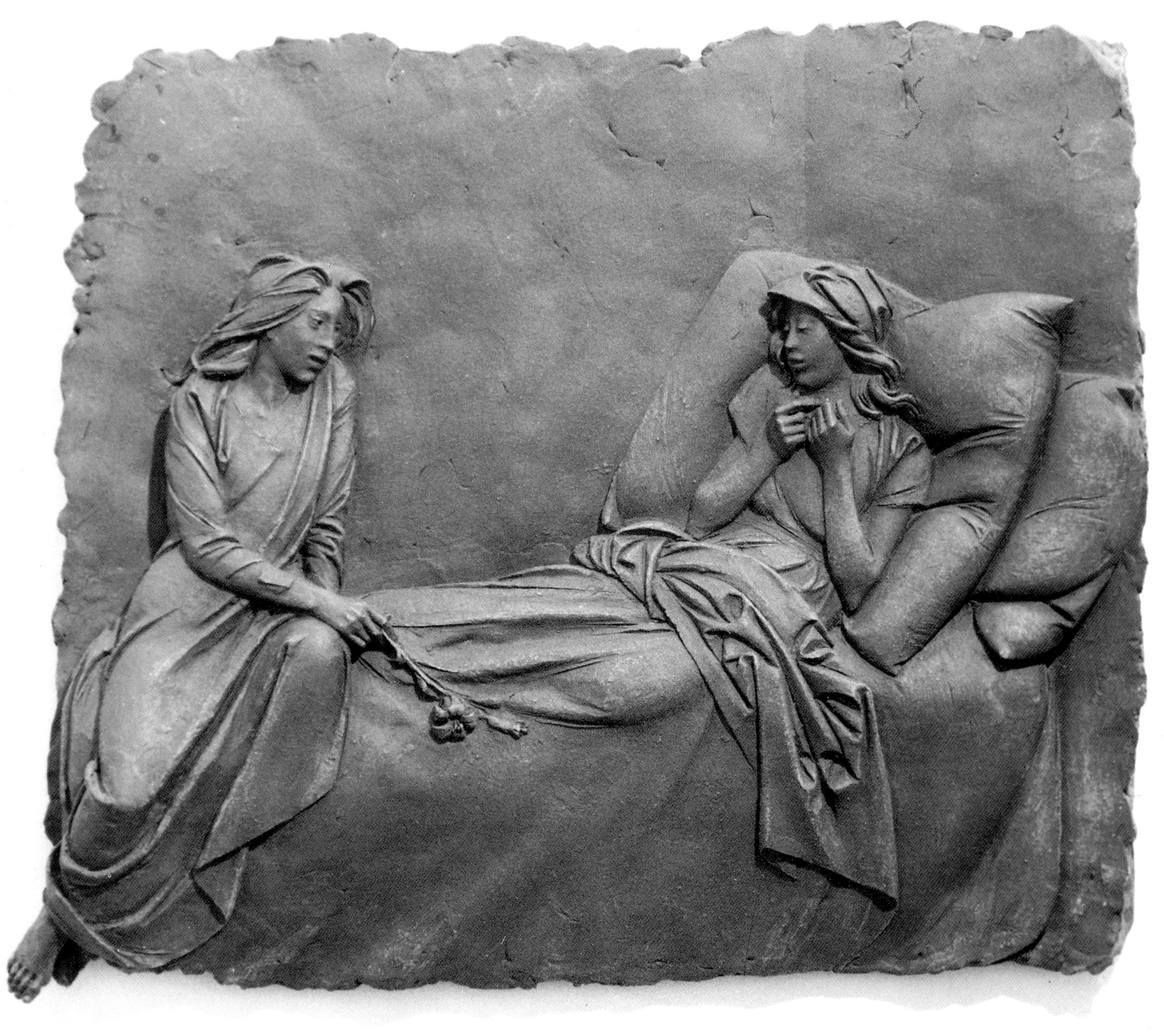

Annunciation, 1980, terra-cotta relief, 16 x 20 inches. Forum Gallery, New York.

Susannah and the Elders, 1980, terra-cotta, 27 x 20 x 14 inches. Forum Gallery, New York.

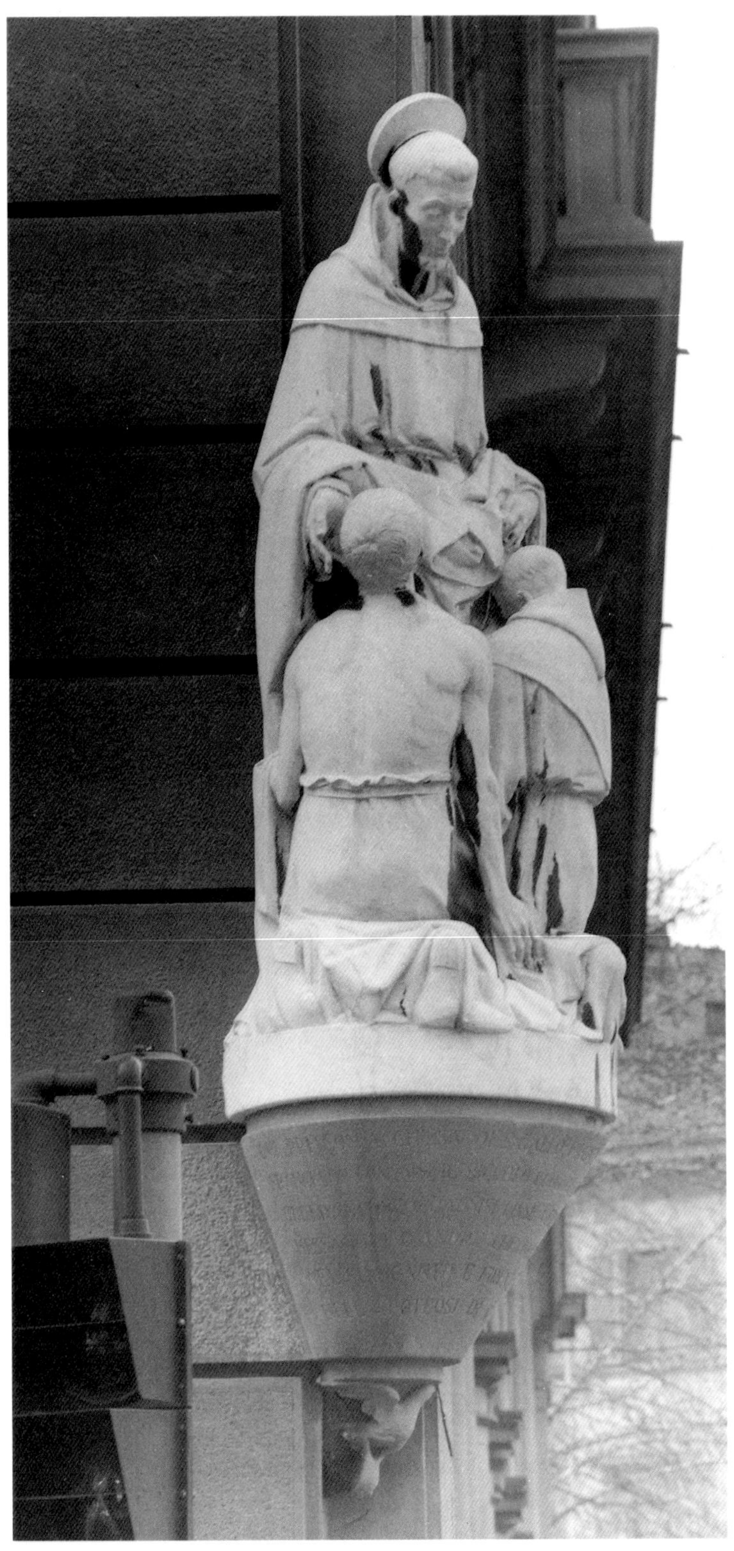

Saint Francis of Assisi, 1956, marble, life-size. Florence. (See also colorplate, page 18.)

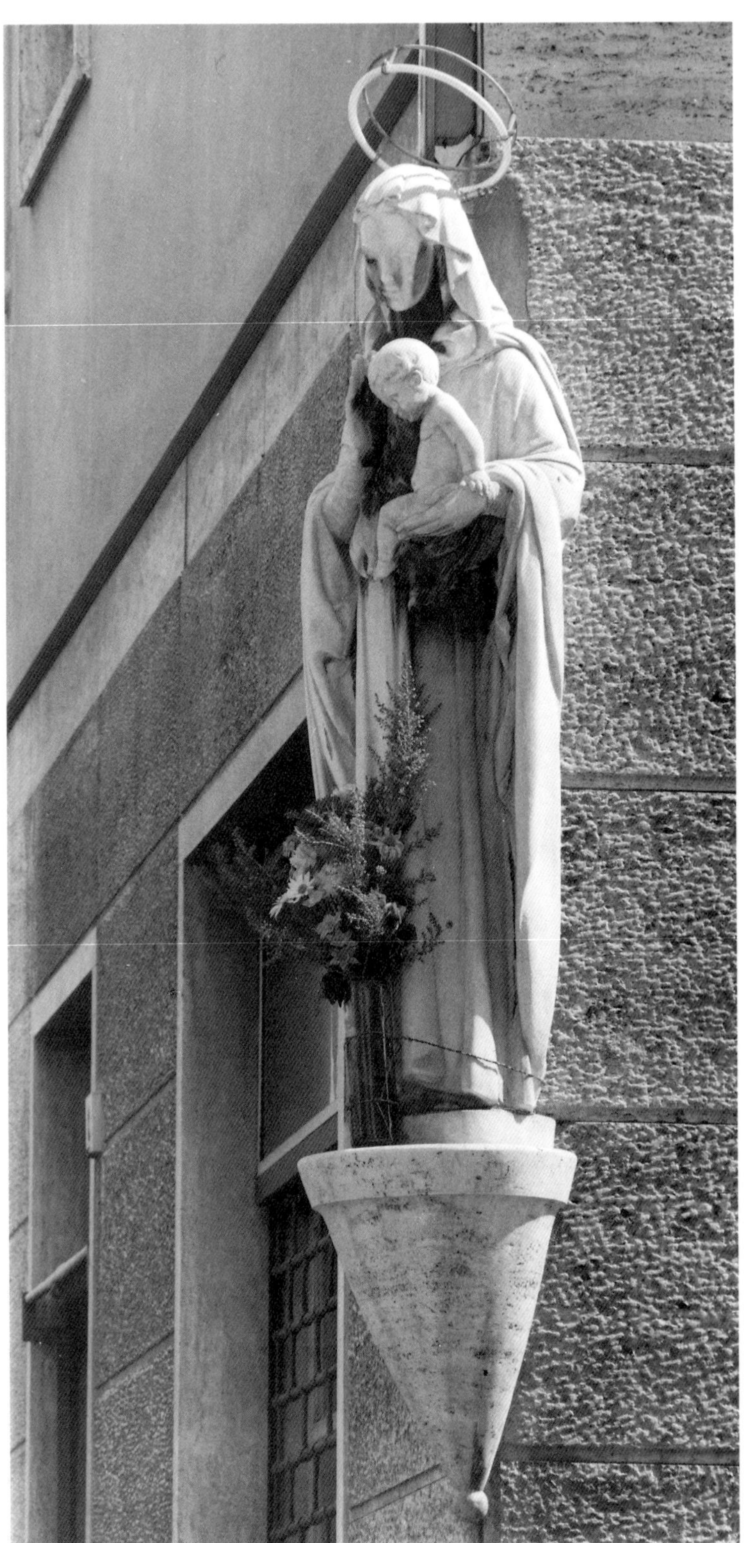

Madonna and Child, 1953, marble, life-size. Florence.

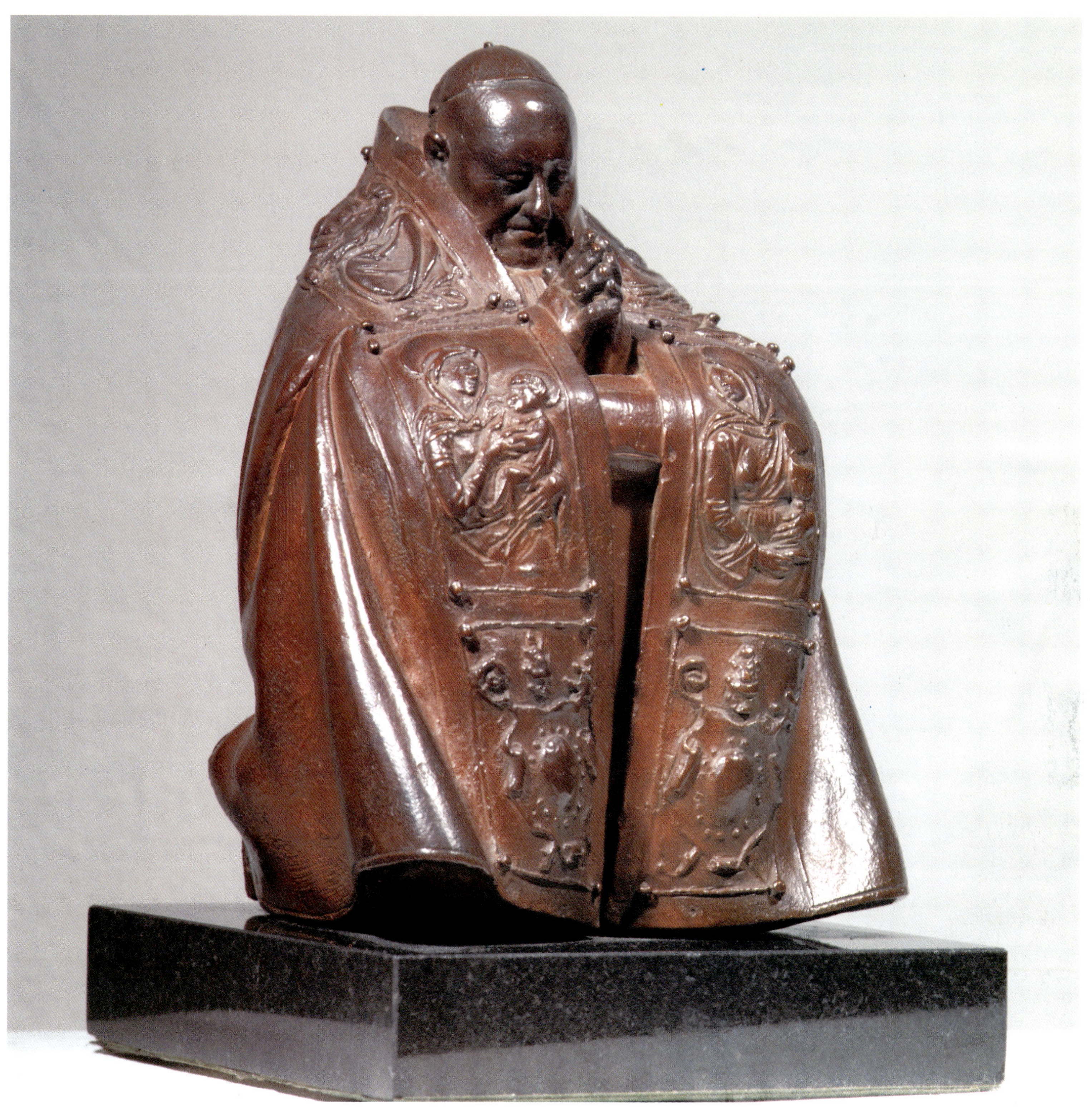

Pope John, 1985, bronze, 7¼ x 5½ x 5½ inches. Private collection.

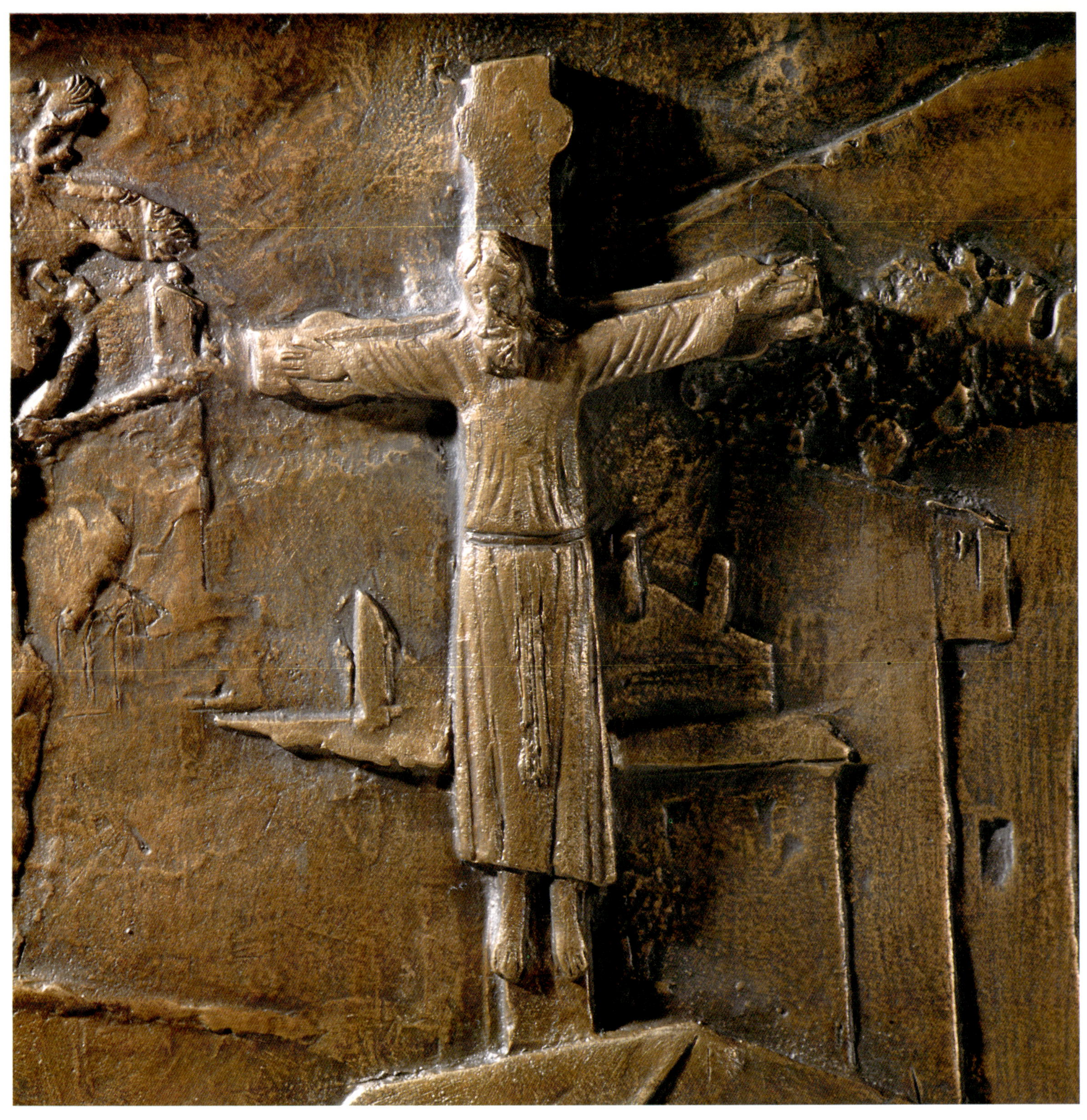

The Legacy of Vescovo Giovanni (detail), 1987, bronze, 4 x 5½ feet. High altar for S. Martino, Lucca. (See also black-and-white illustration, page 183.)

Crucified Christ, 1987, wood, 6 feet high. Church of Massarosa. (See also black-and-white illustration, page 172.)

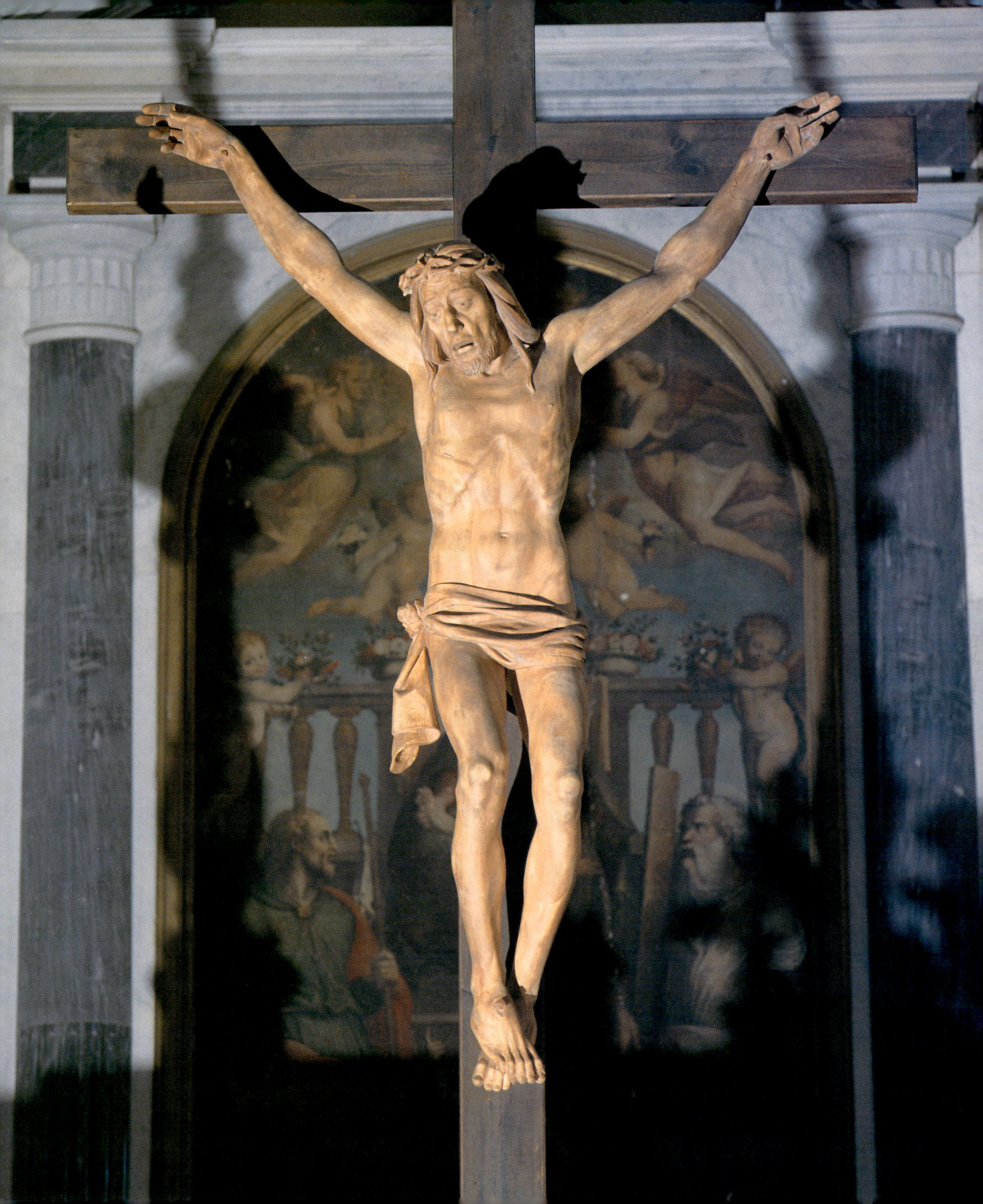

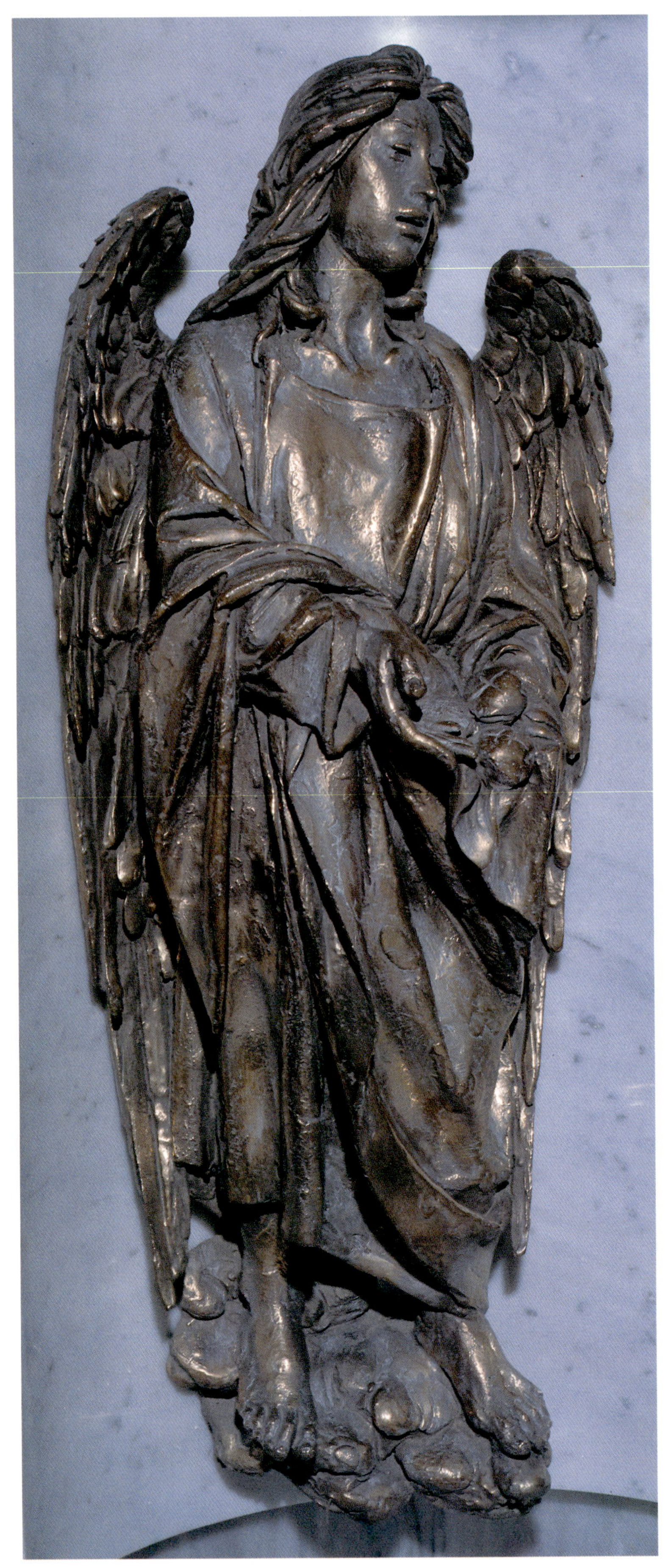

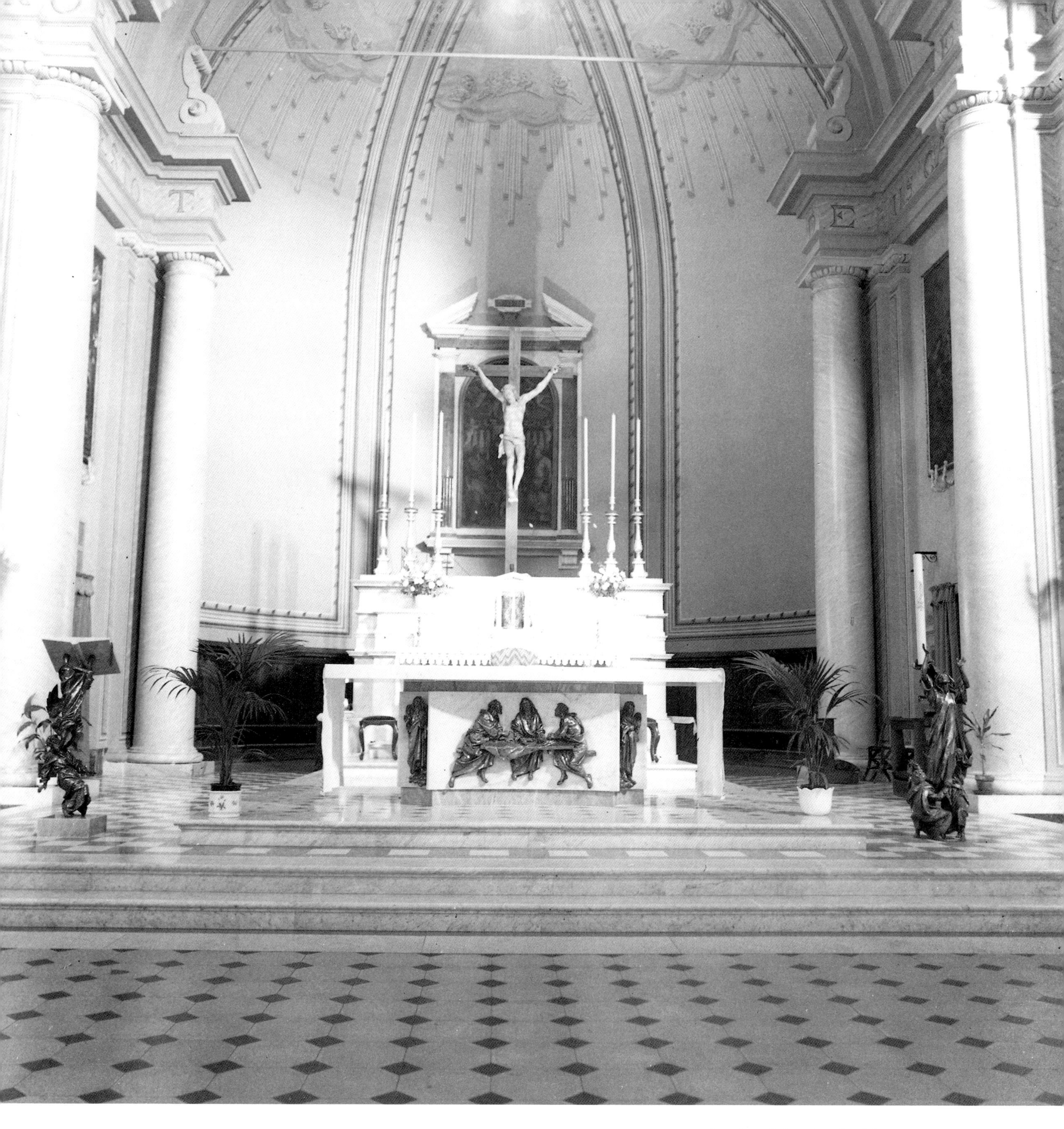

Interior of the church of Massarosa.

Angel, 1985, bronze and marble, 3½ feet high. High altar of the church of Massarosa.

Lectern, 1985, bronze and marble, 5 feet high. Church of Massarosa.

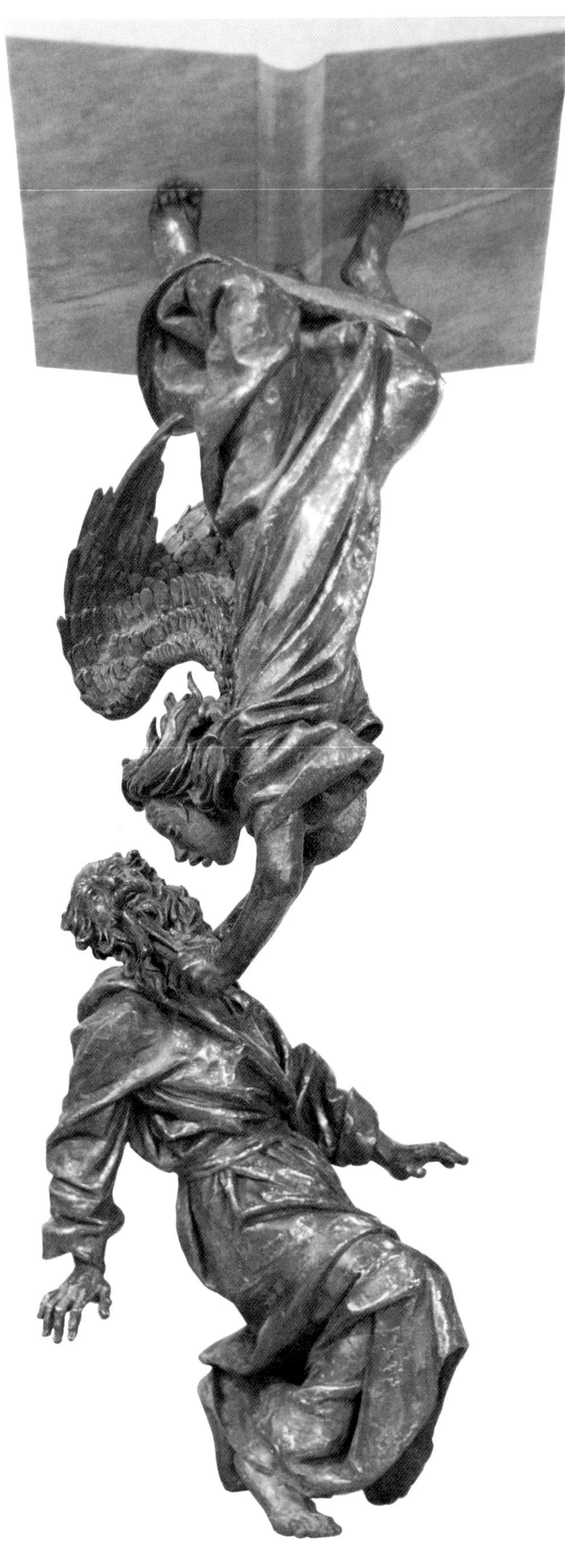

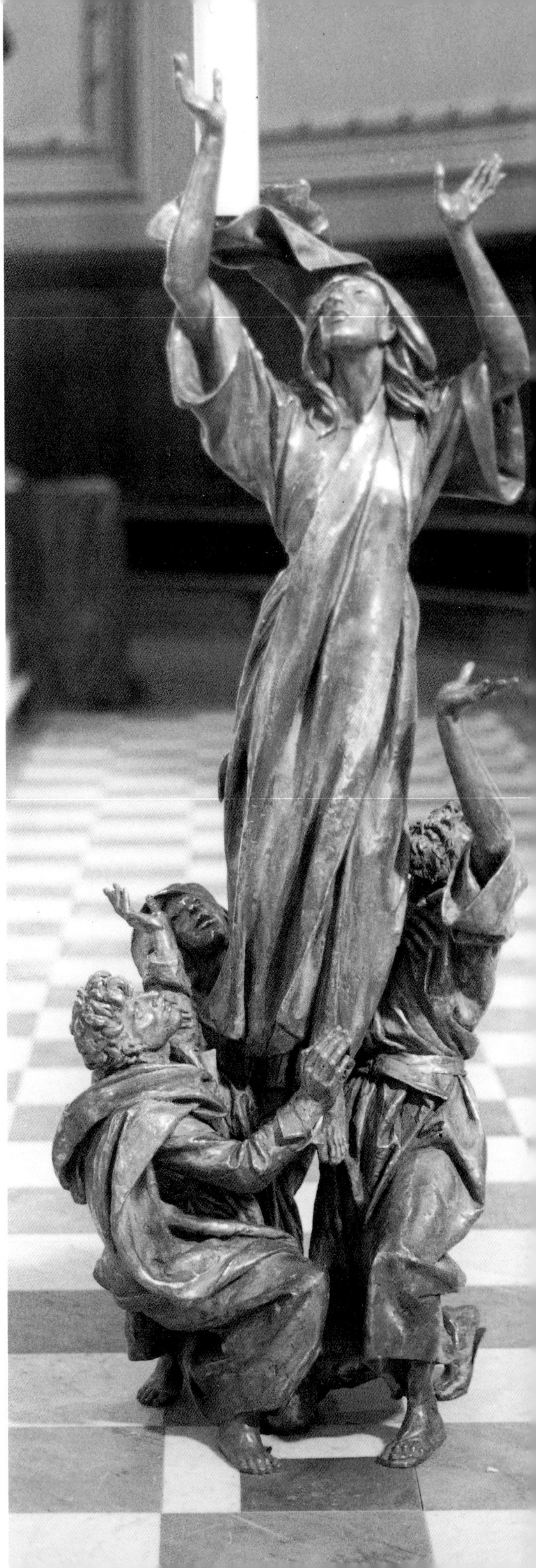

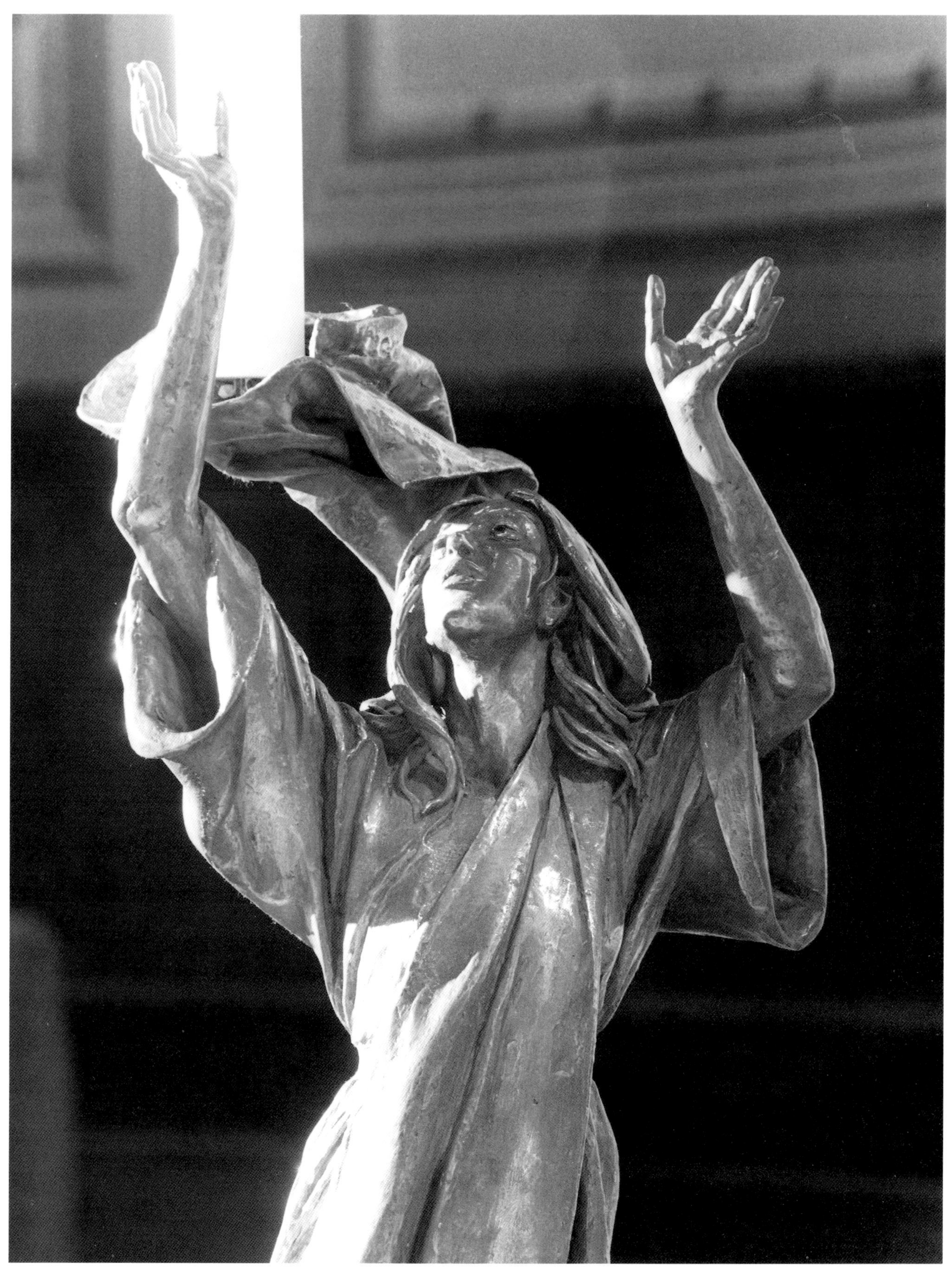

Easter Candle Holder, 1986, bronze, 6 feet high. Church of Massarosa.

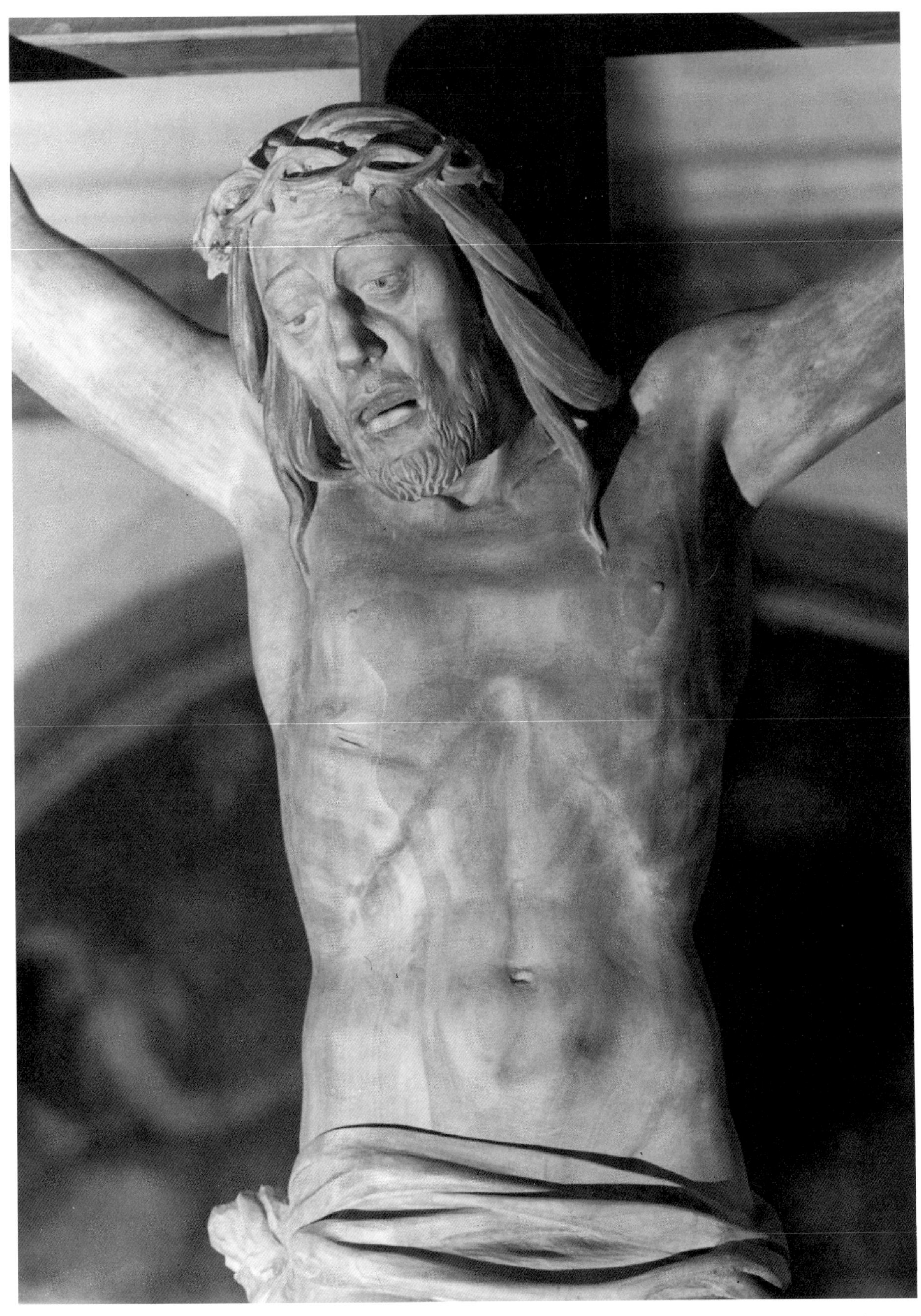

Crucified Christ (detail), 1987, wood, 6 feet high. Church of Massarosa. (See also colorplate, page 167.)

The Supper at Emmaus, 1985, bronze, 3½ feet high. High altar of the church of Massarosa.

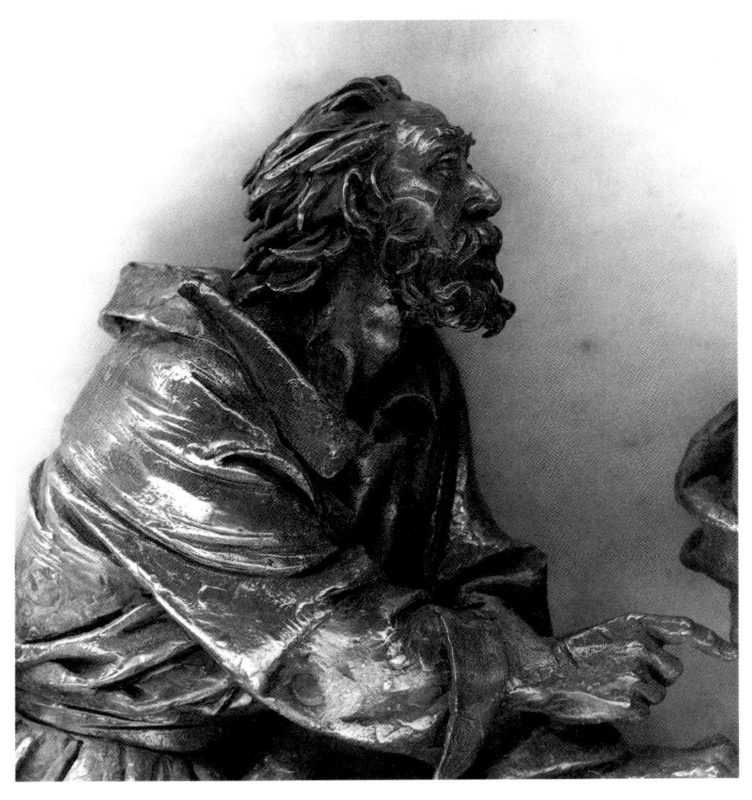

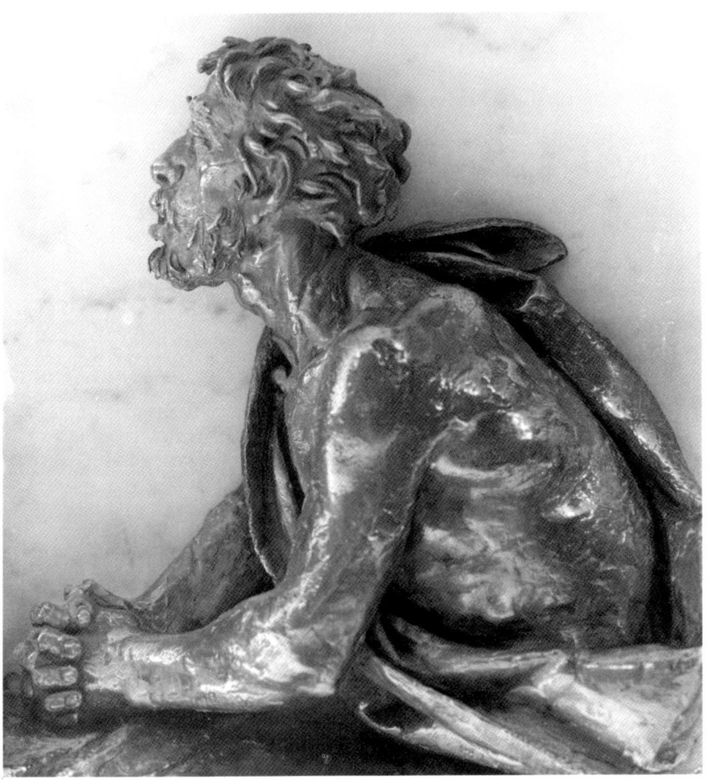

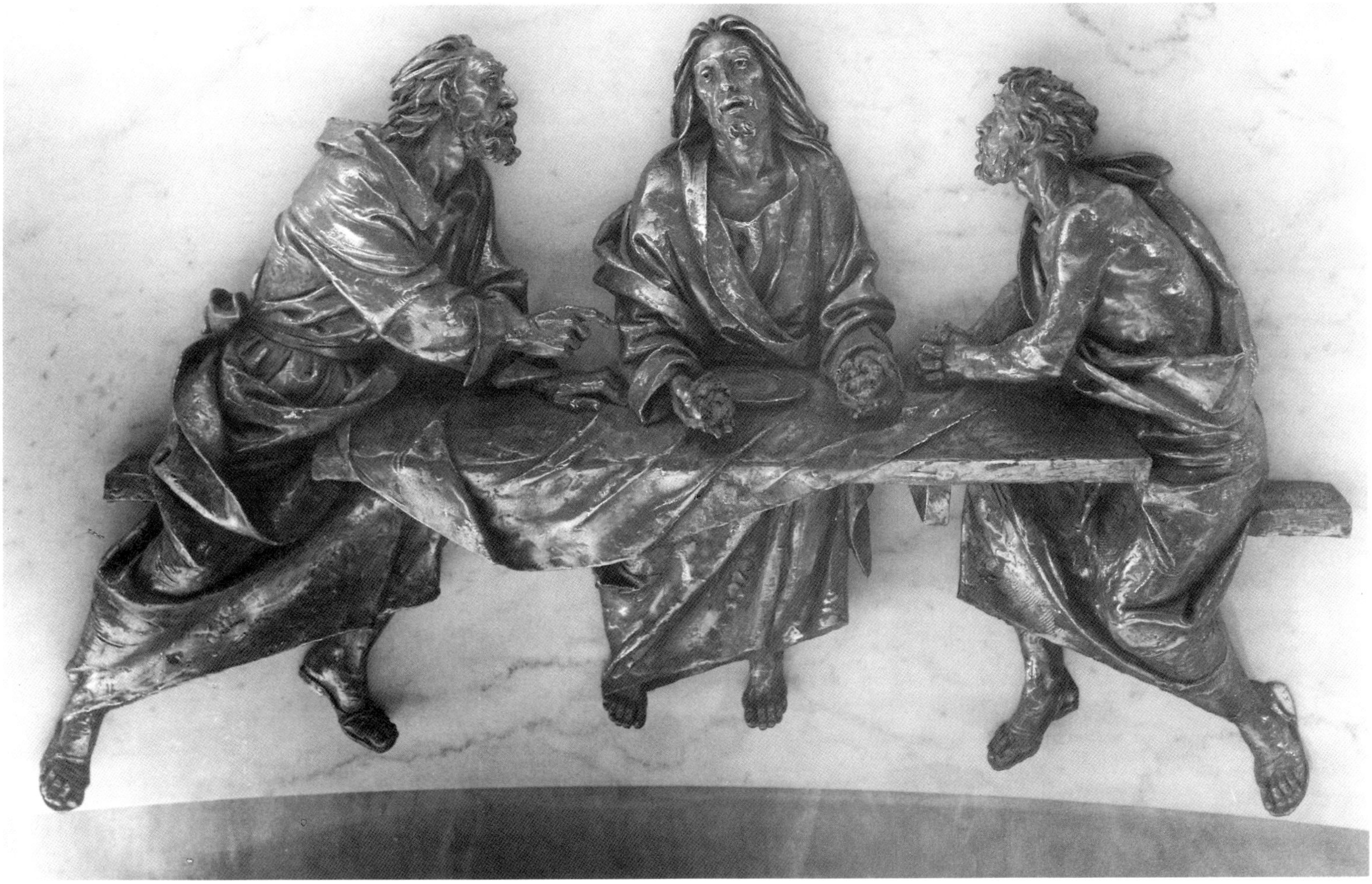

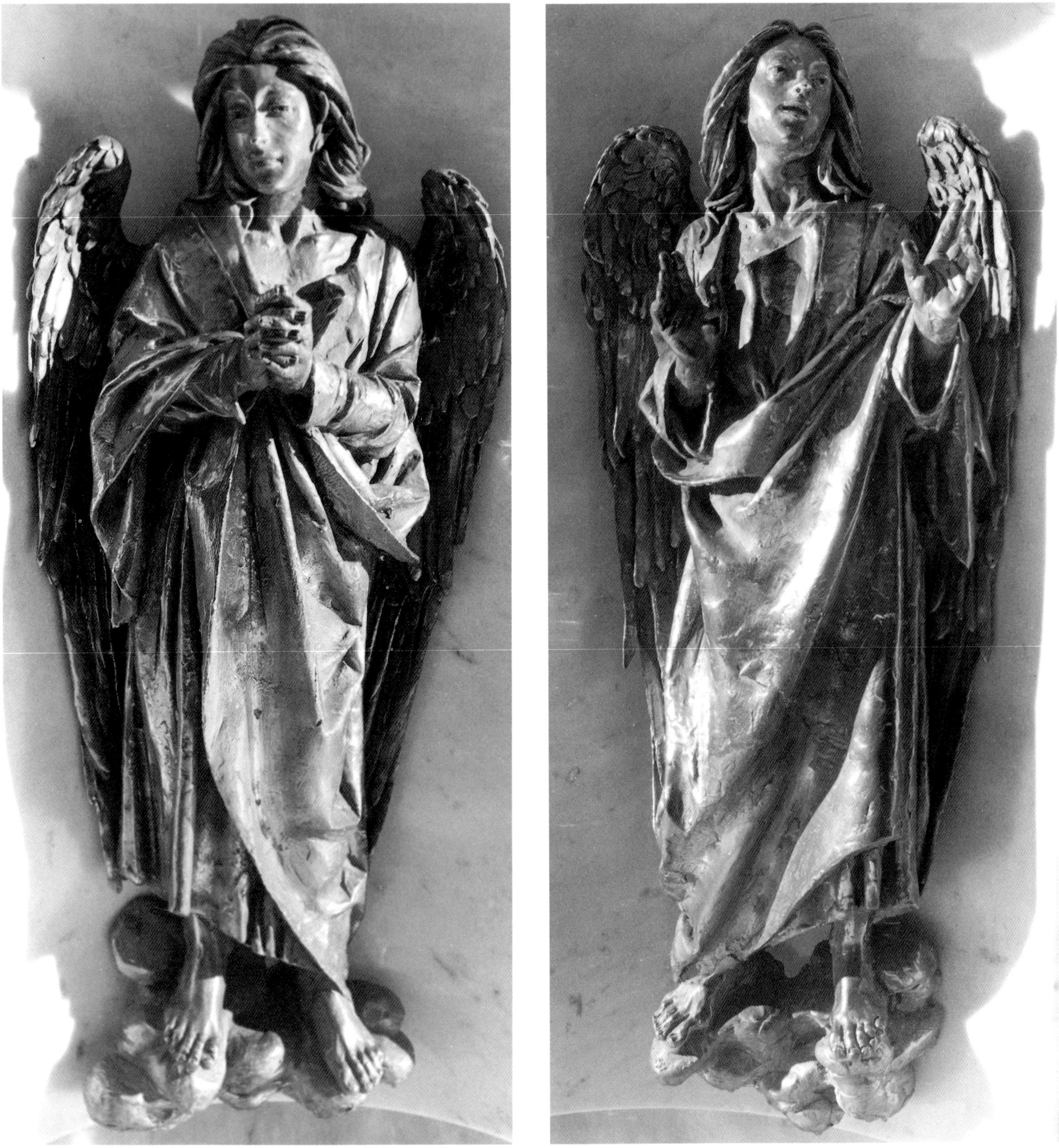

Angels, 1985, bronze, 3½ feet high. High altar of the church of Massarosa.

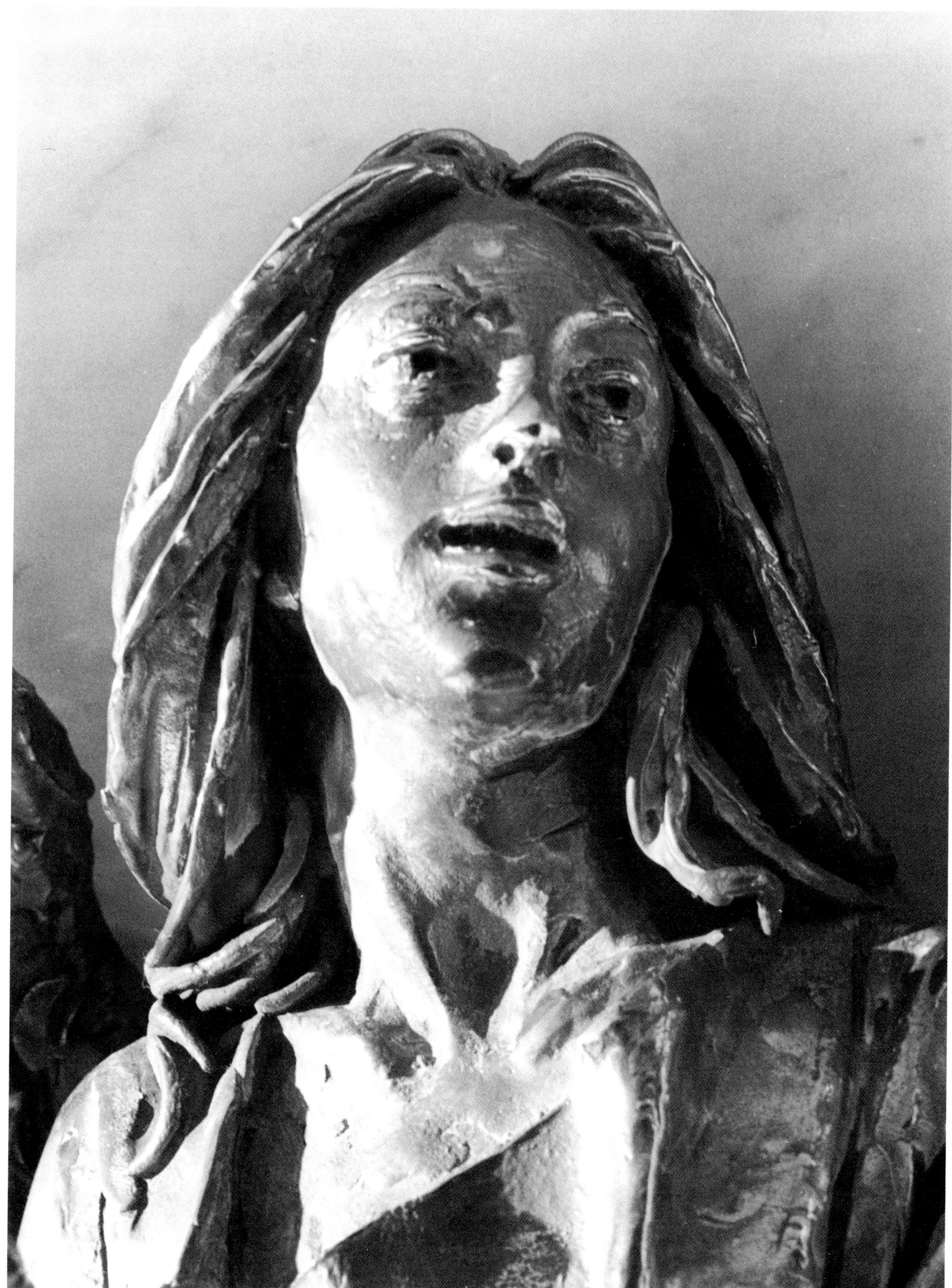

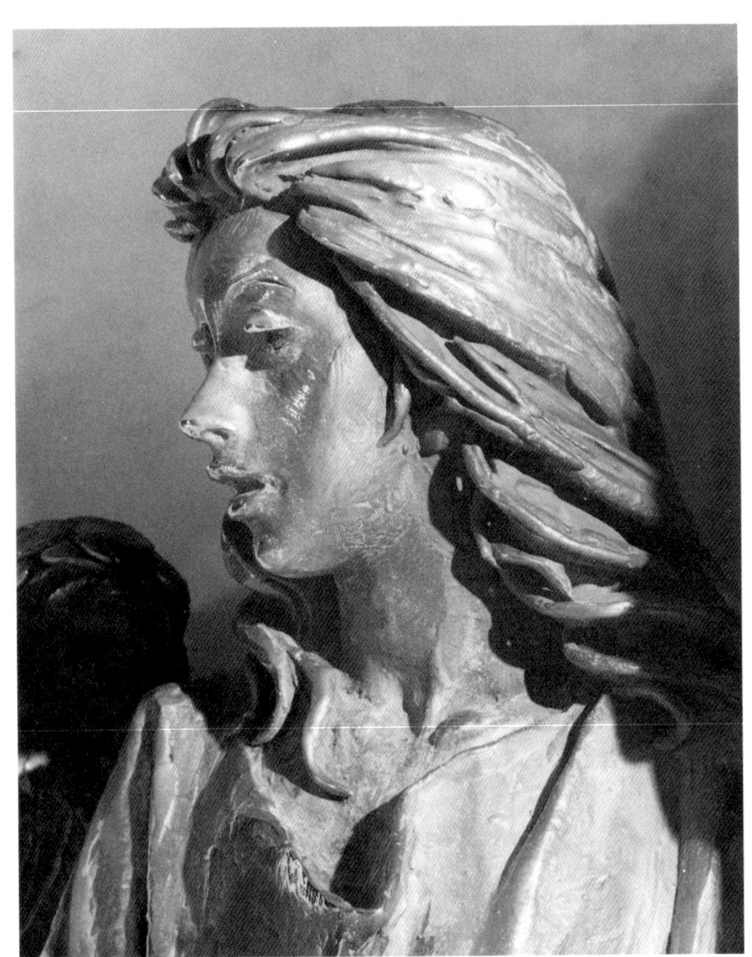

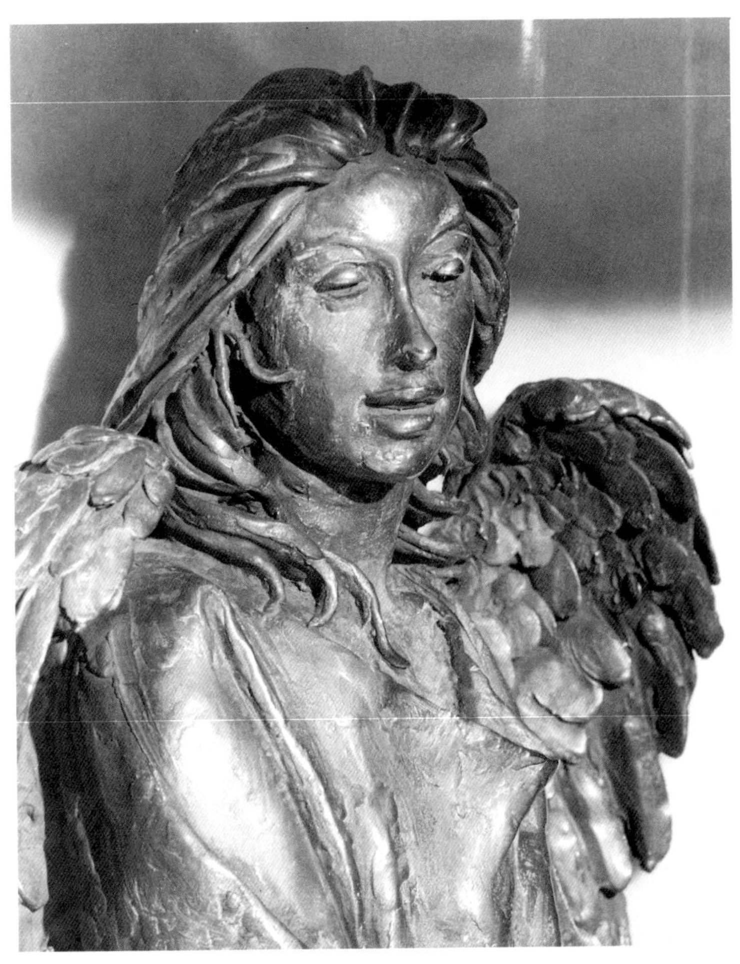

Angels (details)

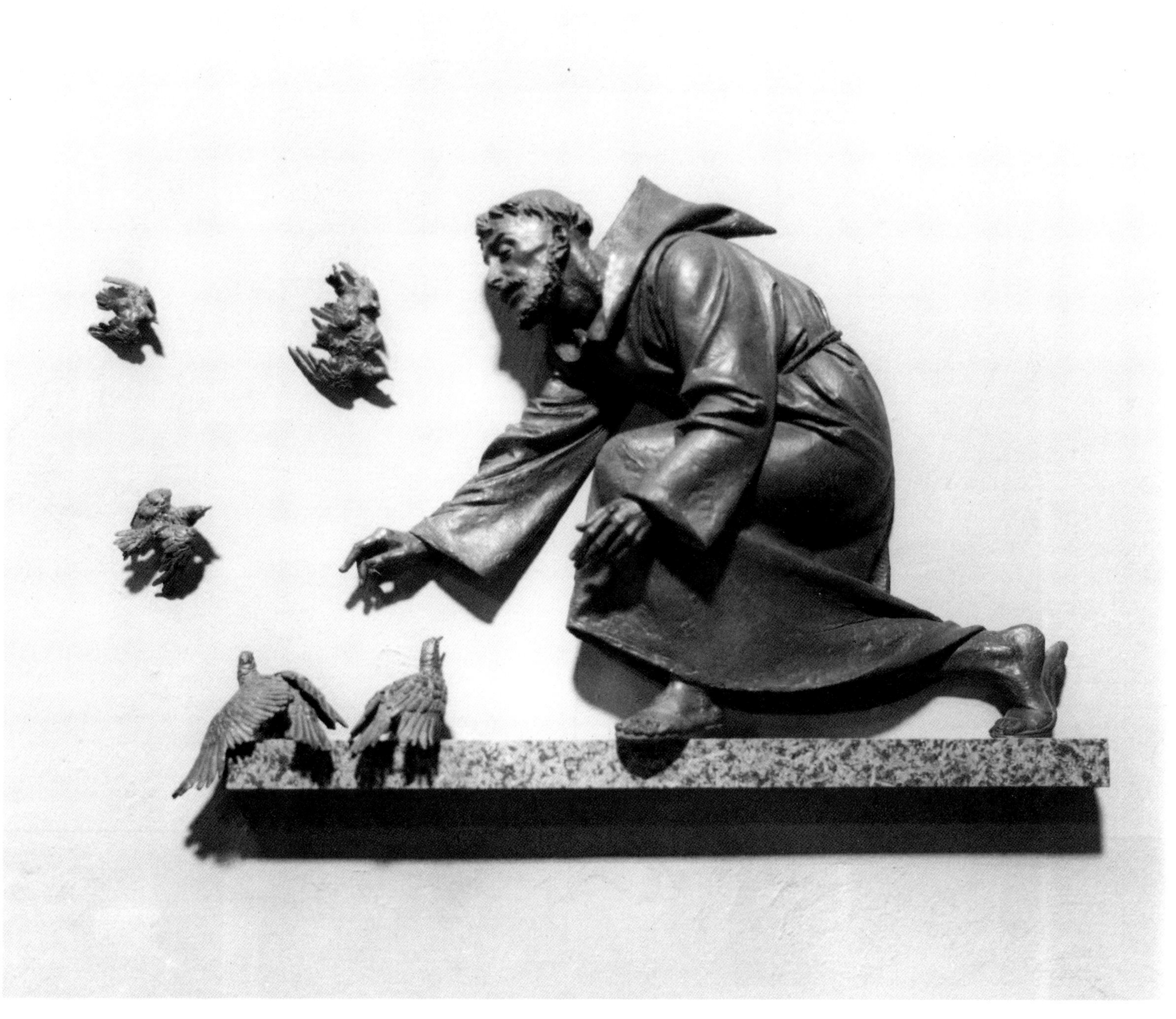

Saint Francis of Assisi, 1984, bronze, 5 feet high. Church of Massarosa.

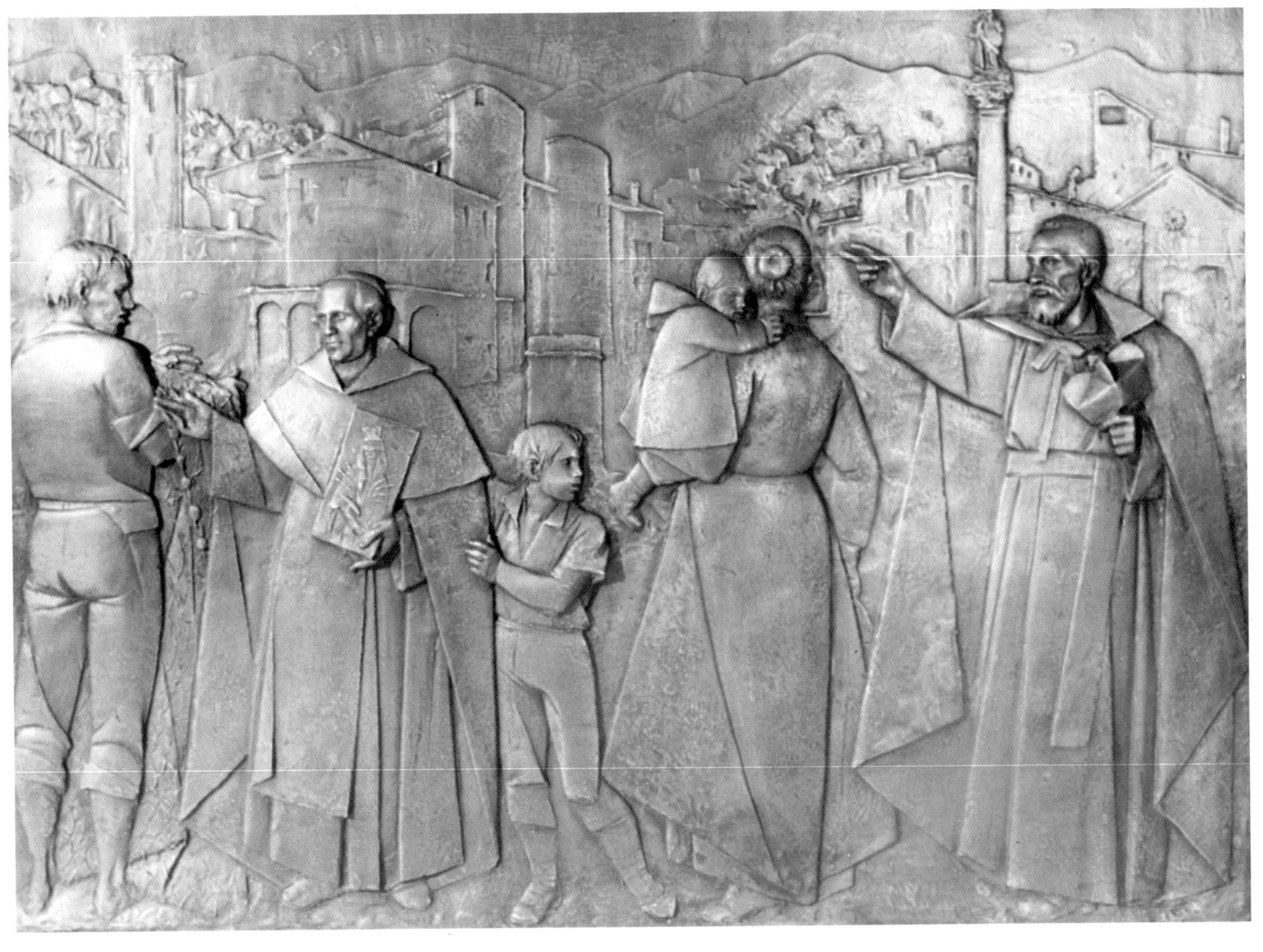

The Blessing, 1987, bronze, 4 x 5½ feet.
High altar for S. Martino, Lucca.

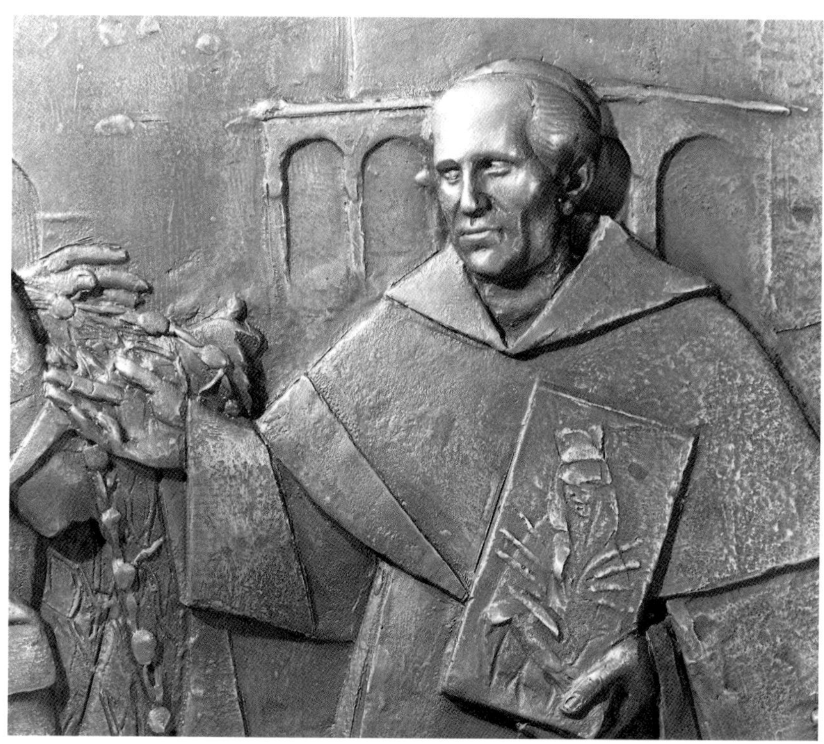

The Curate of Viareggio

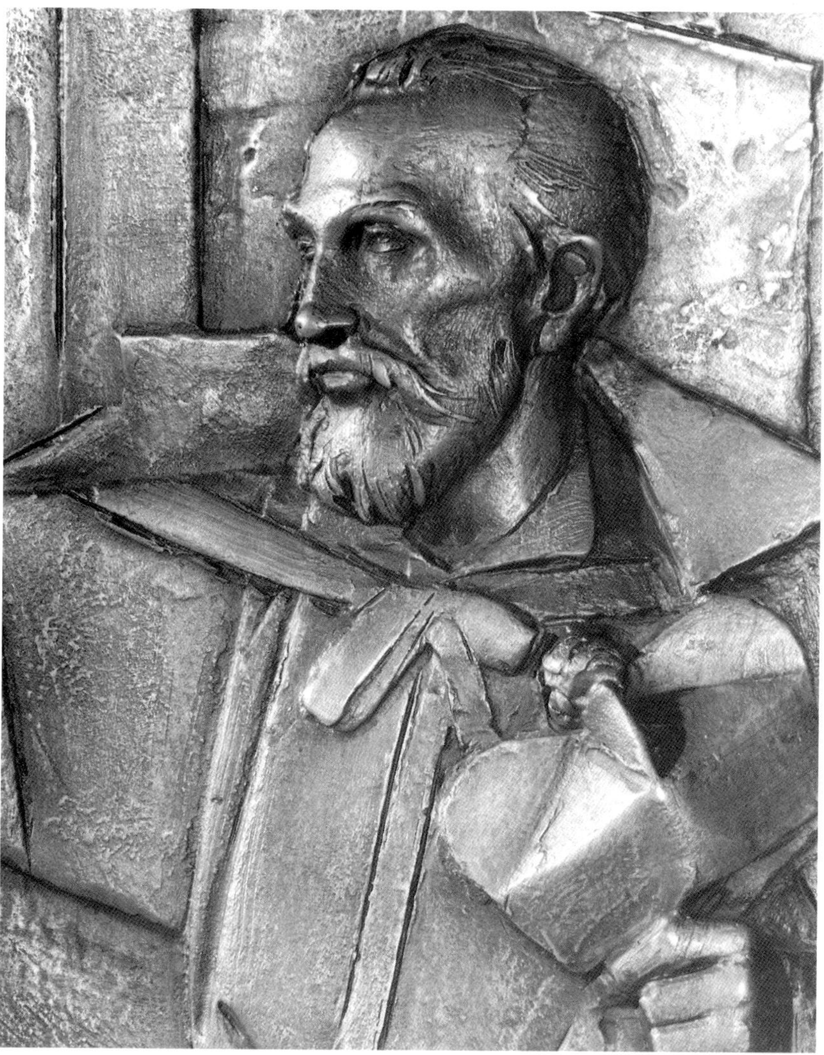

The Preacher

Villager

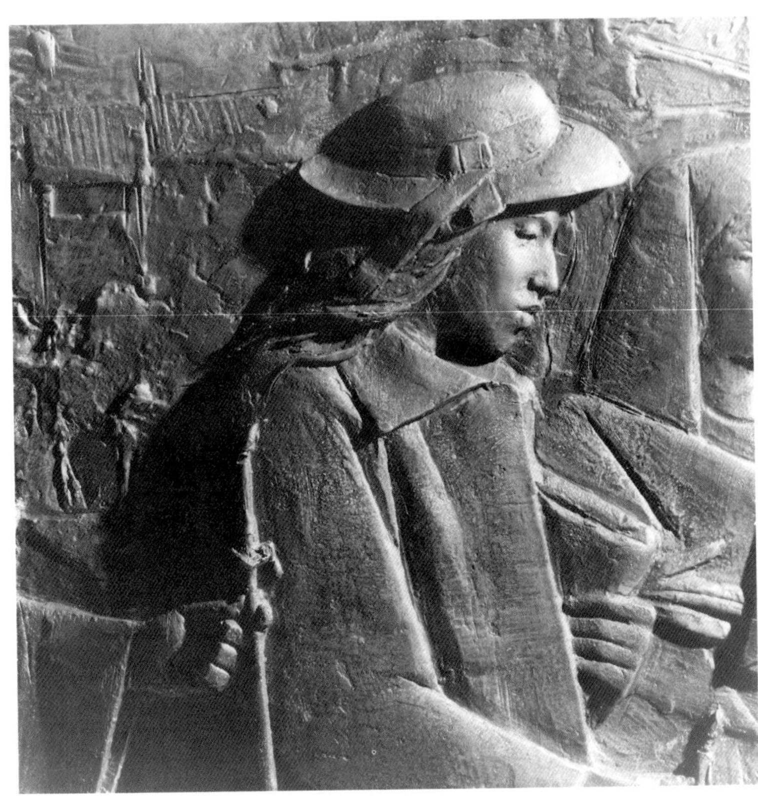

The Procession with Saint Regolo, 1987, bronze, 4 x 10 feet. High altar for S. Martino, Lucca.

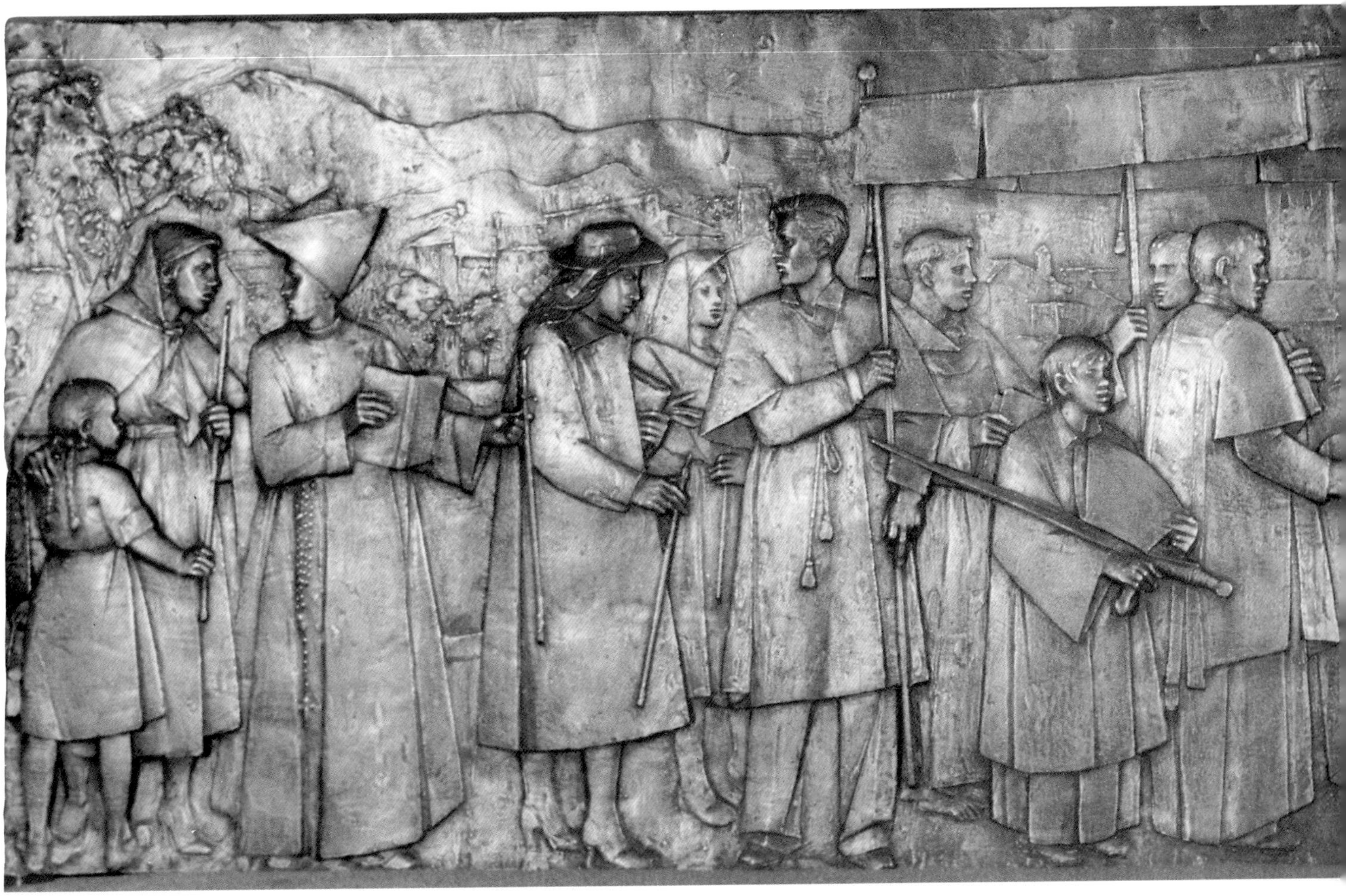

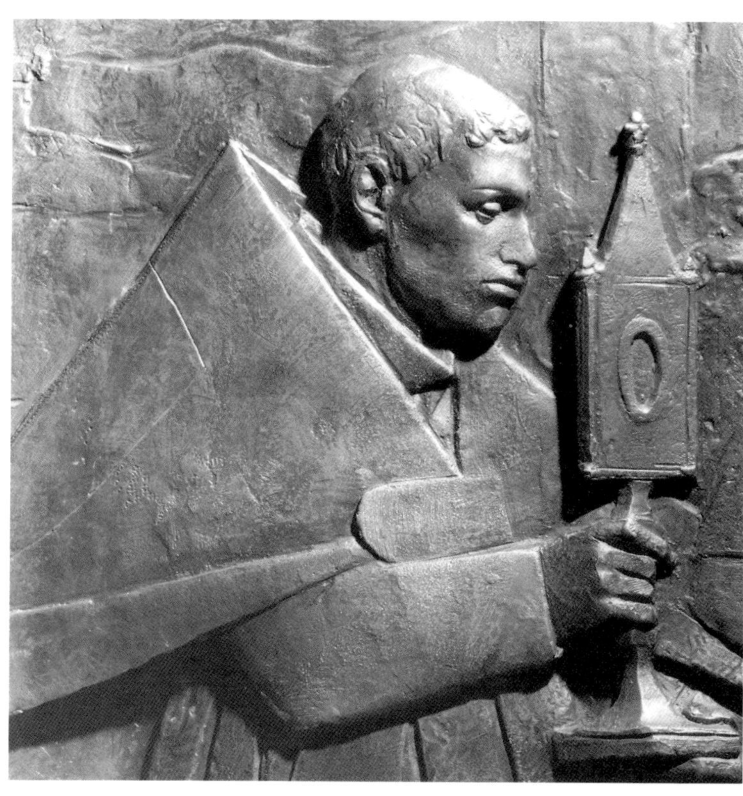

Saint Regolo

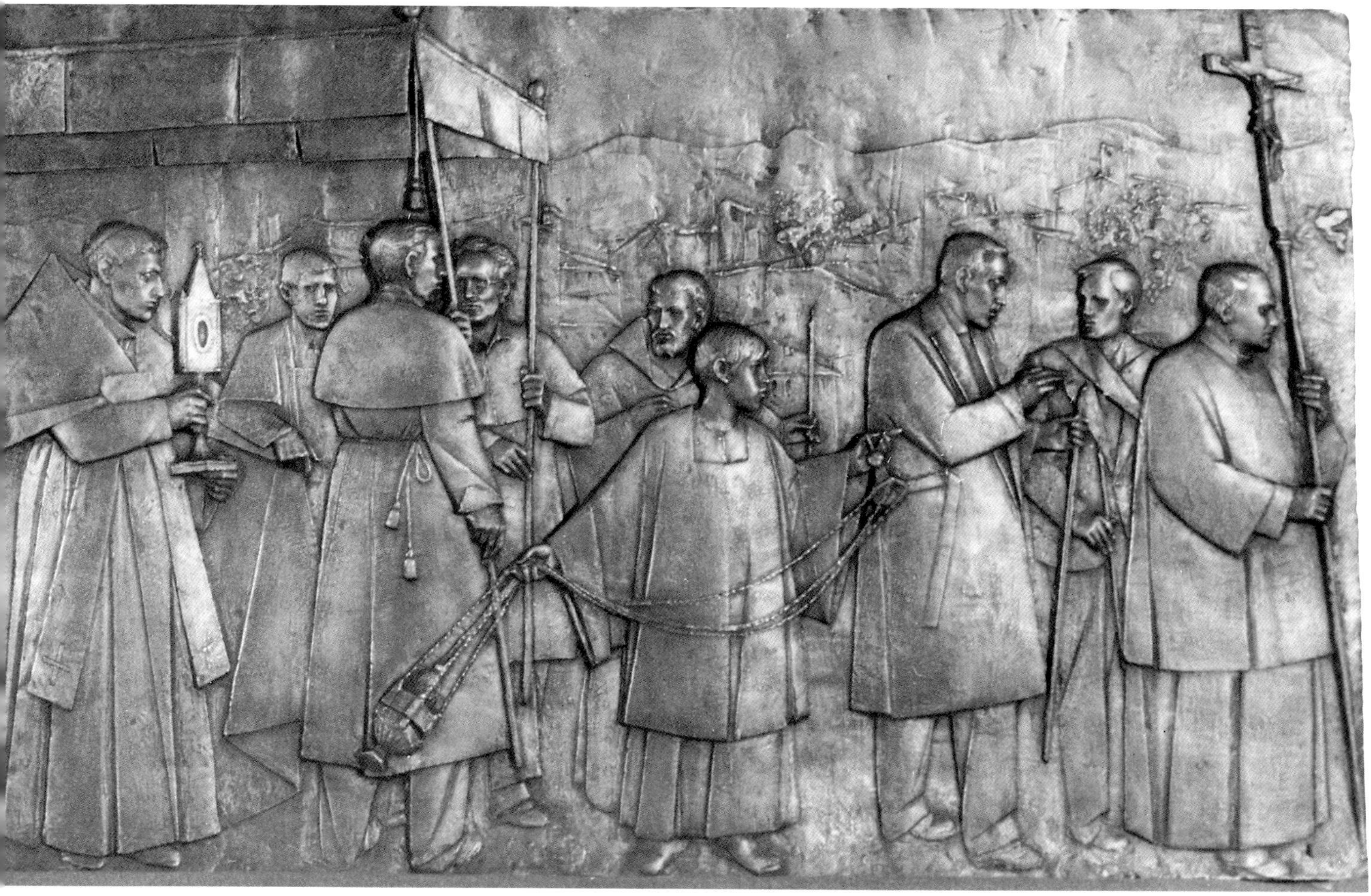

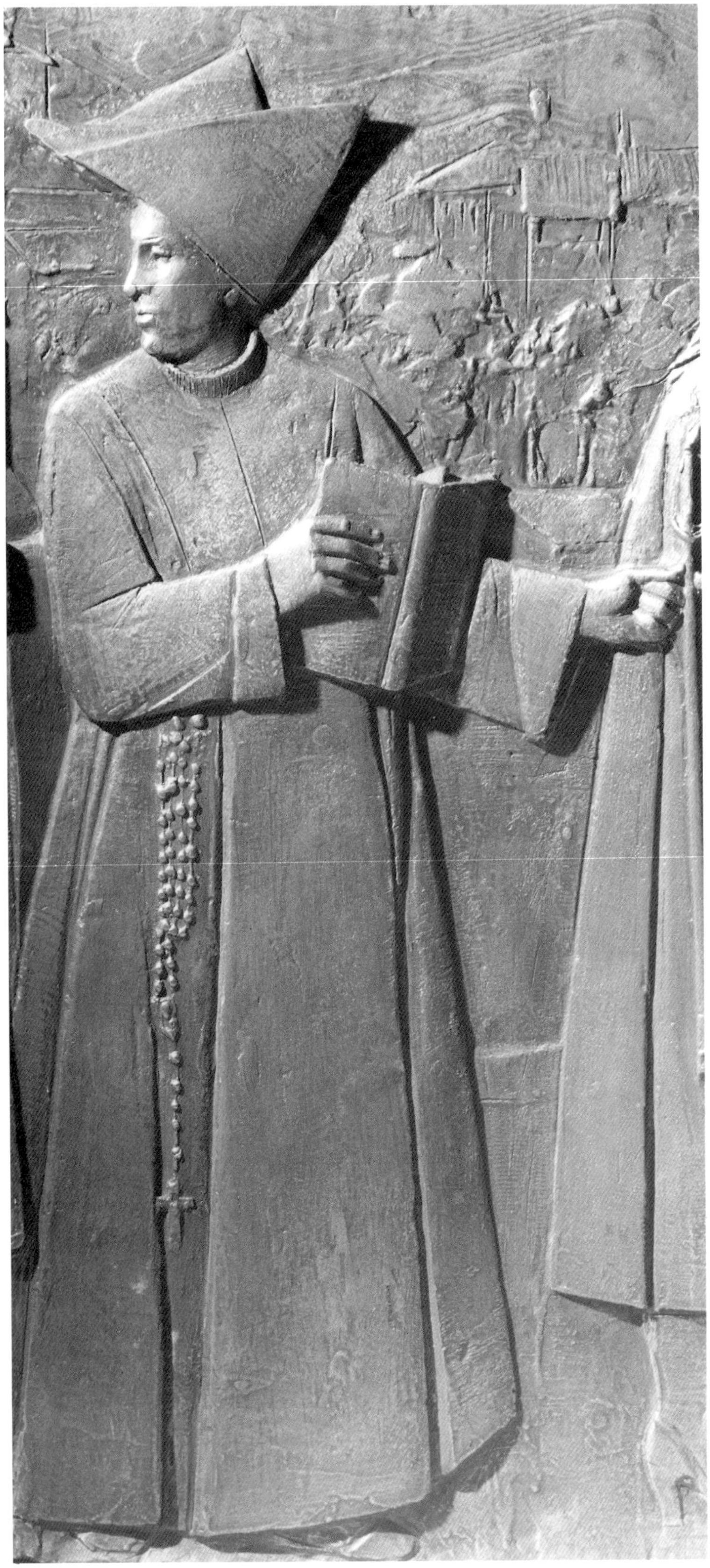

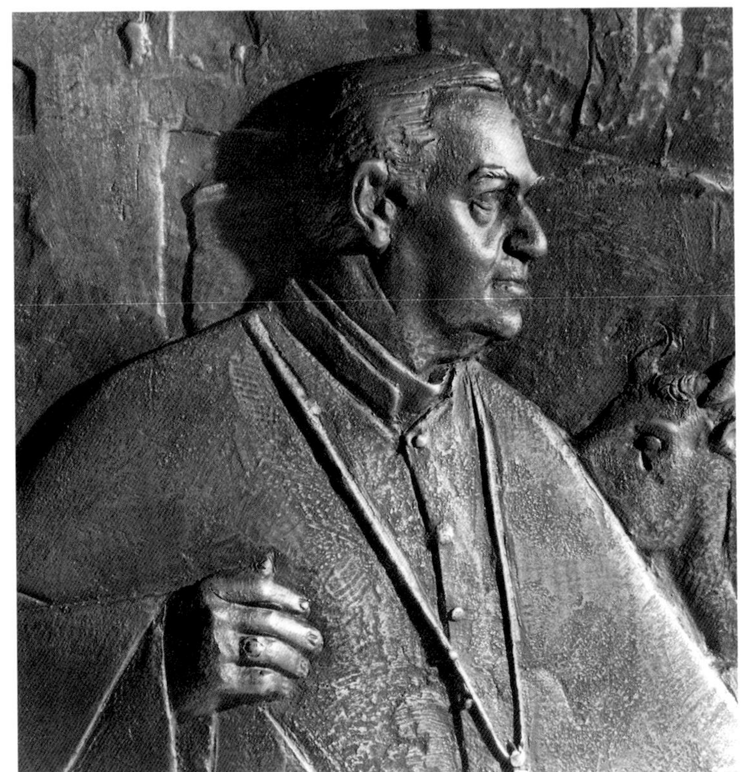

Bishop Giuliano Agresti

Nun

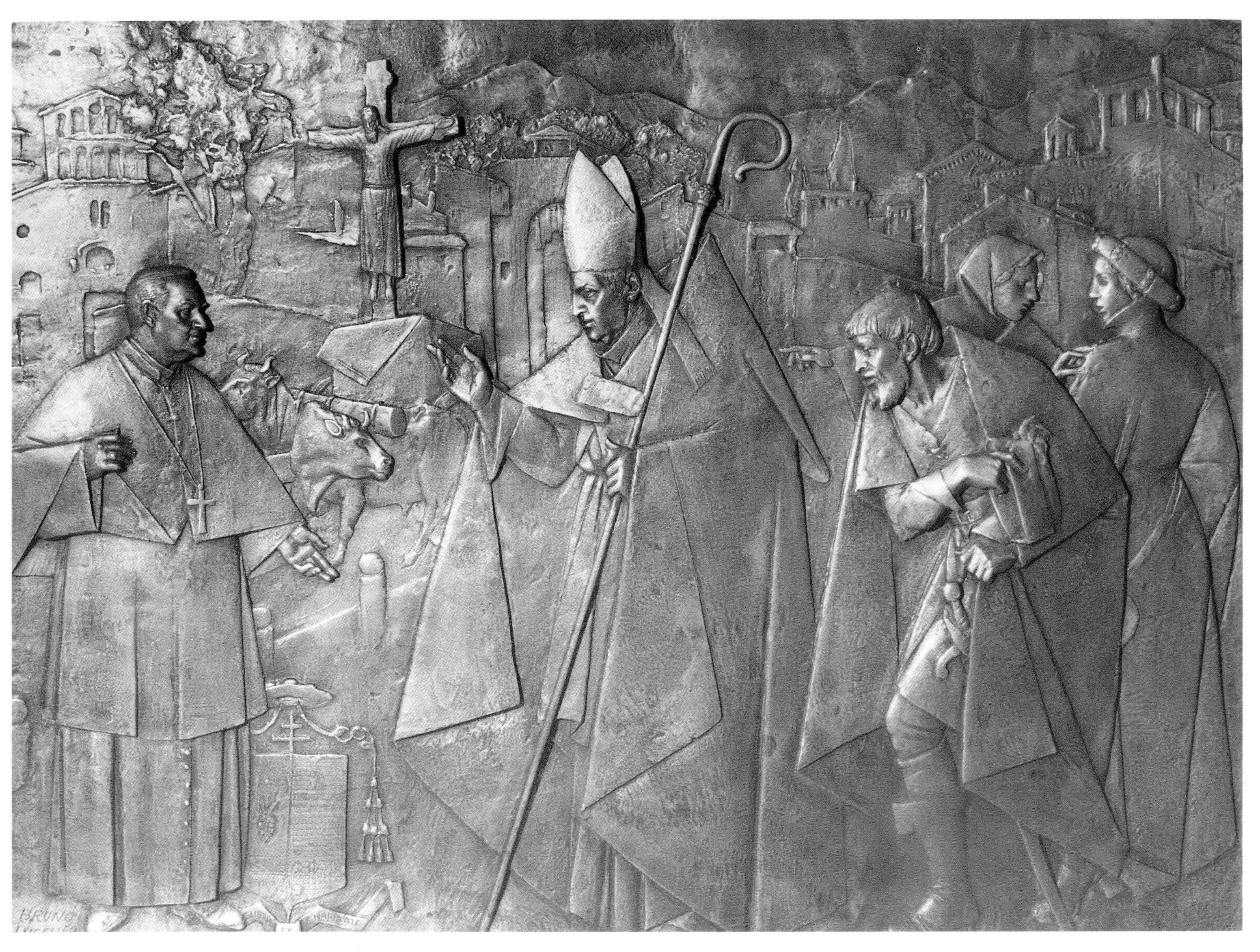

The Legacy of Vescovo Giovanni, 1987, bronze, 4 x $5\frac{1}{2}$ feet. High altar for S. Martino, Lucca. (See also colorplate, page 166.)

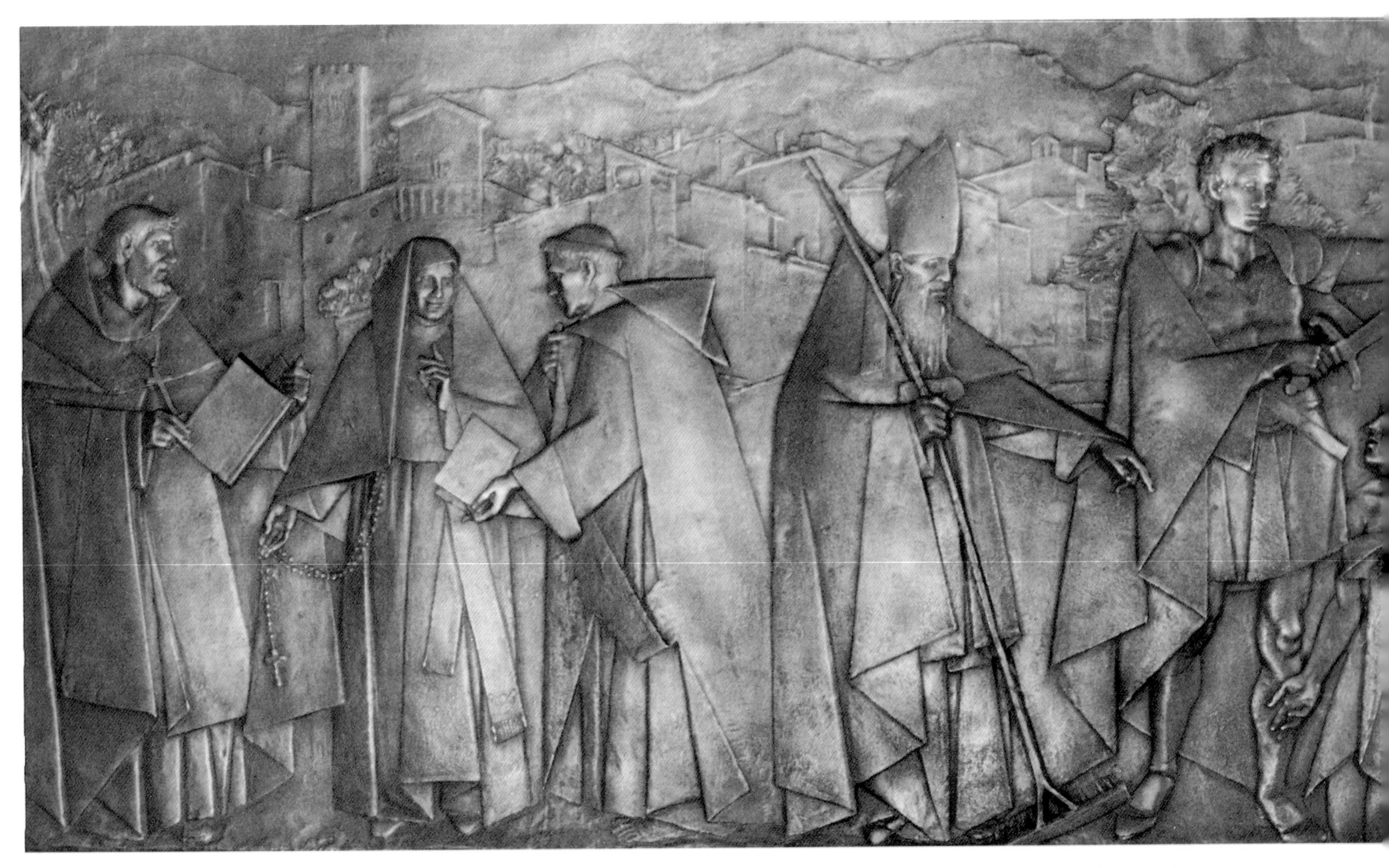

Saint Martin with Saints, 1987, bronze, 4 x 10 feet. High altar for S. Martino, Lucca.

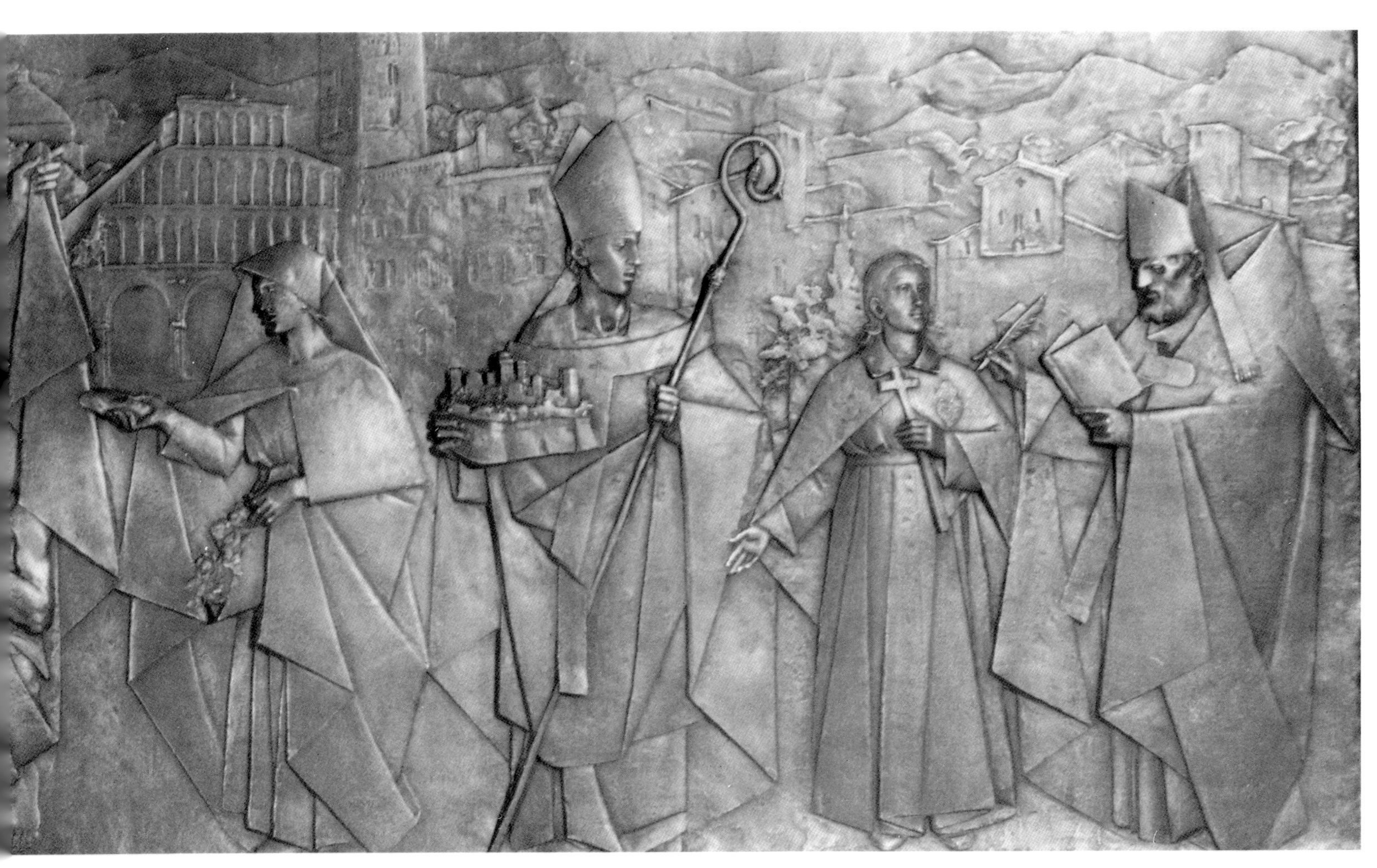

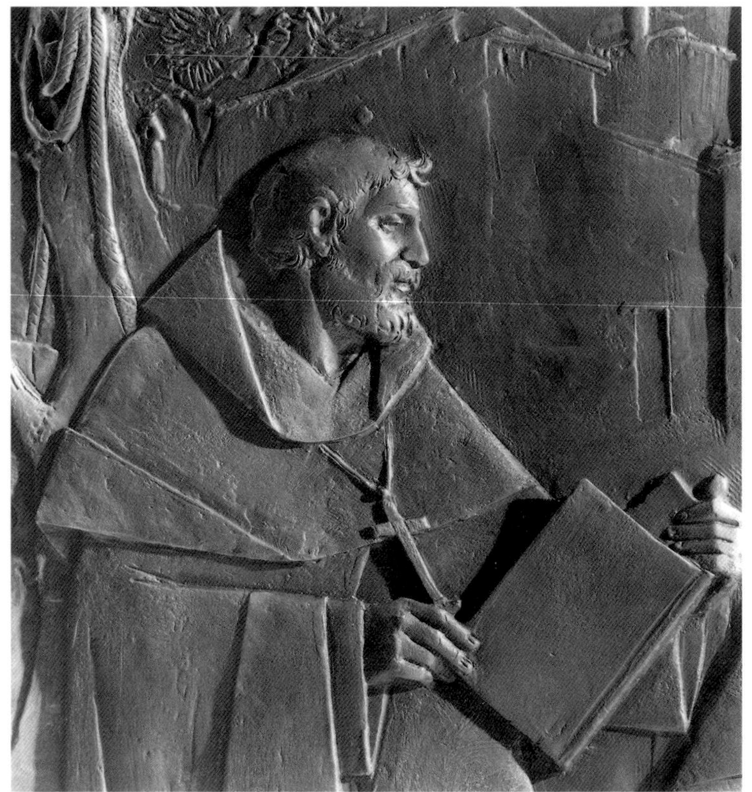
Saint Orsini

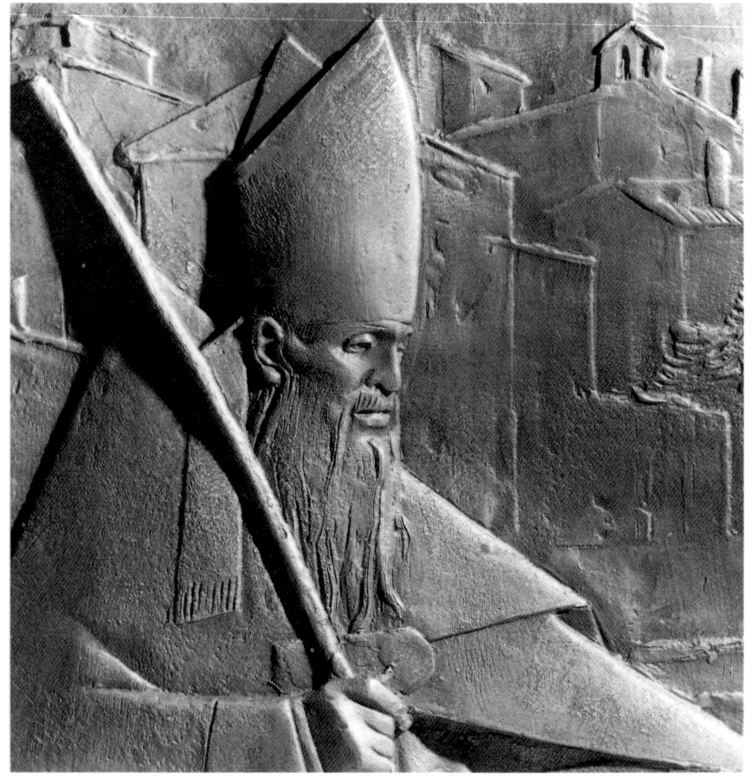
Saint Frediano

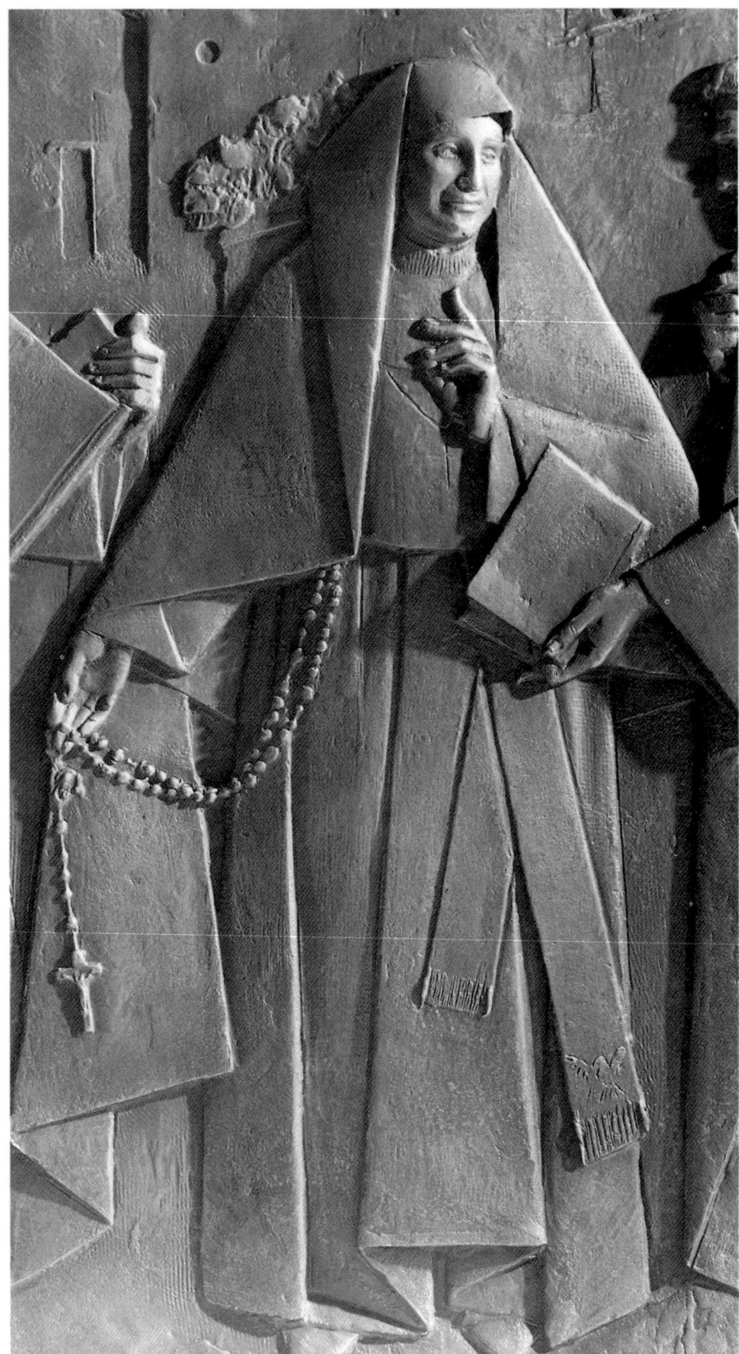
Blessed Helen Guerra

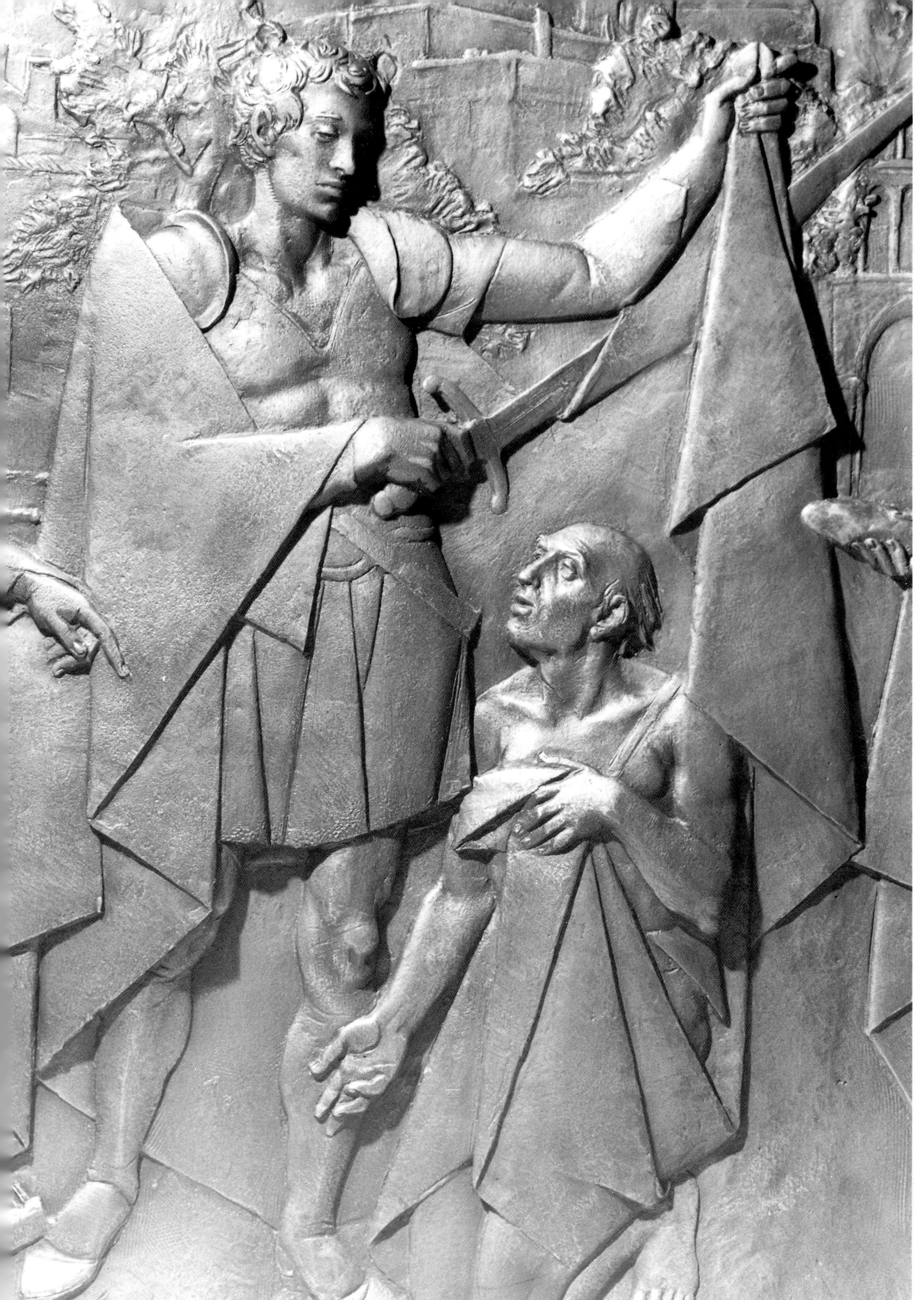

Saint Martin

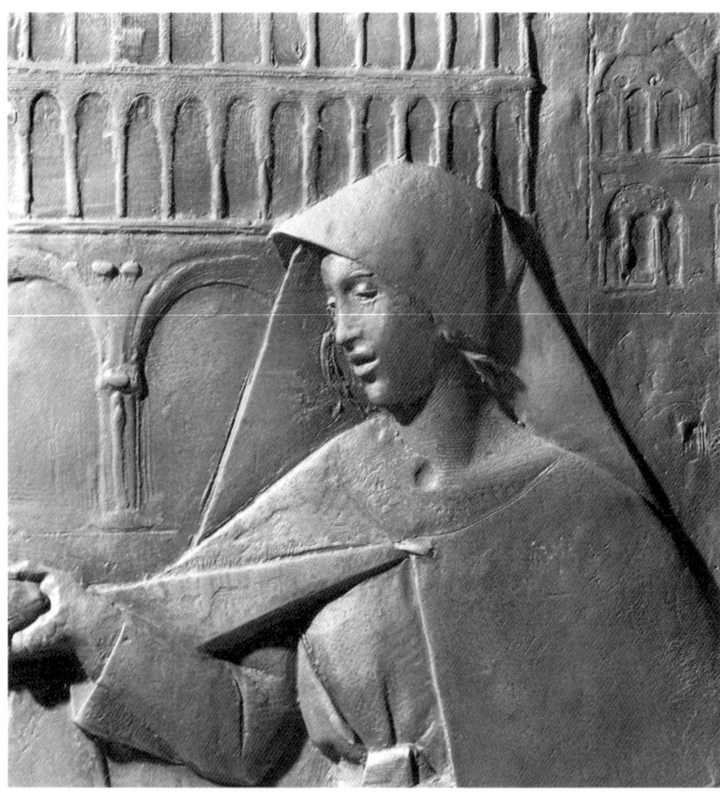
Saint Zita

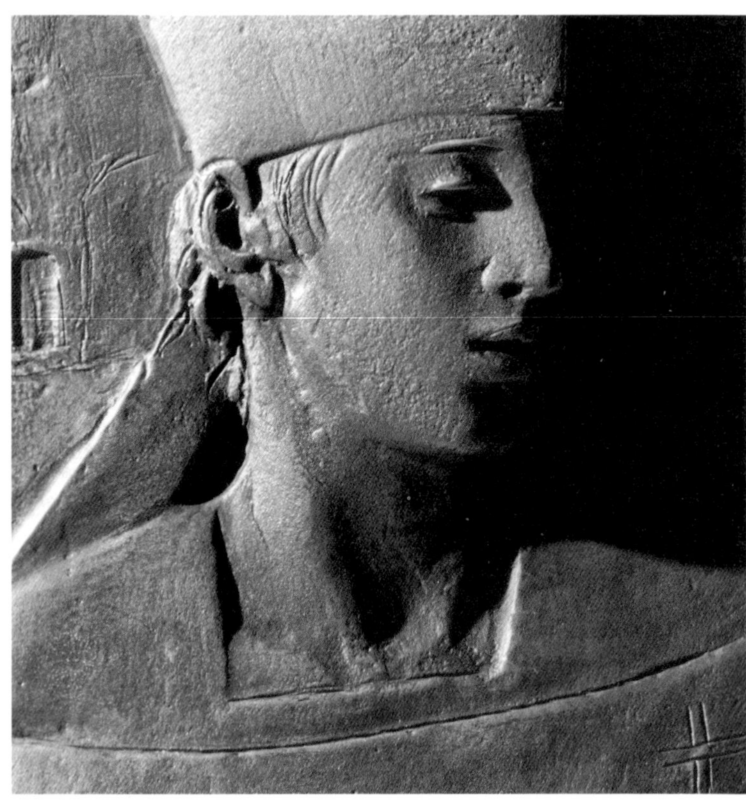
Saint Paulinus of Antioch

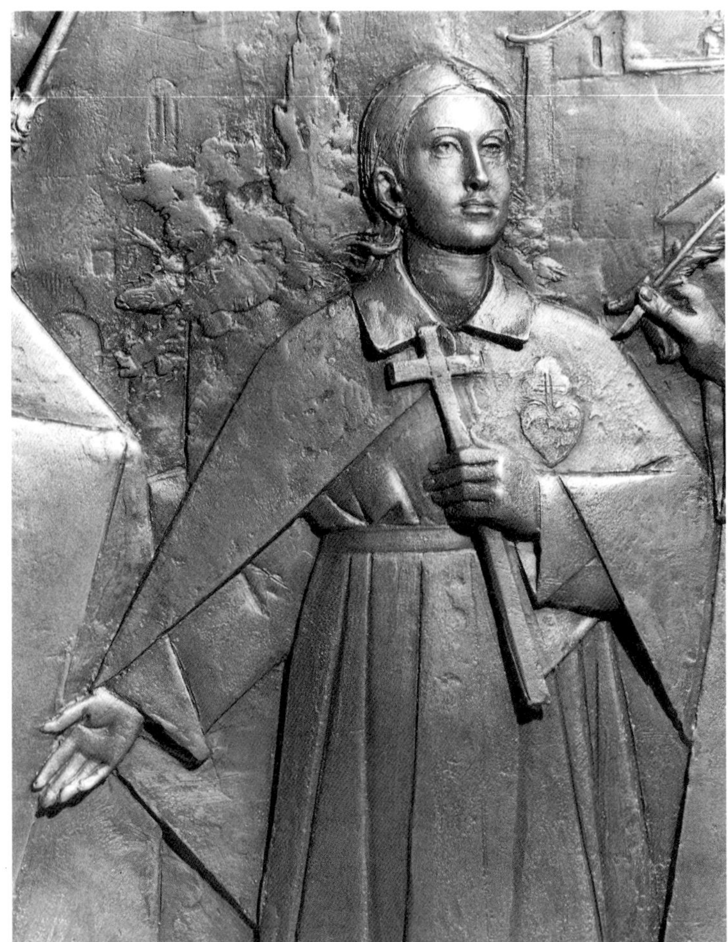
Saint Gemma Galgani

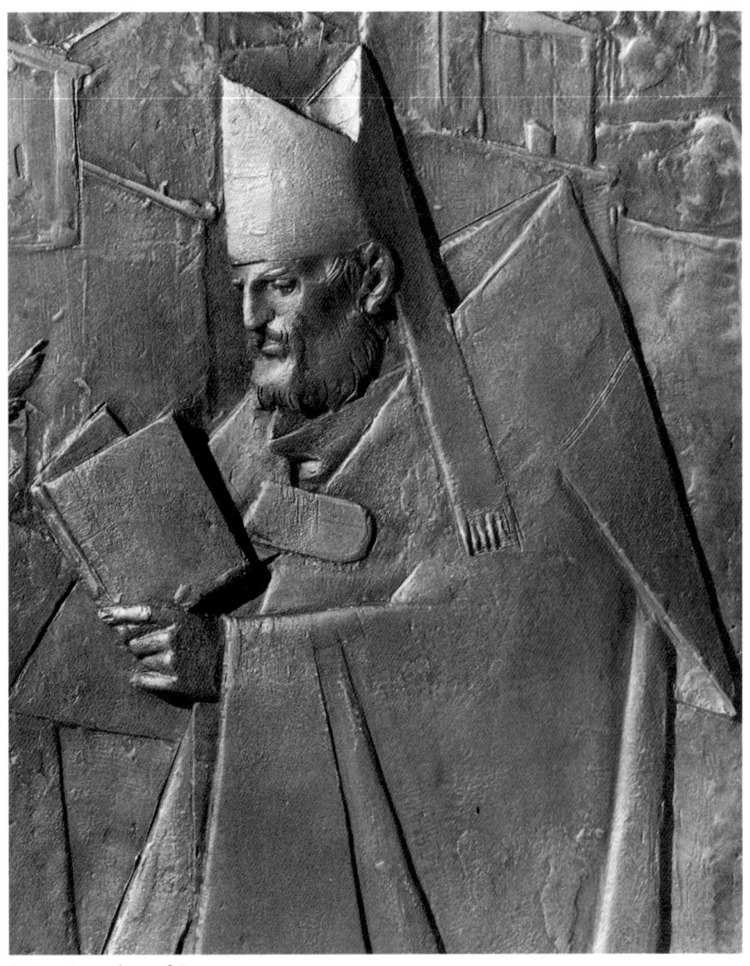
Saint Anselm of Lucca

CHRONOLOGY

1926 Born in village of Fibbiano Montanino, Lucca, Italy.

1945 Begins to study drawing with a local artist in Lucca.

1947 Enrolls in Art Institute of Lucca.

1950 Completes program at the Art Institute and moves to Florence where he continues to study.

1958 Begins teaching career as assistant professor of *plastica ornamentale* at the Art Academy in Florence.
Moves to New York City.

1959 Helen Foster Barnett Prize for Sculpture, National Academy of Design.

1960 Included in the annual exhibition of contemporary American painting and sculpture, Whitney Museum of American Art, New York.
Returns to Florence to work on sculpture for one year.

1961 First one-man exhibition at Forum Gallery, New York.

1962 Guggenheim Fellowship (1962–63).
Receives first U.S. commission for frieze at National Westminster Bank USA, New York.

1963 National Arts Club Gold Medal for sculpture.

1965 Commission for Trade Bank and Trust Company, New York.

1966 Commission for J. Walter Thompson, New York.

1970 Gold Medal, National Academy of Design.

1974 Gold Medal, National Academy of Design.

1976 City of Lucca Medal for honoring Italy abroad.
Commission for *Sir Walter Raleigh* sculpture for city of Raleigh, North Carolina.

1977 Gold Medal, National Sculpture Society.

1980 Commission for *Walt Whitman* bust, Arrow Park, Monroe, New York.

1981 Lion of San Marco Award in Art from the Italian Cultural Society.

1983 Artists' Fund Prize for finest sculpture in annual exhibition, National Academy of Design.

1985 Commission for *Park Bench* for Montana Building, New York.

1986 Commission for bronze friezes for altar of the cathedral of S. Martino, Lucca, Italy.

1987 Commission for award sculpture presented by the American School of Ballet, New York.

1988 Commission for *Ernie Davis* memorial, Elmira, New York.

EXHIBITIONS

One-Man Exhibitions

Forum Gallery, New York, 1961, 1963, 1966, 1972, 1975, 1976, 1980, 1984, 1985.
Canton Art Institute, Canton, Ohio, 1972.
Medici II Gallery, Miami, Florida, 1975.
Sordoni Art Gallery, Wilkes College, Wilkes-Barre, Pennsylvania, 1976.
Prince Arthur Gallery, Toronto, Canada, 1977.
Department of Fine Arts, Washington and Lee University, Lexington, Virginia, 1979.
Foster-Harmon Gallery, Sarasota, Florida, 1980, 1986.
Shirlee Raushbach Gallery, Bay Harbor, Florida, 1983.
Blue Hill Cultural Center, Pearl River, New York, 1984.
Casey Gallery, Scottsdale, Arizona, 1986.

Group Exhibitions

National Academy of Design, New York, *Annual Exhibition*, 1959 and nearly every year thereafter.
Whitney Museum of American Art, New York, *Annual Exhibition 1960: Contemporary American Painting and Sculpture*, 1960.
American Academy of Arts and Letters, New York, *Annual Purchase Program Exhibition*, 1967, 1978.
Root Art Center, Hamilton College, Clinton, New York, *This Is Today*, 1977.
National Council of Jewish Women, Millburn, New Jersey, *Focus on Art*, 1979, 1980, 1981, 1982, 1983.
Harmon Gallery, Naples, Florida, *Contemporary American Realists*, 1980.
Museum of Fine Arts, St. Petersburg, Florida, *The Bronze Figure in Italy*, 1981.
Root Art Center, Hamilton College, Clinton, New York, *Out of New York*, 1981.
Bergen County Museum, Paramus, New Jersey, 1982.
Kaber Gallery, New York, 1982.
Bethune Gallery, State University of New York at Buffalo, *Portrait Sculpture: Contemporary Points of View*, 1983.
Queens Museum, Flushing Meadow, New York, *Ten Twentieth-Century Sculptors*, 1984.
Schulman Sculpture Garden, White Plains, New York, *The Sculptors' Guild Exhibition*, 1986.
National Sculpture Society, Port of History Museum, Philadelphia, *Fifty-fourth Annual Exhibition*, 1987.
Silvermine Guild Arts Center, New Canaan, Connecticut, *The Figure in American Art since Mid-Century*, 1988.
Cavalier Renaissance Gallery, Stamford, Connecticut, *Sculpture Garden Exhibition*, 1988.

PUBLIC COLLECTIONS

Brooklyn Museum, Brooklyn, New York
Columbia Museum, Columbia, South Carolina
Cornell University, Ithaca, New York
Dallas Museum of Art, Dallas, Texas
Hirshhorn Museum and Sculpture Garden, Smithsonian Institution, Washington, D.C.
Lowe Art Gallery, Syracuse University, Syracuse, New York
National Academy of Design, New York
Pennsylvania Academy of the Fine Arts, Philadelphia
Ringling Museum of Art, Sarasota, Florida
Sheldon Memorial Art Gallery, University of Nebraska, Lincoln
Utah Museum of Fine Arts, University of Utah, Salt Lake City
Whitney Museum of American Art, New York

Arrow Park, Monroe, New York
Cathedral of S. Martino, Lucca, Italy
Church of Massarosa, Italy
City of Raleigh, North Carolina
Ernie Davis Junior High School, Elmira, New York
Gasoline station, Piazza Donatello, Florence, Italy
J. Walter Thompson, Graybar Building, New York
Montana Building, New York
National Westminster Bank USA, New York
Trade Bank and Trust Company, New York